Lecture Notes in Control and Information Sciences

Edited by A.V. Balakrishnan and M. Thoma

11

Y. Sawaragi · T. Soeda · S. Omatu

Modeling, Estimation, and Their Applications for Distributed Parameter Systems

Lecture Notes in Control and Information Sciences

Edited by A. V. Balakrishnan and M. Thoma

Vol. 1: Distributed Parameter Systems: Modelling and Identification
Proceedings of the IFIP Working Conference, Rome, Italy, June 21–26, 1976
Edited by A. Ruberti
V, 458 pages. 1978

Vol. 2: New Trends in Systems Analysis
International Symposium, Versailles, December 13–17, 1976
Edited by A. Bensoussan and J. L. Lions
VII, 759 pages. 1977

Vol. 3: Differential Games and Applications
Proceedings of a Workshop, Enschede, Netherlands, March 16–25, 1977
Edited by P. Hagedorn, H. W. Knobloch, and G. J. Olsder
XII, 236 pages. 1977

Vol. 4: M. A. Crane, A. J. Lemoine
An Introduction to the Regenerative Method for Simulation Analysis
VII, 111 pages. 1977

Vol. 5: David J. Clements, Brian D. O. Anderson
Singular Optimal Control: The Linear Quadratic Problem
V, 93 pages. 1978

Vol. 6: Optimization Techniques
Proceedings of the 8th IFIP Conference on Optimization Techniques, Würzburg, September 5–9, 1977
Part 1
Edited by J. Stoer
XIII, 528 pages. 1978

Vol. 7: Optimization Techniques
Proceedings of the 8th IFIP Conference on Optimization Techniques, Würzburg, September 5–9, 1977
Part 2
Edited by J. Stoer
XIII, 512 pages. 1978

Vol. 8: R. F. Curtain, A. J. Pritchard
Infinite Dimensional Linear Systems Theory
VII, 298 pages. 1978

Vol. 9: Y. M. El-Fattah, C. Foulard
Learning Systems:
Decision, Simulation, and Control
VII, 119 pages. 1978

Vol. 10: J. M. Maciejowski
The Modelling of Systems with Small Observation Sets
VII, 241 pages. 1978

Vol. 11: Y. Sawaragi, T. Soeda, S. Omatu
Modeling, Estimation, and Their Applications for Distributed Parameter Systems

Lecture Notes in Control and Information Sciences

Edited by A.V. Balakrishnan and M. Thoma

11

Y. Sawaragi · T. Soeda · S. Omatu

Modeling, Estimation, and Their Applications for Distributed Parameter Systems

Authors
Professor Yoshikazu Sawaragi
Department of Applied Mathematics and Physics
Faculty of Engineering, Kyoto University,
Kyoto, Japan.

Professor Takashi Soeda
Department of Information Science and Systems Engineering,
Faculty of Engineering, University of Tokushima,
Tokushima, Japan.

Assistant Professor Shigeru Omatu
Department of Information Science and Systems Engineering,
Faculty of Engineering, University of Tokushima,
Tokushima, Japan.

ISBN 978-3-540-09142-4 ISBN 978-3-540-35401-7 (eBook)
DOI 10.1007/978-3-540-35401-7

Originally published by Springer-Verlag Berlin Heidelberg New York in 1978

2061/3020-543210

Preface

Recent developments in estimation and control problems have concentrated primarily on systems whose dynamic behavior can be adequately described by ordinary differential equations. In view of the present trend of rapidly advancing science and technology, it is most likely that the control systems call for more stringent design specifications and more complex control objectives, particularly in industrial processes and environmental systems. This generally requires the consideration of a more accurate mathematical description of the systems to be controlled.

In general it seems that all physical systems are intrinsically distributed in nature. However, in many physical situations, the system's spatial energy distribution is sufficiently concentrated or invariant in form during the course of motion so that an approximated lumped parameter description may be adequate. On the other hand, the spatial energy distributions of many practical systems are widely dispersed. For example, we can imagine optical or acoustic waves propagating in the random media. Hence, it is desired to consider the precise estimation and control problems of certain spatially distributed parameter models which are described in terms of stochastic partial differential equations.

In this book, we treat the estimation and control problems for linear stochastic distributed parameter systems. Background material in probability theory and stochastic processes in Hilbert spaces are given in Chapter 2. Chapters 3-4 are devoted to a study of optimal estimation problems for a linear stochastic distributed parameter system and Chapter 5 presents the optimal sensor location problems. Chapter 6 develops the optimal control problems for a linear stochastic distributed parameter system.

ACKNOWLEDGEMENTS

We acknowledge with thanks the valuable comments and criticisms by Professor Yoshiyuki Sakawa of Osaka University and Dr. Ruth F. Curtain of the Mathematics Institute in Groningen, Netherlands. Furthermore, we owe a lot to the many researchers of the University of Tokushima, who have made candid comments on the many experiments for different ways of presenting the material.

Finally, we are indebted to Professor Dr.-Ing. Manfred Thoma, Direktor des Instituts für Regelungstechnik, Technische Universität Hannover, who has been very generous in providing detailed criticisms of our manuscript.

TABLE OF CONTENTS

Chapter 1. Introduction.

Two important problems in technology and applied science are estimation and control of the behavior of physical processes, subject to random disturbances and observation errors, such that a cost functional is optimized. Our concern in this book is with a class of problems within the framework of a general problem of estimation and control for a linear distributed parameter system. The estimation problems are those of obtaining an approximation to the time history of a process's behavior from noisy observation data. The approximation is typically chosen as one which is best in some sense. The control problem is that of determining inputs to a process in order to achieve the desired goals such as maximum yield or minimum expenditure of fuel in spite of the random disturbances which are present. These problems fall within the domain of the stochastic estimation and control theories. They are related each other because the mathematical techniques utilized in approaching one are also relevant in attacking the other and because to solve the estimation problem is usually a first step in implementing a control input, that is, it is necessary to infer a process's behavior before effective control can be applied.

We assume in this book that a physical system has two sets of input variables, that is, a control input which can usually be manipulated as desired and a disturbance input which reflects the presence of internal phenomena which are inherent in the system and its environment, such as noise in electronic circuits, interference due to stray radiation and turbulence in aircraft flight which is caused by random wind gusts.

The system's behavior or responce is then observed with the aid of some suitable collection of sensors termed as the observation system. The sensors are , of course, subject to random and systematic instrument and phenomenon errors.

For example, a multi spectral scanner is used on some satellits to classify the patterns of the objects on the ground for remote sensing problems. However, the instrument gives erroneous results not only because of internal electronic noise but also because irregularities in the earth's atomosphere do not permit a sharp resolvent element.

Then, the observed data yield only crude information about a system's behavior and in themselves, may be unsatisfactory for assessing the system's cost performance. Thus, the estimation problem consists in determining an approximation to the time history of the system's response variables from the erroneous observation data. If a cost functional is introduced to assess the quality of the approximation or estimate, and the estimate is to be chosen so that this functional is either minimized or maximized, the problem is termed as the optimal estimation problem. Implicit here is the development of an algorithm for processing the observation data.

On the other hand, the control problem is that of specifying a manner in which the control input should be manipulated to force the system to behave in some desired fashion. If, as in the estimation problem, a cost functional is introduced to evaluate the quality of the system's behavior , and the control input is to be specified to minimize or maximize this functional, the problem is termed as the optimal control problem. Also, as in the estimation problem, there is implicit here the derivation of an algorithm for control.

This book will be divided into three major sections: first a section on the mathematical aspects of the mathematical models and terminology and concepts necessary to understand our treatment of the estimation and control problems for a stochastic distributed parameter system or for a stochastic system with values in Hilbert spaces; and secondly, the derivations of the optimal estimators, that is, the filtering, smoothing, and prediction estimators for a linear distributed parameter system; and finally, the derivation of the optimal controller.

Chapter 2. MATHEMATICAL PRELIMINARIES.

2.1. Probability theory in Hilbert spaces.

2.1.1. Probability theory in Euclidean spaces.

The underlying concept in probability theory is that of the probability space. Let Ω be a set with elements denoted by ω. Ω is the basic sample space and its elements ω are samples or experiment outcomes. A class $\mathcal{J}$ of ω sets is called a Borel field or σ-field if

i) $\Omega \in \mathcal{J}$

ii) if $\Lambda \in \mathcal{J}$, then $\Lambda^c = \Omega - \Lambda \in \mathcal{J}$

iii) if $\Lambda_i \in \mathcal{J}$, $i = 1,2,\cdots$, then $\bigcup_{i=1}^{\infty} \Lambda_i \in \mathcal{J}$.

It can be proved that given a class $\mathcal{J}_0$ of ω sets there is a unique Borel field of ω sets $\mathcal{B}(\mathcal{J}_0)$ with the properties [1]

i) $\mathcal{J}_0 \subset \mathcal{B}(\mathcal{J}_0)$

ii) if $\mathcal{J}_1$ is a Borel field of ω sets and if $\mathcal{J}_0 \subset \mathcal{J}_1$, then $\mathcal{B}(\mathcal{J}_0) \subset \mathcal{J}_1$.

$\mathcal{B}(\mathcal{J}_0)$ is the smallest Borel field of ω sets which contains all the sets of $\mathcal{J}_0$. It is called the Borel field generated by $\mathcal{J}_0$. $A \in \mathcal{J}$ is called an event and $(\Omega, \mathcal{J})$ is called a measurable space. Now let $\mu(\cdot)$ be a real scalar-valued function on the family of events $\mathcal{J}$. We say that $\mu(\cdot)$ is a probability measure which defines the probability of the events $A \in \mathcal{J}$ if and only if it satisfies the following three axioms:

i) $\mu(A) \geq 0$ for all A

ii) $\mu(\Omega) = 1$

iii) for every collection of events $A_1, A_2, \cdots, A_n, \cdots$ in $\mathcal{J}$ for which

$$A_i \cap A_j = \phi, \; i \neq j,$$

$$\mu\left(\bigcup_{i=1}^{\infty} A_i\right) = \sum_{i=1}^{\infty} \mu(A_i).$$

In axiom iii), the events are said to be mutually exclusive.

Then $(\Omega, \mathcal{J}, \mu)$ is called the probability space.

[DEFINITION 2.1] A finite collection of sets $A_1, A_2, \cdots, A_n$ in $\mathcal{J}$ are independent if

$$\mu\left(\bigcap_{i=1}^{\infty} A_i\right) = \mu(A_1) \cdots \mu(A_n).$$

[DEFINITION 2.2] A real finite-valued function $X(\omega)$ defined on Ω is called a real random variable if for any real number x, the inequality

$$X(\omega) \leqq x$$

defines an ω set whose probability is defined. This means that $\{\omega \,;\, X(\omega) \leqq x\} \in \mathcal{J}$.

[DEFINITION 2.3] A stochastic process $\{X_{t,x}(\omega),\ t \in T,\ x \in D\}$ is a mapping from t,x to a family of real random variables denoted by Mes$[\Omega, \mu\,;\, \mathbf{R}]$, where T denotes the time index and D is the spatial domain.

In what follows, we shall denote $\{X_{t,x}(\omega),\ t \in T,\ x \in D\}$ as $\{X_{t,x}(\omega)\}$ for simplicity. Note that the stochastic process may depend only on the time $t \in T$ or on the spatial parameter $x \in D$.

In view of the definition of a random variable $X(\omega)$, the function

$$F_X(x) = \mu\,\{\omega \mid X(\omega) \leqq x\}$$

is defined for all real x and is called the probability distribution function of the random variable $X(\omega)$. A random variable $X(\omega)$ is called discrete if there exists a mass function $m_X(\zeta) > 0$ such that

$$F_X(x) = \sum_{\zeta \leq x} m_X(\zeta).$$

A random variable $X(\omega)$ is called continuous if there exists a probability density function $f_X(\zeta)$ such that

$$F_X(x) = \int_{-\infty}^{x} f_X(\zeta)\, d\zeta, \qquad -\infty < x < \infty.$$

The probability density function exists if the distribution function is absolutely continuous, that is, the number of points at which $F_X(\cdot)$ is not differentiable is countable. The expectation of a continuous random variable $X(\omega)$ is defined by

$$E[\,X(\omega)\,] = \int_{-\infty}^{\infty} x\, f_X(x)\, dx.$$

If there does not exist a probability density function $f_X(x)$, then we define $E[\,X(\omega)\,]$ by

$$E[\,X(\omega)\,] = \int_{-\infty}^{\infty} x\, dF_X(x).$$

As the probability measure μ is defined on $\mathcal{T}$, we can describe the integral in terms of $\mu(\omega)$ and we have

$$E[\,X(\omega)\,] = \int_{\Omega} X(\omega)\, d\mu(\omega) = \int_{-\infty}^{\infty} x\, dF_X(x)$$

where

$$\int_{\Omega} X(\omega)\, d\mu(\omega) = \lim_{n\to\infty} \left[\sum_{k=-\infty}^{\infty} \frac{k-1}{2^n}\, \mu\left\{\omega\, ;\, \frac{k-1}{2^n} \leq X(\omega) < \frac{k}{2^n}\right\} \right].$$

When we have p random variables $X_1(\omega), \cdots, X_p(\omega)$, we define the joint probability distribution function $F_{X_1\cdots X_p}(x_1, \cdots, x_p)$ by

$$F_{X_1\cdots X_p}(x_1, \cdots, x_p) = \mu\{\omega\, ;\, X_1(\omega) \leq x_1, \cdots, X_p(\omega) \leq x_p\}$$

and the joint probability density function $f_{X_1\cdots X_p}(x_1, \cdots, x_p)$ by

$$F_{X_1 \cdots X_p}(x_1, \cdots, x_p) = \int_{-\infty}^{x_1} \cdots \int_{-\infty}^{x_p} f_{X_1 \cdots X_p}(\zeta_1, \cdots, \zeta_p)\, d\zeta_1 \cdots d\zeta_p .$$

We define the covariance Γ_{12} of $X_1(\omega)$ and $X_2(\omega)$ by

$$\Gamma_{12} = E\{(X_1(\omega) - m_1)(X_2(\omega) - m_2)\}$$

$$= \iint_{\mathbf{R}^2} (x_1 - m_1)(x_2 - m_2)\, dF_{X_1 X_2}(x_1, x_2)$$

where

$$m_1 = E[X_1(\omega)] \text{ and } m_2 = E[X_2(\omega)].$$

[DEFINITION 2.4] The two jointly distributed random variables $X_1(\omega)$ and $X_2(\omega)$ are uncorrelated if $\Gamma_{12} = 0$.

[DEFINITION 2.5] We say that $X_1(\omega)$ and $X_2(\omega)$ are independent if

$$\mu\{\omega ; X_1(\omega) \leq x_1, X_2(\omega) \leq x_2\} = \mu\{\omega; X_1(\omega) \leq x_1\} \mu\{\omega ; X_2(\omega) \leq x_2\} .$$

Let us now consider a stochastic process $X_{t,x}(\omega)$. We define the expectation of the process by

$$m_{t,x} = E[X_{t,x}(\omega)], \text{ for all } t,x.$$

We shall also introduce

$$\Gamma(t_1, t_2; x_1, x_2) = E[(X_{t_1,x_1}(\omega) - m_{t_1,x_1})(X_{t_2,x_2}(\omega) - m_{t_2,x_2})]$$

and Γ is called the correlation function of the process $X_{t,x}(\omega)$.

[DEFINITION 2.6] A random variable $X(\omega)$ is Gaussian, or equivalently, normally distributed if its probability density function is given by

$$f_X(x) = (1/2\Pi\sigma^2)^{1/2} \exp[-\tfrac{1}{2}(\frac{x-m}{\sigma})^2]$$

where m and σ^2 are constant parameters.

An easy computation shows that

$$m = E[X(\omega)], \quad \sigma^2 = E[(X(\omega) - m)^2] = \mathrm{Var}[X(\omega)].$$

σ^2 is called the variance and σ is called the standard deviation of $X(\omega)$. Note that m and σ characterize the Gaussian probability density function. If the random variable $X(\omega)$ is Gaussian with mean m and variance σ^2, we sometimes write

$$X(\omega) \sim N(m, \sigma^2).$$

[DEFINITION 2.6'] n Random variables $X_1(\omega), \cdots, X_n(\omega)$ are n-dimensional Gaussian or equivalently, n jointly normally distributed, if the probability density function is given by

$$f_X(\zeta) = [(2\Pi)^{n/2} |\Gamma|^{1/2}]^{-1} \exp[-\tfrac{1}{2}(\Gamma^{-1}(\zeta - m), \zeta - m)]$$

$$m = \mathrm{Col}[m_1, \cdots, m_n], \quad m_i = E[X_i(\omega)]$$

$$\Gamma = \{\Gamma_{ij}\}, \quad \Gamma_{ij} = E[(X_i(\omega) - m_i)(X_j(\omega) - m_j)]$$

where the $n \times n$ matrix Γ is called the covariance matrix, (,) denotes an inner product in R^n, Γ^{-1} denotes the matrix inverse, $|\cdot|$ denotes the determinant. If for any n and $t_1, \cdots, t_n \in T$, $X_{t_1}(\omega), \cdots, X_{t_n}(\omega)$ are n-dimensional Gaussian, then the stochastic process $\{X_t(\omega)\}$ is said to be Gaussian.

[DEFINITION 2.7] A stochastic process $W(t,\omega)$ is a standard Wiener (or Brounian motion, or Wiener-Lévy) process if

i) $W(0,\omega) = 0$

ii) the random variables $w(t_1,\omega), \cdots, W(t_n,\omega)$ are n-dimensional Gaussian processes whose parameter are

$$E[W(t,\omega)] = 0, \quad E[W(t_i,\omega) W(t_j,\omega)] = \min(t_i, t_j).$$

More generally, we consider a Gaussian stochastic process $W(t,\omega)$ such that

$$E[\, W(t,\omega)\,] = 0 \quad \text{and} \quad E[\, W(t_i,\omega)\, W(t_j,\omega)\,] = \int_0^{\min(t_i,t_j)} q(\tau)d\tau \;, \; q > 0.$$

$W(t,\omega)$ is called a Wiener process.

If we consider also a Gaussian process $W(t,x,\omega)$ such that $E[\, W(t,x,\omega)\,] = 0$ and

$$E[\, W(t_1,x_1,\omega)\, W(t_2,x_2,\omega)\,] = \int_0^{\min(t_1,\, t_2)} q(\tau,x_1,x_2)\, d\tau \;, \; q > 0,$$

then $W(t,x,\omega)$ is called a Wiener process in time. If the correlation function is given by

$$E[\, W(t_1,\, x_1,\omega)\, W(t_2,x_2,\omega)\,] = \int_0^{\min(t_1,t_2)}\int_0^{\min(x_1,x_2)} q(\tau,\zeta)\, d\tau d\zeta, \; q > 0,$$

then $W(t,x,\omega)$ is called a Wiener process in time and in space.

[DEFINITION 2,8] A white Gaussian process $\{\, \xi(t,\omega),\; t \in T,\; \omega \in \Omega \,\}$ is defined as a Gaussian process with

$$E[\, (\, \xi(t_1,\omega) - m_1)(\, \xi(t_2,\omega) - m_2)\,] = \delta(\, t_1 - t_2)$$

where $\delta(\cdot)$ denotes the Dirac delta function and

$$m_1 = E[\, \xi(\, t_1,\omega)\,], \quad m_2 = E[\, \xi(\, t_2,\omega)\,].$$

Let us consider a stochastic process $\xi(t,x,\omega)$ depend on time and space.

A white Gaussian process in time is defined as a Gaussian process with

$$\begin{aligned} \Gamma_{t_1t_2x_1x_2} &= E[\, (\, \xi(t_1,x_1,\omega) - m_1)(\, \xi(t_2,x_2,\omega) - m_2)\,] \\ &= \delta(\, t_1 - t_2)\, q(t_1,x_1,x_2), \quad q > 0 \end{aligned}$$

where

$$m_1 = E[\, \xi(t_1,x_1,\omega)\,] \text{ and } m_2 = E[\, \xi(t_2,x_2,\omega)\,].$$

A white Gaussian process in time and in space is defined by replacing $\Gamma_{t_1t_2x_1x_2}$ by

$$\Gamma_{t_1t_2x_1x_2} = \delta(\, t_1 - t_2)\, \delta(\, x_1 - x_2)\, q(t_1,\, x_1), \quad q > 0.$$

2.1.2. Probability theory in Hilbert spaces.

Based on the results in the previous section, we shall develop the probability theory in Hilbert spaces which plays an essential role in the analysis of the estimation and control problems for a linear stochastic distributed parameter system. These ideas were originally developed by Falb[2], Curtain[3],[4], and Bensoussan[5], and then extended by Omatu et al.[6]-[8].

Let $(\Omega, \mathcal{B}(\Omega), \mu)$ be a complete probability space with Ω as a topological space, $\mathcal{B}(\Omega)$ as the Borel field generated by Ω, and μ as the Radon probability measure on Ω defined by

$$\mu(B) = \sup_{K \subset B} \mu(K), \quad B \in \mathcal{B}(\Omega)$$

where the supremum is taken for all compact subsets K of B. Let Φ be a separable real Hilbert space and let $\langle \, , \, \rangle_\Phi$ be the scalar product between Φ' and Φ.

[DEFINITION 2.9] A function $\chi(\omega)$ defined on Ω is called measurable if $\chi(\omega)$ is essentially separably-valued and $\chi^{-1}(\mathcal{O}) \in \mathcal{B}(\Omega)$ for each open set $\mathcal{O}$ in Φ. Such a measurable function $\chi(\omega)$ is called a random variable with a value in Φ and the space of $\chi(\omega)$ is denoted by Mes$[\Omega, \mu; \Phi]$.

[DEFINITION 2.10] $\chi(\omega)$ is called a second order random variable if $\chi(\omega)$ satisfies

$$E[\, \| \chi(\omega) \|^2 \,] = \int_\Omega \| \chi(\omega) \|^2 \, d\mu(\omega) < \infty \quad ,$$

and the space of $\chi(\omega)$ is denoted by $L^2(\Omega, \mu; \Phi)$.

[DEFINITION 2.11] $\chi(t,\omega)$ is called a stochastic process with values in Φ if $\chi(t,\omega)$ is measurable on $[0, T] \times \Omega$ using the Lebesgue measure on $[0, T]$.

[DEFINITION 2.12] The linear random functional on Φ' is defined by a linear mapping from Φ' into Mes [Ω , μ ; **R**], that is, a family of real random variables $X_\phi(\omega)$ for any $\phi \in \Phi'$ such that

$$X_{\alpha^1\phi^1 + \alpha^2\phi^2}(\omega) = \alpha^1 X_{\phi^1}(\omega) + \alpha^2 X_{\phi^2}(\omega), \quad \text{a.e.}\,\omega \in \Omega$$

for α^1, $\alpha^2 \in R$ and ϕ^1, $\phi^2 \in \Phi'$

where a.e. denotes tha almost everywhere and Φ' denotes the dual space of Φ.
If $X_\phi(\omega)$ is continuous from Φ' into R, then $X_\phi(\omega)$ is given by the following relation [9]:

$$X_\phi(\omega) = < \phi , X(\omega) >_\Phi \quad , X(\omega) \in \text{Mes}\,[\,\Omega , \mu ; \Phi\,].$$

If $X_\phi(\omega)$ is integrable and the mapping from $\phi \in \Phi'$ into $E[\, X_\phi(\omega)\,] \in \mathbf{R}$ is continuous, then there exists $m \in \Phi$ [9] such that

$$E[\, X_\phi(\omega)\,] = < \phi, m >_\Phi . \tag{2.1}$$

m is called the mean value or the expectation of $X(\omega)$ and is denoted by $E[\, X(\omega)\,]$.
Now we define the covariance function $\Gamma(\phi^1,\phi^2)$ for ϕ^1, $\phi^2 \in \Phi'$ by

$$\Gamma(\phi^1,\phi^2) = E[\,(\, X_{\phi^1}(\omega) - m_1)(\, Y_{\phi^2}(\omega) - m_2)\,]$$

where

$$m_1 = E[\, X_{\phi^1}(\omega)\,] \text{ and } m_2 = E[\, Y_{\phi^2}(\omega)\,].$$

If the mapping from $(\phi^1,\phi^2) \in \Phi' \times \Phi'$ into $\Gamma(\phi^1,\phi^2) \in \mathbf{R}$ is continuous, then there exists an operator $\Gamma \in \mathcal{L}(\Phi', \Phi)$ [9] such that

$$\Gamma(\phi^1,\phi^2) = < \phi^1, \Gamma\, \phi^2 >_\Phi . \tag{2.2}$$

Γ is called the covariance operator of $X(\omega)$ and $Y(\omega)$ and denoted by Cov [$X(\omega)$, $Y(\omega)$].
Assume that Φ is identified with its dual Φ'. Then we have the definition of a Wiener process with values in Φ .

[DEFINITION 2.13] Assume that J_n is a finite set of nonnegative integers.

$W(t,\omega)$ is called a Wiener process with values in Φ or a Φ-valued Wiener process if $W(t,\omega)$ is a random variable with values in Φ for any fixed $t \in [0, T]$ and $W_{\phi^j}(t_i,\omega) = (\phi^j, W(t_i,\omega))$ for any $\phi^j \in \Phi$ and $\forall i,j \in J_n$ is a real Gaussian random variable such that

$$E[W(t,\omega)] = 0, \quad t \geqq 0$$

$$E[W_{\phi^j}(t_i,\omega) W_{\phi^k}(t_n,\omega)] = \int_0^{\min(t_i,t_n)} (\phi^j, Q(\tau)\phi^k)_\Phi \, d\tau \qquad (2.3)$$

where $(\ ,\ )_\Phi$ denotes the scalar product in Φ and it equals to that $<\ ,\ >_\Phi$ in the case of $\Phi = \Phi'$. Furthermore, we assume that $Q(\tau)$ satisfies

$$Q(\tau) \in L^\infty(0,T; \mathcal{L}(\Phi, \Phi))$$

and that $Q(\tau)$ is nonnegative, self-adjoint, and nuclear operator for a.e. $\tau \in [0,T]$. Define the notation " $x \circ y$ " for any $x \in \Phi$ and $y \in \Psi'$ [2] by

$$(x \circ y) z = x < y, z >_\Psi, \quad \forall z \in \Psi \qquad (2.4)$$

where Ψ is a Hilbert space.

We observe that if $\Phi = R^n$, i.e., Φ is finite-dimensinal, then $x \circ y$ can be identified with the matrix xy^T where superscript " T " denotes the transpose of the matrix. Moreover, we have the following lemma:

[LEMMA 2.1] Let ϕ be the mapping from $\Phi \times \Psi'$ into $\mathcal{L}(\Psi, \Phi)$ defined by

$$\phi(x, y) = x \circ y.$$

Then ϕ has the following properties:

i) $\phi(x, y)$ is a linear mapping from Ψ into Φ for all x and y,

ii) ϕ is continuous since

$$\|\phi(x, y)\|_{\mathcal{L}(\Psi, \Phi)} = \|x\|_\Phi \, \|y\|_{\Psi'}$$

iii) the adjoint $\phi^*(x,y)$ of $\phi(x,y)$ is $y \circ x$, i.e.,

$$(x \circ y)^{*} = y \circ x \tag{2.5}$$

iv) if $N \varepsilon \mathcal{L}(\Psi', \Psi')$, then

$$(x \circ Ny) = (x \circ y) N^{*}. \tag{2.6}$$

[PROOF] Property i) is obvious from the definition (2.4)

ii) is obtained by noting that

$$\|\phi(x, y)\|_{\mathcal{L}(\Psi, \Phi)} = \sup_{\|z\| \leq 1} \|(x \circ y) z \|_{\Phi} = \sup_{\|z\| \leq 1} \| x < y, z >_{\Psi} \|$$

$$= \|x\|_{\Phi} \sup_{\|z\| \leq 1} |< y, z >_{\Psi}| = \|x\|_{\Phi} \|y\|_{\Psi'} .$$

iii) is proved by noting that

$$< \phi(x, y)^{*} z_1, z_2 >_{\Psi} = < z_1, \phi(x, y) z_2 >_{\Phi}$$

$$= < z_1, x < y, z_2 >_{\Psi} >_{\Phi} = < z_1, x >_{\Phi} < y, z_2 >_{\Psi} = < y < z_1, x >_{\Phi}, z_2 >_{\Psi}$$

$$= < y < x, z_1 >_{\Phi}, z_2 >_{\Psi} = < (y \circ x) z_1, z_2 >_{\Psi} .$$

iv) is proved by noting that

$$(x \circ Ny) z = x < Ny , z >_{\Psi} = x < y, N^{*} z >_{\Psi} = (x \circ y) N^{*} z$$

for any $z \varepsilon \Phi$.

Hence, the proof of the lemma is completed. Q.E.D.

Observe that the property ii) implies that the linear mapping $\phi(x, y)$ is actually an element of $\mathcal{L}(\Psi, \Phi)$.

Using the notation (2.4) and letting $\Phi = \Psi$, it follows that (2.3) can be more simply described by

$$\mathrm{Cov}[W(t_i,\omega), W(t_n,\omega)] = E [W(t_i,\omega) \circ W(t_n,\omega)]$$

$$= \int_0^{\min(t_i,t_n)} Q(\tau)\, d\tau. \tag{2.7}$$

Note that if $W(t,\omega)$ is a Φ-valued Wiener process and $Q(t) = Q$ independent of time t, then it can be shown that there exist stochastic processes $\{ \beta_i(t),\ t \in [0, T]\}$ such that

$$W(t,\omega) = \sum_{i=0}^{\infty} \beta_i(t)\, e_i \quad \text{a.e. in } (t,\omega)$$

where $e_1, e_2, \cdots$ denote the othonormal bases in Φ and $\beta_i(t),\ i = 1,2,\cdots$ are independent scalar-valued Wiener processes.

Then the following theorem can be proved.

[THEOREM 2.1] If $W(t,\omega)$ is a Φ-valued Wiener process, then $W(t,\omega)$ is continuous with respect to time t, i.e.,

$$W(t,\omega) \in C(0, T ; L^2(\Omega, \mu ; \Phi)) \tag{2.8}$$

with independent increments such that

$$E [(W(t_2,\omega) - W(t_1,\omega)) (W(t_4,\omega) - W(t_3,\omega))]$$
$$= E [(W(t_2,\omega) - W(t_1,\omega), W(t_4,\omega) - W(t_3,\omega))_\Phi] = 0 \text{ for } t_1 \leq t_2 \leq t_3 \leq t_4,$$

equivalently

$$(W(t_2,\omega) - W(t_1,\omega), e_1)_\Phi \text{ and } (W(t_4,\omega) - W(t_3,\omega), e_2)_\Phi \text{ are independent}$$
$$\text{real Gaussian random variables for } \forall e_1, e_2 \in \Phi . \tag{2.9}$$

[PROOF] The last statement is obtained by noting that

$$E [(W(t_2,\omega) - W(t_1,\omega), e_1)_\Phi (W(t_4,\omega) - W(t_3,\omega), e_2)_\Phi]$$
$$= \int_0^{\min(t_2,t_4)} (Q(\tau)e_1, e_2)_\Phi\, d\tau - \int_0^{\min(t_2,t_3)} (Q(\tau)e_1, e_2)_\Phi\, d\tau$$
$$- \int_0^{\min(t_1,t_4)} (Q(\tau)e_1, e_2)_\Phi\, d\tau + \int_0^{\min(t_1,t_3)} (Q(\tau)e_1, e_2)_\Phi\, d\tau$$
$$= \int_0^{t_2} (Q(\tau)e_1, e_2)_\Phi\, d\tau - \int_0^{t_2} (Q(\tau)e_1, e_2)_\Phi\, d\tau$$
$$- \int_0^{t_1} (Q(\tau)e_1, e_2)_\Phi\, d\tau + \int_0^{t_1} (Q(\tau)e_1, e_2)_\Phi\, d\tau = 0.$$

The random variables $(W(t_2,\omega) - W(t_1,\omega), e_1)_\Phi$ and $(W(t_4,\omega) - W(t_3,\omega), e_2)_\Phi$ are Gaussian and uncorrelated, hence, the independent property was established. From the Parseval equality we have

$$\|W(t,\omega)\|_\Phi^2 = (W(t,\omega), W(t,\omega))_\Phi = \Sigma_{n=1}^{\infty} (W(t,\omega), e_n)_\Phi^2$$

Let us now define $A_N(\omega)$ by

$$A_N(\omega) = \Sigma_{n=1}^{N} (W(t,\omega), e_n)_\Phi^2 .$$

It is clear that the series $A_N(\omega)$ is a convergent sequence and that

$$E [A_N(\omega)] = \int_0^t \Sigma_{n=1}^{N} (Q(\tau) e_n, e_n)_\Phi \, d\tau \leqq \int_0^t \text{tr } Q(\tau) \, d\tau$$

where tr[ ] denotes the trace of the operator given by

$$\text{tr } Q(t) = \Sigma_{n=1}^{\infty} (Q(t) e_n, e_n)_\Phi .$$

Hence, from Lebesgue's convergence theorem it follows that $E [\|W(t,\omega)\|_\Phi^2]$ exists and

$$E [\|W(t,\omega)\|_\Phi^2] = \lim_{N\to\infty} \int_0^t \Sigma_{n=1}^{N} (Q(\tau) e_n, e_n)_\Phi \, d\tau$$

$$= \int_0^t \text{tr } Q(\tau) \, d\tau.$$

Let ε be arbitrary positive number. Then we shall prove that

$$E [(W(t,\omega), W(t+\varepsilon,\omega))_\Phi] = \int_0^t \text{tr } Q(\tau) \, d\tau .$$

From the Parseval inequality we have

$$(W(t,\omega), W(t+\varepsilon,\omega))_\Phi = \Sigma_{n=1}^{\infty} (W(t,\omega), e_n)_\Phi (W(t+\varepsilon,\omega), e_n)_\Phi .$$

Hence, the series $B_N(\omega)$ given by

$$B_N(\omega) = \Sigma_{n=1}^{N} (W(t,\omega), e_n)_\Phi (W(t+\varepsilon,\omega), e_n)_\Phi$$

is a convergent sequence and

$$\| B_N(\omega) \|_\Phi \leqq \Sigma_{n=1}^{N} | (W(t,\omega), e_n)_\Phi | \, | (W(t+\varepsilon,\omega), e_n)_\Phi |$$

$$\leqq (\Sigma_{n=1}^{N} (W(t,\omega), e_n)^2)^{1/2} (\Sigma_{n=1}^{N} (W(t+\varepsilon,\omega), e_n)^2)^{1/2}$$

$$\leqq \| W(t,\omega) \|_\Phi \, \| W(t+\varepsilon,\omega) \|_\Phi < \infty$$

Hence, from the Lebesgue convergence theorem we have

$$E [\lim_{N \to \infty} B_N(\omega)] = \lim_{N \to \infty} E [B_N(\omega)]$$

hence, we have

$$E [(W(t,\omega), W(t+\varepsilon,\omega))_\Phi] = \lim_{N \to \infty} \int_0^t \Sigma_{n=1}^{N} (Q(\tau)e_n, e_n)_\Phi \, d\tau .$$

On the other hand, it follows from (2.9) that

$$E [\| W(t+\varepsilon,\omega) - W(t,\omega) \|_\Phi^2] = E [\| W(t+\varepsilon,\omega) \|_\Phi^2 + E [\| W(t,\omega) \|_\Phi^2]$$

$$- 2 E [(W(t,\omega), W(t+\varepsilon,\omega))_\Phi]$$

$$= \int_0^{t+\varepsilon} tr \, Q(\tau) \, d\tau + \int_0^t tr \, Q(\tau) \, d\tau - \int_0^t tr \, Q(\tau) \, d\tau$$

$$= \int_t^{t+\varepsilon} tr \, Q(\tau) \, d\tau \to 0 \text{ as } \varepsilon \text{ goes to zero.}$$

Hence, (2.8) was proved. The independent increment property is obvious from (2.9). Thus, the proof of the theorm is completed. Q.E.D.

[COROLLARY 2.1] The Wiener process $W(t,\omega)$ is continuous in probability.

[PROOF] It follows from the Chebyshev inequality that

$$\mu \{ \omega ; \| W(t+\varepsilon,\omega) - W(t,\omega) \|_\Phi > \alpha \} \leqq \frac{1}{\alpha^2} E [\| W(t+\varepsilon,\omega) - W(t,\omega) \|_\Phi^2] .$$

From the continuity of $W(t,\omega)$ as stated in Theorem 2.1 and the above inequality the corollary follows. Q.E.D.

2.1.3. Stochastic integral in Hilbert spaces.

Let us now discuss the stochastic integral and develop some properties of this integral required in the following chapters. Let us suppose that H is a Hilbert space identified with its dual H', that is, $H = H'$, and $(\,,\,)$ and $\|\cdot\|$ denote the inner product in H and the norm in H, respectively. Furthermore, assume that $W(t,\omega)$ denoted by $W(t)$ for simplicity is an H-valued Wiener process, and that $S(t)$ is a step function from $[\,0,\,T\,]$ into $\mathcal{L}(\,H,\,H\,)$. In other words, there exist $t_1 \leqq t_2 \leqq \cdots \leqq t_n$ in $[\,0,\,T\,]$ and S_j, $j = 1,2,\cdots,n$ in $\mathcal{L}(\,H,\,H\,)$ such that

$$S(t) = \begin{cases} 0 & t < t_0 \\ S_j & t_{j-1} \leqq t < t_j \qquad\qquad j = 1,\,2,\,\cdots,\,n \\ 0 & t \geqq t_n \end{cases}$$

Then the stochastic integral of $S(t)$ with respect to $d\,W(t)$, in symbols, $\int_0^T S(t)\,d\,W(t)$ is defined by

$$\int_0^T S(t)\,d\,W(t) = \Sigma_{j=1}^{n}\, S_j \quad [\,W(t_j) - W(t_{j-1})\,]. \tag{2.10}$$

We observe that this integral is an H-valued random variable with zero mean. We shall build up the stochastic integral by an approximation procedure based on (2.10). To this end, we have the following lemma.

[LEMMA 2.2] Let $R(t)$ and $S(t)$ be $\mathcal{L}(\,H,\,H\,)$-valued step functions. Then

$$E\,[\,(\int_0^T R(t)\,d\,W(t)\,)\circ(\,\int_0^T S(t)\,d\,W(t)\,)\,] = \int_0^T R(t)\;Q(t)\;S^*(t)\;dt \tag{2.11}$$

and

$$E\,[\|\int_0^T R(t)\,d\,W(t)\|\;\|\int_0^T S(t)\,d\,W(t)\|\;] \leqq \int_0^T \|\,R(t)\|\;\|\,W(t)\|\;\|S(t)\|\;dt. \tag{2.12}$$

[PROOF] By adding 0's if necessary, we may suppose that there are $t_0 < t_1 < \cdots < t_n$ in [0, T] such that

$$R(t) = \begin{cases} 0, & t < t_0 \\ R_j, & t_{j-1} \leqq t < t_j \\ 0, & t \geqq t_n, \end{cases} \qquad S(t) = \begin{cases} 0, & t < t_0 \\ S_k, & t_{k-1} \leqq t < t_k \\ 0, & t \geqq t_n. \end{cases}$$

It then follows that

$$(\int_0^T R(t)\, dW(t)) \circ (\int_0^T S(t)\, dW(t))$$

$$= \Sigma_{j=1}^{n} \Sigma_{k=1}^{n} R_j [W(t_j) - W(t_{j-1})] \circ S_k [W(t_k) - W(t_{k-1})]$$

and from (2.6) and (2.7) that

$$E [(\int_0^T R(t)\, dW(t)) \circ (\int_0^T S(t)\, dW(t))]$$

$$= \Sigma_{j=1}^{n} \Sigma_{k=1}^{n} R_j E [(W(t_j) - W(t_{j-1})) \circ (W(t_k) - W(t_{k-1}))] S_k^*$$

$$= \Sigma_{j=1}^{n} R_j \int_{t_{j-1}}^{t_j} Q(\tau)\, d\tau \; S_j^* = \int_0^T R(t)\, Q(t)\, S^*(t)\, dt.$$

Similarly, we have from Lemma 2.1 and (2.11) that

$$E [\| \int_0^T R(t)\, dW(t) \| \; \| \int_0^T S(t)\, dW(t) \|]$$

$$= E [\| \int_0^T R(t)\, dW(t) \circ \int_0^T S(t)\, dW(t) \|]$$

$$= \| \int_0^T R(t)\, Q(t)\, S^*(t)\, dt \| \leqq \int_0^T \| R(t) \| \, \| Q(t) \| \, \| S(t) \| \, dt$$

where the equality $\| S(t) \| = \| S^*(t) \|$ was used [9].

Hence, the lemma was proved. Q.E.D.

In view of Lemma 2.2, we can define a stochastic integral in a manner analogous to that used in Doob [1]. In other words, if $S(t)$ is an element of $L^2($ 0, T;

$\mathcal{L}$(H, H)) so that

$$\int_0^T \|S(t)\|^2 \, dt < \infty ,$$

then S(t) is a limit of the step functions $S_m(t)$, i.e.,

$$\lim_{m\to\infty} \int_0^T \| S(t) - S_m(t)\|^2 \, dt = 0 \tag{2.13}$$

and we can define the stochastic integral of S(t) with respect to dw(t), in symbols, $\int_0^T S(t)\,dW(t)$, by letting

$$\int_0^T S(t)\,dW(t) = \underset{m\to\infty}{\text{l.i.m.}} \int_0^T S_m(t)\,dW(t), \tag{2.14}$$

i.e.,

$$\lim_{m\to\infty} E\,[\,\| \int_0^T S(t)\,dW(t) - \int_0^T S_m(t)\,dW(t)\|^2\,] = 0$$

so that $\int_0^T S(t)\,dW(t)$ is the limit in mean square of the $\int_0^T S_m(t)\,dW(t)$. We note that (2.14) follows from (2.13) by virtue of the inequality (2.12). Moreover, $\int_0^T S(t)\,dW(t)$ is also an H-valued random variable with zero mean. Now we have the following lemma.

[LEMMA 2.3] Let S(t) and R(t) be elements of L^2(0, T; $\mathcal{L}$(H, H)). Then

$$E\,[\,(\int_0^T R(t)\,dW(t)) \circ (\int_0^T S(t)\,dW(t))\,] = \int_0^T R(t)\,Q(t)\,S^*(t)\,dt \tag{2.15}$$

and

$$E\,[\| \int_0^T R(t)\,dW(t)\|\,\|\int_0^T S(t)\,dW(t)\|\,]$$

$$\leqq \int_0^T \| R(t)\|\,\|Q(t)\|\,\|S(t)\|\,dt. \tag{2.16}$$

[PROOF] Let $R_m(t)$ and $S_m(t)$ be sequences of step functions that define R(t) and S(t), respectively. Then it follows from (2.11) that

$$\|\,E\,[\,(\int_0^T R(t)\,dW(t)) \circ (\int_0^T S(t)\,dW(t))\,] - \int_0^T R_m(t)\,Q(t)\,S_m^*(t)\,dt\,\|$$

$$\leq \| E[(\int_0^T (R(t) - R_m(t)) dW(t)) \circ \int_0^T S(t) dW(t)] \|$$

$$+ \quad \| E[\int_0^T R_m(t) dW(t) \circ (\int_0^T (S(t) - S_m(t)) dW(t))] \|$$

By virtue of Schwarz's inequality and Lemma 2.1, we have

$$\| E[(\int_0^T (R(t) - R_m(t)) dW(t)) \circ \int_0^T S(t) dW(t)] \|$$

$$\leq E[\|\int_0^T (R(t) - R_m(t)) dW(t)\| \|\int_0^T S(t) dW(t)\|]$$

$$\leq (E[\|\int_0^T (R(t) - R_m(t)) dW(t)\|^2] E[\| \int_0^T S(t) dW(t) \|^2])^{1/2}.$$

The right hand side of the above inequality goes to zero since (2.14) holds when m approaches infinity. Similarly, we have

$$\| E[(\int_0^T R_m(t) dW(t)) \circ (\int_0^T (S(t) - S_m(t)) dW(t))] \| \to 0$$

as $m \to 0$.

On the other hand, we have

$$\varepsilon_m \triangleq \| \int_0^T R(t) Q(t) S^*(t) dt - \int_0^T R_m(t) Q(t) S_m^*(t) dt \|$$

$$\leq \int_0^T \| R(t) - R_m(t)\| \| Q(t) \| \| S_m^*(t)\| dt$$

$$+ \int_0^T \| R(t) \| \| Q(t) \| \| S(t) - S_m(t)\| dt.$$

By virtue of Schwarz's inequality and (2.13), we have

$$\lim_{m \to \infty} \varepsilon_m = 0 .$$

Hence, (2.15) follows from the above relations.

Let us now prove (2.16). Using Lemma 2.1, we have

$$E[\| \int_0^T R(t) dW(t) \| \|\int_0^T S(t) dW(t)\|] = E[\|\int_0^T R(t) dW(t) \circ$$

$$(\int_0^T S(t)\, dW(t)) \|].$$

But, again using Lemma 2.1,

$$E [\| (\int_0^T R(t)\, dW(t)) \circ (\int_0^T S(t)\, dW(t)) \|]$$

$$\leqq E [\| \int_0^T (R(t) - R_m(t))\, dW(t) \| \, \| \int_0^T S(t)\, dW(t) \|]$$

$$+ E [\| \int_0^T R_m(t)\, dW(t) \| \, \| \int_0^T (S(t) - S_m(t))\, dW(t) \|]$$

$$+ E [\| \int_0^T R_m(t)\, dW(t) \| \, \| \int_0^T S_m(t)\, dW(t) \|].$$

By virtue of Schwarz's inequality, we have

$$\lim_{m \to \infty} E [\| \int_0^T (R(t) - R_m(t))\, dW(t) \| \, \| \int_0^T S(t)\, dW(t) \|] = 0,$$

$$\lim_{m \to \infty} E [\| \int_0^T R_m(t)\, dW(t) \| \, \| \int_0^T (S(t) - S_m(t))\, dW(t) \|] = 0,$$

and so, in view of (2.12), we need only show that

$$\lim_{m \to \infty} \int_0^T \| R_m(t) \| \, \| Q(t) \| \, \| S_m(t) \| \, dt$$

$$= \int_0^T \| R(t) \| \, \| Q(t) \| \, \| S(t) \| \, dt$$

or, equivalently, that

$$\lim_{m \to \infty} \int_0^T \| R_m(t) \| \, \| S_m(t) \| \, dt = \int_0^T \| R(t) \| \, \| S(t) \| \, dt.$$

But

$$| \int_0^T \| R(t) \| \, \| S(t) \| \, dt - \int_0^T \| R_m(t) \| \, \| S_m(t) \| \, dt |$$

$$\leqq \int_0^T \| R(t) - R_m(t) \| \, \| S(t) \| \, dt + \int_0^T \| R_m(t) \| \, \| S(t) - S_m(t) \| \, dt.$$

Combining the above relations with Schwarz's inequality, we obtain (2.16). Q.E.D.

The arguement used in proving Lemma 2.3 is quite standard and will be used in various guises in the sequel. Thus, we shall simply use the phrase " by an approximation argument" in the case of applying the method.

Now we observe that if $t \in [0, T]$, then

$$I(t) = \int_0^t R(s)\, dW(s), \quad \forall t \in [0, T] \tag{2.17}$$

may be viewed as an H-valued stochastic process. If R(t) is a step function, then $\int_0^t R(s)\, dW(s)$ has a version which is measurable in the pair (t, ω) in view of the continuity of the sample paths of W(t). We shall see that this is true for the general case in the sequel.

[LEMMA 2.4] Let I(t) be defined by the stochastic integral of (2.17). Then I(t) is an element of $L^2(\Omega, \mu; H)$ and $I(t_2) - I(t_1)$ is orthogonal to I(t) for $t \leqq t_1 < t_2$ in the $L^2(\Omega, \mu; H)$ sense, i.e.,

$$E[(I(t_2) - I(t_1), I(t))] = 0. \tag{2.18}$$

[PROOF] The assertion that I(t) is in $L^2(\Omega, \mu; H)$ is an immediate consequence of the definition of the stochastic integral,(2.17). (2.18) is established by an approximation argument which is omitted. Q.E.D.

[LEMMA 2.5] If $s \leqq t$, then

$$E[\|I(s)\|^2] \leqq E[\|I(t)\|^2]. \tag{2.19}$$

[PROOF] Let us first prove that

$$(I(t), I(t)) = \mathrm{tr}[I(t) \circ I(t)].$$

By virtue of Parseval's equality, we have

$$(I(t), I(t)) = \sum_{i=1}^{\infty} (I(t), e_i)^2$$

where $e_1, e_2, \cdots$ are complete orthonormal bases in H.

On the other hand, we have from the definition of the trace operator

$$\mathrm{tr}[\, I(t) \circ I(t)\,] = \Sigma_{i=1}^{\infty} ((\, I(t) \circ I(t))\, e_i, e_i)$$

$$= \Sigma_{i=1}^{\infty} (\, I(t)\, (\, I(t), e_i), e_i) = \Sigma_{i=1}^{\infty} (\, I(t), e_i)^2$$

Hence, the above relation holds. Then using (2.15) yields

$$E[\, \| I(t) \|^2 \,] = E[\, \mathrm{tr}[\, I(t) \circ I(t)\,]] = \mathrm{tr}[\, E[\, I(t) \circ I(t)\,]]$$

$$= \mathrm{tr}[\, \int_0^t R(\tau)\, Q(\tau)\, R^*(\tau)\, d\tau\,] = \int_0^t \mathrm{tr}[\, R(\tau)\, Q(\tau)\, R^*(\tau)\,]\, d\tau.$$

But the integrand of the last equation is nonnegative since $Q(t) \geqq 0$.
Thus, (2.19) is obvious from the above relations. Q.E.D.

We shall in the sequel have occasion to consider double integrals of the form

$$\int_0^T \int_0^T R(s,t)\, ds\, dW(t), \tag{2.20}$$

where the $\mathcal{L}(\, H, H\,)$-valued function $R(s,t)$ is measurable in s and continuous in t. We shall define this integral in terms of iterated integrals.

[LEMMA 2.6] Suppose that $R(s,t)$ is measurable in s and that

$$\int_0^T \| R(s,t) \|^2\, dt < \infty \tag{2.21}$$

almost everywhere in s. Then the stochastic integral

$$J(s) = \int_0^T R(s,t)\, dW(t)$$

can be defined in such a way that the process $J(s)$ is measurable.

[PROOF] Suppose first that

$$R(s,t) = \Sigma_{j=1}^{k} R_{1j}(s)\, R_{2j}(t)$$

where k is a finite integer and the $R_{1j}(t)$ and $R_{2j}(t)$ are measurable and

$$\int_0^T \| R_{2j}(t)\|^2 \, dt < \infty .$$

Then by the definition of the stochastic integral,

$$J(s) = \Sigma_{j=1}^{k} R_{1j}(s) \int_0^T R_{2j}(t)\, d\,W(t)$$

so that J(s) is measurable in the pair (s,ω), being a finite sum of products of functions measurable in each variable. Then the lemma follows by an approximation argument. Q.E.D.

We are now ready to define the double integral (2.20). Let $[0,S]$ be an interval and suppose that R(s,t) is measurable in s and t. If

$$\int_0^T [\int_0^S \| R(s,t)\| \, ds]^2 \, dt < \infty , \tag{2.22}$$

then

$$L(t) = \int_0^S R(s,t)\, ds$$

is an element of $L^2(0, T ; \mathcal{L}(H, H))$ and so $\int_0^S L(t)\, d\,W(t)$ is defined, i.e., the iterated integral

$$\int_0^T [\int_0^S R(r,t)\, ds]\, d\,W(t) = L_1(\omega), \quad \omega \in \Omega$$

is well-defined. Moreover, using (2.16) yields

$$E [\| L_1(\omega)\|^2] \leqq \int_0^T \| L(t)\|^2 \, \| Q(t)\| \, d\,t < \infty .$$

On the other hand, if

$$\int_0^S [\int_0^T \| R(s,t)\|^2 \, dt]^{1/2} ds < \infty , \tag{2.23}$$

then

$$J_1(s) = \int_0^T R(s,t)\, d\,W(t)$$

may be assumed measurable in the pair (s, ω) by virtue of Lemma 2.6 and $\int_0^S J_1(s)\, ds$

is well-defined, i.e., the iterated integral

$$\int_0^S [\int_0^T R(s,t)\, dW(t)]\, ds = L_2(\omega),$$

is well-defined. Moreover,

$$E[\, \| L_2(\omega) \| \,] \leqq \int_0^S E[\, \| \int_0^T R(s,t)\, dW(t) \| \,]\, ds$$

$$\leqq \int_0^S [\int_0^T \| R(s,t) \|^2 dt]^{1/2} \; \| Q(s) \|^{1/2} \; ds < \infty .$$

We now have

[LEMMA 2.7] Suppose that both (2.22) and (2.23) are valid. Then

$$L_1(\omega) = L_2(\omega) \quad \text{a.e. } \omega \in \Omega .$$

[PROOF] Suppose first of all that

$$R(s,t) = \Sigma_{j=1}^{k} R_{1j}(s)\, R_{2j}(t)$$

with

$$\int_0^S \| R_{1j}(s) \| \, ds < \infty \quad , \quad [\int_0^T \| R_{2j}(t) \|^2 dt]^{1/2} < \infty .$$

Then both (2.22) and (2.23) are valid and it is clear that $L_1(\omega) = L_2(\omega)$. The lemma then follows by an approximation argument. Q.E.D.

The substance of Lemma 2.7 is that the order of integration is immaterial provided that both (2.22) and (2.23) hold. We, of course, define the double integral (2.20) when either (2.22) or (2.23) are valid by means of a suitable iterated integral. We now have

[LEMMA 2.8] Suppose that $[0, S]$ is finite and $R(s,t)$ is an element of $L^2([0,S] \times [0,T] ; \mathcal{L}(H, H))$, i.e.,

$$\int_0^T \int_0^S \| R(s,t) \|^2 \; ds\, dt < \infty . \tag{2.24}$$

Then both (2.22) and (2.23) are valid and hence, the order of integration in (2.20) is immaterial.

[PROOF] Since S is finite, 1 is an element of $L^2(0, S; \mathbf{R})$. It then follows from Schwarz's inequality that

$$\int_0^T [\int_0^S \| R(s,t) \| ds]^2 dt \leqq S \int_0^T [\int_0^S \| R(s,t) \|^2 ds] dt < \infty .$$

Thus, (2.22) holds. On the other hand, if f(s) is given by

$$f(s) = \int_0^T \| R(s,t) \|^2 dt,$$

then $f(s) \geqq 0$ and it will follow from (2.24) that $[f(s)]^{1/2}$ is an element of $L^2(0,S; \mathbf{R})$. In view of Schwarz's inequality, we then observe that $[f(s)]^{1/2}$ is an element of $L^1(0, S; \mathbf{R})$ and that

$$\int_0^S [f(s)]^{1/2} ds = \int_0^S [\int_0^T \| R(s,t) \|^2 dt]^{1/2} ds$$

$$\leqq S^{1/2} \int_0^S \int_0^T \| R(s,t) \|^2 dt\, ds < \infty .$$

Thus, (2.23) holds and the lemma is established. Q.E.D.

Let a regulated mapping be the limit of a uniformly convergent sequence of finite sums of products of step functions. Then by an approximation argument we have

[LEMMA 2.9] Suppose that [0, S] and [0, T] are compact intervals. If R(s,t) is a regulated mapping of $[0, S] \times [0, T]$ into $\mathcal{L}(H, H)$ (in particular, if R(s,t) is continuous), then both (2.22) and (2.23) hold and hence, the order of integration in (2.20) is immaterial.

Now we observe that if S(t) is a step function, then the H-valued stochastic process

$$\tilde{J}(t) = \int_0^t S(s)\, dW(s), \quad \forall t \in [0, T]$$

is continuous in t almost everywhere with respect to ω, and hence, is Lebesgue-integrable with respect to t on any subinterval of [0, T] almost everywhere with respect to ω. In the finite-dimensional case, it is reasonably easy to prove that the stochastic integral

$$K(t) = \int_0^t R(s)\, dW(s)$$

is also continuous in t and therefore, Lebesgue-integrable. Here, in order to avoid considerable complexity relating to the notions of martingale and semimartingale for H-valued stochastic processes, we shall not discuss the continuity of the sample paths of K(t). However, we have the following results:

[LEMMA 2.10] Let $S(t) \varepsilon L^2(0,T;\mathcal{L}(H,H))$ and let $s < t$ be elements of [0, t]. Then

$$E[\,\|\tilde{J}(t) - \tilde{J}(s)\|^2\,] = E[\,\|\int_0^t S(\tau)\,dW(\tau) - \int_0^s S(\tau)\,dW(\tau)\|^2\,]$$

$$\leqq c\,|t - s| \qquad (2.25)$$

where c is a constant independent of s and t.

[PROOF] In view of Lemma 2.3, we have

$$E[\,\|\tilde{J}(t) - \tilde{J}(s)\|^2\,] = E[\,\|\int_s^t S(\tau)\,dW(\tau)\|^2\,]$$

$$\leqq \int_s^t \|S(\tau)\|^2 \|Q(\tau)\|\, d\tau \leqq [\,\underset{\tau \varepsilon [0,T]}{SUP} \|S(\tau)\|^2\, \|Q(\tau)\|\,]\,(t - s).$$

Hence, the lemma was proved. Q.E.D.

[LEMMA 2.11] Let R(t) be an element of $L^2(0,T;\mathcal{L}(H,H))$. Then $\tilde{J}(t,\omega) = \int_0^t R(s)\,dW(s,\omega)$ is measurable in the pair (t,ω) and $\int_0^t \tilde{J}(s,\omega)\,ds$ exists almost everywhere with respect to ω on every finite subinterval of [0, T].

[PROOF] Let F(t) be the mapping of [0, T] into $L^2(\Omega, \mu; H)$ given by

$$F(t) = \tilde{J}(t, \cdot).$$

We claim that F(t) is continuous. Assuming for the moment that this claim is valid and that $[0, T_1]$ is a finite subinterval of [0, T], then there is a function $f(t,\omega)$, measurable in the pair (t,ω) such that i) $f(t,\cdot) = J(t,\cdot)$ almost everywhere in t, ii) $f(\cdot,\omega)$ is integrable in t almost everywhere in ω, iii) $\int_0^T f(t,\omega)\,dt = \int_0^T F(t)\,dt$ (these facts follow from Theorem 17, p.198 of [10]).

In view of the nonuniqueness of the stochastic integral, we can replace $\tilde{J}(t, \omega)$ by $f(t, \omega)$ and the theorem follows.

Now let us verify the claim. Suppose that $s < t$ and that $S_N(t)$ is a step function. Then, letting

$$\tilde{J}_N(t) = \int_0^t S_N(\tau)\, dW(\tau), \quad \forall t \in [0, T],$$

we have

$$E[\, \| F(t) - F(s) \|^2] = E[\, \| \tilde{J}(t) - \tilde{J}(s) \|^2]$$

$$\leq E[\, (\| \tilde{J}(t) - \tilde{J}_N(t) \| + \| \tilde{J}_N(t) - \tilde{J}_N(s) \| + \| \tilde{J}_N(s) - \tilde{J}(s) \|)^2]$$

$$\leq 4 E[\, \| \tilde{J}(t) - \tilde{J}_N(t) \|^2] + 4 E[\, \| \tilde{J}_N(t) - \tilde{J}_N(s) \|^2]$$

$$+ 4 E[\, \| \tilde{J}_N(s) - \tilde{J}(s) \|^2]$$

since $(\| A \| + \| B \|)^2 \leq 2(\| A \|^2 + \| B \|^2)$.

Now let $\varepsilon > 0$ be given. Then since $R(t)$ is a limit of step functions in $L^2(0, T; \mathcal{L}(H, H))$, we can choose an $S_N(\tau)$ such that

$$E[\, \| \tilde{J}(t) - \tilde{J}_N(t) \|^2] < \varepsilon/12, \qquad E[\, \| \tilde{J}_N(s) - \tilde{J}(s) \|^2] < \varepsilon/12$$

as

$$E[\, \| \tilde{J}(t) - \tilde{J}_N(t) \|^2] \leq \int_0^t \| R(\tau) - S_N(\tau) \|^2 \, \| Q(\tau) \| \, d\tau$$

$$\leq \int_0^T \| R(\tau) - S_N(\tau) \|^2 \, \| Q(\tau) \| \, d\tau .$$

In view of Lemma 2.10, it will follow that if $| t - s | < \varepsilon / 12(c_N + 1)$ where c_N is the constant of Lemma 2.10 for $S_N(\tau)$, then

$$E[\, \| F(t) - F(s) \|^2] < \varepsilon/3 + \varepsilon/3 + \varepsilon/3 = \varepsilon$$

and hence, that $F(t)$ is continuous in $L^2(\Omega, \mu; H)$. This completes the proof of the theorem.

Q.E.D.

2.1.4. Ito's stochastic integral in Hilbert spaces.

Let us now discuss Ito's stochastic integral in Hilbert spaces based on the results in the preceding sections. Ito's stochastic integral is the same form as (2.10) except that $S(t)$ or S_j are random variables, that is, functions of ω. In order to make clear the discussion in the sequel, we introduce the new concept of conditional expectation.

[DEFINITION 2.14] A measurable mapping $X(\omega)$ of Ω into a Hilbert space K is integrable on Ω if and only if there is a sequence $\{ X_n(\omega) \}$ of finitely valued measurable mapping from Ω into K such that i) $X_n(\omega)$ converges to $X(\omega)$ almost everywhere, and ii) $\lim_{m,n \to \infty} \int_\Omega \|X_n(\omega) - X_m(\omega)\|_K \, d\mu(\omega) = 0$.

[DEFINITION 2.15] If $X(\omega)$ is integrable on Ω, then the expectation of $X(\omega)$ denoted by $E[X(\omega)]$ is the element of K given by

$$E[X(\omega)] = \int_\Omega X(\omega) \, d\mu(\omega) = \lim_{n \to \infty} \int_\Omega X_n(\omega) \, d\mu(\omega). \tag{2.26}$$

Note that by virtue of Riesz's representation theorem [9] the definition of the expectation of (2.26) is the same as (2.1).

[DEFINITION 2.16] Let $\mathcal{F}$ be a Borel field with $\mathcal{F} \subset \mathcal{B}(\Omega)$ and let $X(\omega)$ be integrable on Ω. The conditional expectation of $X(\omega)$ relative to $\mathcal{F}$ denoted by $E[X(\omega)|\mathcal{F}]$ is a random variable such that

$$\int_F X(\omega) \, d\mu(\omega) = \int_F E[X(\omega)|\mathcal{F}] \, d\mu(\omega) \tag{2.27}$$

for all F in $\mathcal{F}$.

We note that $E[X(\omega)|\mathcal{F}]$ is unique with probability one, is integrable on Ω, and is measurable relative to $\mathcal{F}$.

Then the following lemma follows.

[LEMMA 2.11] Let $\mathcal{J}$ be a Borel field with $\mathcal{J} \subset \mathcal{B}(\Omega)$. Let f, x, and Φ be random variables on Ω to **R**, K, and $\mathcal{L}(K, K)$, respectively. Then the following properties hold.

i) If $E[\,\|X(\omega)\|_K] < \infty$, then $E[\,E[\,X(\omega)|\mathcal{J}\,]] = E[\,X(\omega)\,]$.

ii) If $E[\,\|X(\omega)\|_K] < \infty$ and $X(\omega)$ is measurable relative to $\mathcal{J}$, then

$$E[\,X(\omega)\,|\mathcal{J}\,] = X(\omega) \quad \text{a.e. } \omega \in \Omega .$$

iii) If $E[\,\|X(\omega)\|_K] < \infty$, $E[\,|f(\omega)|\,\|X(\omega)\|_K] < \infty$, and $X(\omega)$ is measurable relative to $\mathcal{J}$, then $E[\,f(\omega)\,X(\omega)|\,\mathcal{J}\,] = E[\,f(\omega)|\mathcal{J}\,]\,X(\omega)$ a.e. $\omega \in \Omega$.

iv) If $E[\,\|X(\omega)\|_K] < \infty$, $E[\,\|X(\omega)\|_K\,\|\Phi(\omega)\|_{\mathcal{L}(K,K)}] < \infty$ and $\Phi(\omega)$ is measurable relative to $\mathcal{J}$, then

$$E[\,\Phi(\omega)\,X(\omega)|\,\mathcal{J}\,] = \Phi(\omega)\,E[\,X(\omega)|\mathcal{J}\,] \text{ a.e. } \omega \in \Omega .$$

v) If $\mathcal{J}_1 \supset \mathcal{J}_2$, then

$$E[\,E[\,X(\omega)|\,\mathcal{J}_1\,]|\mathcal{J}_2\,] = E[\,X(\omega)|\,\mathcal{J}_2\,] \quad \text{a.e. } \omega \in \Omega .$$

[PROOF]

i) Since $\Omega \in \mathcal{J}$, we can take Ω as F in (2.27) and we have

$$\int_\Omega X(\omega)\, d\,\mu(\omega) = \int_\Omega E[\,X(\omega)|\mathcal{J}\,]\, d\,\mu(\omega).$$

Thus, i) was proved.

ii) From (2.27) we have

$$\int_F (\,E[\,X(\omega)|\,\mathcal{J}\,] - X(\omega)\,)\; d\,\mu(\omega) = 0 \quad \text{for all } F \in \mathcal{J} .$$

On the other hand, the integrand $E[\,X(\omega)|\,\mathcal{J}\,] - X(\omega)$ is measurable with respect to $\mathcal{J}$ and hence, it follows that

$$E[\,X(\omega)|\,\mathcal{J}\,] - X(\omega) = 0 \quad \text{a.e. } \omega \in \Omega .$$

Thus, ii) was proved.

iii) Let us devide Ω such that

$$\Omega = B_1 \cup B_2 \cup \cdots, \quad B_i \cap B_j = \phi \quad (i \neq j).$$

Borel field $\mathfrak{J}$ is a family of finite unions of the sets of B_i ($i = 1,2,\cdots$).
Then the measurable function with respect to $\mathfrak{J}$ can be represented as the limit of a sequence of the step functions such that

$$f(\omega) = a_1 I_{B_1} + a_2 I_{B_2} + \cdots,$$

where I_{B_i} denotes the characteristic function given by

$$I_{B_i}(\omega) = \begin{cases} 1 & \text{if } \omega \in B_i \\ 0 & \text{otherwise.} \end{cases}$$

If $F \in \mathfrak{J}$, then $F \cap B_i \in \mathfrak{J}$ ($i = 1, 2, \cdots$) and hence, we have from (2.27) that

$$\int_{F \cap B_i} X(\omega) \, d\mu(\omega) = \int_{F \cap B_i} E[X(\omega) | \mathfrak{J}] \, d\mu(\omega).$$

Hence, we have

$$\int_F I_{B_i}(\omega) X(\omega) \, d\mu(\omega) = \int_F I_{B_i}(\omega) E[X(\omega) | \mathfrak{J}] \, d\mu(\omega).$$

Multiplying both sides of the above equation by a_i and summing up them with respect to i, we have

$$\int_F E[f(\omega) X(\omega) | \mathfrak{J}] \, d\mu(\omega) = \int_F f(\omega) E[X(\omega) | \mathfrak{J}] \, d\mu(\omega), \quad {}^\forall F \in \mathfrak{J} .$$

Since $E[f(\omega) X(\omega) | \mathfrak{J}] - f(\omega) E[X(\omega) | \mathfrak{J}]$ is measurable with respect to $\mathfrak{J}$, the similar discussion to the proof of ii) yields iii).

iv) is obtained by the similar discussion of iii) and hence, the proof is omitted.

v) If $F \in \mathfrak{J}_2$, then $F \in \mathfrak{J}_1$. Hence, from (2.27) we have

$$\int_F E[E[X(\omega) | \mathfrak{J}_1] | \mathfrak{J}_2] \, d\mu(\omega) = \int_F E[X(\omega) | \mathfrak{J}_1] \, d\mu(\omega) = \int_F X(\omega) \, d\mu(\omega)$$

$= \int_F \; E[\, X(\omega) | \mathcal{T}_2] \; d\mu(\omega).$

Since $E[\, E[\, X(\omega) | \mathcal{T}_1] | \mathcal{T}_2]$ and $E[\, X(\omega) | \mathcal{T}_2]$ are measurable with respect to $\mathcal{T}_2$, we have v) by the similar discussion to the proof of ii).

Thus, the proof of the lemma was completed. Q.E.D.

Then the following lemma follows.

[LEMMA 2.12] If $W(t)$ is an H-valued Wiener process, then there is a family $\mathcal{T}_t$, $t \in T$ of Borel fields such that

i) $\mathcal{T}_s \subset \mathcal{T}_t \subset \mathcal{B}(\Omega)$ for $s < t$,

ii) $W(t)$ is measurable relative to $\mathcal{T}_t$ for all t in $[0, T]$,

iii) $W(t) - W(s)$ is independent of $\mathcal{T}_s$ for $s < t$,

iv) $(W(t) - W(s)) \circ (W(t) - W(s))$ is independent of $\mathcal{T}_s$ for $s < t$.

[PROOF] Take, for example, $\mathcal{T}_t$ to be the Borel field generated by the sets $\{ \omega ; W(s) \in \mathcal{O}, s \in [0, T]$ and $s < t \}$ where $\mathcal{O}$ is a Borel set in H. Properties i), ii), and iii) are obvious from this definition of $\mathcal{T}_t$. As for property iv), this is an immediate consequence of iii) and the fact that the mapping ϕ of $H \times H$ into $\mathcal{L}(H, H)$ given by Lemma 2.1 is continuous.

Thus, the proof of the lemma was completed. Q.E.D.

In order to define the stochastic integral of Ito type, we shall introduce the following function spaces.

[DEFINITION 2.17] Let K be a Hilbert space. Then $\mathcal{M}(H, K) = \{ S(t, \omega);$ S is an $\mathcal{L}(H, K)$-valued stochastic process on $[0,T] \times \Omega$ such that $S(t, \omega)$ is $\mathcal{T}_t$-measurable for all t$\}$, $\mathcal{M}_0(H,K) = \{ S(t,\omega);\ S \in \mathcal{L}(H,K)$ and S is a step function of t$\}$, and

$\mathcal{M}_1(H, K) = \{ S(t, \omega) ; \; S(t, \omega) \in \mathcal{L}(H, K)$ and $\int_0^T E[\| S(t, \omega) \|^2_{\mathcal{L}(H,K)}$

$< \infty \}.$

If $S(t,\omega)$ is an element of $\mathcal{M}_1(H, K)$, then the K-valued stochastic integral $\int_0^T S(t,\omega)\,dW(t)$ can be defined in an analogous way to that used in the non-random case in the section 2.1.3. More precisely, if $S(t,\omega)$ is an element of $\mathcal{M}_0(H, K) \cap \mathcal{M}_1(H, K)$, then $\int_0^T S(t,\omega)\,dW(t)$ is given by a finite sum of the form

$$\int_0^T S(t,\omega)\,dW(t) = \Sigma_{i=1}^{N} S(t_i,\omega)(W(t_{i+1}) - W(t_i)) \tag{2.28}$$

where N denotes a finite number.
It is clear from Theorem 2.1 that $W(t_{i+1}) - W(t_i)$ is uncorrelated and Gaussian. Since the Borel field $\mathcal{F}_t$ is generated by $\{W(s), s \leqq t\}$ and $S(t,\omega)$ belongs to $\mathcal{L}(H, K)$, $S(t_i,\omega)$ and $(W(t_{i+1}) - W(t_i))$ are mutually independent. Hence, it is clear from (2.28) that

$$E\left[\int_0^T S(t,\omega)\,dW(t)\right] = 0.$$

Let us now show that for any $S(t,\omega) \in \mathcal{M}_0(H,K) \cap \mathcal{M}_1(H,K)$

$$E\left[\left\|\int_0^T S(t,\omega)\,dW(t)\right\|_K^2\right] \leq \int_0^T E\left[\|S(t,\omega)\|^2_{\mathcal{L}(H,K)}\right]\|Q(t)\|_{\mathcal{L}(H,H)}dt$$

for $S(t,\omega)$ in $\mathcal{M}_0(H,K) \cap \mathcal{M}_1(H,K)$. If $S(t,\omega)$ is any element of $\mathcal{M}_1(H,K)$, then there is a sequence $\{S_n(t,\omega)$ of elements of $\mathcal{M}_0(H,K) \cap \mathcal{M}_1(H,K)$ such that $S_n(t,\omega)$ goes to $S(t,\omega)$ almost everywhere on $[0,T] \times \Omega$ and

$$\lim_{n\to\infty} \int_0^T E\left[\|S(t,\omega) - S_n(t,\omega)\|^2_{\mathcal{L}(H,K)}\right] dt = 0. \tag{2.29}$$

Moreover, $\int_0^T S_n(t,\omega)\,dW(t)$ has a unique limit in $L^2(\Omega, \mu; K)$. This limit is the stochastic integral $\int_0^T S(t,\omega)\,dW(t)$. In what follows, we assume that the subscripts of the norm are omitted in the case without causing confusion as before. Then the following lemma can be obtained.

[LEMMA 2.13] If $S(t,\omega)$ is an element of $\mathcal{M}_1(H, K)$, then

$$E\left[\int_0^T S(t,\omega)\,dW(t)\right] = 0 \tag{2.30}$$

and

$$E\left[\,\|\int_0^T S(t,\omega)\,dW(t)\|^2\right] \leq \int_0^T E\left[\|S(t,\omega)\|^2\right]\|Q(t)\|\ dt. \qquad (2.31)$$

[PROOF] A simple limiting procedure by an approximation argument shows that

$E\left[\int_0^T S(t,\omega)\,dW(t)\right] = 0.$ So let us turn our attention to (2.31). Let $S_n(t,\omega)$ be an approximating sequence of t-step functions used to define $\int_0^T S(t,\omega)\,dW(t)$. Then we have

$$E\left[\,\|\int_0^T S(t,\omega)\,dW(t)\|^2\right] \leq E\left[\|\int_0^T (S(t,\omega) - S_n(t,\omega))\,dW(t)\|\right.$$

$$\left.\|\int_0^T S(t,\omega)\,dW(t)\|\right] + E\left[\,\|\int_0^T S_n(t,\omega)\,dW(t)\|^2\right]$$

$$+\ E\left[\|\int_0^T S_n(t,\omega)\,dW(t)\|\,\|\int_0^T (S(t,\omega) - S_n(t,\omega))\,dW(t)\,\|\right].$$

Suppose, for the moment, that (2.31) holds for elements of

$\mathcal{M}_0(H, K) \cap \mathcal{M}_1(H, K)$.

Then by virtue of Schwarz's inequality and (2.29) we have

$$E\left[\|\int_0^T S(t,\omega)\,dW(t)\|^2\right] \leq \lim_{n\to\infty} \int_0^T E\left[\ \|S_n(t,\omega)\|^2\right]\|Q(t)\|\,dt.$$

However, (2.8) also implies that

$$\lim_{n\to\infty} \int_0^T E\left[\ \|S_n(t,\omega)\|^2\right] dt = \int_0^T E\left[\ \|S(t,\omega)\|^2\right] dt$$

and so, (2.31) follows.

Thus, all that remains is to verify (2.31) for $S(t,\omega)$ in $\mathcal{M}_0(H,K)\cap\mathcal{M}_1(H,K)$. For such a $S(t,\omega)$,

$$\int_0^T S(t,\omega)\,dW(t) = \Sigma_{i=1}^{n-1}\ S(t_i,\omega)(\,W(t_{i+1}) - W(t_i))$$

where $\{t_1, t_2, \cdots, t_n\}$ is a finite partition of $[0,T]$.

Let

$$S_j = S(t_j, \omega), \qquad \Delta W_j = W(t_{j+1}) - W(t_j)$$

and

$$\Delta t_j = t_{j+1} - t_j .$$

Then

$$E [\| \int_0^T S(t, \omega) dW(t) \|^2] = \Sigma_{j,k=1}^{n-1} E [(S_j \Delta W_j, S_k \Delta W_k)_K].$$

But $E [(S_j \Delta W_j, S_k \Delta W_k)_K] = 0$ if $j \neq k$. For if $j > k$, then

$$E [(S_j \Delta W_j, S_k \Delta W_k)_K] = E [E[(S_j \Delta W_j, S_k \Delta W_k)_K | \mathcal{T}_{t_j}]] = 0$$

since the conditional expectation $E [(S_j \Delta W_j, S_k \Delta W_k)_K | \mathcal{T}_{t_j}]$ vanishes by virtue of the measurability of S_j and $S_k \Delta W_k$ relative to $\mathcal{T}_{t_j}$ and the independence of W_j upon $\mathcal{T}_{t_j}$. It follows that

$$E [\| \int_0^T S(t,\omega) dW(t) \|^2] = \Sigma_{j=1}^{n-1} E [\| S_j \Delta W_j \|^2]$$

$$\leqq \Sigma_{j=1}^{n-1} E [\| S_j \|^2] E [\| \Delta W_j \|^2].$$

For the last derivation we used the fact that $\| S_j \|$ and $\| \Delta W_j \|$ are independent since S_j is measurable relative to $\mathcal{T}_{t_j}$. But $E [\| \Delta W_j \|^2] = \int_{t_j}^{t_{j+1}} tr(Q(t))dt$ and so,

$$\Sigma_{j=1}^{n-1} E [\| S_j \|^2] E [\| \Delta W_j \|^2] = \Sigma_{j=1}^{n-1} \int_{t_j}^{t_{j+1}} tr (Q(t)) E[\| S_j \|^2] dt$$

$$= \int_0^T tr (Q(t)) E [\| S(t,\omega) \|^2] dt.$$

Thus, the lemma is established. Q.E.D.

We now prove the convergence property of the stochastic integral.

[LEMMA 2.14] Let $\{ S_n \}$ be a sequence of elements of $\mathcal{M}_1(H, K)$. Suppose that i) there is a $S(t, \omega)$ in $\mathcal{M}_1(H, K)$ such that $S_n \to S(t, \omega)$ almost everywhere on $[0, T] \times \Omega$, and ii) there is an a(t) in $L^2(0, T)$ such that

$$\| S_n(t,\omega) \| \leq a(t) \quad \text{a.e. } \omega \in \Omega$$

for all n. Then

$$\lim_{n \to \infty} \int_0^T S_n(t, \omega) \, dW(t) = \int_0^T S(t, \omega) \, dW(t). \tag{2.32}$$

[PROOF] Since

$$E [\| \int_0^T (S(t, \omega) - S_n(t, \omega)) \, dW(t) \|^2]$$

$$\leq \int_0^T tr(Q(t)) \, E [\| S(t, \omega) - S_n(t, \omega) \|^2] \, dt,$$

the lemma is an immediate consequence of the Lebesgue convergence theorem.
Thus, the lemma is established. Q.E.D.

The other propeties obtained in the preceding section could be proved by the parallel way and hence, we don't mention about them any more.

2.2. Stochastic differential equation in Hilbert spaces.

We are now prepared to discuss stochastic differential equations in the Hilbert space K. So, if we suppose that U_0 is an K-valued random variable with $E[\|U_0\|^2] < \infty$, that A(t) is a regulated mapping of $[0, T]$ into $\mathcal{L}(K, K)$, and that C(t) is an element of $L^2(0, T; \mathcal{L}(H, K))$, then we can consider the following stochastic integral equation:

$$U(t, \omega) = U_0(\omega) + \int_0^t A(s)\, U(s, \omega)\, ds + \int_0^t C(s)\, dW(s, \omega). \qquad (2.33)$$

We often write (2.33) in the form

$$dU(t) = A(t)\, U(t)\, dt + C(t)\, dW(t), \quad U(0) = U_0 \qquad (2.34)$$

and we speak of (2.34) as a stochastic linear differential equation. Intuitively, we write (2.34) in the form

$$d\, U(t)/dt = A(t)\, U(t) + C(t)\, \xi(t), \quad U(0) = U_0$$

where $\xi(t)$ is white Gaussian noise with zero mean and covariance operator given by $Q(t)\, \delta(t - \tau)$. Thus, we shall often denote $\xi(t)$ as $\dot{W}(t)$ where $\cdot = d/dt$. With regard to (2.33), we have the following theorem.

[THEOREM 2.2] Let U_0 be an K-valued random variable with $E[\|U_0\|^2]$. Let A(t) be a regulated mapping from $[0, T]$ into $\mathcal{L}(K, K)$ and let C(t) be an element of $L^2(0, T; \mathcal{L}(H, K))$. Let $\mathcal{L}(t, t_0)$ be the fundamental linear transformation (i.e., resolvent) of the nonstochastic linear differential equation

$$d\, \mathcal{U}(t, t_0)/dt = A(t)\mathcal{U}(t, t_0), \quad \mathcal{U}(t_0, t_0) = \mathcal{J} \qquad (2.35)$$

on H, where $\mathcal{J}$ denotes the identity operator.

Then (2.33) has an essentially unique solution U(t) which is given by

$$U(t) = \mathcal{U}(t, t_0)\left(U_0 + \int_{t_0}^{t} \mathcal{U}(t_0, s)\, C(s)\, dW(s) \right)$$

where $t_0 = 0$.

Moreover, $E[\, \| U(t) \|^2] < \infty$ and $E[\, U(t)\,] = \mathcal{U}(t, t_0)\, E[\, U_0\,]$.

[PROOF] From (2.35) we have

$$U_0(\omega) + \int_{t_0}^{t} A(s)\, \mathcal{U}(s, t_0)\, U_0(\omega)\, ds = \mathcal{U}(t, t_0)\, U_0(\omega).$$

By replacing $U(t)$ by $U(t) - \mathcal{U}(t, t_0)\, U_0(\omega)$, we can suppose without loss of generality that $U_0(\omega) = 0$. Thus, setting

$$Y(s) = \int_{t_0}^{s} \mathcal{U}(t_0, \tau)\, C(\tau)\, dW(\tau)$$

and noting that $Y(s)$ is an H-valued random process in view of Lemma 2.11 and the continuity of $\mathcal{U}(t_0, \tau)$, we want to show that

$$\mathcal{U}(t, t_0)\, Y(t) = \int_{t_0}^{t} A(s)\, \mathcal{U}(s, t_0)\, Y(s)\, ds + \int_{t_0}^{t} C(s)\, dW(s).$$

We note that the first term of the right hand side of the above equation may be viewed as an iterated integral in the following way:

Let $B(s, \tau)$ be given by

$$B(s, \tau) = \begin{cases} A(s)\, \mathcal{U}(s, t_0)\, \mathcal{U}(t_0, \tau)\, C(\tau), & \tau \leqq s, \\ 0 & \tau > s, \end{cases}$$

then

$$\int_{t_0}^{t} A(s)\, \mathcal{U}(s, t_0)\, Y(s)\, ds = \int_{t_0}^{t} \left[\int_{t_0}^{t} B(s, \tau)\, dW(\tau) \right] ds.$$

But in view of Lemma 2.15 (which follows), $B(s, \tau)$ is an element of $L^2(T_1 \times T_1; \mathcal{L}(H, K))$ where T_1 is any finite subinterval of $[0, T]$ of the form $[t_0, t_1]$ with $t_1 \geqq t$. We then deduce from Lemma 2.8 that

$$\int_{t_0}^{t} A(s)\,\mathcal{U}(s, t_0)\, Y(s)\, ds = \int_{t_0}^{t} [\int_{t_0}^{t} B(s,\tau)\, ds]\, dW(\tau)$$

$$= \int_{t_0}^{t} [\int_{\tau}^{t} A(s)\,\mathcal{U}(s, t_0)\, ds]\,\mathcal{U}(t_0, \tau)\, C(\tau)\, dW(\tau).$$

However,

$$A(s)\,\mathcal{U}(s, t_0) = d\,\mathcal{U}(s, t_0)/ ds$$

and

$$\mathcal{U}(a, t_0)\,\mathcal{U}(t_0, b) = \mathcal{U}(a, b), \quad \mathcal{U}(a, a) = \mathcal{I},$$

so that

$$\int_{t_0}^{t} A(s)\,\mathcal{U}(s, t_0)\, Y(s)\, ds = \mathcal{U}(t, t_0) \int_{t_0}^{t} \mathcal{U}(t_0, \tau)\, C(\tau)\, dW(\tau)$$

$$- \int_{t_0}^{t} \mathcal{U}(\tau, \tau)\, C(\tau)\, dW(\tau)$$

$$= \mathcal{U}(t, t_0)\, Y(t) - \int_{t_0}^{t} C(\tau)\, dW(\tau).$$

Thus, the main assertion of the theorem is established. The final point that $E[\ \| U(t) \|^2\ ] < \infty$ and $E[\ U(t)\ ] = \mathcal{U}(t,t_0)\, E[\ U_0\ ]$ is obvious. Hence, by proving the following lemma the proof of the theorem was completed.

Q.E.D.

[LEMMA 2.15] Let T_1 be a compact interval and let X be a Banach space. Let f(t) map T_1 into $\mathcal{L}(X, X)$ and let g(t) map T_1 into $\mathcal{L}(X, X)$ (or X). If one of the maps f,g is in $L^2(T_1 ; \mathcal{L}(X, X))$ (or,in the case of g, $L^p(T_1 ; \mathcal{L}(X, X))$ or $L^p(T_1, X)$) and the other is regulated, then f(t) g(t) is an element of $L^p(T_1, \mathcal{L}(X, X))$ (or $L^p(T_1, X)$).

[PROOF] For example, suppose that f(t) is regulated and that g(t) is in $L^p(T_1; \mathcal{L}(X, X))$. If f(t) is a step function, then the result is clear. On the other hand, if f(t) is regulated then there exists a sequence $f_n(t)$ of step functions such that $f_n(t)$ converges to $f(t)$ uniformly on T_1. It follows that $f_n(t)\, g(t)$ converges to $f(t)\, g(t)$ almost everywhere and that

$$\| f_n(t)\, g(t) \| \leqq M \| g(t) \| \quad \text{almost everywhere for some } M > 0.$$

But $M g(t)$ is in $L^p(T_1; \mathcal{L}(X, X))$ and the lemma follows by the Lebesgue convergence theorem. The other case are treated in a similar manner. Thus, the proof of the lemma was established. Q.E.D.

Furthermore, we have from Theorem 2.2 directly the following corollary.

[COROLLARY 2.2] Let $L(t)$ be a regulated mapping of T_1 into $\mathcal{L}(K, K)$ and let $U(t)$ be generated by (2.33). Then

$$U(t) = \int_{t_0}^{t} L(s)\, A(s)\, U(s)\, ds + \int_{t_0}^{t} L(s)\, C(s)\, d W(s) \qquad (2.36)$$

is a well-defined K-valued stochastic process with $E[\, \| X(t) \|^2 \,] < \infty$.

Now as a generalized version of (2.33) we have

[DEFINITION 2.18] Let $U(t)$, $t \in [0, T]$ be the K-valued stochastic process given by

$$U(t) - U(t_0) = \int_{t_0}^{t} A(s, \omega)\, ds + \int_{t_0}^{t} C(s, \omega)\, d W(s) \qquad (2.37)$$

where $C(s,\omega)$ is an element of $\mathcal{M}_1(H, K)$, and $A(s,\omega)$ is a K-valued stochastic process with $\int_{t_0}^{t} \| A(s,\omega) \| ds < \infty$ with probability one which is measurable relative to $\mathcal{F}_t$ for all t in $[0, T]$. Then $U(t)$ is said to have the stochastic differential $A(t,\omega)\, dt + C(t, \omega)\, d W(t)$.

2.3. Ito's lemma in Hilbert spaces.

Let us now state and prove Ito's lemma in Hilbert spaces. We begin with the following lemma which is an important tool in the proof of the main theorem. First of all, we assume in this section that the covariance operator $Q(t)$ is independent of the time t since this assumption enables us to make the derivation of Ito's lemma very easy. Of course, it is clear from the derivation that Ito's lemma holds in the case of the time-dependent covariance operator.

[LEMMA 2.16] Let H, K and G be Hilbert spaces and let $W(t)$ be an H-valued Wiener process. Suppose that i) $\textcircled{H}(t,\omega)$ is an $\mathcal{L}(K\times K, G)$-valued stochastic process which is measurable relative to $\mathcal{F}_t$ for all t in $[0, T]$, ii) $E[\| H(t)\|^2]$ for all t in $[0, T]$, iii) R_0 is an $\mathcal{L}(H, K)$-valued random variable which is measurable relative to $\mathcal{F}_s$, iv) $E[\|R_0\|^4] < \infty$, and v) $W(t)$ is real on $[0,T]\times\Omega$. Then

$$E[\textcircled{H}(R_0\Delta W, R_0\Delta W)|\mathcal{F}_s] = (t-s)\ \Sigma_{i=0}^{\infty}\textcircled{H}(R_0\sqrt{\lambda_i}\,e_i, R_0\sqrt{\lambda_i}e_i) \text{ a.e. } \omega \tag{2.38}$$

and

$$E[\textcircled{H}(R_0\Delta W, R_0\Delta W)] = (t-s)\,E[\ \Sigma_{i=0}^{\infty}\textcircled{H}(R_0\sqrt{\lambda_i}\,e_i, R_0\sqrt{\lambda_i}e_i)] \tag{2.39}$$

for almost all s, t with $s < t$ where $\textcircled{H} = \textcircled{H}(s,\omega)$, $\Delta W = W(t) - W(s)$, and the $\{e_i\}$ form an orthonormal base of H consisting of eigenvectors of $Q(t) = Q$ and with $\{\lambda_i\}$ as the corresponding eigenvalues.

[PROOF] Clearly, (2.39) follows from (2.38). Now, recall that $W(t) = \Sigma_{i=0}^{\infty}\ \beta_i(t)\,e_i$ and set $\Delta\beta_i = \beta_i(t) - \beta_i(s)$ and $\Delta W_n = W_n(t) - W_n(s)$ for $s < t$ where $W_n(t) = \Sigma_{i=1}^{n}\ \beta_i(t)\,e_i$. We note that since $W(t)$ is real, β_i is also real, and so, it follows from Schwarz's inequality that

$$E[\,|\Delta\beta_i \;\; \Delta\beta_j|\,] \leq E[\,|\Delta\beta_i|^2\,]^{1/2}\, E[\,|\Delta\beta_j|^2\,]^{1/2} \leq (t-s)\sqrt{\lambda_i\,\lambda_j}$$

for all i and j. Since $\|\,\textcircled{H}\,\|\,\|R_0\|^2$ is measurable relative to $\mathcal{J}_s$ and $|\Delta\beta_i\,\Delta\beta_j|$ is independent of $\mathcal{J}_s$ (as $W(t) - W(s)$ is), we have

$$E[\,|\Delta\beta_i\,\Delta\beta_j|\,\|\textcircled{H}\|\,\|R_0\|^2\,] \leq (t-s)\sqrt{\lambda_i\,\lambda_j}\,(\,E[\,\|\textcircled{H}\|^2\,]\,)^{1/2}$$
$$(\,E[\,\|R_0\|^4\,]\,)^{1/2}$$

so that $E[\,|\Delta\beta_i\;\;\Delta\beta_j|\,\|\textcircled{H}\|\,\|R_0\|^2\,]$ is finite. Since $\|\,\textcircled{H}(R_0\,e_i,\,R_0 e_i)\,\| \leq \|\textcircled{H}\|\,\|R_0\|^2$ and since $\textcircled{H}(R_0\,e_i,\,R_0\,e_i)$ is measurable relative to $\mathcal{J}_s$, we have

$$E[\,\textcircled{H}\,(R_0\,\Delta W_n,\,R_0\,\Delta W_n)\,|\,\mathcal{J}_s\,]$$
$$= \Sigma_{i,j=0}^{n}\; E[\,\Delta\beta_i\;\Delta\beta_j\,|\,\mathcal{J}_s\,]\;\textcircled{H}\,(R_0\,e_i,\,R_0\,e_i)$$

with probability one for all n. But $E[\,\Delta\beta_i\,\Delta\beta_j\,|\,\mathcal{J}_s\,] = E[\,\Delta\beta_i\,\Delta\beta_j\,]$ since $\Delta\beta_i\;\;\Delta\beta_j$ is independent of $\mathcal{J}_s$. In view of the property (2.7) and the relation of the eigenfunctions, we have

$$E[\,\Delta\beta_i\,\Delta\beta_j\,] = E[\,(\Delta W,\,e_i)\,(\Delta W,\,e_j)\,] = (e_i,\,Q\,e_j) = \lambda_i\,(e_i,\,e_j)$$
$$= \lambda_i\,\delta_{ij}$$

where δ_{ij} denotes Kronecker's delta.
Thus, we have

$$E[\,\textcircled{H}\,(R_0\,\Delta W_n,\,R_0\,\Delta W_n)\,|\,\mathcal{J}_s\,] = (t-s)\;\Sigma_{i=0}^{n}\,\lambda_i\;\textcircled{H}\,(R_0\,e_i,\,R_0\,e_i).$$

The result then follows by the fact that $\textcircled{H}$ is bilinear operator on $K \times K$ and a simple application of Theorem 2.5 of [11].
As a suggestive shorthand, we write $\tilde{tr}\,(\textcircled{H})\,[\,R_0\,\xi_W\,]$ in place of

$$\Sigma_{i=0}^{\infty}\;\textcircled{H}\,(R_0\sqrt{\lambda_i}\,e_i,\,R_0\sqrt{\lambda_i}\,e_i) \qquad \text{where} \quad \xi_W = \Sigma_{i=0}^{\infty}\,\sqrt{\lambda_i}\,e_i\,.$$

[THEOREM 2.3] (Ito's lemma). Let H, K and G be Hilbert spaces and let $W(t)$ be an H-valued Wiener process. Suppose that $g(t, c)$ is a continuous map of $[0,T] \times K$ into G and that $U(t)$ is a K-valued stochastic process with stochastic differential $dU(t) = A(t,\omega)\,dt + C(t,\omega)\,dW(t)$ such that

i) $g_t(t, c)$ is continuous on $[0,T] \times K$;

ii) $g(t, \cdot)$ is twice differentiable on K for each fixed t in $[0,T]$;

iii) $g_c(t, c)$ and $g_{cc}(t, c)$ are continuous in (t, c) on $[0,T] \times K$;

iv) $A(t, \omega)$ is a K-valued stochastic process which is measurable relative to $\mathcal{F}_t$, $t \in [0,T]$, and integrable on $[0,T]$ with probability one;

v) $C(t,\omega)$ is an element of $\mathcal{M}_1(H, K)$ with $\int_0^T E[\| C(t,\omega)\|^4]\,dt < \infty$; and

vi) $W(t)$ is real, where g_t and g_c denote the partial and Frécht derivatives.

Then $Z(t) = g(t, U(t))$ has the G-valued stochastic differential

$$dZ(t) = \Big(g_t(t, U(t)) + g_c(t, U(t))[A(t, \omega)] + \frac{1}{2}\,\tilde{tr}\,(g_{cc}(t, U(t))) [C(t)\,\xi_W] \Big)\,dt + g_c(t, U(t))[C(t)]\,dW(t). \qquad (2.40)$$

[PROOF] Let us suppose for the moment that the theorem holds if $A(t,\omega)$ and $C(t,\omega)$ are step functions. Then the general case will follow by a straightforward approximation argument. In other words, we consider sequences $A_n(t,\omega)$ and $C_n(t,\omega)$ of t-step functions such that

$$\lim_{n\to\infty} \int_0^T \| A(t,\omega) - A_n(t,\omega)\|\,dt = 0 \quad \text{a.e. } \omega$$

and

$$\lim_{n\to\infty} \int_0^T E[\| C(t,\omega) - C_n(t,\omega)\|^4] = 0 \quad \text{a.e. } \omega$$

where the $A_n(t,\omega)$ satisfies iv) and $C_n(t,\omega)$ satisfies v).

Letting $U_n(t)$ be the K-valued stochastic process with stochastic differential

$$dU_n(t) = A_n(t,\omega)\,dt + C_n(t,\omega)\,dW(t),$$

we can show just as in [12] that $U_n(t)$ converges uniformly to $U(t)$ on $[0,T]$ a.e. ω, i.e., that

$$\lim_{n\to\infty} \sup_{t\in[0,T]} \| U_n(t) - U(t) \| = 0 \quad \text{a.e. } \omega .$$

It follows that there is a subsequence $\{ U_{n_i}(t) \}$ of $\{ U_n(t) \}$ such that

$$g(t, U_{n_i}(t)) \to g(t, U(t)), \quad g_t(t, U_{n_i}(t)) \to g_t(t, U(t)),$$

$$g_c(t, U_{n_i}(t)) \to g_c(t, U(t)), \text{ and } g_{cc}(t, U_{n_i}(t)) \to g_{cc}(t, U(t)),$$

all uniformly on $[0,T]$ with probability one. For simplicity, we also write $U_{n_i}(t)$, $A_{n_i}(t,\omega)$, and $C_{n_i}(t,\omega)$ as $U_i(t)$, $A_i(t)$ and $C_i(t)$, respectively. Then simple inequality computations show that

$$\lim_{i\to\infty} \int_{t_0}^{t} g_s(s, U_i(s))\, ds = \int_{t_0}^{t} g_s(s, U(s))\, ds$$

$$\lim_{i\to\infty} \int_{t_0}^{t} g_c(s, U_i(s))[C_i(s)\, \xi_w]\, ds = \int_{t_0}^{t} g_c(s, U(s))[C(s)\, \xi_w]\, ds$$

and

$$\lim_{i\to\infty} \int_{t_0}^{t} \tilde{tr} (g_{cc}(s, U_i(s))[C_i(s)\, \xi_w]\, ds = \int_{t_0}^{t} \tilde{tr} (g_{cc}(s, U(s))[C(s)\, \xi_w]\, ds$$

where all equalities are valid with probability one.

Thus, to show that $Z(t) = g(t, U(t))$ has the required stochastic differential, it will be enough to prove that

$$\lim_{i\to\infty} \int_{t_0}^{t} g_c(s, U_i(s))[C_i(s)]\, dW(s) = \int_{t_0}^{t} g_c(s, U(s))[C(s)]\, dW(s) \tag{2.41}$$

where the convergence is in probability.

Now let $\chi^{(N)}(\cdot)$ be the real random variable given by

$$\chi^{(N)}(t) = \begin{cases} 1 & \text{if } \| U(s) \| \leqq N \text{ for } t_1 < s < t \\ 0 & \text{otherwise.} \end{cases}$$

Then for sufficiently large i

$$g_c(s, U(s))[C(s) \chi^{(N)}(s)] \text{ and } g_c(s, U_i(s))[C_i(s) \chi^{(N)}(s)]$$

will be elements of $\mathcal{M}_1(H, G)$. It then follows from the inequality (2.31) that

$$\lim_{i \to \infty} \int_{t_0}^{t} g_c(s, U_i(s))[C_i(s) \chi^{(N)}(s)] \, dW(s)$$

$$= \int_{t_0}^{t} g_c(s, U(s)) [C(s) \chi^{(N)}(s)] \, dW(s) \tag{2.42}$$

for all finite N where the convergence is in probability.

But

$$\mu[\omega ;[\| \int_{t_0}^{t} (g_c(s, U_i(s))[C_i(s)] - g_c(s, U(s))[C(s)]) \, dW(s)$$

$$- \int_{t_0}^{t}(g_c(s, U_i(s))[C_i(s) \chi^{(N)}(s)] - g_c(s, U(s))[C(s) \chi^{(N)}(s)])dW(s)\|$$

$$\nrightarrow 0 \quad \text{for} \quad i = 1, 2, \cdots]]$$

$$\leqq \mu [\omega ; \sup_{t \varepsilon [0, T]} \| U(t,\omega)\| > N].$$

Since $\mu [\omega ; \sup_t \| U(t,\omega)\| \geqq N]$ goes to zero as N approaches infinity, (2.42) is established.

Now it remains to prove the theorem for the case of t-step functions $A(s,\omega)$ and $C(t,\omega)$. To do this, it will be enough to prove the theorem for the special case where $A(t,\omega)$ and $C(t,\omega)$ are constant, i.e., are independent of t.

So let us assume that $A(t,\omega)$ and $C(t,\omega)$ are constant. Let t be a fixed but arbitrary element of $(t_0, T_2]$ and let $t_0, t_1, \cdots, t_n$ be elements of $[0, T]$ with

$$0 = t_0 < t_1 < t_2 < \cdots < t_n = t \leqq T_2.$$

We set $\Delta t_k = t_{k+1} - t_k$, $U_k = U(t_k)$, $g_k = g(t_k, U_k)$, $\Delta U_k = U_{k+1} - U_k$, and $\Delta g_k =$

$g_{k+1} - g_k$ for $k = 0, 1, \cdots, n-1$. Then

$$Z(t) - Z(t_0) = g(t, U(t)) - g(t_0, U(t_0))$$

$$= \Sigma_{k=0}^{n-1} (g_{k+1} - g(t_k, U_{k+1}) + g(t_k, U_{k+1}) - g_k)$$

$$= \Sigma_{k=0}^{n-1} \Delta g_k .$$

In view of the differentiability assumptions,

$$\Delta g_k = g_t(t_k, U_{k+1}) \Delta t_k + g_c(t_k, U_k)[\Delta U_k]$$

$$+ \frac{1}{2} g_{cc}(t_k, U_k)[\Delta U_k, \Delta U_k] + \gamma_k + \delta_k$$

where

$$\| \gamma_k \| \leqq \Delta t_k \sup_{0<\theta<1} \| g_t(t_k + \theta \Delta t_k, U_{k+1}) - g_t(t_k, U_{k+1}) \|$$

and

$$\| \delta_k \| \leqq \| \Delta U_k \|^2 \sup_{0<\theta<1} \| g_{cc}(t_k, U_k + \theta \Delta U_k) - g_{cc}(t_k, U_k) \| .$$

Just as in [12], $\Sigma_{k=0}^{n-1} (\| \gamma_k \| + \| \delta_k \|) \to 0$ with probability one as $\max_k \Delta t_k$ goes to zero. It follows that

$$Z(t) - Z(t_0) = \Sigma_{k=0}^{n-1} (g_t(t_k, U_k) \Delta t_k + g_c(t_k, U_k)[\Delta U_k]$$

$$\frac{1}{2} g_{cc}(t_k, U_k)[\Delta U_k, \Delta U_k]) + \theta_n ,$$

where $\| \theta_n \| \to 0$ with probability one as $\max_k \Delta t_k \to 0$. Substituting $\Delta U_k = A(t,\omega) \Delta t_k + C(t,\omega) \Delta W_k$ in the above equation, we obtain the relation

$$Z(t) - Z(t_0) = \Sigma_1 + \Sigma_2 + \Sigma_3 + \Sigma_4 + \Sigma_5 + \theta_n$$

where

$$\Sigma_1 = \Sigma_{k=0}^{n-1} (g_s(t_k, U_k) + g_c(t_k, U_k)[A(s,\omega)]) \Delta t_k$$

$$\Sigma_2 = \Sigma_{k=0}^{n-1} g_c(t_k, U_k)[C(s,\omega)] \Delta W_k$$

$$\Sigma_3 = \Sigma_{k=0}^{n-1} \frac{1}{2} g_{cc}(t_k, U_k)[A(s,\omega), A(s,\omega)](\Delta t_k)^2$$

$$\Sigma_4 = \Sigma_{k=0}^{n-1} \frac{1}{2} g_{cc}(t_k, U_k)[C(s,\omega) \Delta W_k, C(s, \omega) \Delta W_k]$$

$$\Sigma_5 = \Sigma_{k=0}^{n-1} g_{cc}(t_k, U_k)[A(s,\omega) \Delta t_k, C(s,\omega) \Delta W_k].$$

In view of the continuity assumptions and the boundedness of U(t) on [0, T], we immediately deduce that as $\max_k \Delta t_k$ goes to 0,

$$\Sigma_1 \to \int_{t_0}^{t} (g_s(s, U(s)) + g_c(s, U(s))[A(s,\omega)]) ds \quad \text{a.e. } \omega$$

$$\Sigma_3 \to 0 \quad \text{a.e. } \omega$$

$$\Sigma_5 \to 0 \quad \text{a.e. } \omega .$$

In other words, the limiting sums converge to the usual Bochner integral. We now claim that

$$\Sigma_2 \to \int_{t_0}^{t} g_c(s, U(s))[C(s,\omega)] d W(s) \quad \text{in probability} \tag{2.43}$$

$$\Sigma_4 \to \frac{1}{2} \int_{t_0}^{t} \tilde{tr} (g_{cc}(s, U(s)))[C(s,\omega) \xi_W] ds \text{ in probability} \tag{2.44}$$

as $\max_k \Delta t_k \to 0$. Since $X^{(N)}(\cdot)$ is the real random, we have

$$\int_{t_0}^{T} E [\| g_c(t, U(t)) [C(t,\omega) X^{(N)}(t)]\|^2] dt$$

$$\leq \sup_{\| U(t) \| \leq N} (\| g_c(t, U(t))\|^2) \int_{t_0}^{T} E [\| C(t,\omega)\|^2] dt$$

for all N by virtue of assumptions iii) and iv). Since U(t) is bounded with probability one, it follows that $\int_{t_0}^{T} E [\| g_c(t, U(t)) [C(t,\omega)] \|^2] dt < \infty$ and hence, that $g_c(t, U(t))[C(t,\omega)]$ is in $\mathcal{M}_1(H, G)$ as $g_c(t, U(t))[C(t,\omega)]$ is measurable relative to $\mathcal{J}_t$ for all t in [0, T]. Thus, $\int_{t_0}^{t} g_c(s, U(s))$ $[C(s,\omega)] d W(s)$ exists. Consider the sequence $\{ g_c^n(s, U(s))[C(s,\omega)]\}$ where

$$g_c^n(t, U(t))[C(t, \omega)] = g_c(t_j, U_j) [C(t,\omega)]$$

for t in $[t_j, t_{j+1})$, $j = 0,1, \cdots, n-1$. Then $g_c^n(s, U(s))[C(s,\omega)]$ is an element of $\mathcal{M}_1(H,G)$ for every n. Moreover, since g_c is continuous,

$$\| g_c^n (t, U(t))[C(t, \omega)] \| \leqq M$$

for all n and some constant M. Thus, Lemma 2.14 applies and (2.43) is established.

Finally, we prove that (2.44) holds. Let $\chi_k^{(N)}$ be given by

$$\chi_k^{(N)} = \begin{cases} 1 & \text{if} \quad \| U_i \| \leqq N \quad \text{for} \quad i \leqq k \\ 0 & \text{otherwise.} \end{cases}$$

Then

$$E [\| g_{cc}(t_k, U_k) \chi_k^{(N)} \|^2] \leqq \underset{\|U(t)\| \leqq N}{SUP} \| g_{cc}(t, U(t)) \|^2 \qquad \text{for all } N.$$

Since $g_{cc}(t_k, U_k) \chi_k^{(N)}$ is measurable relative to $\mathcal{J}_{t_k}$, we deduce from (2.39) that

$$E [g_{cc}(t_k, U_k) [C(t,\omega) \Delta W_k, C(t,\omega) \Delta W_k] \chi_k^{(N)}]$$

$$= \Delta t_k E [\tilde{tr} (g_{cc}(t_k, U_k)) \chi_k^{(N)} [C(t,\omega) \xi_w]].$$

Setting

$$p_k = g_{cc}(t_k, U_k) [C(t,\omega) \Delta W_k, C(t,\omega) \Delta W_k]$$

and

$$v_k = p_k - \Delta t_k \,\tilde{tr}\,(\, g_{cc}(t_k, U_k))\,[\, C(t,\omega)\, \xi_w \,],$$

we have $E[\, v_k\, x_k^{(N)} \,] = 0$ for all N. Moreover, by virtue of (2.38),

$$E[\, p_k\, x_k^{(N)} | \mathcal{T}_{t_k} \,] = \Delta t_k \,\tilde{tr}\,(\, g_{cc}(t_k, U_k))\,[\, C(t,\omega)\, \xi_w \,]\, x_k^{(N)}$$

and so,

$$E[\, v_k\, x_k^{(N)} \mid \mathcal{T}_{t_k} \,] = 0 \tag{2.45}$$

for all N.

Note that $g_{cc}(t_k, U_k)\,[\, C(t,\omega)\,\Delta W_k,\, C(t,\omega)\,\Delta W_k \,]$ is measurable relative to $\mathcal{T}_{t_k}$ and that

$$E[\, \| g_{cc}(t_k, U_k)\,[\, C(t,\omega)\,\Delta W_k,\, C(t,\omega)\,\Delta W_k \,]\, x_k^{(N)} \| \,]$$

$$\leqq tr\,(\, Q\,)\, E[\| C(t,\omega)\|^2\,] \sup_{\|U(t)\| \leq N} \| g_{cc}(t, U(t))\| \quad \text{for all N.}$$

It is clear that both $E[\, \| p_k\, x_k^{(N)}\|^2 \,]$ and $E[\, \| v_k\, x_k^{(N)}\|^2 \,]$ are finite for all N and k. Thus, if $j > k$, we have (by Lemma 2.11 and (2.45))

$$E[\, (\, v_j\, x_j^{(N)},\, v_k\, x_k^{(N)} \,) | \mathcal{T}_{t_j} \,] = 0$$

since $v_k\, x_k^{(N)}$ is measurable relative to $\mathcal{T}_{t_j}$. It follows that

$$E[\, (\, v_j\, x_j^{(N)},\, v_k\, x_k^{(N)} \,)\,] = 0$$

if $j \neq k$ and hence that

$$E[\, \| \Sigma_{k=0}^{n-1}\, v_k\, x_k^{(N)}\|^2 \,] = \Sigma_{k=0}^{n-1}\, E[\, \| v_k\, x_k^{(N)}\|^2 \,].$$

A simple computation using the independence of $\| C(t,\omega)\|$ and $\|\Delta W_k\|$ leads to the estimate

$$\Sigma_{k=0}^{n-1} E [\| v_k X_k^{(N)} \|^2] \leq 12 \sup_{\|U(t)\| \leq N} [\| g_{cc}(t, U(t)) \|] E [\| C(t,\omega) \|^4] \; tr (Q) \Sigma_{k=0}^{n-1} (\Delta t_k)^2$$

We immediately conclude that $\Sigma_{k=0}^{n-1} v_k X_k^{(N)} \to 0$ in probability as $\max_k \Delta t_k \to 0$. Since

$$\mu[\| \Sigma_{k=0}^{n-1} (v_k - v_k X_k^{(N)}) \| \neq 0] \leq \mu[\sup_t \| U(t) \| > N],$$

we also see that $\Sigma_{k=0}^{n-1} v_k \to 0$ in probability as $\max_k \Delta t_k \to 0$. But

$$\Sigma_{k=0}^{n-1} \Delta t_k \; \tilde{tr} (g_{cc}(t_k, U_k))[C(t,\omega) \xi_W]$$

is an approximating sum for the integral $\int_{t_0}^{t} \tilde{tr}(g_{cc}(s, U(s)))[C(s,\omega)] ds$. Thus, (2.44) is established. Therefore, the theorem was completed. Q.E.D.

[COROLLARY 2.3] Suppose that , in addition to the hypotheses of the theorem, $G = R$. Then $dZ(t)$ can be written in form

$$dZ(t) = (g_t(t, U(t)) + (A(t,\omega), \nabla_c g(t, U(t))) + \frac{1}{2} tr (C(t,\omega) Q(t) C^*(t,\omega) \textcircled{H}_{cc} g(t, U(t))) dt + (C^*(t,\omega) \nabla_c g(t, U(t)), dW(t)) \tag{2.46}$$

where $\nabla_c g$ and $\textcircled{H}_{cc} g$ are the gradient and Hessian, respectively, of g with respect to c.

The proof of the corollary is direct from the fact that $\tilde{tr}$ is identified with tr in the case of the scalar-valued function, and hence, the proof is omitted.

2.4. Stochastic partial differential equations

2.4.1. Deterministic partial differential equations.

We now define the distribution and its derivative. Let (0, T) be an open interval and let L be a Banach space. We denote by $\mathcal{D}((0,T))$ the space of infinitely differentiable real functions with compact support in (0, T) and let

$$\mathcal{D}'(\,(0,T)\,;\,L\,) = \mathcal{L}(\,\mathcal{D}(0,T),\,L\,)$$

be the space of distribution on (0, T) with values in L (cf. [9]).
We now introduce the space $L^2(\,0,\,T\,;\,L\,)$ such that

$$(\,\int_0^T \|\,f(t)\,\|^2\,dt\,)^{1/2} < \infty \quad \text{for} \quad f(t) \in L^2(\,0,\,T\,;\,L\,).$$

In the same manner we define $L^2(\,0,\,T\,;\,L'\,)$. For any element f(t) of $L^2(\,0,\,T\,;\,L\,)$ we can associate a distribution $\tilde{f}$ defined by

$$\tilde{f}\,(\phi) = \int_0^T f(t)\phi(t)\,dt \qquad \text{for all} \quad \phi(t) \in \mathcal{D}(\,(\,0,\,T\,)). \tag{2.47}$$

The mapping from $f \in L^2(\,0,\,T;\,L\,)$ to $\tilde{f} \in \mathcal{D}'(\,(\,0,\,T\,);\,L\,)$ is continuous linear and one-to-one. Hence, we can identify f with $\tilde{f}$ and we have

$$L^2(\,0,\,T\,;\,L\,) \subset \mathcal{D}'(\,(\,0,\,T\,)\,;\,L\,).$$

All the distibution F is diferentiable and the derivative denoted dF/dt is the distribution defined by

$$\frac{dF}{dt}\,(\phi) = -\,F(\,\frac{d\phi}{dt}\,).$$

This formula defines a continuous linear map from $\mathcal{D}(\,(\,0,\,T\,)) \to L$. Hence,

$$\frac{dF}{dt} \in \mathcal{D}'((\,0,\,T\,)\,;\,L\,).$$

In particular, if $f \in L^2(0, T; L)$, we can denote the distribution $df/dt \in \mathcal{D}'((0, T); L)$ by the following relation;

$$\frac{df}{dt}(\phi) = - \int_0^T f(t) \frac{d\phi}{dt} dt.$$

In order to describe the partial differential equations, we now introduce the following notations:

Let D be an open spatial domain with sufficiently smooth boundary B and let H and V be two Hilbert spaces on D. We denote the norm on V (respectively, H) by $\| \ \|$ (respectively, $| \ |$) and the corresponding scalar products by $((\ ,\ ))$ and $(\ ,\ )$, respectively. The index V or H ($\| \ \|_H$, etc.) will be added in the case there is ambiguity. Assume that

$V \subset H$, the injection of V into H is continuous, and V is dense in H. (2.48)

We assume that H will be identified with its dual space. If V' denotes the dual space of V, H may be identified with a subspace of V' and we may write

$$V \subset H \subset V'. \tag{2.49}$$

In (2.49) V is dense in H and H is dense in V' and the corresponding injections are continuous. We denote by $<\ ,\ >$ the duality between V' and V. Then if $h \in H$, h is an element of V' and we have

$$<h, z> = (h, z) \quad \text{for any } z \in V.$$

From (2.49) we have

$$L^2(0, T; V) \subset L^2(0, T; H) \subset L^2(0, T; V') \tag{2.50}$$

where each space is dense in the following space with continuous injection. From (2.50) $f \in L^2(0, T; V')$ and we can consider $df/dt \in \mathcal{D}'((0,T); V')$. Then we can introduce

$$W(0, T) = \{ f ;\ f \in L^2(0, T; V),\ df/dt \in L^2(0, T; V') \}. \tag{2.51}$$

If we endow W(0, T) with the norm

$$\|f\|_{W(0,T)} = \left(\int_0^T \|f(t)\|^2 \, dt + \int_0^T \left\| \frac{d\,f(t)}{dt} \right\|^2_{V'} dt \right)^{1/2} \tag{2.52}$$

then W(0,T) is a Hilbert space.

The following result may be proved (c.f. Chapter 1 of [5]).

[LEMMA 2.17] All functions $f \in W(0,T)$ are, with eventual modification on a set of measure zero, continuous from $[0, T] \to H$. Abbreviating, we shall write

$$W(0,T) \subset \mathcal{C}^0([0, T]; H) = \text{space of continuous functions from } [0, T] \text{ to } H. \tag{2.53}$$

We define by A(t) a family of operator such that

$$A(t) \in L^\infty(0, T; \mathcal{L}(V, V')) \tag{2.54}$$

and

$$\langle A(t)z, z\rangle + \lambda |z|^2 \geqq \alpha \|z\|^2, \quad z \in V, \quad t \in (0, T), \lambda \geqq 0, \alpha > 0. \tag{2.55}$$

We now consider an evolution problem; find $y \in W(0,T)$ such that

$$A(t)\,y + \frac{dy}{dt} = f, \quad f \text{ given in } L^2(0,T; V') \tag{2.56}$$

$$y(0) = y_0, \quad y_0 \text{ given in } H. \tag{2.57}$$

Let us remark that

if $T < \infty$, we may always reduce the problem to a case where (2.55) holds with $\lambda = 0$. In fact, if we set

$$y = \exp(kt)\,z,$$

then (2.56) and (2.57) are equivalent to

$$(A(t) + k\mathcal{I})z + \frac{dz}{dt} = \exp(-kt)\,f, \quad z(0) = y_0,$$

and hence, we have replaced $A(t)$ by $A(t) + k\mathcal{J}$. If $k = \lambda$, (2.55) holds with $\lambda = 0$.

Let us now prove the following theorem.

[THEOREM 2.4] Assuming that (2.54), (2.55) hold, the problem (2.56) and (2.57) admit a unique solution in $W(0,T)$. Furthermore, the solution depends continuously on the data; the bilinear map,

$$f, y_0 \to y$$

is continuous from $L^2(0, T; V') \times H \to W(0, T)$.

[PROOF] In order to prove the uniqueness of the solution, it is sufficient to show that if f, y_0 are zero, then $y = 0$. Let us take the scalar product in (2.56) with $y(t)$ under the duality between V' and V. We obtain

$$< \frac{dy}{dt}(t), y(t) > + < A(t)y(t), y(t) > = 0,$$

Using the following formula with the integration by parts in $W(0,T)$ [5];

$$\int_0^T < \frac{dz(t)}{dt}, y(t) > dt + \int_0^T < \frac{dy(t)}{dt}, z(t) > dt$$

$$= (y(T), z(T)) - (y(0), z(0)),$$

we have

$$\int_0^T < \frac{dy}{dt}(t), y(t) > dt = \frac{1}{2} | y(T)|^2.$$

Hence, we have

$$\frac{1}{2} |y(T)|^2 + \int_0^T < A(t) y(t), y(t) > dt = 0$$

from which we have by virtue of (2.55) with $\lambda = 0$

$$\alpha \int_0^T \| y(t)\|^2 dt + \frac{1}{2} | y(T)|^2 \leqq 0.$$

Thus, $y = 0$ for all $t \in [0, T]$.

Hence, the proof of the uniqueness of the solution was proved.

Let us now prove the existence of the solution. We utilize the discretization procedure to do so. Let $0, k, \cdots, Nk = T$ be a finite partitions of $[0, T]$. We set

$$f_n = \frac{1}{k} \int_{(n-1)k}^{nk} f(\tau)\, d\tau \tag{2.58}$$

and

$$A_n = \frac{1}{k} \int_{(n-1)k}^{nk} A(\tau)\, d\tau . \tag{2.59}$$

We define a sequence y^n by

$$\frac{y^n - y^{n-1}}{k} + A_n y^n = f_n . \tag{2.60}$$

Note that (2.60) is an equation for y^n when y^{n-1} is known and that (2.60) possesses a unique solution in V. In fact, the operator $(\mathcal{J}/k + A_n) \in (V, V')$ is an operator such that

$$< (\frac{\mathcal{J}}{k} + A_n) z, z > \leqq c \| z \|^2, \quad \forall z \in V,$$

and so , the operator is invertible [9]. Then we deduce from (2.60) that

$$\frac{1}{k} (y^n - y^{n-1}, y^n) + < A_n y^n, y^n > = (f_n, y^n),$$

and hence,

$$\frac{1}{2} (|y^n|^2 - |y^{n-1}|^2 + | y^n - y^{n-1}|^2) + k < A_n y^n, y^n > = k (f_n, y^n).$$

We have from (2.55)

$$|y^n|^2 - |y^{n-1}|^2 + | y^n - y^{n-1}|^2 + 2k\alpha \| y^n \|^2$$

$$\leqq 2k (f_n, y^n) \leqq k\alpha |y^n|^2 + \frac{k}{\alpha} |f_n|^2 \leqq k\alpha \| y^n \|^2 + \frac{k}{\alpha} |f_n|^2$$

since $|z|_H \leqq \| z \|_V$.

Summing the above inequality yields

$$|y^n|^2 + k\,\alpha\,\Sigma_{j=1}^{n}\ \|y^j\|^2 \leqq \|y_0\|^2 + \frac{k}{\alpha}\,\Sigma_{j=1}^{n}\,|f_j|^2.$$

on the other hand,

$$|f_j|^2 = \left(\frac{1}{k}\int_{(j-1)k}^{jk} f(\tau)\,d\tau\right)^2 \leqq \frac{1}{k}\int_{(j-1)k}^{jk} |f(\tau)|^2\,d\tau .$$

Hence, we have

$$|y^n|^2 + k\,\alpha\,\Sigma_{j=1}^{n}\ \|y^j\|^2 \leqq |y_0|^2 + \frac{1}{\alpha}\int_0^T |f(\tau)|^2\,d\tau \qquad n = 0, 1, \cdots, N.$$

We have from the above inequality

$$|y^n| \leqq c_0 \qquad n = 0, 1, \cdots, N \tag{2.61}$$

and

$$\Sigma_{j=1}^{N}\ \|y^j\|^2 \leqq c_1 \tag{2.62}$$

where c_0 and c_1 are constants.

Now, we define

$$y_k(t) = y^{n+1}, \quad \text{in } [\ nk,\ (\ n+1\ )k\ ),\ 0 \leqq n \leqq N - 1.$$

Then from (2.61) and (2.62) we have that

$y_k(t)$ ranges in a bounded subset of $L\ (0,T;\ H\ )$ and $L^2(0,T;\ V\ )$ when $k \to 0$.

Let t be fixed in $[\ 0,\ T\ )$ and n_t the integer part of t/k. We suppose that k is sufficiently small so that $t \leqq T - k$. Then $(\ n_t + 1\ )\ k \leqq T$. Hence, from (2.60) we deduce by summing up the both sides of the equation that

$$y^{n_t+1} - y_0 + k\ \Sigma_{n=1}^{n_t+1}\ A_n\,y^n = \int_0^{(\ n_t\ +\ 1\ )k} f(\tau)\,d\tau$$

which can be rewritten as

$$y_k(t) - y_0 + \int_0^{(n_t+1)k} A(\tau)\,y_k(\tau)\,d\tau = \int_0^{(n_t+1)} f(\tau)\,d\tau.$$

From the fact that $y_k(t)$ is bounded in $L\ (0,T;\ H\ )$ and $L^2(\ 0,\ T;\ V\ )$, we can extract a subsequence $y_{k'}$ from a sequence y_k such that

$$y_{k'} \rightarrow y^* \quad \text{weakly in } L^2(\ 0,\ T\ ;\ V) \text{ and } L\ \ (0,T\ ;\ H\ ). \tag{2.63}$$

Let z be any element of V. Then from (2.63) we have

$$(\ y_{k'}(t),\ z) - (\ y_0,\ z\ ) + \int_0^{(n_t+1)k'} (\ f(\tau),\ z\ )\ d\tau. \tag{2.64}$$

But

$$\int_0^{(n_t+1)k'} < A(\tau)\ y_{k'}(\tau),\ z > d\tau \ = \ \int_0^T < A(\tau)\ y_{k'}(\tau),\ \ \chi_{[n_t+1]}(\tau)\ z > d\tau$$

where χ_{n_t+1} denotes the characteristic function of $[\ 0,\ n_t+1\ ]$.
Since $\chi_{n_t+1}(\tau)\ z$ converges strongly to χ_t in $L^2(\ 0,\ T\ ;\ V\ )$, it follows that

$$\int_0^{(n_t+1)\ k'} < A(\tau)\ y_{k'}(\tau),\ z > \ d\tau \ \rightarrow \ \int_0^t < A(\tau)\ y^*(\tau),\ z > d\tau\ ,$$

and

$$\int_0^{(n_t+1)k'} (\ f(\tau),\ z\ )\ d\tau \ \rightarrow \ \int_0^t (\ f(\tau),\ z\ )\ d\tau$$

when k' goes to zero. The convergence in the above equations hold for all t, and therefore, have a sense in the distribution. In fact, for example,

$$\left|\ \int_0^{(n_t+1)k'} < A(\tau)\ y_{k'}(\tau),\ z > d\tau\ \right| \leqq M\ (\ \int_0^{(n_t+1)k'} \|\ y_{k'}(\tau)\|\ \ d\tau\ )\|\ z\| < c$$

where c is a constant.
Then from the Lebesgue convergence theorem we have

$$\int_0^T [\ \int_0^{(n_t+1)k'} < \ A(\tau)\ y_{k'}(\tau),\ z > d\tau\ ]\ \phi(t)\ dt$$

$$\rightarrow \int_0^T [\ \int_0^t < A(\tau)\ y^*(\tau),\ z > d\tau\ ]\ \phi(t)\ dt \qquad \text{for all } \phi \in \mathcal{D}(\ (0,T)\ ).$$

Similarly, we have

$$\int_0^T (\ y_{k'}(t),\ z\ )\ \phi(t)\ dt \ \rightarrow \ \int_0^T (\ y^*(t),\ z\ )\ \phi(t)\ dt.$$

We can pass to the limit in (2.64) in the sense of distribution and we have

$$\int_0^T (y^*(t), z) \phi(t)\, dt + \int_0^T [\int_0^t < A(\tau)\, y^*(\tau), z > d\tau]\, \phi(t)\, dt$$

$$= \int_0^T [\int_0^t (f(\tau), z)\, d\tau]\, \phi(t)\, dt + (y_0, z) \int_0^T \phi(t)\, dt, \forall_\phi \in \mathcal{D}((0,T)).$$

Hence, we have

$$(y^*(t), z) + \int_0^t < A(\tau)\, y^*(\tau), z > d\tau = (y_0, z) + \int_0^t (f(\tau), z)\, d\tau ,$$

for all $z \in V$. (2.65)

We deduce from (2.65) that $(y^*(t), z)$ possesses a derivative in the sense of distribution and

$$\frac{d}{dt} (y^*(t), z) + < A(t)\, y^*(t), z > = (f(t), z) \text{ a.e.} t \in [0, T],$$

which implies that

$$\frac{dy^*}{dt} \in L^2(0, T; V') \text{ and}$$

$$\frac{dy^*(t)}{dt} + A(t)\, y^*(t) = f(t).$$

Since $y^*(0) = y_0$, we can see that $y^*(t)$ is the solution of (2.56).

From the definition of $y_k(t)$ and the inequality used for the derivations of (2.61) and (2.62), we have

$$|y_k(t)|^2 \leqq |y_0|^2 + \frac{1}{\alpha} \int_0^T | f(\tau)|^2\, d\tau, \quad \forall t \in [0, T]$$

and

$$\int_0^T \| y_k(t) \|^2\, dt \leqq |y_0|^2 + \frac{1}{\alpha} \int_0^T |f(\tau)|^2\, d\tau .$$

But $y_k(t) \to y$ in $L^2(0, T; V)$ and in $L\ (0, T ; H)$ weakly, and hence,

$$\operatorname{Ess.Sup}_t |y(t)|^2 \leqq \liminf_{k \to \infty} \operatorname{Ess.Sup}_t |y_k(t)|^2 \leqq |y_0|^2 + \frac{1}{\alpha} \int_0^T |f(\tau)|^2\, d\tau$$

and

$$\int_0^T \|y(t)\|^2 \, dt \leqq \liminf_{k \to \infty} \int_0^T \|y_k(t)\|^2 \, dt$$

$$\leqq |y_0|^2 + \frac{1}{\alpha} \int_0^T \| f(t)\|^2 \, dt,$$

which prove that

y_0, $f \to y$ is continuous from $H \times L^2(0, T; H) \to L^2(0, T; V)$ and

$$L\ (0, T; H). \tag{2.65}$$

From (2.56) we have

$$\int_0^T \|\frac{dy}{dt}\|_{V'}^2 \, dt \leqq 2 \int_0^T \| f(t)\|_{V'}^2 \, dt + 2\int_0^T \| A(t)\, y(t)\|_{V'}^2 \, dt$$

$$\leqq c_1 \int_0^T |f(t)|^2 \, dt + c_2 \int_0^T \| y(t)\|_V^2 \, dt$$

$$\leqq c_3 \int_0^T | f(t)|^2 \, dt + c_4 |y_0|^2 \tag{2.66}$$

where the following relation was used

$$\|f + g\|^2 \leqq 2 (\| f\| + \| g\|).$$

Thus, it was proved from (2.65) and (2.66) that the mapping

y_0, $f \to y$ from $H \times L^2(0, T; H) \to W(0,T)$

is continuous. Hence, the proof of the theorem was completed. Q.E.D.

Remark that there exist a number of methods to prove the existence and uniqueness of the solution for (2.56) and (2.57), in particular, the method by the projection lemma [9] and the Galerkin method by approximating (2.56) and (2.57) by a family of ordinary differential equations [13].

Note that these methods couldn't be applied to the stochastic partial differential equations while the method adopted here by discretizing the partial differential equations enables us to treat the stochastic case by the similar way.

2.4.2.　　　　Stochastic partial differential equations.

　　　　　We will consider the stochastic partial differential equations
analogous to the deterministic case discussed in the preceding section.
Let $(\Omega, \mathcal{B}(\Omega), \mu)$ be the probability space and let $f = f(t, \omega)$ be an element of
$C([0, T]; L^2(\Omega, \mu; H))$ which satisfies the uncorrelation hypothesis given by

$$E[(f(t_2) - f(t_1), \Lambda(f(t_4) - f(t_3)))] = 0, \quad {}^\forall\Lambda \in \mathcal{L}(H, H)$$

for $t_1 < t_2 \leqq t_3 < t_4$.

For simplicity, we assume that $E[f(t)] = 0$, for all t.　　We call the process
$f(t)$ as the stochastic process with independent increments.　　　Furthermore, assume
that the random variable $y_0 \in L^2(\Omega, \mu; H)$ is independent with $f(t)$, so that

$$E[(\Lambda y_0, f(t))] = 0, \quad {}^\forall\Lambda \in \mathcal{L}(H, H), \quad {}^\forall t \in [0, T].$$

We consider the stochastic evolution equation given by

$$y(t, \omega) + \int_0^t A(\tau) y(\tau, \omega) d\tau = y_0(\omega) + f(t, \omega) - f(0, \omega) \qquad (2.67)$$

where the redefined notations and spaces are the same as the preceding section.
Note that the Wiener process with values in the Hilbert space H satisfies the
properties of f(t) and that we denote (2.67) formally as follows:

$$\frac{dy(t)}{dt} + A(t) y(t) = y_0 \delta(t) + \frac{df(t)}{dt} \qquad (2.67')$$

where $df(t)/dt$ is a distribution with values in $L^2(\Omega, \mu; V')$.

Then the following theorem follows.

[THEOREM 2.5]　　　Under the preceding assumptions, there exists a unique stochastic
process $y(t, \omega)$ such that

$$y(t, \omega) \in C([0, t]; L^2(\Omega, \mu; V')) \cap L^\infty(0, T; L^2(\Omega, \mu; H)) \cap L^2(0, T; L^2(\Omega, \mu; V))$$

$$(2.68)$$

for all $t \in [0, T]$, and the equation (2.67) is verified a.e. ω.

[PROOF] Let us first prove the uniqueness of the solution. Suppose that there exist two solutions $y_1(t,\omega)$ and $y_2(t,\omega)$ of (2.67) and we set

$$z(t) = y_1(t) - y_2(t).$$

We can see that z(t) satisfies the equation

$$z(t,\omega) + \int_0^t A(\tau)\, z(\tau,\omega)\, d\tau = 0, \quad \forall t \in [0, T], \text{ a.e.}\omega \tag{2.69}$$

$$z(0,\omega) = 0.$$

But we set

$$\mathcal{H} = L^2(\Omega, \mu; H), \mathcal{V} = L^2(\Omega, \mu; V), \quad \mathcal{V}' = L^2(\Omega, \mu; V')$$

and identify $\mathcal{H}$ with its dual $\mathcal{H}'$, then we have

$$\mathcal{V} \subset \mathcal{H} \subset \mathcal{V}'$$

where each space is dense in the following space with continuous injections. We then define $\mathcal{A}(t) \in \mathcal{L}(\mathcal{V}, \mathcal{V}')$ by

$$\mathcal{A}(t)\zeta = A(t)\zeta, \quad \text{for all } \zeta \in \mathcal{V}.$$

From (2.68) we have

$$Z(t) \in L^2(0,T;\mathcal{V}), \ Z(t) \in C([0,T];\mathcal{V}') \text{ and } Z(t) \in L^\infty(0,T;\mathcal{H}).$$

Thus, (2.69) means that z(t) satisfies

$$z(t) + \int_0^t \mathcal{A}(\tau)\, z(\tau)\, d\tau = o, \text{ for all } t,$$

$$z(0) = 0.$$

By differentiating both sides of the above equation in the sense of distibution with values in $\mathcal{V}'$, we obtain

$$\frac{dz(t)}{dt} + \mathcal{A}(t)\,z(t) = 0, \quad z(0) = 0.$$

On the other hand, $\mathcal{A}(t)$ satisfies the following relation

$$< \mathcal{A}(t)\,z_1,\ z_1 >_{\mathcal{V}} = \int_\Omega < A(t)\,z_1(\omega),\ z_1(\omega) > d\mu(\omega) \geqq \alpha \|z_1\|^2, \quad \forall z_1 \in \mathcal{V}.$$

By the same way as the deterministic case, we can easily show that

$$z(t,\omega) = 0.$$

Thus, the uniqueness property was completed.

In order to prove the existence of the solution, we utilize the discretization procedure as in the preceding section. Let $0, k, \cdots, Nk = T$ be a finite partition of $[\,0,\ T\,]$. We define $f_n(\omega)$ as

$$f_n(\omega) = f(nk,\omega).$$

We take

$$y^0(\omega) = y_0(\omega)$$

and we define a sequence $y^n(\omega)$ by

$$\frac{y^n(\omega) - y^{n-1}(\omega)}{k} + A_n\,y^n(\omega) = \frac{f_n(\omega) - f_{n-1}(\omega)}{k} \qquad (2.70)$$

where A_n is defined by

$$A_n = \frac{1}{k}\int_{(n-1)k}^{nk} A(\tau)\,d\tau.$$

Note that (2.70) determines the $y^n(\omega) \in L^2(\Omega, \mu; V)$ uniquely. In practice, the operator $(\mathcal{J}/k + A_n) \in \mathcal{L}(V, V')$ satisfies the following relation;

$$< \left(\frac{\mathcal{J}}{k} + A_n\right) z,\ z > \ \geqq c\,\|z\|^2, \ \forall z \in V \text{ and for some constant } c.$$

Thus, the operator $(\mathcal{J}/k + A_n)$ is invertible and hence, its inverse is continuous. Therefore, we have

$$y^n(\omega) = \left(\frac{\mathcal{J}}{k} + A_n \right)^{-1} \left(\frac{f_n(\omega) - f_{n-1}(\omega)}{k} + \frac{y^{n-1}(\omega)}{k} \right). \qquad (2.71)$$

Let us introduce the stochastic process defined by

$$y_k(t) = y^{n+1} \qquad \text{for } \forall t \in [\, nk, (n+1)k\,), \quad 0 \leq n \leq N-1,$$

$$y_k(T) = y^N.$$

Then, we now prove that when $k \to 0$, y_k ranges in a bounded set of $L^\infty(0,T; L^2(\Omega, \mu; H))$ and in a bounded set of $L^2(0,T; L^2(\Omega, \mu; V))$. From (2.70) it follows that

$$\frac{1}{k}\left(y^n(\omega) - y^{n-1}(\omega), y^n(\omega)\right) + \langle A_n y^n(\omega), y^n(\omega) \rangle$$

$$= \frac{1}{k}\left(f_n(\omega) - f_{n-1}(\omega), y^n(\omega)\right)$$

and hence, we have

$$\frac{1}{2}\left[|y^n|^2 - |y^{n-1}|^2 + |y^n - y^{n-1}|^2 \right] + k \langle A_n y^n, y^n \rangle = (f_n - f_{n-1}, y^n)$$

from which we obtain

$$|y^n|^2 - |y^{n-1}|^2 + 2k\alpha \| y^n \|_V^2 \leq k\alpha \| y^n \|_V^2 + (f_n - f_{n-1}, y^n)$$

where (2.55) was used.

Taking the expectation of the both sides of the above inequality yields

$$E[\, |y^n|^2] - E[\, |y^{n-1}|^2] + 2k\alpha E[\, \|y^n\|^2] < E[\, (f_n - f_{n-1}, y^n)].$$

On the other hand, from (2.18) we have

$$E[\, (f_n - f_{n-1}, y^n)] = \frac{1}{k} E[\, (f_n - f_{n-1}, (\mathcal{J}/k + A_n)^{-1}(f_n - f_{n-1}))]$$

$$+ \frac{1}{k} E [(f_n - f_{n-1}, (\mathcal{I}/k + A_n)^{-1} y^{n-1})].$$

But from Lemma 2.18 (which follows) the last term of the above equation is zero and hence, we have

$$E [(f_n - f_{n-1}, y^n)] = \frac{1}{k} E [((\mathcal{I}/k + A_n)^{-1}(f_n - f_{n-1}), f_n - f_{n-1})].$$

But from (2.55) and the fact that $(\mathcal{I}/k + A_n)$ is positive and invertible we have

$$|(\mathcal{I}/k + A_n)^{-1}(f_n - f_{n-1}) |_H \leq k |f_n - f_{n-1}|_H,$$

and so,

$$((\mathcal{I}/k + A_n)^{-1}(f_n - f_{n-1}), f_n - f_{n-1}) \leq k | f_n - f_{n-1}|^2.$$

Thus, we have

$$E [(f_n - f_{n-1}, y^n)] \leqq E [| f_n - f_{n-1}|^2].$$

But we have

$$E [|f_n - f_{n-1}|^2] = E [|f_n|^2] + E [|f_{n-1}|^2] - 2 E[(f_n, f_{n-1})].$$

Since it follows from the assumption that f(t) possesses the independent increment, we have

$$E [(f_n - f_{n-1}, f_{n-1})] = 0.$$

Then we obtain

$$E [(f_n, f_{n-1})] = E [|f_{n-1}|^2].$$

Thus, we have

$$E [|f_n - f_{n-1}|^2] = E [|f_n|^2] - E [|f_{n-1}|^2].$$

It follows from the above relations that

$$E [|y^n|^2] - E [|y^{n-1}|^2] + 2k\alpha E [\| y^n\|^2] \leqq E [|f_n|^2] - E [|f_{n-1}|^2].$$

Therefore, we have the following inequality;

$$E[\,|y^n|^2\,] + 2k\alpha\Sigma_{j=1}^{n}\ E[\,\|y^j\|^2\,] \leq E[|y_0|^2] + E[\,|f_n|^2\,] - E[|f_0|\,]$$

$$\leq E[\,|y_0|^2\,] + \underset{t}{SUP}\ E[\,|f(t)|^2\,].$$

Thus, we have from the above inequality that

$$E[|y^n|^2\,] \leq c_0 \quad \text{for all } n \tag{2.72}$$

$$k\alpha\Sigma_{j=1}^{N}\ E[\,\|y^j\|_V^2\,] \leq c_1 \tag{2.73}$$

where c_0 and c_1 are constants.

When $k \to 0$, we have from the above relation that y_k ranges in a bounded set of $L\ (0,T;\ L^2(\Omega, \mu;\ H\ ))$ and in a bounded set of $L^2(0,T;\ L^2(\Omega, \mu;\ H\ ))$.

In order to pass to the limit in (2.70), let t be fixed in [0, T] and let n_t be the integer part of t/k and let

$$n_t\, k \leq t \leq (\, n_t + 1\,)\, k.$$

We assume that k is sufficiently small so that $t \leq T - k$. Then $(\,n_t + 1\,)k \leq T$. Summing up (2.70) from $n = 1$ to $n = n_t + 1$ yields

$$y^{n_t+1} - y_0 + k\,\Sigma_{j=1}^{n_t+1}\ A_j\, y^j = f((n_t+1)k\,) - f(0),$$

which can be rewritten as

$$y_k(t) - y_0 + \int_0^{(n_t+1)k} A(\tau)\, y_k(\tau)\, d\tau = f((\,n_t+1)k) - f(0). \tag{2.74}$$

Let z be any element of $L^2(\Omega, \mu\,; V\,)$ and multiplying the both sides by z as the scalar product and taking the expectation, we have

$$E[(\,y_k(t), z\,)] - E[(y_0, z\,)] + E[\,\int_0^{(n_t+1)k} < A(\tau)\, y_k(\tau), z > d\tau\,]$$

$$= E[(\,f(\,n_t + 1\,)k, z\,)] - E[(\,f(0), z\,)].$$

By virtue of the characteristic function $\chi_{(n_t+1)k}(\tau)$, it follows that

$$E\,[(\,y_k(t),\,z\,)] - E\,[(\,y_0,\,z\,)] + E\,[\,\int_0^T <A(\tau)\,y_k(\tau),\ \ \chi_{(n_t+1)k}\,y_k(\tau)z> d\tau\,]$$

$$= E\,[(f((n_t+1)k),\,z\,)] - E\,[(\,f(0),\,z\,)\,].$$

It is clear that when $k \to 0$, $\chi_{(n_t+1)k}(\tau)\,z \to \chi_t(\tau)\,z$ strongly in $L^2(0,T;$ $L^2(\Omega\,,\mu;V\,))$. But from (2.73) we can extract a subsequence $y_{k'}$ of y_k such that $y_{k'} \to y$ weakly in $L^2(0,T;\,L^2(\Omega\,,\mu\,;V\,))$. Then when $k' \to k$, we have

$$E\,[(\,y_{k'}(t),\,z\,)] \to E\,[(\,y_0,\,z\,)] + E\,[\,\int_0^t <A(\tau)\,y(\tau),\,z> \ d\tau\,]$$

$$+ E\,[\,(\,f(t),\,z\,)] - E\,[(\,f(0),\,z\,)\,]. \qquad (2.74)$$

The convergence of (2.74) is the simple convergence in t and hence, if we designate the right hand side by $\rho(t)$, it is clear that when $k' \to 0$,

$$E\,[(\,y_{k'}(t),\,z\,)] \to \rho(t) \text{ for all } t.$$

From $y \in L^2(\,0,T;\,L^2(\Omega\,,\mu\,;V\,))$ and the fact that $f(t)$ is continuous, it is clear that $\rho(t)$ is bounded. Thus, if $\phi(t) \in \mathcal{D}(\,(0,T\,)\,)$, we deduce from the above relation and the Lebesgue convergence theorem that

$$\int_0^T \ E\,[(\,y_{k'}(t),\,z\,)]\,\phi(t)\,dt \to \int_0^T \ \rho(t)\,\phi(t)\,dt.$$

But since $y_{k'} \to y$ in $L^2(\,0,T;\,L^2(\Omega\,,\mu\,;V\,))$ weakly, the first term of the above relation converges to

$$\int_0^T \ E\,[(\,y(t),\,z\,)]\,\phi(t)\,dt.$$

Hence, we have

$$E\,[(\,y(t),z\,)] = E\,[(\,y_0,z\,)] - E\,[\,\int_0^T <A(\tau)\,y(\tau),z> d\tau] + E\,[(f(t),\,z\,)]$$
$$- E\,[(f(0),\,z\,)]$$

for almost everywhere $t \varepsilon [\ 0,\ T\ ]$.

Since the above relation holds for all $z \varepsilon L^2(\Omega, \mu; V)$, we see that

$$y(t) + \int_0^t A(\tau)\, y(\tau)\, d\tau = y_0 + f(t) - f(0) \tag{2.75}$$

for almost everywhere $\omega \varepsilon \Omega$.

Since (2.75) holds for all $t \varepsilon [\ 0,\ T\ ]$, the existence of the solution is proved if we can prove the following lemma. Q.E.D.

[Lemma 2.18] For all $\Lambda \varepsilon \mathcal{L}(H, H)$, we have

$$E\,[(\Lambda(f_p - f_{p-1}),\ y^n)] = 0 \text{ if } n \leqq p-1,\ p \geqq 1. \tag{2.76}$$

[PROOF] We shall prove this by the mathematical induction. The relation (2.76) is true for n = 0 since the definition of f(t) satisfies the relation given by

$$E\,[\,(\Lambda y_0,\ f(t) - f(t'))\,] = 0,\ \forall \Lambda \varepsilon \mathcal{L}(H, H),\ \forall t,\ t' \varepsilon [0, T].$$

Let $p \geqq 2$ and $n \leqq p - 1$ and let (2.76) hold for n-1. We can describe (2.71) by the following form;

$$y^n(\omega) = b_n + M_n\,(f_n(\omega) - f_{n-1}(\omega)) + N_n\, y^{n-1}(\omega)$$

where b_n, M_n, and N_n are suitable constants associated with (2.71).

If $\Lambda \varepsilon \mathcal{L}(H, H)$, we have

$$E\,[(\Lambda(f_p - f_{p-1}),\ y^n)\,] = E\,[(f(pk) - f((p-1)k),\ \Lambda^* b_n)]$$

$$+ E\,[(f(pk) - f((p-1)k),\ \Lambda^* M_n\,(f(nk) - f((n-1)k)) + E\,[(N_n^* \Lambda\,(f_p - f_{p-1}), y^{n-1})].$$

The first term in the right hand side is zero since $E\,[\,f(t)\,] = 0$ for all t.

The second term is also zero for $nk \leqq (\,p - 1\,)\,k$ and the third term is zero since (2.76) holds for n-1. Thus, the lemma was established. Q.E.D.

[COROLLARY 2.5] The sequence $y_k(t)$ defined before satisfies the following relations:

$$y_k(t) \to y(t) \quad \text{in } L^2(0, T; L^2(\Omega, \mu; V)) \text{ weakly} \tag{2.77}$$

and

$$y_k(t) \to y(t) \quad \text{in } L^2(\Omega, \mu; H)) \text{ weakly for all } t \in [0, T]. \tag{2.78}$$

[PROOF] The property (2.77) follows from the fact that all the subsequences $y_{k'}$ of the sequence y_k converge in $L^2(0, T; V)$ weakly to the solution of (2.67). In order to prove (2.78) we take z as an element of $L^2(\Omega, \mu; V)$. Then from the fact that $E[(y_{k'}(t), z)]$ converges to $\rho(t)$ for all t, it follows that

$$E[(y_{k'}(t), z)] \to E[(y(t), z)].$$

Thus, we have

$$E[(y_k(t), z)] \to E[(y(t), z)].$$

Since $E[|y_k(t)|^2]$ is bounded from (2.72) when $k \to 0$, we can extract a subsequence $y_{k''}(t)$ from the sequence $y_k(t)$, which converges in $L^2(\Omega, \mu; H)$ to an element $\tilde{y}(t) \in L^2(\Omega, \mu; H)$. Then we have

$$E[(\tilde{y}(t), z)] = E[(y(t), z)] \quad \text{for all } z \in L^2(\Omega, \mu; V).$$

Since V is dense in H, $L^2(\Omega, \mu; V)$ is dense in $L^2(\Omega, \mu; H)$ and hence, we have

$$\tilde{y}(t) = y(t).$$

From the fact that the limit of the subsequence extracted is unique, (2.78) was completed. Q.E.D.

Let us now prove the following theorem, so called, energy inequality, which is required in the sequel.

[THEOREM 2.6] Under the same hypotheses with Theorem 2.5, the process $y(t)$

satisfies the following equality.

$$E[|y(t)|^2] + 2\int_0^t E[< A(\tau)\, y(\tau),\, y(\tau) > d\tau]$$

$$= E[|y_0|^2] + E[|f(t)|^2] - E[|f(0)|^2] \quad \text{for all } t \in [0,T]. \quad (2.79)$$

The proof is very long, and so, we divide the proof into two parts, that is, the first part consists of the proof in the case that $f(t) \in C([0,T]; L^2(\Omega,\mu;V))$, and the remaining part consists of the proof in the case that f(t) satisfies the assumption of Theorem 2.5.

[PROOF OF THE FIRST PART] Consider the case where f(t) satisfies the following property

$$f(t) \in C([0,T]; L^2(\Omega,\mu;V)). \quad (2.80)$$

Let us first prove that if (2.80) is satisfied, then we have

$$\frac{1}{2} E[|y(t)|^2] + \frac{1}{2} E[|f(t)|^2] + \int_0^t E[< A(\tau)\, y(\tau),\, y(\tau) >]\, d\tau$$

$$= \frac{1}{2} E[|y_0|^2] + \frac{1}{2} E[|f_0|^2] + E[(y(t), f(t))]$$

$$+ E[\int_0^t < A(\tau)\, y(\tau),\, f(\tau) >]\, d\tau. \quad (2.81)$$

Note that (2.81) has a sense from (2.80) for $< A(\tau)\, y(\tau),\, f(\tau) >$ has a sense and

$$< A(\tau)\, y(\tau),\, f(\tau) > \in L^2(0, T; L^2(\Omega,\mu;R)).$$

Setting

$$z(t,\omega) = y(t,\omega) - f(t,\omega),$$

then $z \in L^2(0, T; L^2(\Omega,\mu;V))$ and from (2.67) we have

$$z(t,\omega) = y_0(\omega) - f(0,\omega) - \int_0^t A(\tau)\, y(\tau,\omega)\, d\tau,$$

and hence,

$$z(0) = y_0 - f(0).$$

If we consider $dz/dt \in \mathcal{D}'((0,T); L^2(\Omega, \mu; V))$, then we see that

$$\frac{dz}{dt} = -A(t)\,y(t) \in L^2(0, T; L^2(\Omega, \mu; V')).$$

In other words, $z \in L^2(0, T; L^2(\Omega, \mu; V))$ and $dz/dt \in L^2(0, T; L^2(\Omega, \mu; V'))$, and hence z ranges in the similar space to $W(0,T)$ where V is changed to $L^2(\Omega, \mu; H)$, H is changed to $L^2(\Omega, \mu; H)$, and V' is changed to $L^2(\Omega, \mu; V')$. By virtue of the integration by parts with values in $W(0, T)$, we have

$$\frac{1}{2} E[|z(t)|^2] - \frac{1}{2} E[|z(0)|^2] = \int_0^t E[\langle dz/dt, z\rangle] d\tau.$$

Hence, it follows that

$$\frac{1}{2} E[|y(t)|^2] + \frac{1}{2} E[|f(t)|^2] - E[(y(t), f(t))]$$

$$= \frac{1}{2} E[|y_0|^2] + \frac{1}{2} E[|f_0|^2] + \int_0^t E[\langle -Ay, y-f\rangle]\, d\tau.$$

Thus, (2.81) was obtained.

Let us prove the following equality:

$$E[(y(t), f(t))] + \int_0^t E[\langle A(\tau)\,y(\tau), f(\tau)\rangle] d\tau$$

$$= E[|f(t)|^2] - E[|f(0)|^2]. \tag{2.82}$$

Multiplying the both sides of (2.70) by f_n as the scalar product yields

$$(y^n - y^{n-1}, f_n) + k\langle A_n y^n, f_n\rangle = (f_n - f_{n-1}, f_n).$$

Hence, it follows that

$$(y^n, f_n) - (y^{n-1}, f_{n-1}) + k\langle A_n y^n, f_n\rangle$$

$$= |f_n - f_{n-1}|^2 + (f_{n-1}, f_n - f_{n-1}).$$

By taking the expectation of the above equation and using the following relations

$E[(f_n - f_{n-1}, f_{n-1})] = 0$ from the definition of f(t)

and

$E[(y^{n-1}, f_n - f_{n-1})] = 0$ from Lemma 2.18,

we have

$$E[(y^n, f_n)] - E[(y^{n-1}, f_{n-1})] + E[<A_n y^n, f_n>]$$

$$= E[|f_n - f_{n-1}|^2] = E[|f_n|^2] - E[|f_{n-1}|^2].$$

Let t be any fixed time in [0, T]. Then by summing up from n = 1 to $n = n_t + 1$ we have

$$E[(y^{n_t+1}, f_{n_t+1})] + k \sum_{n=1}^{n_t+1} E[<A_n y^n, f_n>]$$

$$= E[|f_{n_t+1}|^2] - E[|f_0|^2].$$

Let us introduce stochastic process $f_k(\tau)$ given by

$$f_k(\tau) = f_{n+1} \quad \text{if} \quad nk \leqq \tau < (n+1)k.$$

Then it follows that

$$E[(y_k(t), f((n_t+1)k))] + \int_0^{(n_t+1)k} E[< A(\tau)\, y_k(\tau), f_k(\tau)]\, d\tau$$

$$= E[|f((n_t+1)k)|^2] - E[|f(0)|^2]$$

and hence,

$$E[(y_k(t), f((n_t+1)k))] + \int_0^T E[< A(\tau)\, y_k(\tau), \chi_{(n_t+1)k}(\tau)\, f_k(\tau) >]\, d\tau$$

$$= E[|f((n_t+1)k)|^2] - E[|f(0)|^2]. \tag{2.83}$$

From (2.80) we see easily that

$$\chi_{(n_t+1)k}(\tau)\ f_k(\tau) \ \rightarrow\ \chi_t(\tau)\ f(\tau) \quad \text{in } L^2(0,\ T;\ L^2(\Omega,\mu;V)) \text{ strongly.}$$

Then by using Corollary 2.5 we can pass the limit in (2.83) and it follows that

$$E\,[(\ y(t),\ f(t))] + \int_0^T E\,[<A(\tau)\ y(\tau),\ f(\tau)\ \chi_t(\tau)>]\ d\tau$$

$$= E\,[\ |f(t)|^2\ ] - E\,[|f(0)|^2\ ].$$

Hence, (2.82) was proved.

From (2.81) and (2.82) it follows that (2.79) holds.

Thus, the proof of the first part of the theorem was completed. Q.E.D.

[PROOF OF THE REMAINING PART] Let an orthonormal base of H be w_1, w_2, $\cdots$, which are elements of V. Note that the choice of the base like this is possible since V is dense in H. Let us delete the hypothesis (2.80) in what follows and we associate f(t) with $f_m(t)$ defined by

$$f_m(t) = \Sigma_{i=1}^{m}\ (\ f(t),\ w_i\ )\ w_i. \tag{2.84}$$

Since $f(t) \varepsilon C([0,T];\ L^2(\Omega,\mu;H))$ from the definiton of f(t), it is clear that

$$f_m(t)\ \varepsilon\ C([0,T];L^2(\Omega,\mu;H))$$

and

$$E\,[\ f_m(t)\ ] = 0.$$

Especially, it is seen that $f_m(t)$ is the stochastic process with independent increments since if $\Lambda\ \varepsilon\ \mathcal{L}(\ H,\ H\ )$, we have

$$E\,[(\ f_m(t_2) - f_m(t_1),\ \Lambda(\ f_m(t_4) - f_m(t_3))] = E\,[\ (\Sigma_{i=1}^{m} w_i\ (\ f(t_2) - f(t_1),\ w_i),$$

$$\Sigma_{j=1}^{m} \Lambda\ w_j\ (\ f(t_4) - f(t_3),\ w_j)\ )\ ] = E\,[\ \Sigma_{i,j=1}^{m}\ (\ w_i,\ \Lambda\ w_j)(\ f(t_2) - f(t_1),\ w_i)$$

$$(f(t_4) - f(t_3), w_j)] = E[\Sigma_{i=1}^{m} (f(t_2) - f(t_1), w_i) \Sigma_{j=1}^{m} (\Lambda^* w_j$$

$$(f(t_4) - f(t_3), w_j), w_i)] = E [(f(t_2) - f(t_1), \Lambda_m (f(t_4) - f(t_3)))] = 0$$

where

$$\Lambda_m h = \Sigma_{i=1}^{m} w_i (\Sigma_{j=1}^{m} \Lambda^* w_j (h, w_j), w_i)$$

and $t_1 < t_2 \leqq t_3 < t_4$.

Let us introduce $y_m(t)$ as the solution of the stochastic partial differential equation given by

$$y_m(t) + \int_0^t A(\tau) y_m(\tau) d\tau = y_0 + f_m(t) - f_m(0).$$

Then we have

$$|f_m(t) - f(t)|^2 = \Sigma_{i=m+1}^{\infty} (f(t), w_i)^2 \to 0 \text{ a.e. } \omega \text{ as } m \to \infty$$

and $|f_m(t) - f(t)|^2$ is bounded by $2 |f(t)|^2$ which is integrable with respect to ω . Thus, from the Lebesgue convergence theorem we have

$$E [|f_m(t) - f(t)|^2] \to 0 \quad \text{as} \quad m \to \infty . \tag{2.85}$$

We consider for any m, m'

$$f_{mm'}(t) = f_m(t) - f_{m'}(t) = \Sigma_{i=m+1}^{m'} (f(t), w_i) w_i .$$

Then the process $f_{mm'}(t)$ has the following properties;

$$f_{mm'}(t) \in C([0, T] ; L^2(\Omega, \mu ; V)) \text{ and } E [f_{mm'}(t)] = 0.$$

Furthermore, $f_{mm'}(t)$ possesses the independent increments property for if $\Lambda \in \mathcal{L}(H, H)$ and we set

$$\Lambda_{mm'} h = \Sigma_{i=m+1}^{m'} w_i (\Sigma_{j=m+1}^{m'} \Lambda^* w_j (h, w_j), w_i),$$

then we have

$$E\,[(\,f(t_2) - f(t_1),\ \Lambda_{m\,m'}\,(\,f(t_4) - f(t_3))\,)\,]$$

$$= E\,[\,\Sigma_{i=m+1}^{m'}\,(\,w_i,\ f(t_2) - f(t_1))\ \ \Sigma_{j=m+1}^{m'}\,(\,w_i,\ w_j)(\,w_j,\ f(t_4) - f(t_3))\,]$$

$$= E\,[(\,f_{m\,m'}(t_2) - f_{m\,m'}(t_1),\ \Lambda\,(\,f_{m\,m'}(t_4) - f_{m\,m'}(t_3)))\,] = 0.$$

But the energy equality (2.79) is true for the pair (f_m, y_m) and for the pair ($f_m - f_{m'}$, $y_m - y_{m'}$). Thus, we have

$$E\,[\,|y_m(t)|^2\,] + 2\int_0^t E\,[\,<A(\tau)\,y_m(\tau),\ y_m(\tau)>\,d\tau\,]$$

$$= E\,[\,|y_0|^2\,] + E\,[|f_m(t)|^2\,] - E\,[|f_m(0)|^2\,] \qquad (2.86)$$

and

$$E\,[|y_m(t) - y_{m'}(t)|^2] + 2\int_0^t E\,[<A(\tau)(\,y_m(\tau) - y_{m'}(\tau)),\ y_m(\tau) - y_{m'}(\tau)>\,d\tau\,]$$

$$= E\,[\,|f_m(t) - f_{m'}(t)|^2\,] - E\,[|f_m(0) - f_{m'}(0)|^2\,].$$

But from (2.85) we deduce that

$$E\,[\,|f_m(t) - f_{m'}(t)|^2\,] \to 0 \quad \text{for all } t \text{ as } m,\ m' \to \infty\,.$$

Thus we have that

$$y_m(t) \to y(t) \text{ in } L^2(\Omega,\mu;H) \text{ strongly for all } t$$

and

$$y_m(t) \to y(t) \text{ in } L^2(\Omega,\mu;V) \text{ strongly as } m \to \infty.$$

Then we can pass the limit in (2.86) and the energy equality was proved. Q.E.D.

Let us now prove that the weak convergence of Corollary 2.5 becomes to the strong convergence if f(t) is a Wiener process. In order to prove the strong convergence theorem we use some properties with regard to the nuclear operator and hence, we summarize here some of them.

Let H and H_1 be two Hilbert spaces and let $P \in \mathcal{L}(H, H)$ be a nuclear operator. We define the trace of P by

$$tr(P) = \sum_{n=1}^{\infty} (P e_n, e_n)_H$$

where $e_1, e_2, \cdots$ are an orthonormal base of H.

[LEMMA 2.19] If $P \in \mathcal{L}(H, H)$ is self-adjoint and nuclear and if $Q \in \mathcal{L}(H, H_1)$, then we have

$$tr(Q P Q^*) = tr(Q^* Q P). \tag{2.87}$$

[PROOF] Let us first note that when P is nuclear, $Q P Q^*$ and $Q^* Q P$ are also nuclear. Let f_n be an orthonormal base of H_1. Then we have

$$\sum_{n=1}^{\infty} (Q P Q^* f_n, f_n) = \sum_{n=1}^{\infty} \| P^{1/2} Q^* f_n \|_H^2 .$$

But we have the following relation [9];

$$\sum_{n=1}^{\infty} \| R f_n \|_H^2 = \sum_{n=1}^{\infty} \| R^* e_n \|_{H_1}^2$$

where $R \in \mathcal{L}(H_1, H)$ is any Hilbert-Schmidt operator.

Hence, we have

$$\sum_{n=1}^{\infty} (Q P Q^* f_n, f_n) = \sum_{n=1}^{\infty} \| Q P^{1/2} e_n \|_{H_1}^2 = \sum_{n=1}^{\infty} (Q P^{1/2} e_n, Q P^{1/2} e_n)_{H_1}$$

$$= \sum_{n=1}^{\infty} (P^{1/2} Q^* Q P^{1/2} e_n, e_n)_H .$$

But it follows from [9] that

$$\Sigma_{n=1}^{\infty} (P^{1/2} R P^{1/2} e_n, e_n)_H = \Sigma_{n=1}^{\infty} (R P e_n, e_n)_H$$

where $R \in \mathcal{L}(H, H)$.

Thus, we have

$$\operatorname{tr} (Q P Q^*) = \Sigma_{n=1}^{\infty} (Q P Q^* f_n, f_n) = \Sigma_{n=1}^{\infty} (Q^* Q P e_n, e_n) = \operatorname{tr} (Q^*Q P).$$

Thus, the lemma was completed. Q.E.D.

Let $Q(t) \in L (0, T ; \mathcal{L}(H, H))$ be an operator such that

$Q(t)$ is self-adjoint, nuclear for almost all t, and $t \to \operatorname{tr} Q(t)$

$\in L^\infty (0, T)$. (2.88)

Then we have the strong convergence theorem.

[THEOREM 2.7] Under the same condition with Theorem 2.5, we assume that $f(t)$ is the Wiener process with values in H whose covariance operator $Q(t)$ satisfies (2.88). Then the sequence $y_k(t)$ satisfies the following relations:

When $k \to 0$, $y_k(t) \to y(t)$ in $L^2(\Omega, \mu; H)$ strongly for all $t \in [0, T]$ and $y_k(t) \to y(t)$ in $L^2(0, T; L^2(\Omega, \mu; V))$ strongly. (2.89)

[PROOF] Let t fix in [0, T] and let n_t be the integer part of t/k. Consider the following expression

$$X_k(t) = E [|y_k(t) - y(t)|^2] + \int_{n=1}^{n_t+1} E [| ((\mathcal{I} + k A_n)^{-1} - \mathcal{I}) y^{n-1}|^2]$$

$$+ 2 E [\int_0^{(n_t+1)k} < A_k(\tau) y_k(\tau), y_k(\tau) - y(\tau) > d\tau]$$

where

$$A_k(\tau) = A_{n+1} = \frac{1}{k} \int_{nk}^{(n+1)k} A(\theta) d\theta , \text{ if } \tau \in [nk, (n+1)k).$$

In order to prove (2.89), it is sufficient to show that $X_k(t) \to 0$, for all t.

We can write the above equation as

$$X_k(t) = X_k^1(t) + X_k^2(t) + X_k^3(t),$$

where

$$X_k^1(t) = E[\,|y(t)|^2\,] + 2E[\int_0^{(n_t+1)k} < A_k(\tau)\, y(\tau),\, y(\tau) > d\tau],$$

$$X_k^2(t) = -2E[(y(t), y_k(t))] - 2E[\int_0^{(n_t+1)k} A_k(\tau)y(\tau),\, y(\tau)\, d\tau]$$
$$- 2E[\int_0^{(n_t+1)k} < A_k(\tau)y(\tau),\, y_k(\tau) > d\tau],$$

and

$$X_k^3(t) = E[|y_k(t)|^2] + \Sigma_{n=1}^{n_t+1} E[\,|\,((\mathcal{I} + k A_n)^{-1} - \mathcal{I})\, y^{n-1}\,|^2\,]$$
$$+ 2E[\int_0^{(n_t+1)k} < A_k(\tau)y_k(\tau),\, y_k(\tau) > d\tau].$$

By virtue of Corollary 2.5, it is clear [9] that

$$X_k^1(t) \to E[|y(t)|^2] + 2\int_0^t E[< A(\tau)y(\tau), y(\tau) >]d\tau = X^1(t)$$

and

$$X_k^2(t) \to -2E[|y(t)|^2] - 4\int_0^t E[< A(\tau)y(\tau), y(\tau) >]\, d\tau = X^2(t).$$

It is necessary to study the term $X_k^3(t)$. From (2.70) we have

$$|y^n|^2 - |y^{n-1}|^2 + |y^n - y^{n-1}|^2 + 2k < A_n\, y^n, y^n > = 2\,(y^n, f_n - f_{n-1}),$$

and summing up the above equation with respect to n from 1 to n_t+1 yields

$$|y^{n_t+1}|^2 - |y_0|^2 + \Sigma_{n=1}^{n_t+1} |y^n - y^{n-1}|^2 + 2\int_0^{(n_t+1)k} < A_k(\tau)y_k(\tau), y_k(\tau)> d\tau$$
$$= 2\,\Sigma_{n=1}^{n_t+1}\,(y^n, f_n - f_{n-1}),$$

which can be again rewritten as

$$|y_k(t)|^2 - |y_0|^2 + \Sigma_{n=1}^{n_t+1} |y^n - y^{n-1}|^2 + 2 \int_0^{(n_t+1)k} < A_k(\tau) y_k(\tau), y_k(\tau)> d\tau$$

$$= 2 \Sigma_{n=1}^{n_t+1} (y^n, f_n - f_{n-1}).$$

Taking the expectation of the both sides of the above equation, and using (2.70), we have

$$E [|y_k(t)|^2] - E [|y_0|^2] + \Sigma_{n=1}^{n_t+1} E [|y^n - y^{n-1}|^2]$$

$$+ 2 \int_0^{(n_t+1)k} E [(\mathcal{J} + k A_n)^{-1}((f_n - f_{n-1}), f_n - f_{n-1})] .$$

On the other hand, we have from (2.70)

$$y^n - y^{n-1} = (\mathcal{J} + k A_n)^{-1} y^{n-1} + (\mathcal{J} + k A_n)^{-1}(f_n - f_{n-1}) - y^{n-1}.$$

Taking the expectation of the squares of the above equation and using Lemma 2.18, we have

$$E [|y^n - y^{n-1}|^2] = E [| ((\mathcal{J} + k A_n)^{-1} - \mathcal{J}) y^{n-1}|^2]$$

$$+ E [|(\mathcal{J} + k A_n)^{-1}(f_n - f_{n-1})|^2].$$

Thus, we have

$$X_k^3(t) = E [|y_0|^2] + 2 \Sigma_{n=1}^{n_t+1} E [((\mathcal{J} + k A_n)^{-1}(f_n - f_{n-1}), f_n - f_{n-1})]$$

$$- \Sigma_{n=1}^{n_t+1} E [|(\mathcal{J} + k A_n)^{-1}(f_n - f_{n-1})|^2].$$

But if $e_1, e_2, \cdots$ designate an orthonormal base of H, then we have

$$| (\mathcal{J} + k A_n)^{-1}(f_n - f_{n-1}) |^2 = \Sigma_{i=1}^{\infty} (f_n - f_{n-1}, (\mathcal{J} + k A_n^*)^{-1} e_i)^2,$$

from which

$$E[|(\mathcal{J}+kA_n)^{-1}(f_n-f_{n-1})|^2] = \Sigma_{i=1}^{\infty}\int_{(n-1)k}^{nk}(Q(\tau)(\mathcal{J}+kA_k^*(\tau))^{-1}e_i, (\mathcal{J}+kA_k^*(\tau))^{-1}e_i)d\tau = \mathrm{tr}\{\int_{(n-1)k}^{nk}(\mathcal{J}+kA_k^*(\tau))^{-1}Q(\tau)(\mathcal{J}+kA_k^*(\tau))^{-1}d\tau\}.$$

On the other hand, it holds that

$$((\mathcal{J}+kA_n)^{-1}(f_n-f_{n-1}), f_n-f_{n-1}) \leqq |f_n-f_{n-1}|^2,$$

from which

$$E[(\mathcal{J}+kA_n)^{-1}((f_n-f_{n-1}), f_n-f_{n-1})] \leqq \int_{(n-1)k}^{nk}\mathrm{tr}(Q(\tau))\,d\tau .$$

Then we obtain

$$X_k^3(t) \leqq X_{k'}^3(t) = E[|y_0|^2] + 2\int_0^{(n_t+1)k}\mathrm{tr}(Q(\tau))\,d\tau$$

$$- \int_0^{(n_t+1)k}\mathrm{tr}(\mathcal{J}+kA_k(\tau))^{-1}Q(\tau)(\mathcal{J}+kA_k^*(\tau))^{-1}d\tau.$$

Setting

$$X_{k'}(t) = X_k^1(t) + X_k^2(t) + X_{k'}^3(t),$$

we have

$$0 \leqq X_k(t) \leqq X_{k'}(t).$$

Let us define $\rho_k(t)$ as

$$\rho_k(t) = \int_0^{(n_t+1)k}(\mathrm{tr}(\mathcal{J}+kA_k(\tau))^{-1}Q(\tau)(\mathcal{J}+kA_k^*(\tau))^{-1})\,d\tau.$$

On the other hand, from Lemma 2.20 and 2.21 (which follow) as $k \to 0$, we have

$$(\mathcal{J}+kA_k(\tau))^{-1}\phi \to \phi \quad \text{in } H \text{ strongly for all } \phi \in H, \tag{2.90}$$

and

$$\mathrm{tr}(\mathcal{J}+kA_k(\tau))^{-1}Q(\tau)(\mathcal{J}+kA_k^*(\tau))^{-1} \to \mathrm{tr}(Q(\tau)) \text{ almost all } t. \tag{2.91}$$

Then we can determine the limit of $X_{k'}(t)$. From Lemma 2.21 and the Lebesgue convergence theorem, we have

$$\rho_k(t) \to \int_0^t \mathrm{tr}\,(\,Q(\tau)\,)\,d\tau \qquad \text{as} \quad k \to 0.$$

But then

$$X_{k'}^3\,(t) \to E\,[|y_0|^2\,] + \int_0^t \mathrm{tr}\,(\,Q(\tau))\,d\tau\,.$$

Then we have

$$\begin{aligned} X_{k'}(t) \to\ & E\,[\,|y(t)|^2\,] + 2\int_0^t E\,[\,< A(\tau)\,y(\tau),\,y(\tau)>\,]\,d\tau \\ & - 2\,E\,[\,|y(t)|^2\,] - 4\int_0^t E\,[\,< A(\tau)\,y(\tau),\,y(\tau)>]\,d\tau \\ & + E\,[\,|y_0|^2\,] + \int_0^t \mathrm{tr}\,(\,Q(\tau)\,)\,d\tau\,. \end{aligned}$$

But from the energy equality the right hand side of the above equation is zero. Hence, it follows that as $k \to 0$,

$$0 \leqq X_k(t) \leqq X_{k'}(t) \to 0\,.$$

Hence, if we prove Lemma 2.20 and 2.21, the proof of the theorem is completed.

Q.E.D.

[LEMMA 2.20] As $k \to 0$, it follows that

$$(\,\mathcal{J} + k\,A_k(\tau))^{-1}\phi \to \phi \quad \text{in } H \text{ strongly for all } \phi \in H. \tag{2.90}$$

[PROOF] Let τ fix and consider the relations

$$z_{n_t} = \phi,$$

$$z_{n_t+1} - z_{n_t} + k\,A_{n_t+1}\,z_{n_t+1} = 0,$$

from which we have

$$|z_{n_t+1}|^2 - |z_{n_t}|^2 + 2k < A_{n_t+1} z_{n_t+1}, z_{n_t+1} > + |z_{n_t+1} - z_{n_t}|^2 = 0.$$

Using the assumption (2.55) yields

$$|z_{n_t+1}| \leqq |\phi| \text{ and } k \|z_{n_t+1}\|_V^2 \leqq |\phi| / 2\alpha .$$

Hence, we can extract a subsequence from z_{n_t+1}, which is denoted also by z_{n_t+1}, such that

$$z_{n_t+1} \to w_1 \text{ in H weakly and } \sqrt{k}\, z_{n_t+1} \to w_2 \text{ in V weakly.}$$

Then we can show that

$$w_1 = \phi.$$

In fact, let w be any element of V. Then we obtain

$$(z_{n_t+1}, w) - (\phi, w) + \sqrt{k} < \sqrt{k}\, z_{n_t+1}, A^*_{n_t+1} w > = 0.$$

But

$$(\sqrt{k}\, z_{n_t+1}, A^*_{n_t+1} w) \quad \text{ranges in a bounded set as } k \to 0,$$

from which

$$(w_1, w) = (\phi, w) \text{ for all } w \in V.$$

Since V is dense in H, we obtain $w_1 = \phi$.

But we have

$$|z_{n_t+1}|^2 + 2k < A_{n_t+1} z_{n_t+1}, z_{n_t+1} > + | z_{n_t+1} - z_{n_t}|^2 = |\phi|^2.$$

Using the fact that $z_{n_t+1} \to \phi$ in H weakly and the above equation yields

$$\operatorname*{Lim\,Inf}_{k \to 0} |z_{n_t+1}| \leqq \operatorname*{Lim\,Sup}_{k \to 0} |z_{n_t+1}| \leqq |\phi|,$$

from which we have

$$|z_{n_t+1}| \to |\phi| \quad .$$

Hence, we obtain

$$z_{n_t+1} = (\mathcal{J} + k A_{n_t+1})^{-1} z_{n_t} = (\mathcal{J} + k A_k(t))^{-1}\phi \to \phi \quad \text{in H strongly.}$$

Thus, the proof of the lemma was established. Q.E.D.

[LEMMA 2.21] For almost all t, we have

$$\text{tr}\ (\mathcal{J} + k A_k(t))^{-1} Q(t) (\mathcal{J} + k A_k^*(t))^{-1} \to \text{tr}\ (Q(t)). \tag{2.91}$$

[PROOF] From Lemma 2.19, we have

$$\text{tr}((\mathcal{J} + k A_k(t))^{-1} Q(t) (\mathcal{J} + k A_k(t))^{-1}) = \text{tr}\ ((\mathcal{J} + k A_k^*(t))^{-1}$$

$$(\mathcal{J} + k A_k^*(t))^{-1} Q(t)) = \text{tr}\ (Q^{1/2}(t)(\mathcal{J} + k A_k^*(t))^{-1}(\mathcal{J} + k A_k(t))^{-1} Q^{1/2}(t)).$$

Setting

$$S_N^k = \Sigma_{i=1}^{N} |(\mathcal{J} + k A_k(t))^{-1} Q^{1/2}(t)\, e_i|^2$$

where e_1, e_2, $\cdots$ are an orthonormal base of H and

$$S^k = \Sigma_{i=1}^{\infty} |(\mathcal{J} + k A_k(t))^{-1} Q^{1/2}(t)\, e_i|^2.$$

For all N fixed, we have from Lemma 2.20 that as $k \to 0$ and $N \to \infty$,

$$S_N^k \to \Sigma_{i=1}^{N} |Q^{1/2}(t)\, e_i|^2 = S_N \to \text{tr}\ (Q(t)) = S.$$

In particular, $S_N^k \to S^k$ uniformly in k as $N \to \infty$ since

$$S^k - S_N^k = \Sigma_{i=N+1}^{\infty} |(\mathcal{J} + k A_k(t))^{-1} Q^{1/2}(t)\, e_i|^2$$

$$\leqq \Sigma_{i=N+1}^{\infty} |Q^{1/2}(t)\, e_i|^2 \to 0 \quad \text{as } N \to \infty .$$

But then we have

$$0 \leqq S - S^k = S - S_N + S_N - S_N^k + S_N^k - S^k.$$

For fixed $\varepsilon > 0$, we can take $N(\varepsilon)$ independent of k such that

$$S - S_{N(\varepsilon)} < \varepsilon/3 \quad \text{and} \quad S^k_{N(\varepsilon)} - S^k < \varepsilon/3.$$

For the chosen $N(\varepsilon)$, we choose $K(\varepsilon)$ such that

$$|S_{N(\varepsilon)} - S^k_{N(\varepsilon)}| < \varepsilon/3 \quad \text{for} \quad k < K(\varepsilon).$$

Then it follows that

$$|S - S^k| < \varepsilon \quad \text{for} \quad k < K(\varepsilon).$$

Thus, the proof of the lemma was completed. Q.E.D.

Therefore, we have obtained the results with the stochastic partial differential equations and proved that the approximated solution of the partial differential equation converges to the true solution strongly under the appropriate assumptions. However, the existence and uniqueness of the solution for the partial differential equation holds in the sense of the distribution and hence, it is desired to prove that the results hold in the sense of the usual function. For the deterministic case, this was proved by using the Radon-Nikodym theorem [14],but for the stochastic case, this is the open problem. In what follows, we treat only the case that the solution of the stochastic partial differential equation exists uniquely in the sense of the distribution.

2.5. Abstract evolution theory.

Let us discuss in this section about the theory of the abstract evolution which is used frequently in the sequel to derive the optimal estimator. Let us first consider the partial differential equation described by

$$\frac{d\,z(t)}{dt} + A(t)\,z(t) = 0, \qquad {}^{\forall}t \in (s, T) \tag{2.92}$$

$$z(s) = \xi, {}^{\forall}\xi \in H. \tag{2.92'}$$

From Theorem 2.4, (2.92) and (2.92') admit a unique solution $z(t)$ such that

$$z(t) \in L^2(s, T; V) \text{ and } d\,z(t)/dt \in L^2(s, T; V').$$

Hence, we can describe the solution $z(t)$ as

$$z(t) = \mathcal{U}(t, s)\,\xi, \qquad \text{where} \quad \mathcal{U}(t, s) \in \mathcal{L}(H, H).$$

We call $\mathcal{U}(t, s)$ evolution operator associated with $A(t)$.   Then we can represent the solution of (2.56) and (2.57) as the following form;

$$y(t) = \mathcal{U}(t,0)\,y_0 + \int_0^t \mathcal{U}(t,s)\,f(s)\,ds.$$

The evolution operator $\mathcal{U}(t,s)$ satisfies the following properties:

i) $\mathcal{U}(t,t_1)\,\mathcal{U}(t_1,t_0) = \mathcal{U}(t, t_0)$ for $t \geq t_1 \geq t_0$ and

$$\mathcal{U}(s, s) = \mathcal{J}. \tag{2.93}$$

ii) If $\xi \in H$, the function $t \to \mathcal{U}(t,s)$ belongs to $L^2(s,T; V)$,

d $\mathcal{U}(t,s)\xi\,/dt \in L^2(s, T; V')$, and we have

d $\mathcal{U}(t,s)\xi/dt + A(t)\mathcal{U}(t,s)\,\xi = 0$ for almost all $t \in (s, T)$ and

$$\mathcal{U}(s,s)\,\xi = \xi. \tag{2.94}$$

Note that in the case of A(t) being independent of time t, we have

$$\mathcal{U}(t, s) = T(t - s).$$

The function $t \to T(t)$ defined for all $t \geqq 0$, is then the semi-group in H.(For the detail of the semi-group see [5],[9],[15].)

Let us now discuss the additional properties with the evolution operator. From (2.92) we have

$$\int_s^t < \frac{d\, z(\tau)}{d} , z(\tau) > d\tau \quad + \int_s^t < A(\tau)\, z(\tau), z(\tau) > d\tau = 0.$$

Thus, we obtain

$$\frac{1}{2} |z(t)|^2 + \int_s^t < A(\tau)\, z(\tau), z(\tau) > d\tau = \frac{1}{2} |z(s)|^2$$

from which we deduce by considering (2.55) that

$$|z(t)| \leqq |z(s)|.$$

Thus, we have

$$||\mathcal{U}(t,s)||_{\mathcal{L}(H,H)} \leqq 1, \text{ for } t \geqq s. \tag{2.95}$$

The evolution operator $\mathcal{U}(t,s)$ belongs to $\mathcal{L}(H,H)$, and hence, to $\mathcal{L}(H,V')$ since the injection of H into V' is continuous. Then we have the following result:

[LEMMA 2.22] For $t \geqq s$, it follows that

$$|| \mathcal{U}(t,s) - \mathcal{I} ||_{\mathcal{L}(H,V')} \leqq 1. \tag{2.96}$$

[PROOF] We consider (2.92). Since $dz/dt \in L^2(0,T ; V')$, we have

$$z(t) - z(s) = \int_s^t dz(\tau)/d\tau \; d\tau = - \int_s^t A(\tau)\, z(\tau)\, d\tau \quad \text{in } V'.$$

Hence, we have

$$(\mathcal{U}(t,s) - \mathcal{I})\xi = -\int_s^t A(\tau)\, z(\tau)\, d\tau, \text{ in } V'$$

and

$$\|(\mathcal{U}(t,s) - \mathcal{I})\xi\|_{V'} \leqq \int_s^t \|A(\tau)\, z(\tau)\|_{V'}\, d\tau \leqq M \int_s^t \|z(\tau)\|_V\, d\tau$$

$$\leqq M\sqrt{t-s}\ \sqrt{\int_s^t \|z(\tau)\|_V^2\, d\tau}$$

where

$$M = \|A(\tau)\|_{L^\infty(0,T;\mathcal{L}(V,V'))}.$$

But

$$|z(t)|^2 + 2\int_s^t \langle A(\tau)\, z(\tau),\, z(\tau)\rangle\, d\tau = |\xi|^2,$$

from which we obtain by virtue of (2.55)

$$2\alpha \int_s^t \|z(\tau)\|_V^2\, d\tau \leqq |\xi|^2.$$

Thus, we have

$$\|(\mathcal{U}(t,s) - \mathcal{I})\xi\|_{V'} \leqq (M/\sqrt{2\alpha})\sqrt{t-s}\ |\xi| .$$

Thus, the proof of the lemma was completed. Q.E.D.

[LEMMA 2.23] As $\varepsilon \to 0$, it follows for all t that

$$\mathcal{U}^*(t+\varepsilon, t)\, h - h \to 0 \text{ in H strongly.} \qquad (2.97)$$

[PROOF] Note that

$$\mathcal{U}(t+\varepsilon, t)\, h - h \to 0 \text{ in H strongly as } \varepsilon \to 0$$

since the evolution operator $\mathcal{U}(t,s)$ possesses the continuity property in t [9].

We deduce by transposing the above relation that

$$\mathcal{U}^*(\,t+\varepsilon,\ t\,)\,h\ -\ h \to 0 \text{ in } H \text{ weakly as } \varepsilon \to 0.$$

Let $\psi_\varepsilon(\tau)$ be the solution of the following equation;

$$\frac{d\,\psi_\varepsilon(\tau)}{d\,\tau} + A^*(\tau)\ \psi_\varepsilon(\tau) = 0 \quad \text{for all } \tau \in (\,t,\ t+\varepsilon\,)$$

$$\psi_\varepsilon(\,t+\varepsilon\,) = h, \qquad h \in H.$$

Then we have

$$\psi_\varepsilon(\tau) = \mathcal{U}^*(\,t+\varepsilon,\ \tau)\ h$$

and from the energy equality and the above equation with $\psi_\varepsilon(\tau)$ we obtain

$$\frac{1}{2}|\psi_\varepsilon(t)|^2 + \int_t^{t+\varepsilon} \langle A^*(\tau)\ \psi_\varepsilon(\tau),\ \psi_\varepsilon(\tau)\rangle\, d\tau = \frac{1}{2}\,|h|^2. \tag{2.98}$$

Since $\psi_\varepsilon(t) \to h$ weakly, we have

$$\operatorname*{Lim\ Inf}_{\varepsilon \to 0}|\psi_\varepsilon(t)|^2 \geqq |h|^2$$

and from (2.98)

$$\operatorname*{Lim\ Sup}_{\varepsilon \to 0}|\psi_\varepsilon(t)|^2 \leqq |h|^2$$

from which we have

$$\operatorname{Lim}|\psi_\varepsilon(t)| = |h|$$

which proves (2.97) by combining the fact that $\psi_\varepsilon(t)$ converges weakly to h.
Thus, the proof of the lemma was completed. Q.E.D.

2.6. Concluding remarks.

We have introduced the concepts of the probability space in Hilbert spaces and the random variable with values in Hilbert spaces and then have discussed some properties of them, which will be required to solve the estimation and control problems for a linear distributed parameter system in the following chapters. These results were first introduced by Falb [2], Curtain & Falb [16], and Scalora [11], and then some extensions were done by Omatu et al.[8] and [17]. More recently, Bensoussan [5] proved the existence and uniqueness theorem concerning the solution of the stochastic partial differential equation based on the variational inequality originated by Lions [13].

The results stated in this chapter are mainly obtained by combining the results of [2], [8], [13], and [17]. For further detailed discussions for the existence and uniqueness theorem, Bensoussan's book [5] will be helpful.

Chapter 3. OPTIMAL ESTIMATION PROBLEMS FOR A DISTRIBUTED PARAMETER SYSTEM.

3.1. Formal derivations for the optimal estimators.

3.1.1. Optimal filtering problems.

Let D be a connected bounded open domain of an r-dimensional Euclidean space $\mathbf{R}^r$ and let S be the sufficiently smooth boundary of D. The spatial coordinate vector will be denoted by $x = (x_1, x_2, \cdots, x_r) \in D$. Consider a linear stochastic distributed parameter system which is described by the partial differential equation

$$\frac{\partial U(t,x)}{\partial t} = A_x U(t,x) + C(t,x) \xi_d(t,x) \tag{3.1}$$

defined for all $t \geqq t_0$ on the spatial domain D where $U(t,x) = \mathrm{Col}[u_1(t,x),\cdots, u_n(t,x)]$ is an n-dimensional state vector function of the system, $\xi_d(t,x)$ is a vector-valued white Gaussian process, A_x is a matrix linear spatial differential operator whose parameter may depend on x, and $C(t,x)$ is a known matrix function. The operator A_x is assumed to be elliptic and self-adjoint and of the form

$$A_x u = \Sigma_{i=1}^{r} \frac{\partial}{\partial x^i} (\Sigma_{j=1}^{r} A_{ij}(x) \frac{\partial u}{\partial x^j}) + A_0(x) u,$$

where A_{ij} and A_0 are $n \times n$ symmetric matrix functions satisfying $A_{ij} = A_{ji}$.

The initial and boundary conditions are given by

$$U(t_0, x) = U_0(x) \tag{3.2}$$

$$F(\xi) U(t,\xi) + \frac{\partial U(t,\xi)}{\partial n_A} = B(t,\xi) \xi_b(t,\xi), \forall \xi \in S, \tag{3.3}$$

where $U_0(x)$ is a Gaussian stochastic vector function, $F(\xi)$ is a known symmetric $n \times n$ matrix function, $\xi_b(t,\xi)$ is a vector-valued white Gaussian process defined on S, and $B(t,\xi)$ is a known matrix function. $\partial /\partial n_A$ denotes the derivative with respect to the co-normal of the surface S relative to the operator A_x and is given by

$$\frac{\partial}{\partial n_A} = \Sigma_{j=1}^{r} \left(\Sigma_{i=1}^{r} A_{ij}(\xi) \cos(\nu, x^i) \right) \frac{\partial}{\partial x^j}$$

where ν is the exterior normal to the surface S at a point $\xi \varepsilon$ S and $\cos(\nu, x^i)$ is the ith direction cosine of ν. The mean and covariance of $U_0(x)$ is given as

$$E[\, U_0(x) \,] = 0$$

$$E[\, U_0(x)\, U_0'(y) \,] = P_0(x,y). \tag{3.4}$$

Let us assume that the measurement data are taken at fixed m points x^1, x^2, $\cdots$, x^m of $\bar{D} = D \cup S$. Furthermore, let us define an mn-dimensional column vector

$$U_m(t) = \mathrm{Col}\, [\, U(t,x^1), \cdots, U(t,x^m) \,] = \begin{bmatrix} U(t,x^1) \\ \vdots \\ U(t,x^m) \end{bmatrix}. \tag{3.5}$$

Then the measurement equation is given by

$$Z(t) = H(t)\, U_m(t) + \zeta(t) \tag{3.6}$$

where z(t) is a p-dimensional measurement vector at the points x^1, $\cdots$, x^m, H(t) is a known $p \times mn$ matrix function, and $\zeta(t)$ is a p-dimensional vector-valued white Gaussian process. The white Gaussian processes $\xi_d(t,x)$, $\xi_b(t,\xi)$, and $\zeta(t)$ are assumed to be statistically independent of each other and also independent of the stochastic initial condition $U_0(x)$. Their means and covariances are given by

$$E[\, \xi_d(t,x) \,] = 0, \quad E[\, \xi_b(t, \;) \,] = 0$$

$$E[\, \xi_d(t,x)\, \xi_d'(s,y) \,] = Q_d(t,x,y)\, \delta(t-s)$$

$$E\,[\,\xi_b(t,\xi)\,\xi_b'(s,\eta)] = Q_b(t,\xi,\eta)\delta(t-s) \tag{3.7}$$

$$E\,[\,\zeta(t)\,] = 0, \quad E\,[\,\zeta(t)\,\zeta'(s)\,] = R(t)\delta(t-s) \tag{3.8}$$

where $x, y \in D$, $\xi, \eta \in S$, $R(t)$ is a symmetric positive-definite matrix, and $Q_d(t,x,y)$ and $Q_b(t,\xi,\eta)$ are nonnegative-definite matrices satisfying

$$Q_d'(t,x,y) = Q_d(t,y,x), \qquad Q_b'(t,\xi,\eta) = Q_b(t,\eta,\xi). \tag{3.9}$$

Now let us make the following assumptions:

i) The problem given by (3.1)-(3.3) is well-posed in the sense of Hadamard, i.e., the solution exists uniquely and depends continuously on the initial and boundary data.

ii) There exists a fundamental $n \times n$ matrix $\mathcal{U}(t,x,y)$ of (3.1) and (3.3), defined for $t \geqq 0$ and $x,y \in \overline{D}$ such that

$$\mathcal{U}(t,x,y) = \mathcal{U}(t,y,x) \tag{3.10}$$

$$\frac{\partial\,\mathcal{U}(t,x,y)}{\partial t} = A_x\,\mathcal{U}(t,x,y) = A_y\,\mathcal{U}(t,x,y) \tag{3.11}$$

$$\mathcal{U}(0,x,y) = I\delta(x-y) \tag{3.12}$$

$$F(\xi)\,\mathcal{U}(t,\xi,y) + \frac{\partial\,\mathcal{U}(t,\xi,y)}{\partial n_A} = 0, \quad \forall\xi \in S \tag{3.13}$$

and that the solution of (3.1)-(3.3) is expressed as

$$U(t,x) = \int_D \mathcal{U}(t-t_0, x,y)\,U_0(y)\,dy + \int_{t_0}^{t} d\tau \int_D \mathcal{U}(t-\tau,x,y)\,C(\tau,y)$$

$$\xi_d(\tau,y)\,dy + \int_{t_0}^{t} d\tau \int_S \mathcal{U}(t-\tau,x,\xi)\,B(\tau,\xi)\,\xi_b(\tau,\xi)\,dS_\xi\,, \tag{3.14}$$

where $dy = dy_1 \cdots dy_r$, and dS_ξ is the surface element on S at $\xi \in S$. In the case where $U(t,x)$ is a scalar function and

$$A_x = \frac{\partial^2}{(\partial x_1)^2} + \cdots + \frac{\partial^2}{(\partial x_r)^2} - q(x), \quad q(x) \text{ is Hölder continuous} \tag{3.15}$$

it is well-known that the above assumptions are satisfied [18].
Let the boundary S be represented locally by the equation

$$\Psi(x) = \Psi(x_1, \cdots, x_r) = 0 \tag{3.16}$$

in a neighborhood of the point $\xi \in S$ where $\Psi(x)$ is a scalar function, and let $\Psi(x) \geqq 0$ if $x \in \bar{D}$. Furthermore, let $\delta(\Psi(x))$ be a generalized function concentrated on the boundary S, an $(r - 1)$-dimensional manifold [9]. Then by use of the formula [9]

$$\int_D \delta(\Psi(x))\phi(x)\, dx = \int_S \phi(\xi)\, dS_\xi , \tag{3.17}$$

(3.14) can be written as

$$U(t,x) = \int_D \mathcal{U}(t-t_0, x,y)\, U_0(y)\, dy + \int_{t_0}^{t} d\tau \int_D \mathcal{U}(t-\tau,x,y) \Big(C(\tau,y)\, \xi_d(\tau,y) + \delta(\Psi(y))B(\tau,y)\, \xi_b(\tau,y) \Big)\, dy. \tag{3.18}$$

In view of (3.14) and (3.18), it is seen that the solution in the sense of the distribution of the equation

$$\frac{\partial U(t,x)}{\partial t} = A_x U(t,x) + C(t,x)\, \xi_d(t,x) + \delta(\Psi(x))B(t,x)\, \xi_b(t,x) \tag{3.19}$$

with the homogeneous boundary condition

$$F(\xi)\, U(t,\xi) + \frac{\partial U(t,\xi)}{\partial n_A} = 0, \quad \forall \xi \in S \tag{3.20}$$

and the initial condition

$$U(t_0,x) = U_0(x) \tag{3.21}$$

coincides with that of (3.1)-(3.3), where the value of $B(t,\xi)\, \xi_b(t,x)$ may be arbitrary if $\Psi(x) > 0$. In this case, the boundary noise input has been replaced by a distributed noise input that has the same effect on the system. In what follows, (3.19)-(3.21) will be considered in place of (3.1)-(3.3).

Now, the problem is to estimate $U(t,x)$ on the basis of the measurement data $Z(\tau)$, $t_0 \leqq \tau \leqq t$. As in the Kalman-Bucy approach, an estimate $\hat{U}(t,x)$ of $U(t,x)$ is sought through a linear operation on the past of the measurement data of the form

$$\hat{U}(t,x) = \int_{t_0}^{t} L(t,x,\tau)\, Z(\tau)\, d\tau, \quad {}^{\forall}x \in \bar{D}, \tag{3.22}$$

where $L(t,x,\tau)$ is an $n \times p$ matrix kernel function whose elements are continuously differentiable in t and x. The estimation error will be denoted by

$$\tilde{U}(t,x) = U(t,x) - \hat{U}(t,x). \tag{3.23}$$

The estimate $\hat{U}(t,x)$ which minimizes the covariance

$$E[\ \| U(t,x) - \hat{U}(t,x) \|^{2}\ ] = E[\ \| \tilde{U}(t,x) \|^{2}\ ] \tag{3.24}$$

is said to be optimal, where $\| \ \|$ denotes the Euclidean norm.
Then the following theorem which is called the Wiener-Hopf theorem is obtained.

[THEOREM 3.1] (Wiener-Hopf theorem). A necessary and sufficient condition for the estimate (3.22) to be optimal is that the Wiener-Hopf equation

$$\int_{t_0}^{t} L(t,x,s)\, E[\ Z(s)\, Z'(\tau)\ ]\, ds = E[\ U(t,x)\, Z'(\tau)\ ] \tag{3.25}$$

holds for $t_0 \leqq \tau < t$, ${}^{\forall}x \in \bar{D}$.

(3.25) is equivalent to

$$E[\ \tilde{U}(t,x)\, Z'(\tau)\ ] = 0, \quad t_0 \leqq \tau < t, \quad {}^{\forall}x \in \bar{D}. \tag{3.26}$$

[PROOF] Let $M(t,x,s)$ be an $n \times p$ matrix function and ε be a scalar-valued parameter. The covariance for the estimate

$$\hat{U}_{\varepsilon}(t,x) = \int_{t_0}^{t} [L(t,x,s) + \varepsilon M(t,x,s)] Z(s) ds \tag{3.27}$$

is given by

$$E [\| U(t,x) - \int_{t_0}^{t} L(t,x,\tau) Z(\tau) d\tau - \varepsilon \int_{t_0}^{t} M(t,x,\tau) Z(\tau) d\tau \|^2]$$

$$= E [\| \tilde{U}(t,x)\|^2] - 2\varepsilon E [\tilde{U}'(t,x) \int_{t_0}^{t} M(t,x,\tau) Z(\tau) d\tau]$$

$$+ \varepsilon^2 E [\| \int_{t_0}^{t} M(t,x,\tau)Z(\tau) d\tau \|^2]. \tag{3.28}$$

The necessary and sufficient condition for the estimate given by (3.22) to be optimal is that

$$E [\tilde{U}'(t,x) \int_{t_0}^{t} M(t,x,\tau)Z(\tau) d\tau] = \mathrm{tr} (\int_{t_0}^{t} E [\tilde{U}(t,x) Z'(\tau)] M'(t,x,\tau) d\tau) = 0 \tag{3.29}$$

for any matrix function $M(t,x,\tau)$.
By assuming $M(t,x,\tau) = E [\tilde{U}(t,x) Z'(\tau)]$, (3.26) is obtained as a necessary condition. Sufficiency of (3.26) is obvious from (3.29). Thus, the proof of the theorem was completed. Q.E.D.
The following corollary can be obtained immediately from (3.26).
[COROLLARY 3.1] (Orthogonal projection lemma). The following relation holds.

$$E [\tilde{U}(t,x) \hat{U}'(t,y)] = 0 \quad \text{for all } x,y \in \bar{D}. \tag{3.30}$$

[LEMMA 3.1] Let $L(t,x,\tau)$ be the optimal kernel function, and let $L(t,x,\tau) + M(t,x,\tau)$ be also the optimal kernel function satisfying the Wiener-Hopf equation (3.25). Then $M(t,x,\tau) = 0$ for all $t_0 \leqq \tau \leqq t$, and $x \in \bar{D}$.

[PROOF] From (3.25) it follows that

$$E\,[\| \int_{t_0}^{t} M(t,x,\tau)\, Z(\tau)\, d\tau \|^2\,] = 0. \tag{3.31}$$

(3.31) is rewritten as

$$tr(\int_{t_0}^{t} \int_{t_0}^{t} M(t,x,\tau)\, E\,[\, Z(\tau)\, Z'(s)\,]\, M'(t,x,s)\, d\tau\, ds) = 0. \tag{3.32}$$

On the other hand, since $U_m(t)$ and $\zeta(t)$ are uncorrelated, it follows from (3.6) and (3.8) that

$$E\,[\, Z(\tau)\, Z'(s)\,] = H(\tau)\, E\,[\, U_m(\tau)\, U_m'(s)\,]\, H'(s) + R(\tau)\delta(\, \tau - s\,). \tag{3.33}$$

Substituting (3.33) into (3.32) yields

$$tr\,(\int_{t_0}^{t} \int_{t_0}^{t} M(t,x,\tau)\, H(\tau)\, E\,[\, U_m(\tau)\, U_m'(s)\,]\, H'(s)\, M'(t,x,s)\, d\tau ds\,)$$

$$+ tr\,(\int_{t_0}^{t} M(t,x,\tau)\, R(\tau)\, M'(t,x,\tau)\, d\tau\,) = 0. \tag{3.34}$$

Since the first term of (3.34) is nonnegative and the second term is positive-definite, it follows that

$$M(t,x,\tau) = 0 \quad \text{for} \quad t_0 \leqq \tau \leqq t,\ \forall x \in \bar{D}. \tag{3.35}$$

Thus, the proof of the lemma was completed. Q.E.D.

Now we derive the optimal filter by using the Wiener-Hopf equation obtained above. Differntiating (3.25) with respect to t and substituting (3.19) yields

$$\int_{t_0}^{t} \frac{\partial L(t,x,s)}{\partial t}\, E\,[\, Z(s)\, Z'(\tau)\,]\, ds + L(t,x,t)\, E\,[\, Z(t)\, Z'(\tau)\,]$$

$$= E\,[\, \frac{\partial U(t,x)}{\partial t}\, Z'(\tau)\,] = A_x\, E\,[\, U(t,x)\, Z'(\tau)] + C(t,x)\, E\,[\, \xi_d(t,x)\, Z'(\tau)\,]$$

$$+ \quad \delta(\,\Psi(x))\; B(t,x)\; E\,[\; \xi_b(t,x)\; Z'(\tau)\;]$$

$$= \int_{t_0}^{t} A_x\, L(t,x,s)\; E\,[\; Z(s)\; Z'(\tau)\;]\, ds, \qquad t_0 \leqq \tau < t, \tag{3.36}$$

where the relations

$$\left.\begin{aligned} &E\,[\; \xi_d(t,x)\; Z'(\tau)\;] = 0 \\ &E\,[\; \xi_b(t,x)\; Z'(\tau)\;] = 0 \end{aligned}\right. \qquad t_0 \leqq \tau < t \tag{3.37}$$

and (3.25) was used.

Since

$$E\,[\; \zeta(t)\; Z'(\tau)\;] = 0, \quad t_0 \leqq \tau < t, \tag{3.38}$$

it follows that

$$L(t,x,t)\; E\,[\; Z(t)\; Z'(\tau)\;] = L(t,x,t)\; H(t)\; E\,[\; U_m(t)\; Z'(\tau)\;]$$

$$= L(t,x,t)\; H(t)\; E\left[\begin{pmatrix} U(t,x^1)\; Z'(\tau) \\ \vdots \\ U(t,x^m)\; Z'(\tau) \end{pmatrix}\right]$$

$$= L(t,x,t)\; H(t) \int_{t_0}^{t} L_m(t,s)\; E\,[\; Z(s)\; Z'(\tau)\;]\, ds, \tag{3.39}$$

where

$$L_m(t,s) = \begin{pmatrix} L(t,x^1,s) \\ \vdots \\ L(t,x^m,s) \end{pmatrix}$$

is an mn × p matrix and (3.25) was used again.

From (3.36) and (3.39), it follows that

$$\int_{t_0}^{t} \left(\frac{\partial L(t,x,s)}{\partial t} - A_x L(t,x,s) + L(t,x,t)\, H(t)\, L_m(t,s) \right) E\,[\, Z(s)\, Z'(\tau)\,]\, ds$$

$$= 0 \qquad \text{for} \quad t_0 \leqq \tau < t. \tag{3.40}$$

Let $\Delta(t,x,s)$ denote the expression inside the bracket of (3.40). Then it is clear that $L(t,x,s) + \Delta(t,x,s)$ is also an optimal kernel function satisfying the Wiener-Hoph equation (3.25). Therefore, from Lemma 3.1, it follows that

$$\frac{\partial L(t,x,\tau)}{\partial t} = A_x\, L(t,x,\tau) - L(t,x,t)\, H(t)\, L_m(t,\tau) \quad \text{for } t_0 \leqq \tau < t. \tag{3.41}$$

Thus, the following lemma is obtained.

[LEMMA 3.2] The optimal kernel $L(t,x,\tau)$ must satisfy (3.41).

Now differentiating (3.22) with respect to t and making use of (3.41) yields

$$\frac{\partial \hat{U}(t,x)}{\partial t} = A_x\, \hat{U}(t,x) + L(t,x,t)\,[\, Z(t) - H(t)\, \hat{U}_m(t)\,]. \tag{3.42}$$

Let $P(t,x,y)$ denote the covariance matrix of the estimation error defined by

$$P(t,x,y) = E\,[\, \tilde{U}(t,x)\, \tilde{U}'(t,y)\,] \triangleq P(t,x,y|t). \tag{3.43}$$

Clearly

$$P(t,x,y) = P'(t,y,x). \tag{3.44}$$

Substituting the equations

$$\begin{aligned} E\,[\, Z(s)\, Z'(\tau)\,] &= E\,[\, Z(s)\, U_m'(\tau)\,]\, H'(\tau) + R(\tau)\delta(\tau - s) \\ E\,[\, U(t,x)\, Z'(\tau)\,] &= E\,[\, U(t,x)\, U_m'(\tau)\,]\, H'(\tau) \end{aligned} \tag{3.45}$$

into (3.25) yields

$$\int_{t_0}^{t} L(t,x,s)\, E\,[\, Z(s)\, U_m'(\tau)\,]\, H'(\tau)\, ds + L(t,x,\tau)\, R(\tau)$$

$$= E [U(t,x) U_m'(\tau)] H'(\tau), \qquad t_0 \leqq \tau < t. \tag{3.46}$$

By virtue of (3.22), (3.46) can be rewritten as

$$L(t,x,\tau) R(\tau) = E [U(t,x) U_m'(\tau)] H'(\tau) - E [\hat{U}(t,x) U_m'(\tau)] H'(\tau)$$

$$= E [\tilde{U}(t,x) U_m'(\tau)] H'(\tau) \tag{3.47}$$

for $t_0 \leqq \tau < t$, where the relation

$$E [\tilde{U}(t,x) \hat{U}_m'(\tau)] = 0, \quad t_0 \leqq \tau < t \tag{3.48}$$

was employed. Let

$$P_m(t,x) = [P(t,x,x^1), \cdots , P(t,x,x^m)] \tag{3.49}$$

be an $n \times mn$ matrix. Letting $\tau \to t$ in (3.47) yields

$$L(t,x,t) = P_m(t,x) H'(t) R^{-1}(t). \tag{3.50}$$

Therefore, substituting (3.50) into (3.42) gives

$$\frac{\partial \hat{U}(t,x)}{\partial t} = A_x \hat{U}(t,x) + P_m(t,x) H'(t) R^{-1}(t) [Z(t) - H(t) \hat{U}_m(t)]. \tag{3.51}$$

Now, let $x = \xi \in S$ in (3.25). Then by use of (3.20), it follows that

$$\int_{t_0}^{t} \left(F(\xi) L(t,\xi,s) + \frac{\partial L(t,\xi,s)}{\partial n_A} \right) E [Z(s) Z'(\tau)] ds = 0. \tag{3.52}$$

By using Lemma 3.1 and the same argument as before, for $t_0 \leqq \tau < t$ it holds that

$$F(\xi) L(t,\xi,s) + \frac{\partial L(t,\xi,s)}{\partial n_A} = 0. \tag{3.53}$$

Therefore, we obtain the following boundary condition;

$$F(\xi) \hat{U}(t,\xi) + \frac{\partial \hat{U}(t,\xi)}{\partial n_A} = 0. \tag{3.54}$$

From (3.22), it follows that

$$\hat{U}(t_0,x) = 0. \tag{3.55}$$

Then the following theorem is obtained.

[THEOREM 3.2] The optimal estimate $\hat{U}(t,x)$ satisfies the differential equation (3.51), the boundary condition (3.54), and the initial condition (3.55), that is,

$$\frac{\partial \hat{U}(t,x)}{\partial t} = A_x \hat{U}(t,x) + P_m(t,x)\, H'(t)\, R^{-1}(t)\, [\, Z(t) - H(t)\, \hat{U}_m(t)\,], \tag{3.51}$$

$$F(\xi)\, \hat{U}(t,\xi) + \frac{\partial \hat{U}(t,\xi)}{\partial n_A} = 0, \tag{3.54}$$

$$\hat{U}(t_0,x) = 0. \tag{3.55}$$

Let us derive the covariance equation. From (3.19) and (3.51), it follows that

$$\frac{\partial \tilde{U}(t,x)}{\partial t} = A_x \tilde{U}(t,x) - P_m(t,x)\, H'(t)\, R^{-1}(t)\, [\, Z(t) - H(t)\, \hat{U}_m(t)\,]$$

$$+ C(t,x)\, \xi_d(t,x) + B(t,x)\, \xi_b(t,x) \delta(\, \Psi(x)). \tag{3.56}$$

Now, differentiating (3.43) with respect to t yields

$$\frac{\partial P(t,x,y)}{\partial t} = E\, [\, \frac{\partial \tilde{U}(t,x)}{\partial t}\, \tilde{U}'(t,y)\,] + E\, [\, \tilde{U}(t,x)\, \frac{\partial \tilde{U}'(t,y)}{\partial t}\,]. \tag{3.57}$$

From (3.56) we obtain

$$E\, [\, \frac{\partial \tilde{U}(t,x)}{\partial t}\, \tilde{U}'(t,y)\,] = A_x\, P(t,x,y) - P_m(t,x)\, H'(t)\, R^{-1}(t)\, E\, [(Z(t)$$

$$- H(t)\, \hat{U}_m(t))\tilde{U}'(t,y)\,] + C(t,x)\, E\, [\, \xi_d(t,x)\, \tilde{U}'(t,y)\,]$$

$$+ B(t,x)\, E\, [\, \xi_b(t,x)\, \tilde{U}'(t,y)\,]\, \delta(\, \Psi(x)). \tag{3.58}$$

The values of the expectations contained in the right hand side of (3.58) can be calculated as follows:

$$E\,[(\,Z(t)\,-\,H(t)\,\hat{U}_m(t))\,\tilde{U}'(t,y)] = H(t)\,E\,[\,\tilde{U}_m(t)\,\tilde{U}'(t,y)\,] + E\,[\,\zeta(t)$$

$$\tilde{U}'(t,y)\,] = H(t)\,P_m'(t,y) - E\,[\,\zeta(t)\int_{t_0}^{t} Z'(\tau)\,L'(t,y,\tau)\,d\tau\,]$$

$$= H(t)\,P_m'(t,y) - \int_{t_0}^{t} R(t)\,\delta(t-\tau)\,L'(t,y,\tau)\,d\tau$$

$$= \frac{1}{2}\,H(t)\,P_m'(t,y), \qquad (3.59)$$

where properties of the delta function and (3.50) were employed for deriving the last equation.

$$E\,[\,\tilde{U}(t,y)\,\xi_d'(t,x)\,] = E\,[\,\tilde{U}(t,y)\,\xi_d'(t,x)\,]$$

$$= \int_{t_0}^{t} d\tau \int_D \mathcal{U}(\,t-\tau\,,y,z\,)\,C(\tau,z)\,Q_d(t,z,x)\delta(t-\tau)\,dz$$

$$= \frac{1}{2}\int_D \mathcal{U}(\,0,\,y,\,z\,)\,C(t,z)\,Q_d(t,z,x)\,dz = \frac{1}{2}\,C(t,y)\,Q_d(t,y,x) \qquad (3.60)$$

where the property of the fundamental matrix as given by (3.12) was employed. On the other hand, from (3.37) we have

$$E\,[\,\tilde{U}(t,y)\,\xi_b'(t,x)\,] = E\,[\,U(t,y)\,\xi_b'(t,x)\,]$$

$$= \int_D \int_{t_0}^{t} \mathcal{U}(\,t-\tau\,,y,z)\,B(\tau,z)\,Q_b(t,z,x)\delta(t-\tau\,)\delta(\,\Psi(z))\,d\tau\,dz$$

$$= \frac{1}{2}\int_D \mathcal{U}(\,0,\,y,z\,)\,B(t,z)\,Q_b(t,z,x\,)\delta(\Psi(z))\,dz$$

$$= \frac{1}{2}\,B(t,y)\,Q_b(t,y,x)\delta(\Psi(y)). \qquad (3.61)$$

Substituting (3.59), (3.60) and (3.61) into (3.58), the first term of the right hand side of (3.57) can be evaluated. Analogously, the second term is evaluated. Thus, we obtain the covariance equation given by

$$\frac{\partial P(t,x,y)}{\partial t} = A_x P(t,x,y) + (A_y P(t,y,x))' - P_m(t,x) H'(t) R^{-1}(t) H(t) P_m'(t,y)$$

$$+ C(t,x) Q_d(t,x,y) C'(t,y) + B(t,x) Q_b(t,x,y) B'(t,y)\delta(\Psi(x))\delta(\Psi(y)). \tag{3.62}$$

The boudary condition for P(t,x,y) is obtained as follows. First, from (3.20) and (3.54) it follows that

$$F(\xi) \tilde{U}(t,\xi) + \frac{\partial \tilde{U}(t,\xi)}{\partial n_A} = 0, \forall \xi \in S. \tag{3.63}$$

Consequently, by virtue of the definition (3.43) of P(t,x,y), we have

$$F(\xi) P(t,\xi,y) + \frac{\partial P(t,\xi,y)}{\partial n_A} = 0 \tag{3.64}$$

for $\forall \xi \in S$ and $\forall y \in \bar{D}$. It is clear that the initial condition for P(t,x,y) is given by

$$P(t_0,x,y) = P_0(x,y). \tag{3.65}$$

Thus, the following theorem is obtained.

[THEOREM 3.3] The covariance matrix function P(t,x,y) satisfies the differential equation (3.62), the boundary condition (3.64), and the initial condition (3.65), that is,

$$\frac{\partial P(t,x,y)}{\partial t} = A_x P(t,x,y) + (A_y P(t,y,x))' - P_m(t,x)H'(t)R^{-1}(t)H(t)P_m'(t,y)$$

$$+ C(t,x)Q_d(t,x,y)C'(t,y) + B(t,x)Q_b(t,x,y)B'(t,y)\delta(\Psi(x))\delta(\Psi(y)), \tag{3.62}$$

$$F(\xi) P(t,\xi,y) + \frac{\partial P(t,\xi,y)}{\partial n_A} = 0 \quad \text{for } \forall \xi \in S \text{ and } \forall y \in \bar{D}, \tag{3.64}$$

and

$$P(t_0,x,y) = P_0(x,y). \tag{3.65}$$

In order to obtain the optimal estimate $\hat{U}(t,x)$, it is necessary to solve simultaneously both the covariance equation (3.62) with the boundary and initial conditions (3.64) and (3.65), and the estimate equation (3.51) with the boundary and initial conditions (3.54) and (3.55). The most common approach to this initial and boundary value problem is to apply the eigenfunction expansion and to derive the ordinary differential equations for coefficient functions.

Now, let us assume that there exists a sequence $\{ \phi_i(x) \}$ of the eigen-functions and a sequence $\{ \lambda_i \}$ of eigenvalues such that

$$A_x \phi_i(x) = - \lambda_i \phi_i(x), \tag{3.66}$$

$$F(\xi) \phi_i(\xi) + \frac{\partial \phi_i(\xi)}{\partial n_A} = 0, \forall \xi \in S, \tag{3.67}$$

$$\lambda_1 \leqq \lambda_2 \leqq \lambda_3 \leqq \cdots ,$$

and $\phi_i(x)$ is a complete orthonormal system in $L_2(D)$, the space of n-dimensional vector-valued functions square integrable over D. Consequently,

$$\int_D \phi_i'(x) \phi_j(x) dx = \begin{cases} 1 & (i = j) \\ 0 & (i \neq j). \end{cases}$$

In the case where $U(t,x)$ is a scalar function and the differential operator A_x is of the form as given in (3.15), it is well-known that the above assumption is satisfied [5],[9]. Assuming that the solutions of (3.51) and (3.62) are of the form

$$\hat{U}(t,x) = \Sigma_{i=1}^{\infty} \hat{u}_i(t) \phi_i(x), \tag{3.68}$$

$$P(t,x,y) = \Sigma_{i,j=1}^{\infty} p_{ij}(t) \phi_i(x) \phi_j'(y) \tag{3.69}$$

where the coefficient functions are given by

$$\hat{u}_i(t) = \int_D \phi_i'(x)\ \hat{U}(t,x)\ dx$$

$$p_{ij}(t) = \int_D \int_D \phi_i'(x)\ P(t,x,y)\ \phi_j(y)\ dx\ dy. \tag{3.70}$$

Thus, we have only to determine $\hat{u}_i(t)$ and $p_{ij}(t)$ ($i,j = 1,2,\cdots$). It is clear that the assumed solutions (3.68) and (3.69) satisfy the boundary conditions (3.54) and (3.64), respectively. Also, it follows from (3.44) that $p_{ij}(t) = p_{ji}(t)$. Let Φ_i denote an mn vector defined by

$$\Phi_i = \begin{pmatrix} \phi_i(x^1) \\ \cdot \\ \cdot \\ \cdot \\ \phi_i(x^m) \end{pmatrix} . \tag{3.71}$$

Then, $\hat{U}_m(t)$ and $P_m(t,x)$ can be expressed as

$$\hat{U}_m(t) = \Sigma_{i=1}^{\infty}\ \hat{u}_i(t)\ \Phi_i,$$

$$P_m(t,x) = \Sigma_{i=1}^{\infty}\ \phi_i(x)\ \Sigma_{j=1}^{\infty}\ p_{ij}(t)\ \Phi_j'. \tag{3.72}$$

Now, substituting (3.68), (3.69), and (3.72) into (3.51) and (3.62), and comparing the coefficients of the eigenfunctions, we obtain the ordinary differential equations given by

$$d\,\hat{u}_i(t)/dt = -\lambda_i\ \hat{u}_i(t) + (\ \Sigma_{j=1}^{\infty}\ p_{ij}(t)\ \Phi_j'\ )\ H'(t)\ R^{-1}(t)$$

$$[\ Z(t) - H(t)\ \ \Sigma_{k=1}^{\infty}\ \hat{u}_k(t)\ \Phi_k\ ], \tag{3.73}$$

and

$$d\,p_{ij}(t)/dt = -\ (\ \lambda_i + \lambda_j\ )\ p_{ij}(t) + a_{ij}(t) + b_{ij}(t)$$

$$-\ \Sigma_{k,m=1}^{\infty}\ p_{ik}(t)\ p_{mj}(t)\ \Phi_k'\ H'(t)\ R^{-1}(t)\ H(t)\ \Phi_m\ . \tag{3.74}$$

where

$$a_{ij}(t) = \int_D \int_D \phi_i'(x)\ C(t,x)\ Q_d(t,x,y)\ C'(t,y)\ \phi_j(y)\ dx\ dy \quad (3.75)$$

and

$$b_{ij}(t) = \int_D \int_D \phi_i'(x)B(t,x)Q_b(t,x,y)B'(t,y)\phi_j(y)\delta(\Psi(x))\delta(\Psi(y))\ dx\ dy$$

$$= \int_S \int_S \phi_i'(\xi)\ B(t,\xi)\ Q_b(t,\xi,\eta)\ B'(t,\eta)\ \phi_j(\eta)\ d\,S_\xi\ d\,S_\eta . \quad (3.76)$$

The initial conditions are given by

$$\hat{u}_i(t_0) = 0, \quad p_{ij}(t_0) = \int_D \int_D \phi_i'(x)\ P_0(x,y)\ \phi_j(y)\ dx\ dy. \quad (3.77)$$

Let us approximate the infinite series (3.72) by the first N terms and define the following matrices:

$$\hat{U}(t) = \mathrm{Col}\ [\ \hat{u}_1(t),\ \cdots,\ \hat{u}_N(t)\ ]\ ,\ -\Lambda = \mathrm{Diag}\ [\lambda_1,\ \cdots,\ \lambda_N\ ]$$

$$P(t) = \begin{bmatrix} p_{11}(t) & \cdots & p_{1N}(t) \\ \vdots & & \vdots \\ p_{N1}(t) & \cdots & p_{NN}(t) \end{bmatrix}, \quad \Phi = [\ \Phi_1,\ \cdots,\ \Phi_N\ ] = \begin{bmatrix} \phi_1(x^1) \cdots & \phi_N(x^1) \\ \vdots & \vdots \\ \phi_1(x^m) \cdots & \phi_N(x^m) \end{bmatrix}$$

$$A(t) = \begin{bmatrix} a_{11}(t) & \cdots & a_{1N}(t) \\ \vdots & & \\ a_{N1}(t) & \cdots & a_{NN}(t) \end{bmatrix}, \quad B(t) = \begin{bmatrix} b_{11}(t) & \cdots b_{1N}(t) \\ \vdots & \\ b_{N1}(t) & \cdots b_{NN}(t) \end{bmatrix}. \quad (3.78)$$

Then the system of (3.73) and (3.74) can be approximated by

$$d\hat{U}(t)/dt = \Lambda\ \hat{U}(t) + P(t)\ \Phi'\ H'(t)\ R^{-1}(t)\ [\ Z(t) - H(t)\ \Phi\ \hat{U}(t)\ ] \quad (3.79)$$

$$d\,P(t)/dt = \Lambda\ P(t) + P(t)\Lambda' - P(t)\ \Phi'\ H'(t)\ R^{-1}(t)\ H(t)\ \Phi\, P(t)$$
$$+ A(t) + B(t), \quad (3.80)$$

which are the ordinary Kalman-Bucy filter equations and can be integrated by a computer in the usual way.

3.1.2. Optimal smoothing problems.

Let D be a bounded open domain of an r-dimensional Euclidean space $\mathbf{R}^r$ and let S, the boundary of D, consist of a finite number of (r - 1)-dimensional hypersurfaces of class C^3. The spatial coordinate vector will be denoted by $x = (x_1, x_2, \cdots, x_r) \in D$. Consider a linear distributed parameter system which is described by the partial differential equation of the real-valued variables

$$\frac{\partial U(t,x)}{\partial t} = A_x U(t,x) + C(t,x) \dot{W}(t,x), \quad \cdot = d/dt \tag{3.81}$$

where U(t,x) is a state of the system, $\dot{W}(t,x)$ is a white Gaussian process, A_x is a spatial differential operator, and C(t,x) is a known function. The operator A_x is assumed to be of the form

$$A_x u = (\Delta - q(x)) u \tag{3.82}$$

where q(x) is a nonnegative and Hölder continuous function on the spatial domain $\overline{D} = D \times S$ and Δ denotes the Laplacian given by

$$\Delta = \frac{\partial^2}{\partial x_1^2} + \cdots + \frac{\partial^2}{\partial x_r^2} .$$

The initial and boundary conditions are given by

$$U(t_0,x) = U_0(x) \tag{3.83}$$

$$\Gamma_\xi U(t,\xi) = 0, \ \forall \xi \in S \tag{3.84}$$

$$\Gamma_\xi u = \alpha(\xi) u + (1 - \alpha(\xi)) \partial u/\partial \mathbf{n}$$

where $U_0(x)$ is a Gaussian random function, $\partial u/\partial \mathbf{n}$ denotes the derivative with respect to the co-normal of the surface S relative to the operator A_x, and $\alpha(\xi)$ is a function such that $0 \leqq \alpha(\xi) \leqq 1$. The mean and covariance functions of $U_0(x)$ are given by

$$E[\,U_0(x)\,] = 0, \quad E[\,U_0(x)\,U_0(y)\,] = P_0(x,y). \tag{3.85}$$

Let us assume that the observation data are taken at fixed m points $x^1, \cdots, x^m \in \overline{D}$. Further, let us define an m-dimensional column vector $U_m(t)$ by

$$U_m(t) = \mathrm{Col}\,[\,U(t,x^1), \cdots, U(t,x^m)\,]. \tag{3.86}$$

Then the observation equation is given by

$$Z(t) = H(t)\,U_m(t) + \dot{V}(t), \quad \cdot = d/dt \tag{3.87}$$

where $Z(t)$ is a p-dimensional observed vector at the points $x^1, \cdots, x^m$, $H(t)$ is a $p \times m$ matrix, and $\dot{V}(t)$ is a p-dimensional vector white Gaussian process. The white Gaussian processes $W(t,x)$ and $V(t)$ are assumed to be statistically independent of each other and also independent of the initial state $U_0(x)$. Their means and covariance functions are given by

$$E[\,\dot{W}(t,x)\,] = 0, \quad E[\,\dot{V}(t)\,] = 0 \tag{3.88}$$

$$E[\,\dot{W}(t,x)\,\dot{W}(s,y)\,] = Q(t,x,y)\,\delta(t-s) \tag{3.89}$$

$$E[\,\dot{V}(t)\,\dot{V}'(s)\,] = R(t)\,\delta(t-s) \tag{3.90}$$

where $\delta(\cdot)$ is the Dirac delta function, " ' " denotes the transpose of the matrix, and $R(t)$ is a symmetric positive-definite matrix. It was proved in Theorem 2.5 that there exists a unique solution $U(t,x)$ for (3.81), (3.83), and (3.84) in the sense of the distribution. Further, it is well-known that the eigenvalues λ_i and the corresponding normalized eigenfunctions $\phi_i(x)$ of the operator A_x exist and satisfy the following conditions [18]:

$$A_x\,\phi_i(x) = \lambda_i\,\phi_i(x), \quad i = 1, 2, \cdots \tag{3.91}$$

$$C > \lambda_1 > \lambda_2 > \cdots > \lambda_i > \cdots, \quad \lim_{i \to \infty} \lambda_i = -\infty \tag{3.92}$$

$$C = -\min_{x \in D} q(x) \tag{3.93}$$

and that the family of the eigenfunctions $\{\phi_i(x),\ i = 1,2,\cdots\}$ is complete and orthonormal in $L^2(D)$. Then it was proved in [18] that under the preceding condition on A_x there exists a unique fundamental solution $\mathcal{U}_A(t,x,\sigma,y)$ of (3.81) such that

$$\frac{\partial \mathcal{U}_A(t,x,\sigma,y)}{\partial t} = A_x\ \mathcal{U}_A(t,x,\sigma,y), \qquad \sigma < t \tag{3.94}$$

$$\mathcal{U}_A(\sigma,x,\sigma,y) = \delta(x-y) \tag{3.95}$$

$$\Gamma_\xi \mathcal{U}_A(t,\xi,\sigma,y) = 0, \ \forall \xi \in S, \ \forall y \in \bar{D}. \tag{3.96}$$

Furthermore, it was proved in [18] that $\mathcal{U}_A(t,x,\sigma,y)$ possesses the following property:

$$\mathcal{U}_A(t,x,\sigma,y) = \Sigma_{i=1}^{\infty} \exp(\lambda_i(t-\sigma))\ \phi_i(x)\ \phi_i(y), \quad t > \sigma \tag{3.97}$$

where $\{\phi_i(x),\ \lambda_i,\ i = 1, 2, \cdots\}$ are given by (3.91) and (3.92).
Note that in the case of time invariant systems $\mathcal{U}_A(t,x,\sigma,y) = \mathcal{U}_A(t-\sigma,x,0,y)$. Hence, we can denote the fundamental solution as $\mathcal{U}_A(t-\sigma,x,y)$.

Now the smoothing problem is to find the best estimate of the state $U(\tau,x)$ based on the observed data $Z(\sigma)$, $t_0 \leqq \sigma \leqq t$, for $\tau < t$, which has the form

$$\hat{U}(\tau,x|t) = \int_{t_0}^{t} A(t,\tau,x,\sigma)\ Z(\sigma)\ d\sigma, \ \forall x \in \bar{D} \tag{3.98}$$

where $A(t,\tau,x,\sigma)$ is a p-dimensional row vector kernel function whose elements are continuously differentiable in t, τ, and x. The smoothing error will be denoted by

$$\tilde{U}(\tau,x|t) = U(\tau,x) - \hat{U}(\tau,x|t). \tag{3.99}$$

The estimate $\hat{U}(\tau,x|t)$ which minimizes the variance function J given by

$$J = E[\ |\ \tilde{U}(\tau,x|t)\ |^2\ ] \tag{3.100}$$

is said to be optimal. Note that setting $\tau = t$ implies that (3.98) reduces to the filtering problem which was discussed in Section 3.1.1.

Wiener-Hopf equation

Let us prove the following Wiener-Hopf theorem for the smoothing problem which plays an important role in the derivation of the optimal smoothing estimator.

[THEOREM 3.4] A necessary and sufficient condition for the estimate (3.98) to be optimal is that the Wiener-Hopf equation

$$\int_{t_0}^{t} A(t,\tau,x,\sigma)\, E[\, Z(\sigma)\, Z'(\alpha)\,]\, d\sigma = E[\, U(\tau,x)\, Z'(\alpha)\,] \tag{3.101}$$

holds for $t_0 \leqq \alpha < t$ and $\forall x \in \bar{D}$. (3.101) is equivalent to

$$E[\, \tilde{U}(\tau,x|t)\, Z'(\alpha)\,] = 0, \quad t_0 \leqq \alpha < t \text{ and } \forall x \in \bar{D}. \tag{3.102}$$

[PROOF] Let $M(t,\tau,x,\sigma)$ be a p-dimensional row vector kernel function and let ε be a scalar parameter. The variance of the estimate

$$\hat{U}_\varepsilon(\tau,x|t) = \int_{t_0}^{t} \{\, A(t,\tau,x,\alpha) + M(t,\tau,x,\alpha)\,\}\, Z(\alpha)\, d\alpha$$

is given by

$$J_\varepsilon = E[\, |\, U(\tau,x) - \hat{U}_\varepsilon(\tau,x|t)\,|^2\,].$$

The necessary and sufficient condition for the estimate $\hat{U}(\tau,x|t)$ given by (3.98) to be optimal is that J_ε has an extremum at $A(t,\tau,x,\sigma)$, that is,

$$\left(\frac{d J_\varepsilon}{d\varepsilon}\right)\Big|_{\varepsilon=0} = 2\, E[\, \tilde{U}(\tau,x|t) \int_{t_0}^{t} M(t,\tau,x,\alpha)\, Z(\alpha)\, d\alpha\,] = 0.$$

Hence, we have

$$\int_{t_0}^{t} E[\, \tilde{U}(\tau,x|t)\, Z'(\alpha)\,]\, M'(t,\tau,x,\alpha)\, d\alpha = 0. \tag{3.103}$$

Letting $M(t,\tau,x,\alpha) = E[\tilde{U}(\tau,x|t)\, Z'(\alpha)]$ yields (3.102). Thus, (3.102) is the necessary condition for $\hat{U}(\tau,x|t)$ to be optimal.

On the other hand, the sufficiency is clear by substituting (3.102) into (3.103). Since it is clear from (3.98) and (3.99) that (3.102) is equivalent to (3.101), the proof of the theorem is completed. Q.E.D.

It follows from (3.98) and (3.22) that

$$E[\tilde{U}(\tau,x|t)\, \hat{U}(\tau,x|t)] = 0 \qquad (3.104)$$

which is the orthogonal projection lemma for the distributed parameter system. By using the same way as the filtering problem in the previous section, we have the following theorem.

[THEOREM 3.5] Let $A(t,\tau,x,\sigma)$ be the optimal kernel function and let $A(t,\tau,x,\sigma) + M(t,\tau,x,\sigma)$ be also the optimal kernel function satisfying the Wiener-Hopf equation (3.101). Then $M(t,\tau,x,\sigma) = 0$ for all σ, $t_0 \leqq \alpha < t$ and $\forall x \in \bar{D}$, that is, the optimal kernel function for the smoothing problem is unique.

Let $\hat{U}(t,x|t)$ be the optimal filtering estimate based on the observed data $Z(\sigma)$, $t_0 \leqq \sigma \leqq t$ and given by

$$\hat{U}(t,x|t) = \hat{U}(t,x) = \int_{t_0}^{t} L(t,x,\sigma)\, Z(\sigma)\, d\sigma. \qquad (3.105)$$

Then from the Wiener-Hopf equation for the filtering problem, Theorem 3.1, it follows that

$$\int_{t_0}^{t} L(t,x,\sigma)\, E[Z(\sigma)\, Z'(\alpha)]\, d\sigma = E[U(t,x)\, Z'(\alpha)] \qquad (3.106)$$

for $t_0 \leqq \alpha < t$ and $\forall x \in \bar{D}$.

Derivation of the optimal smoothing estimator

Let us now derive the optimal smoothing estimator based on the Wiener-Hopf theory discussed above. The following lemma will be proved.

[LEMMA 3.3] The optimal kernel function $A(t,\tau,x,\sigma)$ must satisfy the following equation:

$$\frac{\partial A(t,\tau,x,\sigma)}{\partial t} + A(t,\tau,x,t)\ H(t)\ L_m(t,\sigma) = 0 \tag{3.107}$$

$$L_m(t,\sigma) = \text{Col}\ [\ L(t,x^1,\sigma),\ \cdots,\ L(t,x^m,\sigma)\ ] \quad \text{for } t_0 \leqq \sigma < t.$$

[PROOF] Differentiating (3.101) with respect to t yields

$$A(t,\tau,x,t)\ E\ [\ Z(t)\ Z'(\alpha)\ ] + \int_{t_0}^{t} \frac{\partial A(t,\tau,x,\sigma)}{\partial t}\ E\ [\ Z(\sigma)\ Z'(\alpha)\ ]\ d\sigma = 0.$$

It follows from (3.87) that

$$E\ [\ Z(t)\ Z'(\alpha)\ ] = H(t)\ E\ [\ U_m(t)\ Z'(\alpha)\ ] \quad \text{for } t_0 \leqq \alpha < t.$$

From (3.86) and the Wiener-Hopf equation (3.106) for the filtering problem we have

$$E\ [\ U_m(t)\ Z'(\alpha)\ ] = \int_{t_0}^{t} L_m(t,\sigma)\ E\ [\ Z(\sigma)\ Z'(\alpha)\ ]\ d\sigma\ .$$

Hence, we have

$$\int_{t_0}^{t} [\ \frac{\partial A(t,\tau,x,\sigma)}{\partial t} + A(t,\tau,x,t)\ H(t)\ L_m(t,\sigma)\ ]\ E\ [\ Z(\sigma)\ Z'(\alpha)\ ]\ d\sigma = 0.$$

Applying Theorem 3.5 to the above equation yields

$$\frac{\partial A(t,\tau,x,\sigma)}{\partial t} + A(t,\tau,x,t)\ H(t)\ L_m(t,\sigma) = 0 \quad \text{for } t_0 \leqq \sigma < t.$$

Thus, the proof of the lemma is completed. Q.E.D.

Then we have the following theorem concerning the optimal smoothing estimator.

[THEOREM 3.6] The optimal smoothing estimate $\hat{U}(\tau,x|t)$ is given by

$$\frac{\partial \hat{U}(\tau,x|t)}{\partial t} = A(t,\tau,x,t)\ \nu(t) \tag{3.108}$$

$$\nu(t) = Z(t) - H(t)\ \hat{U}_m(t) \tag{3.109}$$

$$\hat{U}_m(t) = \mathrm{Col}\ [\ \hat{U}(t,x^1|t),\ \cdots,\ \hat{U}(t,x^m|t)\ ] \tag{3.110}$$

$$A(t,\tau,x,t) = B_m(\tau,x|t)\ H'(t)\ R^{-1}(t) \tag{3.111}$$

$$B_m(\tau,x|t) = (\ B(\tau,x,x^1|t),\ \cdots,\ B(\tau,x,x^m|t)) \tag{3.112}$$

where $B(\tau,x,y|t)$ denotes the optimal smoothing gain function given by

$$B(\tau,x,y|t) = E\ [\ \tilde{U}(\tau,x|t)\ U(t,y)\ ]. \tag{3.113}$$

[PROOF] Differentiating (3.98) with respect to t and using (3.105),(3.107), and (3.110) yields

$$\frac{\partial \hat{U}(\tau,x|t)}{\partial t} = A(t,\tau,x,t)\ Z(t) + \int_{t_0}^{t} \frac{\partial A(t,\tau,x,\sigma)}{\partial t}\ Z(\sigma)\ d\sigma$$

$$= A(t,\tau,x,t)\ [\ Z(t) - H(t) \int_{t_0}^{t} L_m(t,\sigma)\ Z(\sigma)\ d\sigma\ ] = A(t,\tau,x,t)\ \nu(t).$$

From (3.90) and the observation equation (3.87), we have

$$E\ [\ Z(\sigma)\ Z'(\alpha)\ ] = E\ [\ Z(\sigma)\ U_m'(\alpha)\ ]\ H'(\alpha) + R(\alpha)\ \delta(\alpha - \sigma\ ).$$

It follows from (3.87) and the Wiener-Hopf equation (3.101) that

$$E\ [\ U(\tau,x)\ Z'(\alpha)\ ] = E\ [\ U(\tau,x)\ U_m'(\alpha)\ ]\ H'(\alpha)$$

$$= \int_{t_0}^{t} A(t,\tau,x,\sigma)\ E\ [\ Z(\sigma)\ Z'(\alpha)\ ]\ d\sigma\ .$$

Then using (3.98) yields

$$E[\,U(\tau,x)\,U_m'(\alpha)\,]\,H'(\alpha) = \int_{t_0}^{t} A(t,\tau,x,\sigma)\,E[\,Z(\sigma)\,U_m'(\alpha)\,]\,H'(\alpha)\,d\sigma$$

$$+\,A(t,\tau,x,\alpha)\,R(\alpha) = E[\,\hat{U}(\tau,x|t)\,U_m'(\alpha)\,]\,H'(\alpha) + A(t,\tau,x,\alpha)\,R(\alpha).$$

From (3.99) and the above relation, we have

$$E[\,\tilde{U}(\tau,x|t)\,U_m'(\alpha)\,]\,H'(\alpha) = A(t,\tau,x,\alpha)\,R(\alpha).$$

Letting $\alpha \to t$ yields

$$B_m(\tau,x|t)\,H'(t) = A(t,\tau,x,t)\,R(t).$$

Since $R(t)$ is positive-definite, the proof of the theorem is completed. Q.E.D.

If the equation satisfied by $B(\tau,x,y|t)$ is derived, the optimal smoothing estimator can be determined. Using the orthogonarity between $\tilde{U}(\tau,x|t)$ and $\hat{U}(t,y|t)$ which follows from (3.102), $B(\tau,x,y|t)$ is rewritten as follows:

$$B(\tau,x,y|t) = E[\,\tilde{U}(\tau,x|t)\,\tilde{U}(t,y|t)\,] = E[\,\tilde{U}(\tau,x|\tau)\,\tilde{U}(t,y|t)\,] + \Delta_1$$

where

$$\Delta_1 = E[\,(\,\tilde{U}(\tau,x|t) - \tilde{U}(\tau,x|\tau))\,\tilde{U}(t,y|t)\,]$$

$$\tilde{U}(t,y|t) = U(t,y) - \hat{U}(t,y|t).$$

Thus, Δ_1 is written as

$$\Delta_1 = E[\,(\,\hat{U}(\tau,x|\tau) - \hat{U}(\tau,x|t))\,\tilde{U}(t,y|t)\,].$$

Hence, using the orthogonality between the optimal estimate and the optimal filtering error function, it follows that $\Delta_1 = 0$ and $B(\tau,x,y|t)$ is given by

$$B(\tau,x,y|t) = E[\,\tilde{U}(\tau,x|\tau)\,\tilde{U}(t,y|t)\,]. \tag{3.114}$$

On the other hand, from (3.56) it follows that the optimal filtering error function $\tilde{U}(t,y|t)$ satisfies

$$\frac{\partial \tilde{U}(t,y|t)}{\partial t} = A_y \tilde{U}(t,y|t) + C(t,y)\, W(t,y) - P_m(t,y)\, \tilde{R}(t)\, \tilde{U}_m(t)$$

$$- P_m(t,y)\, H'(t)\, R^{-1}(t)\, \dot{V}(t) \tag{3.115}$$

$$\tilde{U}(t_0,y|t_0) = U_0(y) \tag{3.116}$$

$$\Gamma_\xi \tilde{U}(t,\xi|t) = 0, \quad \forall \xi \in S \tag{3.117}$$

where

$$P_m(t,y) = (\, P(t,y,x^1|t),\ \cdots,\ P(t,y,x^m|t)) = (\, P(t,y,x^1),\ \cdots,\ P(t,y,x^m)\,)$$

$$P(\theta,x,y|t) = E\,[\, \tilde{U}(\theta,x|t)\, \tilde{U}(\theta,y|t)\,], \quad \theta \leqq t \tag{3.118}$$

$$\tilde{R}(t) = H'(t)\, R^{-1}(t)\, H(t).$$

Let $\mathcal{U}(t,y,\sigma,z)$ be the fundamental solution of (3.115), that is,

$$\frac{\partial\, \mathcal{U}(t,y,\sigma,z)}{\partial t} = A_y\, \mathcal{U}(t,y,\sigma,z) - P_m(t,y)\, \tilde{R}(t)\, \mathcal{U}'_m(t,z,\sigma) \tag{3.119}$$

$$\mathcal{U}_m(t,z,\sigma) = (\, \mathcal{U}(t,x^1,\sigma,z),\ \cdots,\ \mathcal{U}(t,x^m,\sigma,z)) \tag{3.120}$$

$$\mathcal{U}(\sigma,y,\sigma,z) = \delta(\, y - z\,) \tag{3.121}$$

$$\Gamma_\xi \mathcal{U}(t,\xi,\sigma,z) = 0, \quad \forall \xi \in S, \quad \forall z \in \bar{D}. \tag{3.122}$$

Then the following theorem is obtained.

[THEOREM 3.7] $B(\tau,x,y|t)$ satisfies the following equations:

$$\frac{\partial B(\tau,x,y|t)}{\partial t} = A_y\, B(\tau,x,y|t) - B_m(\tau,x|t)\, \tilde{R}(t)\, P'_m(t,y) \tag{3.123}$$

or

$$\frac{\partial B(\tau,x,y|t)}{\partial\tau} = A_x\, B(\tau,x,y|t) + \int_D \mathcal{U}(t,y,\tau,\alpha)\ \tilde{Q}(\tau,\alpha,x)\, d\alpha \tag{3.124}$$

$$B(\tau,x,y|\tau) = P(\tau,x,y|\tau) \tag{3.125}$$

$$\Gamma_\xi\, B(\tau,\xi,y|t) = 0, \quad \forall_\xi \in S, \quad \forall_y \in \bar{D} \tag{3.126}$$

where

$$\tilde{Q}(\tau,\alpha,x) = C(\tau,\alpha)\ Q(\tau,\alpha,x)\ C(\tau,x). \tag{3.127}$$

[PROOF] Using the orthogonality between $\hat{U}(\tau,x|\tau)$ and $\tilde{U}(t,y|t)$, $B(\tau,x,y|t)$ or (3.114) are given by

$$B(\tau,x,y|t) = E\ [\ U(\tau,x)\ \tilde{U}(t,y|t)\ ].$$

Differentiating the above equation with respect to τ and using (3.115) and the independent assumption between $V(t)$ and $U(\tau,x)$ yields

$$\frac{\partial B(\tau,x,y|t)}{\partial\tau} = A_x\ B(\tau,x,y|t) + C(\tau,x)\ \Delta_2 \tag{3.128}$$

$$\Delta_2 = E\ [\ \dot{W}(\tau,x)\ \tilde{U}(t,y|t)\ ].$$

The solution $\tilde{U}(t,y|t)$ of (3.115)-(3.117) is given by

$$\tilde{U}(t,y|t) = \int_D \mathcal{U}(t,y,t_0,\alpha)\ U_0(\alpha)\ d\alpha + \int_{t_0}^t \int_D \mathcal{U}(t,y,\sigma,\alpha)\ [\ C(\sigma,\alpha)\ \dot{W}(\sigma,\alpha)$$

$$-\ P_m(\sigma,\alpha)\ H'(\sigma)\ R^{-1}(\sigma)\ \dot{V}(\sigma)\ ]\ d\alpha d\sigma.$$

From the assumption that $W(\tau,x)$ is independent of $U_0(\alpha)$ and $V(\sigma)$, Δ_2 is given by

$$\Delta_2 = \int_{t_0}^t \int_D \mathcal{U}(t,y,\sigma,\alpha)\ C(\tau,\alpha)\ E\ [\ \dot{W}(\tau,x)\ \dot{W}(\sigma,\alpha)\ ]\ d\alpha d\sigma$$

$$= \int_D \mathcal{U}(t,y,\tau,\alpha)\; C(\tau,\alpha)\; Q(\tau,x,\alpha)\; d\alpha. \qquad (3.129)$$

Hence, (3.124)is obtained from (3.128) and (3.129).

Differentiating (3.114) with respect to t yields

$$\frac{\partial B(\tau,x,y|t)}{\partial t} = E\left[\, \tilde{U}(\tau,x|\tau)\, \frac{\partial \tilde{U}(t,y|t)}{\partial t} \,\right].$$

Substituting (3.115) into the above equation and using the same procedure as the derivation of (3.124) yields (3.123). Since it is clear that the initial condition (3.125) and the boundary condition (3.126) are satisfied, the proof of the theorem is completed. Q.E.D.

Then the following lemma holds.

[LEMMA 3.4] $B(\tau,x,y|t)$ is given by

$$B(\tau,x,y|t) = \int_D \mathcal{U}(t,y,\tau,\alpha)\; P(\tau,\alpha,x|\tau)\; d\alpha. \qquad (3.130)$$

[PROOF] Since (3.123) is a linear partial differential equation, it is easily proved that there exists a unique solution of (3.123), (3.125), and (3.126) [8,19]. By direct differentiation of (3.130) with respect to t, it is clear that (3.130) satisfies (3.123). It is easily seen from (3.117),(3.118), and (3.121) that $B(\tau,x,y|t)$ given by (3.130) satisfies the initial condition (3.125) and the boundary condition (3.126). Hence, the unique solution of (3.123), (3.125), and (3.126) is given by (3.130). Thus, the proof of the lemma is completed.

Q.E.D.

Then the following theorem will be obtained.

[THEOREM 3.8] The optimal smoothing estimate $\hat{U}(\tau,x|t)$ is given by

$$\hat{U}(\tau,x|t) = \hat{U}(\tau,x|\tau) + \int_\tau^t B_m(\tau,x|\sigma)\; \nu_m(\sigma)\; d\sigma \qquad (3.131)$$

where

$$\nu_m(\sigma) = H'(\sigma)\ R^{-1}(\sigma)\ \nu(\sigma). \tag{3.132}$$

[PROOF] Substituting (3.111) into (3.108) and integrating (3.108) with respect to t yields (3.131). Thus, the proof of the theorem is completed. Q.E.D.

Then the following theorem holds.

[THEOREM 3.9] The optimal smoothing estimation error covariance function $P(\tau,x,y|t)$ satisfies

$$\frac{\partial P(\tau,x,y|t)}{\partial t} = -\ B_m(\tau,x|t)\ \tilde{R}(t)\ B_m'(\tau,y|t) \qquad \text{for} \quad \tau < t \tag{3.133}$$

$$\Gamma_\xi\ P(\tau,\xi,y|t) = 0, \quad \forall_\xi \in S, \quad \forall y \in \bar{D} \tag{3.134}$$

with initial condition $P(\tau,x,y|\tau)$, that is,

$$P(\tau,x,x|t) = P(\tau,x,y|\tau) - \int_\tau^t B_m(\tau,x|\sigma)\ \tilde{R}(\sigma)\ B_m'(\tau,y|\sigma)\ d\sigma. \tag{3.135}$$

[PROOF] Using the orthogonality between $\tilde{U}(\tau,y|t)$ and $\hat{U}(\tau,y|t)$ yields

$$P(\tau,x,y|t) = E\ [\ \tilde{U}(\tau,x|t)\ U(\tau,y)\ ]. \tag{3.136}$$

Differentiating (3.136) with respect to t and using the relation

$$\frac{\partial\tilde{U}(\tau,x|t)}{\partial t} = -\ \frac{\partial\hat{U}(\tau,x|t)}{\partial t},$$

we have from (3.108)

$$\frac{\partial P(\tau,x,y|t)}{\partial t} = -\ A(t,\tau,x,t)\ H(t)\ E\ [\ \tilde{U}_m(t)\ U(\tau,y)\ ].$$

Using the orthogonality conditions between $\tilde{U}_m(t)$ and $\hat{U}(\tau,y|t)$ and between $\tilde{U}(\tau,y|t)$ and $\hat{U}_m(t)$ yields

$$E\ [\ \tilde{U}_m(t)\ U(\tau,y)\ ] = E\ [\ U_m(t)\ \tilde{U}(\tau,y|t)\ ] = B_m'\ (\tau,y|t).$$

Hence, (3.133) is obtained. Multiplying each side of (3.101) by $\alpha(\xi)$ and

$(1 - \alpha(\xi))\, \partial/\partial \mathbf{n}$ and summing them yields

$$\int_{t_0}^{t} \Gamma_\xi A(t,\tau,\xi,\sigma)\, E[\, Z(\sigma)\, Z'(\alpha)\,]\, d\sigma = E[\, \Gamma_\xi U(\tau,\xi)\, Z'(\alpha)\,] = 0, \quad \forall \xi \in S.$$

Hence, from Theorem 3.5 we have

$$\Gamma_\xi A(t,\tau,\xi,\sigma) = 0, \quad \forall \xi \in S. \tag{3.137}$$

Multiplying each side of (3.137) by $Z(\sigma)$ and integrating with respect to σ from t_0 to t yields

$$\Gamma_\xi \hat{U}(\tau,\xi|t) = 0, \quad \forall \xi \in S. \tag{3.138}$$

From (3.84), (3.99), and (3.138) we have

$$\Gamma_\xi \tilde{U}(\tau,\xi|t) = 0, \quad \forall \xi \in S. \tag{3.139}$$

Multiplying each side of (3.139) by $\tilde{U}(\tau,y|t)$, and taking the expectation yields (3.134). It is clear from the definition of $P(\tau,x,y|t)$ that the initial condition of $P(\tau,x,y|t)$ is $P(\tau,x,y|\tau)$. Integrating (3.133) with respect to t yields (3.135). Thus, the proof of the theorem is completed. Q.E.D.

Note that the smoothing estimator given by (3.130), (3.131), and (3.135) is an extension of the results for the finite dimensional linear system by using the innovation theory [20] to the results for the linear distributed parameter system. A new feature of the derivation of this section is that the present method by using the Wiener-Hopf theory does not necessitate the innovation theory or Kalman's formal limiting procedure and that the method clarifies the relation between the innovation theory and the Wiener-Hopf theory as shown in Theorem 3.6. Furthermore, the present method shows that the Wiener-Hopf theory provides a powerful technique for the derivation of the optimal smoothing estimator as well as the optimal filtering estimator in the previous section.

Fixed-Point smoothing

Let t_1 be a fixed time such that $t_1 < t$. Letting $\tau = t_1$ in Theorems 3.6, 3.7 yields the following theorem.

[THEOREM 3.10] The optimal fixed-point smoothing estimate $\hat{U}(t_1,x|t)$ and the error covariance function $P(t_1,x,y|t)$ are given by

$$\frac{\partial \hat{U}(t_1,x|t)}{\partial t} = B_m(t_1,x|t)\ \nu_m(t) \tag{3.140}$$

$$\frac{\partial P(t_1,x,y|t)}{\partial t} = - B_m(t_1,x|t)\ \tilde{R}(t)\ B_m'(t_1,y|t) \tag{3.141}$$

$$\frac{\partial B(t_1,x,y|t)}{\partial t} = A_x\ B(t_1,x,y|t) - B_m(t_1,x|t)\ \tilde{R}(t)\ P_m(t,y) \tag{3.142}$$

$$B(t_1,x,y|t_1) = P(t_1,x,y|t_1) \tag{3.143}$$

$\Gamma_\xi\ (\cdot) = 0,\quad (\cdot) = \hat{U}(t_1,\xi|t),\ P(t_1,\xi,y|t)$ or $B(t_1,\xi,y|t)$ for $\forall \xi \in S$ and $\forall x \in \bar{D}$. (3.144)

Fixed-interval smoothing

Letting T be a fixed time and setting $\tau = t$ and $t = T$ in (3.131) and (3.135) yields

$$\hat{U}(t,x|T) = \hat{U}(t,x|t) + \int_t^T B_m(t,x|\sigma)\ \nu_m(\sigma)\ d\sigma \tag{3.145}$$

$$P(t,x,y|T) = P(t,x,y|t) - \int_t^T B_m(t,x|\sigma)\ \tilde{R}(\sigma)\ B_m'(t,y|\sigma)\ d\sigma. \tag{3.146}$$

Then we have the following theorem.

[THEOREM 3.11] The optimal fixed-interval smoothing estimate $\hat{U}(t,x|T)$ and the error covariance function $P(t,x,y|T)$ are given by

$$\frac{\partial \hat{U}(t,x|T)}{\partial t} = A_x \hat{U}(t,x|T) + \int_D \int_D (\hat{U}(t,\alpha|T) - \hat{U}(t,\alpha|t)) \overline{P}(t,\alpha,\beta|t) \tilde{Q}(t,\beta,x) \, d\alpha d\beta \tag{3.147}$$

$$\frac{\partial P(t,x,y|T)}{\partial t} = (A_x + A_y) P(t,x,y|T) - \tilde{Q}(t,x,y) + \int_D \int_D \tilde{Q}(t,x,\beta)$$

$$\overline{P}(t,\beta,\alpha|t) P(t,\alpha,y|T) \, d\alpha d\beta + \int_D \int_D P(t,x,\alpha|T) \overline{P}(t,\alpha,\beta|t) \tilde{Q}(t,\beta,y) \, d\alpha d\beta \tag{3.148}$$

$$\Gamma_\xi (\cdot) = 0, \quad (\cdot) = \hat{U}(t,\xi|T) \text{ or } P(t,\xi,y|T) \text{ for } \forall \xi \in S \text{ and } \forall y \in \overline{D} \tag{3.149}$$

where the initial conditions for (3.147) and (3.148) are $\hat{U}(T,x|T)$ and $P(T,x,y|T)$, respectively and $\overline{P}(t,\alpha,\beta|t)$ denotes the inverse kernel function of $P(t,\alpha,\beta|t)$ such that

$$\int_D P(t,\beta,\alpha|t) \overline{P}(t,\alpha,x|t) \, d\alpha = \delta(\beta - x). \tag{3.150}$$

[PROOF] Differentiating (3.145) with respect to t yields

$$\frac{\partial \hat{U}(t,x|T)}{\partial t} = \frac{\partial \hat{U}(t,x|t)}{\partial t} - B_m(t,x|t) \nu_m(t) + \int_t \frac{\partial B_m(t,x|\sigma)}{\partial t} \nu_m(\sigma) \, d\sigma.$$

The optimal filtering estimate $\hat{U}(t,x|t)$ satisfies the following relation as shown in (3.51):

$$\frac{\partial \hat{U}(t,x|t)}{\partial t} = A_x \hat{U}(t,x|t) + P_m(t,x) \nu_m(t). \tag{3.151}$$

It follows from (3.112) and (3.124) that

$$\frac{\partial B_m(t,x|\sigma)}{\partial t} = A_x B_m(t,x|\sigma) + \int_D \mathcal{U}_m(\sigma,\beta,t) \tilde{Q}(t,\beta,x) \, d\beta. \tag{3.152}$$

From (3.130) and (3.145) we have

$$\hat{U}(t,\alpha|T) - \hat{U}(t,\alpha|t) = \int_t^T \int_D \mathcal{U}_m(\sigma,\zeta,t) P(t,\zeta,\alpha|t) \nu_m(\sigma) \, d\zeta d\sigma.$$

Multiplying the above equation by $\bar{P}(t,\alpha,\beta|t)$ and integrating each side with respect to α yields from (3.150)

$$\int_t^T \mathcal{U}_m(\sigma,\beta,t)\ \nu_m(\sigma)\ d\sigma = \int_D (\ \hat{U}(t,\alpha|T) - \hat{U}(t,\alpha|t))\ \bar{P}(t,\alpha,\beta|t)\ d\alpha. \quad (3.153)$$

Thus, (3.147) is obtained. Differentiating (3.146) with respect to t yields

$$\frac{\partial P(t,x,y|T)}{\partial t} = \frac{\partial P(t,x,y|t)}{\partial t} + B_m(t,x|t)\ \tilde{R}(t)\ B_m'(t,y|t)$$
$$- \int_t^T \partial B_m(t,x|\sigma)/\partial t\ \tilde{R}(\sigma)\ B_m'(t,y|\sigma)\ d\sigma$$
$$- \int_t^T B_m(t,x|\sigma)\ \tilde{R}(\sigma)\ \partial B_m'(t,y|\sigma)/\partial t\ d\sigma.$$

On the other hand, the optimal filtering error covariance function $P(t,x,y|t)$ satisfies the following equation as shown in (3.62):

$$\frac{\partial P(t,x,y|t)}{\partial t} = (\ A_x + A_y\ )\ P(t,x,y|t) + \tilde{Q}(t,x,y) - P_m(t,x)\ \tilde{R}(t)\ P_m'(t,y) \quad (3.154)$$

$$P(t_0,x,y|t_0) = P_0(x,y)$$
$$\Gamma_\xi\ P(t,\xi,y|t) = 0, \forall\xi \in S, \quad \forall y \in \bar{D}.$$

Using (3.125) and (3.154) yields

$$\frac{\partial P(t,x,y|T)}{\partial t} = (\ A_x + A_y\ )\ P(t,x,y|T) + \tilde{Q}(t,x,y)$$
$$- \int_t^T \int_D \mathcal{U}_m(\sigma,\beta,t)\ \tilde{Q}(t,\beta,x)\ \tilde{R}(\sigma)\ B_m'(t,y|\sigma)\ d\beta d\sigma$$
$$- \int_t^T \int_D B_m(t,x|\sigma)\ \tilde{R}(\sigma)\ \tilde{Q}(t,\beta,y)\,\mathcal{U}_m'(\sigma,\beta,t)\ d\beta d\sigma. \quad (3.155)$$

Multiplying (3.130) by $\bar{P}(\tau,x,\beta|\tau)$ and integrating each side with respect to x yields from (3.150)

$$\mathcal{U}(t,y,\tau,\beta) = \int_D B(\tau,x,y|t)\ \bar{P}(\tau,x,\beta|\tau)\ dx. \quad (3.156)$$

From (3.120) we have

$$\mathcal{U}_m(\sigma,\beta,t) = \int_D B_m(t,\alpha|\sigma)\,\overline{P}(t,\alpha,\beta|t)\,d\alpha. \tag{3.157}$$

Using the orthogonality condition (3.150), it follows from (3.146) and (3.157) that

$$\tilde{Q}(t,x,y) - \int_t^T \int_D \mathcal{U}_m(\sigma,\beta,t)\,\tilde{Q}(t,\beta,x)\,\tilde{R}(t)\,B_m'(t,y|\sigma)\,d\beta d\alpha$$

$$= \int_D \int_D \tilde{Q}(t,\beta,x)\,\overline{P}(t,\alpha,\beta|t)\,[\,P(t,\alpha,y|t) - \int_t^T B_m(t,\alpha|\sigma)\,\tilde{R}(\sigma)\,B_m'(t,y|\sigma)d\sigma]d\alpha d\beta$$

$$= \int_D \int_D \tilde{Q}(t,\beta,x)\,\overline{P}(t,\alpha,\beta|t)\,P(t,\alpha,y|T)\,d\alpha d\beta.$$

Since $\tilde{Q}(t,\beta,x) = \tilde{Q}(t,x,\beta)$ and $\overline{P}(t,\alpha,\beta|t) = \overline{P}(t,\beta,\alpha|t)$, (3.148) follows from (3.155). It is easily seen that the initial condition and the boundary condition of the theorem are satisfied. Thus, the proof of the theorem is completed.

Q.E.D.

Fixed-lag smoothing

Let ∇ be a fixed time interval. Setting $\tau = t$ and $t = t + \nabla$ in (3.131) and (3.135) yields

$$\hat{U}(t,x|t+\nabla) = \hat{U}(t,x|t) + \int_t^{t+\nabla} B_m(t,x|\sigma)\,\nu_m(\sigma)\,d\sigma \tag{3.158}$$

and

$$P(t,x,y|t+\nabla) = P(t,x,y|t) - \int_t^{t+\nabla} B_m(t,x|\sigma)\,\tilde{R}(\sigma)\,B_m'(t,y|\sigma)\,d\sigma. \tag{3.159}$$

Then we have the following theorem.

[THEOREM 3.12] The optimal fixed-lag smoothing estimate $\hat{U}(t,x|t+\nabla)$ and the error covariance function $P(t,x,y|t+\nabla)$ are given by

$$\frac{\partial \hat{U}(t,x|t+\nabla)}{\partial t} = A_x\,\hat{U}(t,x|x+\nabla) + B_m(t,x|t+\nabla)\,\nu_m(t+\nabla)$$

$$+ \int_D \int_D \tilde{Q}(t,x,\alpha)\ \overline{P}(t,\alpha,\beta|t)(\ \hat{U}(t,\beta|t+\nabla) - \hat{U}(t,\beta|t))\ d\alpha d\beta \qquad (3.160)$$

$$\frac{\partial B(t,x,y|t+\nabla)}{\partial t} = (\ A_x + A_y\ )\ B(t,x,y|t+\nabla) - B_m(t,x|t+\nabla)\ \tilde{R}(t+\nabla)\ P_m'(t+\nabla,y)$$

$$+ \int_D \int_D B(t,\alpha,y|t+\nabla)\ \overline{P}(t,\alpha,\beta|t)\ \tilde{Q}(t,\beta,x)\ d\alpha d\beta \qquad (3.161)$$

$$\frac{\partial P(t,x,y|t+\nabla)}{\partial t} = (\ A_x + A_y\ )\ P(t,x,y|t+\nabla) - \tilde{Q}(t,x,y)$$

$$+ \int_D \int_D \tilde{Q}(t,x,\alpha)\ \overline{P}(t,\alpha,\beta|t)\ P(t,\beta,y|t+\nabla)\ d\alpha d\beta$$

$$+ \int_D \int_D \tilde{Q}(t,y,\alpha)\ \overline{P}(t,\alpha,\beta|t)\ P(t,\beta,x|t+\nabla)\ d\alpha d\beta$$

$$- B_m(t,x|t+\nabla)\ \tilde{R}(t+\nabla)\ B_m'(t,y|t+\nabla) \qquad (3.162)$$

$$(\cdot) = 0, \quad (\cdot) = \hat{U}(t,\xi|t+\nabla),\ B(t,\xi,y|t+\nabla) \text{ or } P(t,\xi,y|t+\nabla) \text{ for } \forall\xi \in S \text{ and } \forall y \in \overline{D}$$

where the initial conditions for (3.160), (3.161), and (3.162) are $\hat{U}(t_0,x|t_0+\nabla)$, $B(t_0,x,y|t_0+\nabla)$, and $P(t_0,x,y|t_0+\nabla)$, respectively.

[PROOF] Differentiating (3.158) with respect to t yields

$$\frac{\partial \hat{U}(t,x|t+\nabla)}{\partial t} = \frac{\partial \hat{U}(t,x|t)}{\partial t} - B_m(t,x|t)\ \nu_m(t) + B_m(t,x|t+\nabla)\ \nu_m(t+\nabla)$$

$$+ \int_t^{t+\nabla} \partial B_m(t,x|\sigma)/\partial t\ \ \nu_m(\sigma)\ d\sigma.$$

From (3.124) and (3.153) we have

$$\int_t^{t+\nabla} \partial B_m(t,x|\sigma)/\partial t\ \ \nu_m(\sigma)\ d\sigma = \int_t^{t+\nabla} A_x\ B_m(t,x|\sigma)\ \nu_m(\sigma)\ d\sigma$$

$$+ \int_D \int_D (\ \hat{U}(t,\alpha|t+\nabla) - \hat{U}(t,\alpha|t))\ \overline{P}(t,\alpha,\beta|t)\ \tilde{Q}(t,\beta,x)\ d\alpha d\beta.$$

Using (3.125), (3.151), (3.158), and the above equation yields

$$\frac{\partial \hat{U}(t,x|t+\nabla)}{\partial t} = A_x\ \hat{U}(t,x|t+\nabla) + B_m(t,x|t+\nabla)\ \nu_m(t+\nabla)$$

$$+ \int_D \int_D\ (\ \hat{U}(t,\alpha|t+\nabla) - \hat{U}(t,\alpha|t))\ \overline{P}(t,\alpha,\beta|t)\ \tilde{Q}(t,\beta,x)\ d\alpha d\beta.$$

Since $Q(t,\beta,x) = Q(t,x,\beta)$ and $\overline{P}(t,\alpha,\beta|t) = \overline{P}(t,\beta,\alpha|t)$, (3.160) is obtained. From (3.123) and (3.124) we have

$$\frac{\partial B(t,x,y|t+\nabla)}{\partial t} = A_y\ B(t,x,y|t+\nabla) - B_m(t,x|t+\nabla)\ \tilde{R}(t+\nabla)\ P_m(t+\nabla,y)$$

$$+ A_x\ B(t,x,y|t+\nabla) + \int_D \mathcal{U}\,(t+\nabla,y,t,\alpha)\ \tilde{Q}(t,\alpha,x)\ d\alpha. \qquad (3.163)$$

Substituting (3.156) into (3.163) yields (3.161). Differentiating (3.159) with respect to t,and using (3.124), (3.154), and (3.159) yields

$$\frac{\partial P(t,x,y|t+\nabla)}{\partial t} = A_x\ P(t,x,y|t+\nabla) + A_y\ P(t,x,y|t+\nabla) + \tilde{Q}(t,x,y)$$

$$- \int_t^{t+\nabla}\int_D \mathcal{U}_m(\sigma,\beta,t)\ \tilde{Q}(t,\beta,x)\ \tilde{R}(\sigma)\ B_m'(t,y|\sigma)\ d\beta d\sigma$$

$$- B_m(t,x|t+\nabla)\ \tilde{R}(t+\nabla)\ B_m'(t,y|t+\nabla)$$

$$- \int_t^{t+\nabla}\int_D\ B_m(t,x|\sigma)\ \tilde{R}(\sigma)\ \mathcal{U}_m'(\sigma,\alpha,t)\ \tilde{Q}(t,\alpha,y)\ d\alpha d\sigma.$$

Then we have from (3.157) and (3.159)

$$\int_t^{t+\nabla}\int_D \int_D\ B_m(t,\alpha|\sigma)\ \overline{P}(t,\alpha,\beta|t)\ \tilde{Q}(t,\beta,x)\ \tilde{R}(\sigma)\ B_m'(t,y|\sigma)\ d\alpha d\beta d\sigma$$

$$= \int_D \int_D\ \overline{P}(t,\alpha,\beta|t)\ \tilde{Q}(t,\beta,x)\ [\ P(t,\alpha,y|t) - P(t,\alpha,y|t+\nabla)\ ]\ d\alpha d\beta$$

$$= \tilde{Q}(t,y,x) - \int_D \int_D\ \tilde{Q}(t,\beta,x)\ \overline{P}(t,\beta,\alpha|t)\ P(t,\alpha,y|t+\nabla)\ d\alpha d\beta.$$

Thus, (3.162) is obtained. It is easily seen that the initial and boundary conditions of (3.160)-(3.162) are satisfied. Thus, the proof of the theorem is completed. Q.E.D.

Let us define $G(t+\nabla,x,z)$ as the solution of the following equation:

$$\frac{\partial G(t+\nabla,x,z)}{\partial t} = A_x G(t+\nabla,x,z) + \int_D \int_D \tilde{Q}(t,x,\alpha)\, \bar{P}(t,\alpha,\beta|t)\, G(t+\nabla,\beta,z)\, d\alpha d\beta$$

$$- A_z G(t+\nabla,x,z) - \int_D \int_D G(t+\nabla,x,\alpha)\, \tilde{Q}(t+\nabla,\alpha,\beta)\, \bar{P}(t+\nabla,\beta,z|t+\nabla)\, d\alpha d\beta \tag{3.164}$$

$$G(t_0+\nabla,x,z) = \int_D B(t_0,x,\alpha|t_0+\nabla)\, \bar{P}(t_0+\nabla,\alpha,z|t_0+\nabla)\, d\alpha.$$

$$\Gamma_\xi\, G(t+\nabla,\xi,z) = 0, \quad \forall \xi \in S, \quad \forall z \in \bar{D}.$$

Then it is easily shown that

$$B(t,x,y|t+\nabla) = \int_D G(t+\nabla,x,\alpha)\, P(t+\nabla,\alpha,\, y|t+\nabla)\, d\alpha. \tag{3.165}$$

Thus, the following corollary holds.

[COROLLARY 3.2] The optimal smoothing estimator is given by

$$\frac{\partial \hat{U}(t,x|t+\nabla)}{\partial t} = A_x \hat{U}(t,x|t+\nabla) + \int_D G(t+\nabla,x,\alpha)\, P_m(t+\nabla,\alpha)\, d\, \nu_m(t+\nabla)$$

$$+ \int_D \int_D \tilde{Q}(t,x,\alpha)\, \bar{P}(t,\alpha,\beta|t)(\hat{U}(t,\beta|t+\nabla) - \hat{U}(t,\beta|t))\, d\alpha d\beta. \tag{3.166}$$

Therefore, three kinds of the smoothing estimator were derived by using the Wiener-Hopf theory. A new feature of the present derivation for the smoothing estimators is that three kinds of the smoothing estimators can be derived only from the Wiener-Hopf theoretical viewpoints although this fact was not clarified even for a finite dimensional system in the original works by Kalman [21, 22].

Solution of the smoothing estimator equations

In general, the smoothing estimator equations can be solved by the numerical approximation methods. The Fourier expansion method is adopted here. Let us assume that $\hat{U}(\theta,x|t)$, $B(\theta,x|t)$, and $P(\theta,x,y|t)$ can be expanded in $L^2(D)$ or in $L^2(D \times D)$ as

$$\hat{U}(\theta,x|t) = \Sigma_{i=1}^{\infty} \hat{u}_i(\theta|t)\, \phi_i(x) \tag{3.167}$$

$$B(\theta,x,y|t) = \Sigma_{i,j=1}^{\infty} b_{ij}(\theta|t)\, \phi_i(x)\, \phi_j(y) \tag{3.168}$$

$$P(\theta,x,y|t) = \Sigma_{i,j=1}^{\infty} p_{ij}(\theta|t)\, \phi_i(x)\, \phi_j(y) \tag{3.169}$$

where $\theta = t$ or $\theta < t$.
Then $B_m(\theta,x|t)$ and $P_m(t,x)$ are represented as

$$B_m(\theta,x|t) = \Sigma_{i,j=1}^{\infty} b_{ij}(\theta|t)\, \phi_i(x)\, \Phi_j' \tag{3.170}$$

$$P_m(t,x) = \Sigma_{i,j=1}^{\infty} p_{ij}(t|t)\, \phi_i(x)\, \Phi_j' \tag{3.171}$$

$$\Phi_j = \text{Col}\,[\, \phi_j(x^1), \cdots, \phi_j(x^m)\,] \tag{3.172}$$

where $p_{ij}(t|t)$ denotes the (i,j)-th component of the Fourier expansion of $P(t,x,y|t)$.

For the fixed-point smoothing estimator, we obtain from Theorem 3.10 and (3.167)-(3.172) the following relations:

$$\frac{d\,\hat{u}_i(t_1|t)}{dt} = \Sigma_{k=1}^{\infty} b_{ik}(t_1|t)\, \Phi_k'\, H'(t)\, R^{-1}(t)\, (\, Z(t) - \Sigma_{n=1}^{\infty} H(t)\, \Phi_n\, \hat{u}_n(t|t)) \tag{3.173}$$

$$\hat{u}_i(t_1|t_1) = \int_D \hat{U}(t_1,x|t_1)\, \phi_i(x)\, dx, \quad i = 1, 2, \cdots,$$

$$\frac{d\, b_{ij}(t_1|t)}{dt} = - \Sigma_{k,n=1}^{\infty} \; b_{ik}(t_1|t)\, \Phi_k' \, \tilde{R}(t)\, \Phi_n \, p_{nj}(t|t) + \lambda_j \, b_{ij}(t_1|t) \tag{3.174}$$

$$b_{ij}(t_1|t_1) = p_{ij}(t_1|t_1), \quad i, j = 1, 2, \cdots$$

$$\frac{d\, p_{ij}(t_1|t)}{dt} = - \Sigma_{k,n=1}^{\infty} \; b_{ik}(t_1|t)\, \Phi_k' \, \tilde{R}(t)\, \Phi_n \, b_{nj}(t_1|t) \tag{3.175}$$

$$p_{ij}(t_1|t_1) = b_{ij}(t_1|t_1), \quad i, j = 1, 2, \cdots.$$

Let us define the following matrices:

$$\hat{U}(\theta|t) = \text{Col}\,[\, \hat{u}_1(\theta|t), \cdots, \hat{u}_N(\theta|t) \,], \; \Lambda = \text{Diag}\,[\, \lambda_1, \cdots, \lambda_N \,]$$

$$B(\theta|t) = [\, b_{ij}(\theta|t) \,]_N, \quad P(\theta|t) = [\, p_{ij}(\theta|t) \,]_N$$

$$\Phi = [\, \Phi_1, \cdots, \Phi_N \,]$$

where $[\, g_{ij} \,]_N$ denotes the $N \times N$ matrix with g_{ij} as the (i,j)-th element. If the infinite series (3.167)-(3.169) can be approximated by the first N terms, then the system of (3.173)-(3.175) is represented as

$$\frac{d\, \hat{U}(t_1|t)}{dt} = B(t_1|t)\, \Phi' \, H'(t)\, R^{-1}(t)\, [\, Z(t) - H(t)\, \Phi\, \hat{U}(t|t) \,]$$

$$\frac{d\, B(t_1|t)}{dt} = B(t_1|t)\, [\, \Lambda - \Phi' \, \tilde{R}(t)\, \Phi\, P(t|t) \,]$$

$$\frac{d\, P(t_1|t)}{dt} = - B(t_1|t)\, \Phi' \, \tilde{R}(t)\, \Phi\, B'(t_1|t).$$

These relations have the same form as those of the finite dimensional system [23, 24] except that the present smoothing estimator equations contain the new matrix Φ which reflects the effect of the sensor location.

For the fixed-interval smoothing, we obtain from Theorem 3.11 and (3.167)-(3.172) the following relations:

$$\frac{d\,\hat{u}_i(t|T)}{dt} = \lambda_i\,\hat{u}_i(t|T) + \Sigma_{j,k=1}^{\infty}\,(\,\hat{u}_j(t|T) - \hat{u}_j(t|t))\,\bar{p}_{kj}(t|t)\,q_{ik}(t)) \tag{3.176}$$

$$\frac{d\,p_{ij}(t|T)}{dt} = (\,\lambda_i + \lambda_j\,)\,p_{ij}(t|T) - q_{ij}(t) + \Sigma_{\,k,n=1}^{\infty}\,q_{in}(t)\,\bar{p}_{nk}(t|t)\,p_{kj}(t|T)$$
$$+\;\Sigma_{k,n=1}^{\infty}\;q_{ij}(t)\,\bar{p}_{kn}(t|t)\,p_{ik}(t|T) \tag{3.177}$$

where

$$\bar{p}_{nk}(t|t) = \int_D \int_D \quad \phi_n(x)\,\bar{P}(t,x,y|t)\,\phi_k(y)\,dx\,dy$$

$$q_{nk}(t) = \int_D \int_D \quad \phi_n(x)\,\tilde{Q}(t,x,y)\,\phi_k(y)\,dx\,dy.$$

Defining $\bar{P}(t)$ and $Q(t)$ by the following relation;

$$\bar{P}(t) = P^{-1}(t) = [\,\bar{p}_{ij}(t|t)\,]_N, \quad Q(t) = [\,q_{ij}(t)\,]_N,$$

we obtain from (3.176)-(3.177)

$$\frac{d\,\hat{U}(t|T)}{dt} = \Lambda\,\hat{U}(t|T) + Q(t)\,\bar{P}(t)(\,\hat{U}(t|T) - \hat{U}(t|t))$$

$$\frac{d\,P(t|T)}{dt} = (\,\Lambda + Q(t)\,\bar{P}(t|t))\,P(t|T) - Q(t) + P(t|T)(\,\Lambda + Q(t)\,\bar{P}(t))'.$$

For the fixed-lag smoothing estimator, we obtain from Corollary 3.2, Theorem 3.12, and (3.167)-(3.172) the following relations:

$$\frac{d\,\hat{u}_i(t|t+\,)}{dt} = \lambda_i\,\hat{u}_i(t|t+\nabla) + \Sigma_{k,n=1}^{\infty}\,g_{ik}(t+\nabla)\,p_{kn}(t+\nabla)\,\phi_n'\,H'(t+\nabla)\,R^{-1}(t+\nabla)$$
$$(\,Z(t+\nabla) - \Sigma_{m=1}^{\infty}\,H(t+\nabla)\,\phi_m\,\hat{U}_m(t+\nabla|t+\nabla)\,)$$
$$+\;\Sigma_{k,n=1}^{\infty}\;q_{ik}(t)\,\bar{p}_{kn}(t|t)(\,\hat{u}_n(t|t+\nabla) - \hat{u}_n(t|t)) \tag{3.178}$$

$$\frac{d\, g_{ij}(t|t+\nabla)}{dt} = \Sigma_{k,n=1}^{\infty} \; q_{in}(t)\, \overline{p}_{nk}(t|t)\, g_{kj}(t|t+\nabla)$$

$$- \; \Sigma_{k,n=1}^{\infty} \; g_{in}(t|t+\nabla)\, q_{nk}(t+\nabla)\, \overline{p}_{kj}(t+\nabla|t+\nabla)$$

$$+ \; \lambda_i \, g_{ij}(t|t+\nabla) \; - \; \lambda_j \, g_{ji}(t|t+\nabla) \qquad (3.179)$$

$$\frac{d\, p_{ij}(t|t+\nabla)}{dt} = (\, \lambda_i + \lambda_j \,)\, p_{ij}(t|t+\nabla) + \Sigma_{k,n=1}^{\infty} \; q_{in}(t)\, \overline{p}_{nk}(t|t)\, p_{kj}(t|t+\nabla)$$

$$- \; \Sigma_{n,m,h,k=1}^{\infty} \; g_{in}(t|t+\nabla)\, p_{nk}(t+\nabla|t+\nabla)\, \Phi_k^{'}\, \tilde{R}(t)\, \Phi_h\, p_{hm}(t+\nabla|t+\nabla)$$

$$g_{mj}(t|t+\nabla) - q_{ij}(t) + \Sigma_{k,n=1}^{\infty} p_{ik}(t|t+\nabla)\, \overline{p}_{kn}(t|t)\, q_{nj}(t) \qquad (3.180)$$

where

$$g_{ij}(t|t+\nabla) = \int_D \int_D \; \phi_i(x)\, G(t+\nabla,x,y)\, \phi_j(y)\, dx\, dy.$$

Defining $G(t+\nabla)$ as

$$G(t+\nabla) = [\, g_{ij}(t|t+\nabla) \,]_N,$$

we have from (3.178)-(3.179)

$$\frac{d\, \hat{U}(t|t+\nabla)}{dt} = \hat{U}(t|t+\nabla) + G(t+\nabla)\, P(t+\nabla)\, \Phi^{'}\, H^{'}(t+\nabla)\, R^{-1}(t+\nabla)$$

$$(\, Z(t+\nabla) - H(t+\nabla)\, \Phi\, \hat{U}(t+\nabla|t+\nabla))$$

$$+ \; Q(t)\, \overline{P}(t)(\, \hat{U}(t|t+\nabla) - \hat{U}(t|t))$$

$$\frac{d\, G(t+\nabla)}{dt} = Q(t)\, \overline{P}(t)\, G(t+\nabla) - G(t+\nabla)\, Q(t+\nabla)\, \overline{P}(t+\nabla)$$

$$\Phi\, G(t+\nabla) - G^{'}(t+\nabla)\, \Phi^{'}.$$

$$\frac{d\, P(t|t+\nabla)}{dt} = \Lambda\, P(t|t+\nabla) + P(t|t+\nabla)\, \Lambda + Q(t)\, \overline{P}(t)\, P(t|t+\nabla) + P(t|t+\nabla)\, \overline{P}(t)\, Q(t)$$

$$- \; G(t+\nabla)\, P(t+\nabla)\, \Phi^{'}\, \tilde{R}(t)\, \Phi\, P^{'}(t+\nabla)\, G^{'}(t+\nabla) - Q(t).$$

Numerical examples

Let us consider the following heat conduction system with the observation at one measurement point x^1:

$$\frac{\partial U(t,x)}{\partial t} = \left(a \frac{\partial^2 U(t,x)}{\partial x^2} + b\, U(t,x) \right) + \dot{W}(t,x)$$

$$Z(t) = H(t)\, U(t,x^1) + \dot{V}(t)$$

where

$x, x^1 \varepsilon D = (0, 1), \quad t \varepsilon (0, 0.085).$

The noise covariance functions of $\dot{W}(t,x)$ and $\dot{V}(t)$ are assumed to be

$$Q(t,x,y) = 0.5 \exp(-(x-y)^2), \quad R(t) = r_0$$

where r_0 is a constant.

Numerical computations were carried out for the following two cases:

Case 1.

$a = 1,\ b = 0,\ r_0 = 0.1,\ U(t,0) = U(t,1) = 0,\ H(t) = 4.5,\ t_1 = 0.005,$

$\nabla = 0.005,\ T = 0.085,\ P_0(x,y) = 0.1\ \phi_1(x)\,\phi_1(y) + 0.05\,\phi_2(x)\,\phi_2(y).$

Case 2.

$a = b = 1,\ r_0 = 1.0,\ \partial U(t,0)/\partial x = \partial U(t,1)/\partial x + 1.5\, U(t,1) = 0,$

$H(t) = 4.5,\ t_1 = 0.005,\ \nabla = 0.005,\ T = 0.085,\ P_0(x,y) = 1.03\ \phi_1(x)\ \phi_1(y)$

$+ 0.39\ \phi_2(x)\ \phi_2(y).$

Then the eigenfunctions $\{\phi_i(x),\ i = 1, 2, \cdots\}$ and the eigenvalues $\{\lambda_i,\ i = 1, 2, \cdots\}$ are given by

$$\phi_i(x) = \sqrt{2}\ \sin \pi i x, \quad \lambda_i = -(\pi i)^2 \quad \text{for Case 1} \quad \text{and}$$

$$\phi_i(x) = \sqrt{3/(1.5 + \sin^2 \omega_i)}\ \cos \omega_i x, \quad \omega_i \tan \omega_i = 1.5, \quad \omega_i = \sqrt{1 - \lambda_i}$$

for Case 2.

The expansion coefficients for the truncation number N = 2 are solved by the Runge-Kutta method and the trajectories of the error covariance functions for $x^1 = 0.5$ for Case 1 and $x^1 = 0.1$ for Case 2 are depicted in Figs. 3-1 and 3-2 where $P_{t|t}$, $P_{t_1|t}$, $P_{t|T}$, and $P_{t|t+\nabla}$ denote $P(t,0.5,o.5|t)$, $P(t_1,0.5,0.5|t)$, $P(t,0.5,0.5|T)$, and $P(t,0.5,0.5|t+\nabla)$, respectively.

These figures show that the sufficient improvement of the estimation accuracy is obtained by using the smoothing estimators. Tables III-1 and III-2 show the optimal estimation error covariance functions for $x^1 = 0.1$ for Case 1 and $x^1 = 0.9$ for Case 2. In this case, the estimation acurracy decreases compared with the previous results as shown in Figs. 3-1 and 3-2. This decrease comes from the fact that the observation at the point where the greatest value of the amplitude of the wave form is attained in the spatial domain yields the minimum estimation error covariance function as shown in the following chapter.

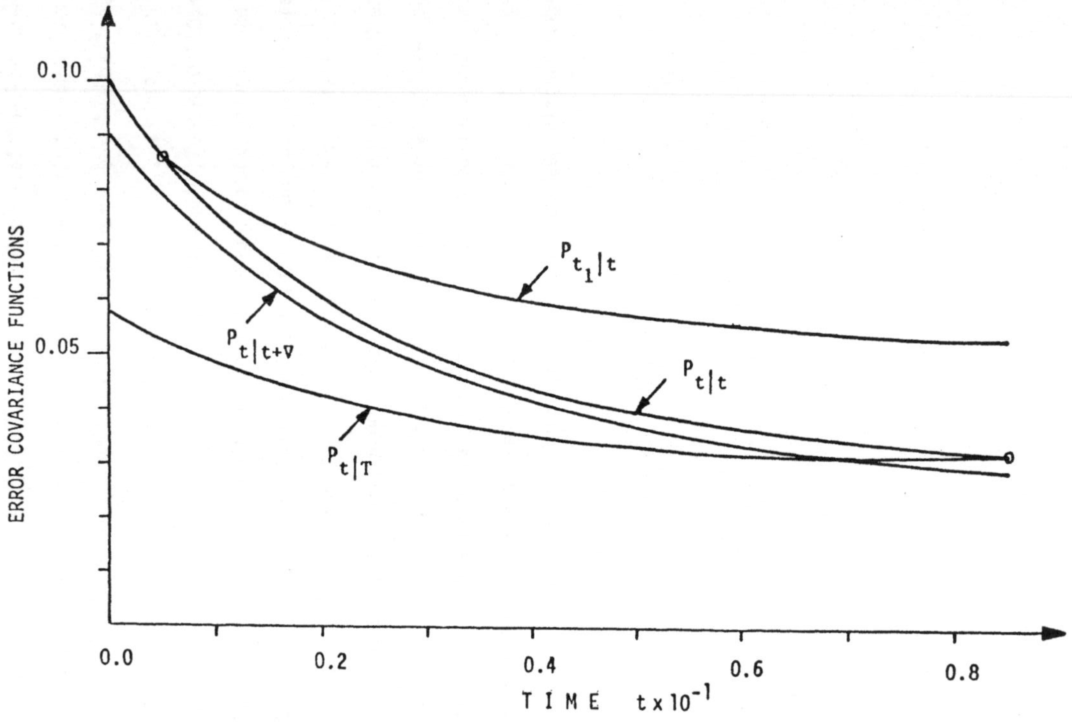

Fig. 3-1. Estimation error covariance functions for Case 1 with $x^1 = 0.5$.

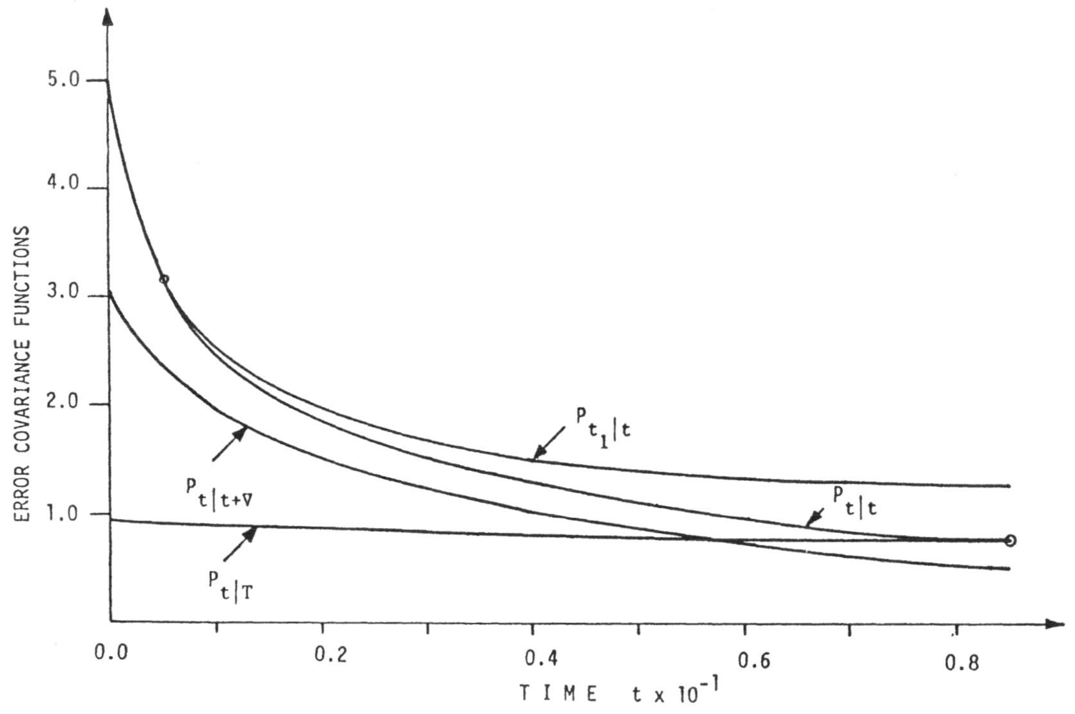

Fig. 3-2. Estimation error covariance functions for Case 2 with $x^1 = 0.1$.

TABLE III-1. Estimation error covariance functions for Case 1 with $x^1 = 0.1$.

Time t x 10^{-1}	$P_{t\|t}$ x 10^{-1}	$P_{t_1\|t}$ x 10^{-1}	$P_{t\|T}$ x 10^{-1}	$P_{t\|t+\nabla}$ x 10^{-1}
0.00	1.0000	******	0.9241	0.9909
0.05	0.9324	0.9324	0.8675	0.9242
0.10	0.8724	0.9247	0.8166	0.8648
0.15	0.8190	0.9178	0.7708	0.8118
0.20	0.7713	0.9118	0.7296	0.7644
0.25	0.7287	0.9065	0.6926	0.7220
0.30	0.6906	0.9017	0.6594	0.6841
0.35	0.6566	0.8975	0.6296	0.6500
0.40	0.6261	0.8937	0.6029	0.6195
0.45	0.5987	0.8904	0.5789	0.5922
0.50	0.5742	0.8873	0.5575	0.5676
0.55	0.5523	0.8846	0.5383	0.5455
0.60	0.5326	0.8821	0.5212	0.5256
0.65	0.5149	0.8800	0.5059	0.5077
0.70	0.4990	0.8781	0.4924	0.4916
0.75	0.4848	0.8763	0.4804	0.4771
0.80	0.4719	0.8747	0.4698	0.4639
0.85	0.4605	0.8733	0.4605	0.4521

TABLE III-2. Estimation error covariance functions for Case 2 with $x^1 = 0.9$.

Time t x 10^{-1}	$P_{t\|t}$ x 10	$P_{t_1\|t}$ x 10	$P_{t\|T}$ x 10	$P_{t\|t+\nabla}$ x 10
0.00	0.4973	******	0.1120	0.3709
0.05	0.3767	0.3767	0.1131	0.3059
0.10	0.3153	0.3114	0.1143	0.2662
0.15	0.2773	0.2720	0.1154	0.2390
0.20	0.2509	0.2453	0.1165	0.2187
0.25	0.2311	0.2259	0.1176	0.2027
0.30	0.2154	0.2111	0.1186	0.1895
0.35	0.2025	0.1995	0.1196	0.1783
0.40	0.1914	0.1900	0.1206	0.1685
0.45	0.1818	0.1823	0.1216	0.1598
0.50	0.1732	0.1758	0.1226	0.1519
0.55	0.1654	0.1703	0.1235	0.1447
0.60	0.1583	0.1657	0.1245	0.1780
0.65	0.1517	0.1617	0.1255	0.1318
0.70	0.1455	0.1583	0.1264	0.1260
0.75	0.1398	0.1554	0.1274	0.1204
0.80	0.1344	0.1529	0.1283	0.1151
0.85	0.1293	0.1508	0.1293	0.1102

3.1.3. Optimal prediction problems.

The optimal prediction problem requires to find an estimate $\hat{U}(\tau,x|t)$ of $U(\tau,x)$ for $\tau > t$ which minimizes the following variance function J given by

$$J = E[\,|\tilde{U}(\tau,x|t)|^2\,]$$

where

$$\tilde{U}(\tau,x|t) = U(\tau,x) - \hat{U}(\tau,x|t) \quad \text{for } \tau > t. \tag{3.181}$$

Assume that the optimal prediction estimate $\hat{U}(\tau,x\ t)$ is given by

$$\hat{U}(\tau,x|t) = \int_{t_0}^{t} M(t,\tau,x,\sigma)\, Z(\sigma)\, d\sigma. \tag{3.182}$$

Then the following Wiener-Hopf theorem holds.

[THEOREM 3.13] A necessary and sufficient condition for the estimate (3.182) to be optimal is that the Wiener-Hopf equation

$$\int_{t_0}^{t} M(t,\tau,x,\sigma)\, E[\, Z(\sigma)\, Z'(\alpha)\,]\, d\sigma = E[\, U(\tau,x)\, Z'(\alpha)\,] \tag{3.183}$$

holds for $t_0 \leqq \alpha < t$ and $x \in \bar{D}$. (3.183) is equivalent to

$$E[\,\tilde{U}(\tau,x|t)\, Z'(\alpha)\,] = 0, \quad t_0 \leqq \alpha < t \text{ and } \forall x \in \bar{D}. \tag{3.184}$$

Furthermore, the optimal kernel $M(t,\tau,x,\sigma)$ is unique.

The proof of this theorem is directly obtained by using the variational calculus as shown in Theorems 3.4 and 3.5. Thus, the proof is omitted here.

Then the following theorem holds.

[THEOREM 3.14] The optimal prediction estimate $\hat{U}(\tau,x|t)$ is given by the following relation:

$$\frac{\partial \hat{U}(\tau,x|t)}{\partial \tau} = A_x\, \hat{U}(\tau,x|t) \tag{3.185}$$

$$\Gamma_\xi \hat{U}(\tau,\xi|t) = 0, \quad \forall \xi \in S \tag{3.186}$$

where the initial condition of (3.185) is $\hat{U}(t,x|t)$.

[PROOF] Differentiating (3.183) with respect to τ yields

$$\int_{t_0}^{t} \partial M(t,\tau,x,\sigma)/\partial\tau \; E[\, Z(\sigma)\, Z'(\alpha)\,]\, d\sigma = E[\, \partial U(\tau,x)/\partial\tau \; Z'(\alpha)]$$

$$= E[\, A_x\, U(\tau,x)\, Z'(\alpha)\,].$$

Using the Wiener-Hopf equation (3.183) yields

$$\int_{t_0}^{t} (\, \partial M(t,\tau,x,\sigma)/\partial\tau + A_x\, M(t,\tau,x,\sigma))\, E[\, Z(\sigma)\, Z'(\alpha)\,]\, d\sigma = 0.$$

From the uniqueness of the kernel function $M(t,\tau,x,\sigma)$, we have

$$\frac{\partial M(t,\tau,x,\sigma)}{\partial\tau} = A_x\, M(t,\tau,x,\sigma) \tag{3.187}$$

Then differentiating (3.182) with respect to τ and substituting (3.187), we have

$$\frac{\partial \hat{U}(\tau,x|t)}{\partial\tau} = \int_{t_0}^{t} A_x\, M(t,\tau,x,\sigma)\, Z(\sigma)\, d\sigma = A_x\, \hat{U}(\tau,x|t).$$

The boundary condition (3.166) is easily obtained from the Wiener-Hopf equation (3.183) as shown in the derivation of the filtering estimate in (3.54).

Thus, the proof of the theorem is completed. Q.E.D.

Then the following theorem holds.

[THEOREM 3.15] The optimal prediction error covariance function $P(\tau,x,y|t)$ is given by the following relation:

$$\frac{\partial P(\tau,x,y|t)}{\partial\tau} = (\, A_x + A_y)\, P(\tau,x,y|t) + \tilde{Q}(\tau,x,y) \tag{3.188}$$

$$\Gamma_\xi P(\tau,\xi,y|t) = 0, \quad \forall\xi \in S, \quad \forall y \in \bar{D} \tag{3.189}$$

where the initial condition of (3.188) is $P(t,x,y|t)$.

[PROOF] From (3.81), (3.84), (3.181), (3.185), and (3.186), we have

$$\frac{\partial \tilde{U}(\tau,x|t)}{\partial \tau} = A_x \tilde{U}(\tau,x|t) + C(\tau,x)\hat{W}(\tau,x) \tag{3.190}$$

$$\Gamma_\xi \tilde{U}(\tau,\xi|t) = 0, \quad \forall \xi \in S. \tag{3.191}$$

Noting that $P(\tau,x,y|t) = E[\tilde{U}(\tau,x|t)\tilde{U}(\tau,y|t)]$ and differentiating the both sides with respect to τ, we have

$$\frac{\partial P(\tau,x,y|t)}{\partial \tau} = E\left[\frac{\partial \tilde{U}(\tau,x|t)}{\partial \tau}\tilde{U}(\tau,y|t)\right] + E\left[\tilde{U}(\tau,x|t)\frac{\partial \tilde{U}(\tau,y|t)}{\partial \tau}\right].$$

Substituting (3.190) into the above equation and using (3.89), we have (3.188). Since (3.189) is clear from (3.191) and the definition of $P(\tau,x,y|t)$, the proof of the theorem is completed. Q.E.D.

As the integral forms of Theorems 3.14, 3.15, we have the following corollary.

[COROLLARY 3.3] The optimal prediction estimate and prediction error covariance function are given by the following relation:

$$\hat{U}(\tau,x|t) = \int_D \mathcal{U}(\tau,x,t,y)\,\hat{U}(t,y|t)\,dy \tag{3.192}$$

$$P(\tau,x,y|t) = \int_D \int_D \mathcal{U}(\tau,x,t,\alpha)\,P(t,\alpha,\beta|t)\,\mathcal{U}(\tau,\beta,t,y)\,d\alpha d\beta$$

$$+ \int_{t_0}^{\tau}\int_D \int_D \mathcal{U}(\tau,x,\sigma,\alpha)\,\tilde{Q}(\sigma,\alpha,\beta)\,\mathcal{U}(\tau,\beta,\sigma,y)\,d\alpha d\beta d\sigma. \tag{3.193}$$

3.2. Optimal estimators in Hilbert spaces

3.2.1. Optimal filtering problems.

Let us suppose that the state $U(t,\omega)$ is generated by the stochastic linear differential equation in the Hilbert space $\mathcal{H}$

$$d\,U(t,\omega) = A(t)\,U(t,\omega)\,dt + C(t)\,d\,W(t,\omega) \tag{3.194}$$

$$U(t_0,\omega) = U_0(\omega) \tag{3.195}$$

and that the observation $Z(t)$ is generated by the stochastic linear differential equation in the Hilbert space $\mathcal{K}$

$$d\,Z(t,\omega) = H(t)\,U(t,\omega)\,dt + d\,V(t,\omega) \tag{3.196}$$

where $C(\cdot) \in L^\infty(t_0,t_f;\mathcal{L}(\mathcal{H},\mathcal{H}))$, $H(\cdot) \in L^\infty(t_0,t_f;\mathcal{L}(\mathcal{H},\mathcal{K}))$, U_0 is an $\mathcal{H}$-valued random variable independent of $W(t,\omega)$ and $V(t,\omega)$ and has zero expectation and covariance operator P_0. $W(t,\omega)$ and $V(t,\omega)$ are independent of Wiener processes on $\mathcal{H}$ and $\mathcal{K}$ with covariance operators $\mathcal{W}(t)$ and $\mathcal{V}(t)$, respectively, i.e.,

$$\mathrm{Cov}\,[\,W(t,\omega) - W(s,\omega),\ W(t,\omega) - W(s,\omega)\,] = \int_s^t \mathcal{W}(\tau)\,d\tau, \tag{3.197}$$

$$\mathrm{Cov}\,[\,V(t,\omega) - V(s,\omega),\ V(t,\omega) - V(s,\omega)\,] = \int_s^t \mathcal{V}(\tau)\,d\tau, \tag{3.198}$$

where $\mathcal{W}(t)$ and $\mathcal{V}(t)$ are nuclear, positive and symmetric operators for almost all $t \in (t_0, t_f)$ and

$$\int_{t_0}^{t_f} \mathrm{tr}\,\mathcal{W}(\tau)\,d\tau < \infty .$$

Furthermore, $\mathcal{V}(t)$ is assumed to be invertible. Thus, $\mathcal{K}$ is a finite dimensional space since $\mathcal{V}(t)$ denotes the invertible nuclear operator.
Assume that $A(t)$ is a linear operator in $\mathcal{H}$, satisfying the following relation;

(i) the domain $\mathcal{D}(A)$ of $A(t)$ is dense in $\mathcal{H}$ and independent of t, and $A(t)$ is a closed operator;

(ii) $(\lambda\mathcal{J} - A(t))^{-1}$ exists for Re $\lambda \geqq 0$ and $\|(\lambda\mathcal{J} - A(t))^{-1}\| \leqq c/(1+|\lambda|)$ where c is constant and $\mathcal{J}$ denotes the identity operator;

(iii) $\|(A(t) - A(\tau))A^{-1}(\tau)\| \leqq C\,|t-\tau|^{\alpha}$ for all $t, \tau \geqq t_0$ where C and α are positive constants.

Then note that there exists the evolution operator $\mathcal{U}(t,s)$ with the following properties as shown in Chapter 2:

(1) $\mathcal{U}(t,s) : [t_0, t_f] \times [t_0, t_f] \to \mathcal{L}(\mathcal{H}, \mathcal{H})$ and is strongly continuous in s and t for $t_0 \leqq s \leqq t \leqq t_f$.

(2) $\mathcal{U}(t,s) = \mathcal{U}(t,\tau)\,\mathcal{U}(\tau, s)$ if $t_0 \leqq s \leqq \tau \leqq t \leqq t_f$, and $\mathcal{U}(s,s) = \mathcal{J}$.

(3) $\mathcal{U}(t,s)$ is strongly continuously differentiable in t for $t > s$ and

$$\frac{\partial\,\mathcal{U}(t,s)}{\partial t} = A(t)\,\mathcal{U}(t,s) \tag{3.199}$$

where

$\|A(t)\,\mathcal{U}(t,s)\| \leqq c_1/|t-s|$ for $t_0 \leqq s < t \leqq t_f$ and some constant c_1.

In what follows we shall often delete the explicit ω-dependence of the random variables. The filtering problem can be stated as follows:

Given $Z(s)$, $t_0 \leqq s \leqq t$, find an estimate $\hat{U}(t|t)$ of the state $U(t)$, which has the form

$$\hat{U}(t|t) = \int_{t_0}^{t} L(t,s)\, dZ(s), \tag{3.200}$$

and which minimizes the following filtering error variance function J

$$J = E[\langle h, \tilde{U}(t|t)\rangle^2] \tag{3.201}$$

$$\tilde{U}(t|t) = U(t) - \hat{U}(t|t) \tag{3.202}$$

where $L(t,\cdot) \in L^2(t_0,t_f ; \mathcal{L}(\mathcal{K},\mathcal{H}))$ for almost all t and L(t,s) is regulated in both arguments t and s.

Then the following Wiener-Hopf theorem holds:

[THEOREM 3.16] Let $\hat{U}(t|t)$ be given by

$$\tilde{U}(t|t) = U(t) - \hat{U}(t|t). \tag{3.203}$$

Then $\hat{U}(t|t)$ is a solution of the filtering problem if and only if

$$\mathrm{Cov}\,[\,U(t),\, Z(\sigma) - Z(\tau)\,] = \mathrm{Cov}\,[\textstyle\int_{t_0}^{t} L(t,s)\, d\,Z(s),\, Z(\sigma) - Z(\tau)\,] \tag{3.204}$$

for all σ, τ with $t_0 \leqq \tau < \sigma < t$, or equivalently, if and only if

$$E\,[\,\tilde{U}(t|t) \circ [\,Z(\sigma) - Z(\tau)\,]\,] = 0 \tag{3.205}$$

for all σ, τ with $t_0 \leqq \tau < \sigma < t$.

[PROOF] Since $E\,[\,U_0\,] = 0$, $E\,[\,Z(\sigma) - Z(\tau)\,] = 0$ and so it is clear that (3.204) and (3.205) are equivalent. Now let h be a fixed element of $\mathcal{H}$ and let U(h) be the space of all real random variables of the form $< h, U >$ where U $\in L^2(\Omega, \mu; \mathcal{H})$. Define an inner product on U(h) by $E\,[< h, U >< h, U >]$ and let Y(h) denote the subspace of U(h) generated by elements of the form

$$< h, y(a) > = < h, \textstyle\int_{t_0}^{a} B(t,s)\, d\,Z(s) > \quad , a \leqq t, \tag{3.206}$$

where B(t,s) is regulated. By the well-known orthogonal projection lemma [10] $\hat{U}(t|t)$ will be a solution of the filtering problem if and only if $\tilde{U}(t|t)$ is orthogonal to Y(h) in U(h) for every h. In other words, $\hat{U}(t|t)$ is a solution of the filtering problem if and only if

$$E\,[\,< h, \tilde{U}(t|t)> < h, y(a)>] = 0 \tag{3.207}$$

for all h where

$$y(a) = \int_{t_0}^{a} B(t,s)\, d\, Z(s), \quad a \leq t \tag{3.208}$$

and B(t,s) is regulated.

So let us first assume that (3.205) holds. We observe that, in view of the definition of the operator " $\circ$ " in (2.4)

$$< h, (h_1 \circ h_2) h > = < h, h_1 >< h, h_2 > \tag{3.209}$$

for any $h, h_1, h_2 \in \mathcal{H}$.

Thus, we have

$$E [< h, \tilde{U}(t|t) > < h, y(a) >] = < h, E[\tilde{U}(t|t) \circ y(a)] h >. \tag{3.210}$$

Taking into consideration that y(a) is given by (3.208) and assuming that B(t,s) is a step function, we have

$$E [\tilde{U}(t|t) \circ y(a)] = \Sigma_{j=1}^{n} E [\tilde{U}(t|t) \circ B_j [Z(\sigma_j) - Z(\tau_j)]]$$

$$= \Sigma_{j=1}^{n} E [\tilde{U}(t|t) \circ [Z(\sigma_j) - Z(\tau_j)]] B_j^{*} = 0 \tag{3.211}$$

where n denotes the maximum point of the time with the jump as shown in (2.10) since (3.205) is satisfied. It follows by an approximation argument as shown in Lemma 2.3 that $E [\tilde{U}(t|t) \circ y(a)] = 0$ for any y(a) given by (3.212) and hence, that

$$< h, E [\tilde{U}(t|t) \circ y(a)] h > = 0 \tag{3.212}$$

for all h. Therefore, $\hat{U}(t|t)$ is a solution of the filtering problem.

On the other hand, let us assume that $\hat{U}(t|t)$ is a solution of the filtering problem. If we assume that (3.205) does not hold, then

$$E [\tilde{U}(t|t) \circ [Z(\sigma) - Z(\tau)]] = \mathrm{Cov} [\tilde{U}(t|t), Z(\sigma) - Z(\tau)] \neq 0 \tag{3.213}$$

for some σ , τ with $t_0 \leq \tau < \sigma \leq t$.

If we let B(t,s) be given by

$$B(t,s) = \begin{cases} 0, & s < \tau , \\ \mathrm{Cov}\ [\ \tilde{U}(t|t),\ Z(\sigma) - Z(\tau)\ ], & \tau \leqq s \leqq \sigma , \\ 0, & s > \sigma , \end{cases}$$

then B(t,s) is regulated (in fact, a step function) and

$$y(t) = \int_{t_0}^{t} B(t,s)\ d\ Z(s) = \mathrm{Cov}\ [\ \tilde{U}(t|t),\ Z(\sigma) - Z(\tau)]\ (\ Z(\sigma) - Z(\tau)).$$

Thus,

$$E\ [\ <h,\ \tilde{U}(t|t)><h,\ y(t)>\ ] = <h,\ E\ [\ \tilde{U}(t|t)\circ y(t)\ ]\ h>$$

$$= <h,\ E\ [\ \tilde{U}(t|t)\circ \mathrm{Cov}\ [\ \tilde{U}(t|t),\ Z(\sigma) - Z(\tau)](\ Z(\sigma) - Z(\alpha))\ ]\ h> \quad (3.214)$$

$$= <h,\ \mathrm{Cov}\ [\ \tilde{U}(t|t),\ Z(\sigma) - Z(\tau)\ ]\ \mathrm{Cov}\ [\ \tilde{U}(t|t),\ Z(\sigma) - Z(\tau)\ ]^{*}\ h>.$$

But (3.213) implies that there is some h for which the right hand side of (3.214) is not zero. This contradicts that $\tilde{U}(t|t)$ is a solution of the optimal filtering problem. By an approximation argument the only if part is proved.
Thus, the proof of the theorem is completed. Q.E.D.

Derivations of the optimal filter

Let us now derive the equation governing the optimal filter by using some properties of covariance operators and hence, let us begin with some lemmas.

[LEMMA 3.5] Let $\Phi(s)$ and $\Psi(s)$ be elements of $L^2(t_0,t_f\ ;\ \mathcal{L}(\mathcal{H},\mathcal{H}))$ and $L^2(t_0,t_f\ ;\ \mathcal{L}(\mathcal{K},\mathcal{K}))$, respectively. Then

$$\mathrm{Cov}\ [\ \int_{t_0}^{t} \Phi(s)\ d\ W(s),\ \int_{t_0}^{t} \Psi(s)\ d\ V(s)\ ] = 0 \quad (3.215)$$

and

$$\mathrm{Cov}\ [\ \int_{t_0}^{t} \Phi(s)\ d\ W(s),\ \int_{t_0}^{t} \Psi(s)\ d\ W(s)\ ] = \int_{t_0}^{t} \Phi(s)\mathcal{W}(s)\ \Psi^{*}(s)\ ds. \quad (3.216)$$

[PROOF] In view of Lemma 2.2 and the fact that

$$E\left[\int_{t_0}^{t} \Phi(s)\, d\, W(s)\right] = 0 \tag{3.217}$$

we can see that (3.216) holds by an approximation argument . As for (3.215), we can only need to establish that

$$E\left[\left(\int_{t_0}^{t} \Phi(s)\, d\, W(s)\right) \circ \left(\int_{t_0}^{t} \Psi(s)\, d\, V(s)\right)\right] = 0 \tag{3.218}$$

for step functions $\Phi(s)$ and $\Psi(s)$ since the general result will then follow by an approximation argument. By adding 0's if necessary, we can suppose that there are $a_0 \leqq a_1 \leqq \cdots \leqq a_n$ in $[\ t_0,\ t_f\ ]$ such that

$$\Phi(a) = \begin{cases} 0, & a < a_0 \\ \Phi_j, & a_{j-1} \leqq a < a_j \\ 0, & a \geqq a_n, \end{cases} \qquad \Psi(a) = \begin{cases} 0, & a < a_0 \\ \Psi_k, & a_{k-1} \leqq a < a_k \\ 0, & a > a_n. \end{cases} \tag{3.219}$$

It then follows that

$$\left[\int_{t_0}^{t} \Phi(a)\, d\, W(a)\right] \circ \left[\int_{t_0}^{t} \Psi(a)\, d\, V(a)\right]$$

$$= \sum_{j,k=1}^{n} \Phi_j \left[\ W(a_j) - W(a_{j-1})\ \right] \circ \left[\ V(a_k) - V(a_{k-1})\ \right] \Psi_k^*$$

and hence that (3.218) holds since $\mathrm{Cov}\,[\ W(t),\ V(s)\ ] = 0$ for all t, s. Thus, the proof of the lemma is completed. Q.E.D.

Now , for simplicity of exposition, let us set $\Delta Z(\sigma) = Z(\sigma) - Z(t_0)$ where $t_0 \leqq \sigma \leqq t$. Then

$$\Delta Z(\sigma) = \int_{t_0}^{\sigma} H(s)\, U(s)\, ds + \int_{t_0}^{\sigma} d\, V(s).$$

Using Theorem 2.2, we have

$$\Delta Z(\sigma) = \int_{t_0}^{\sigma} H(s)\, \mathcal{U}(s,t_0)\, U_0\, ds + \int_{t_0}^{\sigma} H(s) \left[\int_{t_0}^{s} \mathcal{U}(s,t_0)\, C(a)\, d\, W(a)\right] ds$$

$$+ \int_{t_0}^{\sigma} d\, V(s) \tag{3.220}$$

where $\mathcal{U}(\cdot, \cdot)$ is the fundamental linear transformation of the system, that is, the evolution operator of $A(t)$. Since $H(t)$ and $\mathcal{U}(s,a)$ are regulated and $C(a)$ is in $L^2(t_0,t_f; \mathcal{L}(\mathcal{H},\mathcal{H}))$, we can deduce from Lemma 2.8 that

$$\Delta Z(\sigma) = \int_{t_0}^{\sigma} H(s)\, \mathcal{U}(s, t_0)\, U_0\, ds + \int_{t_0}^{\sigma} d\, V(a)$$

$$+ \int_{t_0}^{\sigma} [\int_{a}^{\sigma} H(s)\, \mathcal{U}(s,a)\, ds]\, C(a)\, d\, W(a).$$

To simplify notation, we shall let $\phi_\sigma(a)$ be given by

$$\phi_\sigma(a) = \int_{a}^{\sigma} H(s)\, \mathcal{U}(s, a)\, ds. \tag{3.221}$$

We have the following lemma:

[LEMMA 3.6] Suppose that $\mathrm{Cov}\, [W(t), U_0] = 0$ for all t and that $K(t,s)$ is in $L^2([t_0,t_f] \times [t_0,t_f], \mathcal{L}(\mathcal{H},\mathcal{H}))$. Then

$$\mathrm{Cov}\, [\int_{t_0}^{t} K(t,s)\, d\, W(s),\ \Delta Z(\sigma)] = \int_{t_0}^{\sigma} K(t,s)\, \mathcal{W}(s)\, C^*(s)\, \phi_\sigma^*(s)\, ds. \tag{3.222}$$

[PROOF] Setting $\Psi(a) = \phi_\sigma(a)\, C(a)$ for $a \le \sigma$ and $\Psi(a) = 0$ for $a > \sigma$ and noting that

$$\mathrm{Cov}\, [\int_{t_0}^{t} K(t,s)\, d\, W(s),\ U_0] = 0,$$

we have from Lemma 3.5

$$\mathrm{Cov}\, [\int_{t_0}^{t} K(t,s)\, d\, W(s),\ \Delta Z(\sigma)]$$

$$= \mathrm{Cov}\, [\int_{t_0}^{t} K(t,s)\, d\, W(s),\ \int_{t_0}^{t} \Psi(s)\, d\, W(s)] = \int_{t_0}^{t} K(t,s)\, \mathcal{W}(s)\, \Psi^*(s)\, ds.$$

The lemma follows immediately. Thus, the proof of the lemma is completed.

Q.E.D.

Now if a(t) and b(t) are random processes with Cov [a(t), b(t)] = h(t) (a sure function), then it is natural to set

$$\frac{d}{dt} \text{ Cov } [\ a(t),\ b(t)\ ] = \frac{d}{dt} h(t) = \dot{h}(t)$$

whenever $\dot{h}(t)$ exists. Bearing this in mind, we have the following corollary:

[COROLLARY 3.4] If Cov [W(t), U_0] = 0, if K(t,s) is in $L^2([t_0,t_f] \times [t_0,t_f];$ $\mathcal{L}(\mathcal{H},\mathcal{H}))$ and if $\partial K(t,s)/\partial t$ exists, is regulated in t,and is L^2 in s, then

$$\frac{d}{dt} \text{ Cov } [\ \int_{t_0}^{t} K(t,s)\, d\, W(s),\ \Delta Z(\sigma)\ ]$$

$$= \text{Cov } [\ \int_{t_0}^{t} \frac{\partial K(t,s)}{\partial t}\, d\, W(s),\ \Delta Z(\sigma)\ ] \qquad \text{for } \sigma < t.$$

Then we have the following corollary:

[COROLLARY 3.5] If Cov [V(t), U_0] = 0, then for $\sigma < t$

$$\frac{d}{dt} \text{ Cov } [\ U(t),\ \Delta Z(\sigma)\ ] = \text{ Cov } [\ A(t)\, U(t),\ \Delta Z(\sigma)\ ]. \tag{3.223}$$

[PROOF] Let $K(t,s) = \mathcal{U}(\, t,\ s)\, C(s)$ and let apply Corollary 3.5. Thus, the proof of the corollary is completed. Q.E.D.

We then have the following lemma:

[LEMMA 3.7] Suppose that L(t,s) is regulated. Then

$$\text{Cov } [\ \int_{t_0}^{t} L(t,s)\, d\, Z(s),\ \Delta Z(\sigma)\ ]$$

$$= \int_{t_0}^{t} \psi(t,s)\, C(s)\, \mathcal{W}(s)\, C^*(s)\ \phi_\sigma^*(s)\, ds + \int_{t_0}^{t} L(t,s)\, \mathcal{V}(s)\, ds$$

$$+ \int_{t_0}^{t} L(t,s)\, H(s)\, \mathcal{U}(s,t_0)\, ds\, P_0\ \phi_\sigma^*(t_0) \tag{3.224}$$

where

$$\psi(t,s) = \int_{s}^{t} L(t,a)\, H(a)\, \mathcal{U}(a,s)\, da \tag{3.225}$$

$$P_0 = \text{Cov}\,[\,U_0,\ U_0\,]$$

and $\phi_\sigma(a)$ is given by (3.221).

[PROOF] First of all, we note that

$$\int_{t_0}^{t} L(t,s)\, d\,Z(s) = \int_{t_0}^{t} L(t,s)\, H(s)\, (\ \mathcal{U}(s,t_0)\, U_0$$

$$+ \int_{t_0}^{s} \mathcal{U}(s,a)\, C(a)\, d\,W(a)\ )\, ds\ +\ \int_{t_0}^{t} L(t,s)\, d\,V(s).$$

However, in view of (3.220), Lemma 3.5, the independence of U_0 and both $W(t)$ and $V(t)$, and Lemma 2.8, we readily see that

$$\text{Cov}\,[\ \int_{t_0}^{t} L(t,s)\, d\,Z(s),\ \ \Delta Z(\sigma)\ ]$$

$$= \text{Cov}\,[\ \int_{t_0}^{t} \psi(t,s)\, C(s)\, d\,W(s),\ \Delta Z(\sigma)\ ] + \int_{t_0}^{t} L(t,s)\, \mathcal{V}(s)\, ds$$

$$+ \int_{t_0}^{t} L(t,s)\, H(s)\, \mathcal{U}(s,t_0)\, ds\ P_0\ \ \phi_\sigma^{*}(t_0).$$

The lemma then follows immediately from Lemma 3.6.

Thus, the proof of the lemma is completed. Q.E.D.

[COROLLARY 3.6] If $\partial L(t,s)/\partial t$ exists and is regulated, then for $\sigma < t$

$$\frac{d}{dt}\, \text{Cov}\,[\ \int_{t_0}^{t} L(t,s)\, d\,Z(s),\ \ \Delta Z(\sigma)\ ]$$

$$= \text{Cov}\,[\int_{t_0}^{t} \frac{\partial L(t,s)}{\partial t}\, d\,Z(s) + L(t,t)\, H(t)\, U(t),\ \Delta Z(\sigma)\ ]. \tag{3.226}$$

The proof of the corollary is a straightforward calculation and is therefore omitted.

These lemmas and corollaries lead to the following theorem:

[THEOREM 3.17] Suppose that there is a solution of the filtering problem of the form

$$\hat{U}(t|t) = \int_{t_0}^{t} L(t,s)\, d\,Z(s) \tag{3.227}$$

with $\partial L(t,s)/\partial t$ regulated. Then

$$\frac{\partial L(t,s)}{\partial t} = A(t)\,L(t,s) - L(t,t)\,H(t)\,L(t,s) \tag{3.228}$$

for $t_0 \leq s \leq t$.

[PROOF] Since $\hat{U}(t|t)$ is a solution of the filtering problem, we have by virtue of Theorem 3.16

$$\frac{d}{dt}\,\mathrm{Cov}\,[\,U(t),\ \Delta Z(\sigma)\,] = \frac{d}{dt}\,\mathrm{Cov}\,[\,\int_{t_0}^{t} L(t,s)\,d\,Z(s),\ \ \Delta Z(\sigma)\,].$$

It follows from Corollaries 3.5, 3.6, and Theorem 3.16 that

$$\mathrm{Cov}\,[\,\int_{t_0}^{t}\ (\,A(t)\,L(t,s) - \frac{\partial L(t,s)}{\partial t} - L(t,t)\,H(t)\,L(t,s)\,)\,d\,Z(s),\ \Delta Z(\sigma)\,]$$

$$= 0$$

and hence that

$$\mathrm{Cov}\,[\,\int_{t_0}^{t}\ (\,A(t)\,L(t,s) - \frac{\partial L(t,s)}{\partial t} - L(t,t)\,H(t)\,L(t,s)\,)\,d\,Z(s),$$

$$Z(\sigma) - Z(\tau)\,] = 0 \tag{3.229}$$

since $Z(\sigma) - Z(\tau) = \Delta Z(\sigma) - \Delta Z(\tau)$. Setting

$$\Delta(t,s) = A(t)\,L(t,s) - \frac{\partial L(t,s)}{\partial t} - L(t,t)\,H(t)\,L(t,s), \tag{3.230}$$

we observe that (3.229) implies that

$$\hat{y}(t|t) = \int_{t_0}^{t} [\,L(t,s) + \Delta(t,s)\,]\,d\,Z(s)$$

satisfies (3.204) and hence is a solution of the filtering problem. As a consequence of the orthogonal projection lemma [2,10],

$$E\,[\,<h,\ \hat{y}(t|t) - \hat{U}(t|t)>^2\,] = 0 \qquad \text{for all } h \in \mathcal{H}\,. \tag{3.231}$$

In other words,

$$< h, \mathrm{Cov} [\int_{t_0}^{t} \Delta(t,s) \, d Z(s), \int_{t_0}^{t} \Delta(t,s) \, d Z(s)] h > = 0 \tag{3.232}$$

for all $h \in \mathcal{H}$. But

$$\mathrm{Cov} [\int_{t_0}^{t} \Delta(t,s) \, d Z(s), \int_{t_0}^{t} \Delta(t,s) \, d Z(s)]$$

$$= \int_{t_0}^{t} \Delta(t,s) \, \mathcal{V}(s) \, \Delta^*(t,s) \, ds + \mathrm{Cov} [\int_{t_0}^{t} \Delta(t,s) H(s) U(s) \, ds,$$

$$\int_{t_0}^{t} \Delta(t,s) H(s) U(s) \, ds].$$

Since $\mathcal{V}(s)$ is positive definite for all s, we immediately conclude that $\Delta(t,s) = 0$. Thus, the proof of the theorem is completed. Q.E.D.

Then we have the following lemma.

[LEMMA 3.8] Under the same hypotheses as Theorem 3.17, $\hat{U}(t|t)$ satisfies the linear stochastic differential equation in Hilbert space ;

$$d \hat{U}(t|t) = [A(t) - L(t,t) H(t)] \hat{U}(t|t) \, dt + L(t,t) \, d Z(t)$$

$$= A(t) \hat{U}(t|t) \, dt + L(t,t) \, d \nu(t) \tag{3.233}$$

where

$$d \nu(t) = d Z(t) - H(t) \hat{U}(t|t) \, dt \tag{3.234}$$

$$\hat{U}(t_0|t_0) = 0. \tag{3.235}$$

[PROOF] We know that

$$\hat{U}(t|t) = \int_{t_0}^{t} L(t,s) \, d Z(s) = \int_{t_0}^{t} L(t,s) H(s) U(s) \, ds + \int_{t_0}^{t} L(t,s) \, d V(s)$$

and hence that

$$\int_{t_0}^{t} [A(s) - L(s,s) H(s)] \hat{U}(s|s) \, ds = \int_{t_0}^{t} D(s) [\int_{t_0}^{t} L(s,a) H(a) U(a) \, da] \, ds$$

$$+ \int_{t_0}^{t} D(s) \left[\int_{t_0}^{t} L(s,a) \, d\, V(a) \right] ds$$

where

$$D(s) = A(s) - L(s,s)\, H(s).$$

Applying Lemma 2.8 and the standard Fubini theorem, we have

$$\int_{t_0}^{t} D(s) \left[\int_{t_0}^{s} L(s,a)\, H(a)\, U(a)\, da \right] ds$$

$$= \int_{t_0}^{t} \left[\int_{a}^{t} D(s)\, L(s,a)\, ds \right] da,$$

$$\int_{t_0}^{t} D(s) \left[\int_{t_0}^{s} L(s,a)\, d\, V(a) \right] ds = \int_{t_0}^{t} \left[\int_{a}^{t} D(s)\, L(s,a)\, ds \right] d\, V(a).$$

It then follows from (3.228) that

$$\int_{t_0}^{t} D(s)\, U(s\ s)\, ds = \int_{t_0}^{t} \left[\int_{a}^{t} \frac{\partial L(s,a)}{\partial s}\, ds \right] d\, Z(a)$$

$$= \int_{t_0}^{t} (L(t,a) - L(a,a))\, d\, Z(a) = \hat{U}(t|t) - \int_{t_0}^{t} L(a,a)\, d\, Z(a).$$

Differentiating each side with respect to t, we obtain (3.223).

Thus, the proof of the lemma is completed. Q.E.D.

[LEMMA 3.9] Under the same hypotheses as Theorem 3.17, $\tilde{U}(t|t)$ satisfies the following linear stochastic differential equation in the Hilbert space $\mathcal{H}$;

$$d\, \tilde{U}(t|t) = [A(t) - L(t,t)\, H(t)]\, \tilde{U}(t|t)\, dt + C(t)\, d\, W(t)$$

$$- L(t,t)\, d\, V(t) \tag{3.236}$$

with $\tilde{U}(t_0|t_0) = U_0$.

Lemmas 3.8 and 3.9 are at the heart of the development of Kalman and Bucy [22]. Continuing in the same vein, we have the following theorem:

[THEOREM 3.18] Suppose that the conditions of the Theorem 3.17 are satisfied. Then

$$L(t,t) = P(t|t)\, H^*(t)\, \mathcal{V}^{-1}(t) \tag{3.237}$$

where $P(t|t)$ is a solution of the Riccati-type equation

$$\frac{d\,P(t|t)}{dt} = A(t)\, P(t|t) + P(t|t)\, A^*(t) - P(t|t)\, \tilde{R}(t)\, P(t|t) + \tilde{Q}(t) \tag{3.238}$$

$$\tilde{R}(t) = H^*(t)\, \mathcal{V}^{-1}(t)\, H(t)$$

$$\tilde{Q}(t) = C(t)\, \mathcal{W}(t)\, C^*(t)$$

with $P(t_0|t_0) = P_0 = \mathrm{Cov}\,[\, U_0,\, U_0\,]$. (3.239)

[PROOF] Let us set

$$y(\sigma) = \int_{t_0}^{\sigma} H(s)\, U(s)\, ds = \Delta Z(\sigma) - \int_{t_0}^{\sigma} d\,V(s).$$

Then we have by direct computation

$$\frac{d\,\mathrm{Cov}\,[\,\tilde{U}(t|t),\, y(\sigma)\,]}{d\sigma} = \mathcal{U}(t,t_0)\, P_0\, \mathcal{U}^*(\sigma,t_0)\, H^*(\sigma)$$

$$+ \int_{t_0}^{\sigma} \mathcal{U}(t,s)\, Q(s)\, \mathcal{U}^*(t_0,s)\, ds\ \ \mathcal{U}^*(\sigma,t_0)\, H^*(\sigma)$$

$$- \psi(t,t_0)\, P_0\, \mathcal{U}^*(\sigma,t_0)\, H^*(\sigma)$$

$$- \int_{t_0}^{\sigma} \psi(t,s)\, \tilde{Q}(s)\, \mathcal{U}^*(t_0,s)\, ds\ \ \mathcal{U}^*(\sigma,t_0)\, H^*(\sigma)$$

and by Theorem 3.16

$$\mathrm{Cov}\,[\,\tilde{U}(t|t),\, y(\sigma)\,] = \int_{t_0}^{\sigma} L(t,s)\, \mathcal{V}(s)\, ds$$

where $\psi(t,s)$ is given by (3.225).

It follows that for $\sigma < t$

$$L(t,\sigma)\,\mathcal{V}(\sigma) = [\,(\,\mathcal{U}(t,t_0) - \psi(t,t_0)\,)\,P_0$$

$$+ \int_{t_0}^{\sigma} (\,\mathcal{U}(t,s) - \psi(t,s))\,Q(s)\,\mathcal{U}^*(t_0,s)\,ds\,]\,\mathcal{U}^*(\sigma,t_0)\,H^*(\sigma). \quad (3.240)$$

Since any regulated function is equivalent to a function continuous on the left in an almost everywhere sense, we can take limits as σ approaches t from below in the above equation and thus deduce that

$$L(t,t) = P(t|t)\,H^*(t)\,\mathcal{V}^{-1}(t)$$

where

$$P(t|t) = [\,(\,\mathcal{U}(t,t_0) - \psi(t,t_0)\,)\,P_0$$

$$+ \int_{t_0}^{t} (\,\mathcal{U}(t,s) - \psi(t,s))\,\tilde{Q}(s)\,\mathcal{U}^*(t_0,s)\,ds\,]\,\mathcal{U}^*(t,t_0). \quad (3.241)$$

Clearly

$$P(t_0|t_0) = P_0.$$

Now we note that

$$\frac{\partial\,\mathcal{U}(t,s)}{\partial t} = A(t)\,\mathcal{U}(t,s), \qquad \frac{\partial\,\mathcal{U}^*(t,t_0)}{\partial t} = \mathcal{U}^*(t,t_0)\,A^*(t)$$

and that

$$\frac{\partial\psi(t,s)}{\partial t} = L(t,t)\,H(t)\,\mathcal{U}(t,s) + \int_s^t (\,A(t)\,L(t,a) - L(t,t)\,H(t)\,L(t,a))\,H(a)\,\mathcal{U}(a,s)\,da \quad (3.242)$$

by Theorem 3.17. Moreover, $L(t,t)\,H(t) = P(t|t)\,\tilde{R}(t)$. Then , the theorem follows from these relations by direct differentiation of (3.240). Thus, the proof of the theorem is completed. Q.E.D.

[LEMMA 3.10] $P(t|t)$ is symmetric.

[PROOF] If $P(t|t)$ satisfies (3.238), then $P^*(t|t)$ also satisfies (3.238). As $P_0 = P_0^*$, the result follows from the uniqueness of solutions of (3.238). Thus, the proof of the lemma is completed. Q.E.D.

[LEMMA 3.11] $P(t|t) = \mathrm{Cov}\,[\,\tilde{U}(t|t),\ \tilde{U}(t|t)\,]$.

[PROOF] We have

$$\mathrm{Cov}\,[\,\tilde{U}(t|t),\ \tilde{U}(t|t)\,] = \mathrm{Cov}\,[\,\tilde{U}(t|t),\ U(t)\,] - \mathrm{Cov}\,[\,\tilde{U}(t|t),\ \hat{U}(t|t)\,]$$

$$\mathrm{Cov}\,[\,\tilde{U}(t\ t),\ U(t)] = \mathrm{Cov}\,[\,U(t),\ U(t)] - \mathrm{Cov}\,[\,\hat{U}(t|t),\ U(t)\,]$$

where

$$\mathrm{Cov}\,[\,U(t),\ U(t)\,] = [\,\mathcal{U}(t,t_0)\,P_0 + \int_{t_0}^{t} \mathcal{U}(t,s)\,Q(s)\,\mathcal{U}^*(t_0,s)\,ds\,]\,\mathcal{U}^*(t,t_0)$$

$$\mathrm{Cov}\,[\,\hat{U}(t|t),\ U(t)\,] = [\,\psi(t,t_0)\,P_0 + \int_{t_0}^{t} \psi(t,s)\,Q(s)\,\mathcal{U}^*(t_0,s)\,ds\,]\,\mathcal{U}^*(t,t_0).$$

By Lemma 3.12 which follows Lemma 3.11, we have

$$\mathrm{Cov}\,[\,\tilde{U}(t|t),\ \hat{U}(t|t)\,] = 0.$$

Thus, the proof of the lemma is completed. Q.E.D.

[LEMMA 3.12] $\mathrm{Cov}\,[\,\tilde{U}(t|t),\ \hat{U}(t|t)\,] = 0.$ (3.243)

[PROOF] We have

$$\mathrm{Cov}\,[\,\tilde{U}(t|t),\ \hat{U}(t|t)\,] = \mathrm{Cov}\,[\,U(t),\ \hat{U}(t|t)\,] - \mathrm{Cov}\,[\,\hat{U}(t|t),\ \hat{U}(t|t)\,]$$

$$\mathrm{Cov}\,[\,U(t),\ \hat{U}(t|t)\,] = \int_{t_0}^{t} \mathcal{U}(t,s)\,Q(s)\,\psi^*(t,s)\,ds + \mathcal{U}(t,t_0)\,P_0\,\psi(t,t_0)^*$$

$$\mathrm{Cov}\,[\,\hat{U}(t|t),\ \hat{U}(t|t)\,] = \int_{t_0}^{t} L(t,s)\,\mathcal{V}(s)\,L^*(t,s)\,ds + \psi(t,t_0)\,P_0\,\psi^*(t,t_0)$$

$$+ \int_{t_0}^{t} \psi(t,s)\,\tilde{Q}(s)\,\psi^*(t,s)\,ds\ .$$

However, $L(t,s)\mathcal{W}(s)$ is given by (3.240) and also the lemma follows by a straightforward calculation and the standard Fubini theorem.

Thus, the proof of the lemma is completed. Q.E.D.

We note that the operator Riccati equation (3.238) is discussed in Kalman et al. [25] and in Falb and Kleinman [26]. In particular, it is shown that (3.238) has a unique solution which is defined on the entire interval of the definition of $A(t)$, $H(t)$, $\mathcal{V}(t)$ and $\mathcal{W}(t)$ in these references. Let us denote this solution by $P(t|t)$ again and $L(t,t) = P(t|t)\, H^*(t)\, \mathcal{V}^{-1}(t)$.

Then the linear stochastic differential equation in the Hilbert space

$$d\,\hat{U}(t|t) = [\, A(t) - L(t,t)\, H(t)\,]\, \hat{U}(t|t)\, dt + L(t,t)\, d\,V(t)$$
$$+ L(t,t)\, H(t)\, U(t)\, dt \tag{3.244}$$

has a solution $\hat{U}(t|t)$ with $\hat{U}(t_0|t_0) = 0$. If $\Psi(t,s)$ is the fundamental linear transformation, that is, the evolution operator of $A(t) - L(t,t)\, H(t)$,

$$\frac{d\,\Psi(t,t_0)}{dt} = [\, A(t) - L(t,t)\, H(t)\,]\, \Psi(t,t_0), \quad \Psi(t_0, t_0) = \mathcal{J}\,, \tag{3.245}$$

then

$$\hat{U}(t|t) = \int_{t_0}^{t} L_1(t,s)\, d\,Z(s) \tag{3.246}$$

where

$$L_1(t,s) = \Psi(t,s)\, L(t,t). \tag{3.247}$$

We observe that $L_1(t,t) = L(t,t)$ and that

$$\frac{\partial L_1(t,s)}{\partial t} = A(t)\, L_1(t,s) - L_1(t,t)\, H(t)\, L_1(t,s). \tag{3.248}$$

Then the following theorem holds:

[THEOREM 3.19] $\hat{U}(t|t)$ is a solution of the filtering problem.

[PROOF] Let us set $\tilde{U}(t|t) = U(t) - \hat{U}(t|t)$. Then, by Theorem 3.16 we need only show that

$$\text{Cov}\ [\ \tilde{U}(t|t),\ \Delta Z(\sigma)\ ] = 0 \quad \text{for } \sigma < t.$$

If $\psi_1(t,s)$ is given by

$$\psi_1(t,s) = \int_s^t L_1(t,a)\, H(a)\, \mathcal{U}(a,s)\, da,$$

then it will follow from (3.248) and the definition of the evolution operator $\mathcal{U}(t,s)$, by direct differentiation that

$$P(t|t) = [\ (\ \mathcal{U}(t,t_0) - \psi_1(t,t_0)\ )\ P_0 + \int_{t_0}^t (\ \mathcal{U}(t,s) - \psi_1(t,s))\ Q(s)\ \mathcal{U}^*(t_0,s)\ ds\ ]\ \mathcal{U}^*(t,t_0). \quad (3.249)$$

Now, a direct computation shows that

$$\frac{d}{d\sigma}\text{Cov}\ [\ \tilde{U}(t|t),\ y(\sigma)\ ] = \text{Cov}\ [\ \tilde{U}(t|t),\ H(\sigma)\ U(\sigma)\ ]$$

$$= \text{Cov}\ [\ U(t),\ H(\sigma)\ U(\sigma)\ ] - \text{Cov}\ [\ \hat{U}(t|t),\ H(\sigma)\ U(\sigma)]$$

$$= \mathcal{U}(t,t_0)\ P_0\ \mathcal{U}^*(\sigma,t_0)\ H^*(\sigma) + \int_{t_0}^{\sigma} \mathcal{U}(t,s)\ \tilde{Q}(s)\ \mathcal{U}^*(t_0,s)\ ds\ \mathcal{U}^*(\sigma,t_0)\ H^*(\sigma)$$

$$- \psi_1(t,t_0)\ P_0\ \mathcal{U}^*(\sigma,t_0)\ H^*(\sigma) - \int_{t_0}^{\sigma} \psi_1(t,s)\ \tilde{Q}(s)\ \mathcal{U}^*(t_0,s)\ ds\ \mathcal{U}^*(\sigma,t_0)\ H^*(\sigma)$$

and that

$$\frac{d}{d\sigma}\text{Cov}\ [\ \hat{U}(t|t),\ \int_{t_0}^{\sigma} d\,V(s)\ ] = -\,L_1(t,\sigma)\,\mathcal{V}(\sigma).$$

Letting $\phi(t,\sigma)$ be given by

$$\phi(t,\sigma) = \frac{d\ \text{Cov}\ [\ \tilde{U}(t|t),\ \Delta Z(\sigma)\ ]}{d\sigma},$$

we have $\phi(\sigma,\sigma) = 0$ and after some straigrtforward computations,

$$\frac{\partial\phi(t,\sigma)}{\partial t} = \frac{d}{d\sigma}\left(\text{Cov}\,[\,\tilde{U}(t|t),\, y(\sigma)\,] + \text{Cov}\,[\,\tilde{U}(t|t),\, \int_{t_0}^{\sigma} d\,V(s)\,]\right)$$

$$= (\,A(t) - L_1(t,t)\,H(t))\,\phi(t,\sigma).$$

Thus, it follows that

$$\phi(t,\sigma) = \Psi(t,\sigma)\,\phi(\sigma,\sigma) = 0.$$

Hence, we have

$$\text{Cov}\,[\,\tilde{U}(t|t),\, \Delta Z(\sigma)\,] = \text{Cov}\,[\,\tilde{U}(t|t),\, \Delta Z(t_0)\,] = \text{Cov}\,[\,\tilde{U}(t|t),\, 0\,] = 0.$$

Thus, the proof of the theorem is completed. Q.E.D.

Theorem 3.19 shows that (3.238) provides the basis for a complete solution to the filtering problem as shown in (3.249). Moreover, this implies that the duality theorem of Kalman and Bucy [22] also holds in the infinite dimensional case. Thus, we have the following theorem:

[THEOREM 3.20] The optimal filtering estimate $\hat{U}(t|t)$ satisfies the linear stochastic differential equation in Hilbert space $\mathcal{H}$;

$$d\,\hat{U}(t|t) = (\,A(t) - L(t,t)\,H(t)\,)\,\hat{U}(t|t)\,dt$$
$$+ L(t,t)\,H(t)\,U(t)\,dt + L(t,t)\,d\,V(t) \tag{3.250}$$

where

$$L(t,t) = P(t|t)\,H^*(t)\,\mathcal{V}^{-1}(t) \tag{3.251}$$

$$P(t|t) = [\,(\mathcal{U}(t,t_0) - \psi(t,t_0))\,P_0$$
$$+ \int_{t_0}^{t} (\,\mathcal{U}(t,s) - \psi(t,s))\,Q(s)\,\mathcal{U}^*(t_0,s)\,ds\,]\,\mathcal{U}^*(t,t_0) \tag{3.251}$$

$$\psi(t,s) = \int_s^t L(t,\tau)\,H(\tau)\,\mathcal{U}(\tau,s)\,d\tau. \tag{3.252}$$

3.2.2. Optimal smoothing problems.

Let us suppose that the state $U(t)$ and the observation $Z(t)$ are given by (3.194) and (3.196), respectively. Then the smoothing problem we consider is to find the best estimate of the state $U(\tau)$ based on the observations $Z(s)$, $t_0 \leqq s \leqq t$, $\tau < t$, which has the form

$$\hat{U}(\tau|t) = \int_{t_0}^{t} K(t,\tau,s)\, d\,Z(s) \tag{3.253}$$

where $K(t,\tau,\cdot) \in L^2([t_0,t_f]\,;\,\mathcal{L}(\mathcal{K},\mathcal{H}))$ for almost all t and τ, and which minimizes the following smoothing estimation error variance function J;

$$J = E\,[\,<h,\,\tilde{U}(\tau|t)>^{2}\,]\,,\ \forall h \in \mathcal{H} \tag{3.254}$$

$$\tilde{U}(\tau|t) = U(\tau) - \hat{U}(\tau|t) \tag{3.255}$$

Note that setting $\tau = t$ implies that (3.253) reduces to the filtering problem which has been discussed in Section 3.2.1.

Derivations of the smoothing estimators

Let us derive the optimal smoothing estimator by using the results of the optimal filtering problem in the preceding section. The following theorem and lemma which involve the Wiener-Hopf equation give the basic necessary and sufficient condition for $\hat{U}(\tau|t)$ to be the optimal smoothing estimate.

[THEOREM 3.21] The smoothing estimate $\hat{U}(\tau|t)$ given by (3.253) is optimal if and only if

$$\mathrm{Cov}\,[\,U(\tau),\,(\,Z(\sigma) - Z(\zeta))\,] = \mathrm{Cov}\,[\,\int_{t_0}^{t} K(t,\tau,s)\, d\,Z(s),\,(\,Z(\sigma) - Z(\zeta))\,] \tag{3.256}$$

for all σ, ζ such that $t_0 \leqq \zeta < \sigma < t$, or equivalently, if and only if

$$E\,[\,\tilde{U}(\tau|t)\ \ (Z(\sigma) - Z(\zeta))\,] = 0 \tag{3.257}$$

for all σ, ζ such that $t_0 \leqq \zeta < \sigma < t$.

[LEMMA 3.13] Let $K(t,\tau,s)$ be the optimal smoothing kernel and let $K(t,\tau,s) + N(t,\tau,s)$ satisfy the Wiener-Hopf equation. Then $N(t,\tau,s) = 0$ for all s such that $t_0 \leqq s \leqq t$.

Theorem 3.21 can be proved by the same way as Theorem 3.16 except that $\tilde{U}(t|t)$ is replaced by $\tilde{U}(\tau|t)$. Furthermore, Lemma 3.13 can be proved by the same way as Lemma 3.1. Thus, the proofs of Theorem 3.21 and Lemma 3.13 are omitted here. Then the next theorem follows.

[THEOREM 3.22] Suppose that there is a solution of the optimal smoothing problem of the form

$$\hat{U}(\tau|t) = \int_{t_0}^{t} K(t,\tau,s)\, d\, Z(s)$$

with $\partial K(t,\tau,s)/\partial t$ regulated. Then

$$\frac{\partial K(t,\tau,s)}{\partial t} = -\,K(t,\tau,t)\, H(t)\, L(t,s) \tag{3.258}$$

where $L(t,s)$ has been given by Theorem 3.17.

[PROOF] Since $\hat{U}(\tau|t)$ is an optimal solution of the smoothing problem, we have by virtue of Theorem 3.21,

$$\frac{d}{dt}\,\mathrm{Cov}\,[\,U(\tau),\ \Delta Z(\sigma)\,] = \frac{d}{dt}\ \mathrm{Cov}\,[\,\int_{t_0}^{t} K(t,\tau,s)\, d\, Z(s),\ \Delta Z(\sigma)\,]$$

where

$$\Delta Z(\sigma) = Z(\sigma) - Z(t_0).$$

It follows from Corollary 3.6 and Theorem 3.21 that

$$\mathrm{Cov}\,[\,\int_{t_0}^{t} \frac{\partial K(t,\tau,s)}{\partial t}\, d\, Z(s) + K(t,\tau,t)\, H(t)\, U(t),\ \ \Delta Z(\sigma)\,]$$

$$= \mathrm{Cov}\left[\int_{t_0}^{t} \left(\frac{\partial K(t,\tau,s)}{\partial t} + K(t,\tau,t)\, H(t)\, L(t,s) \right) d\, Z(s),\ \Delta Z(\sigma) \right] = 0.$$

Hence, from Lemma 3.13 we have

$$\frac{\partial K(t,\tau,s)}{\partial t} + K(t,\tau,s)\, H(t)\, L(t,s) = 0.$$

Thus, the proof of the theorem is completed. Q.E.D.

This leads us to the following theorem.

[THEOREM 3.23] Under the hypotheses of Theorem 3.22, $\hat{U}(\tau|t)$ satisfies the following linear stochastic differential equation in the Hilbert space $\mathcal{H}$:

$$\begin{aligned} d\, \hat{U}(\tau|t) &= K(t,\tau,t) \left[d\, Z(t) - H(t)\, \hat{U}(t|t)\, dt \right] \\ &= K(t,\tau,t)\, d\, \nu(t) \end{aligned} \tag{3.259}$$

where

$$d\, \nu(t) = d\, Z(t) - H(t)\, \hat{U}(t|t)\, dt.$$

[PROOF] Applying the standard Fubini theorem, Lemma 2.8, and Theorem 3.22, we have

$$- \int_{t_0}^{t} K(s,\tau,s)\, H(s)\, \hat{U}(s|s)\, ds = - \int_{t_0}^{t} K(s,\tau,s)\, H(s) \left[\int_{t_0}^{s} L(s,\zeta)\, d\, Z(\zeta) \right] ds$$

$$= \int_{t_0}^{t} \left[\int_{\zeta}^{t} \frac{\partial K(s,\tau,\zeta)}{\partial s}\, ds \right] d\, Z(\zeta) = \int_{t_0}^{t} \left[K(t,\tau,\zeta) - K(\zeta,\tau,\zeta) \right] d\, Z(\zeta)$$

$$= \hat{U}(\tau|t) - \int_{t_0}^{t} K(\zeta,\tau,\zeta)\, d\, Z(\zeta).$$

Hence, the theorem follows from this relation by direct differentiation.

Thus, the proof of the theorem is completed. Q.E.D.

Then from (3.255) and (3.259) we have the following corollary.

[COROLLARY 3.7] Under the same hypotheses as Theorem 3.22, $\tilde{U}(\tau|t)$ satisfies the following linear stochastic differential equation in the Hilbert space $\mathcal{H}$:

$$d\, \tilde{U}(\tau|t) = - K(t,\tau,t) \left[d\, Z(t) - H(t)\, \hat{U}(t|t)\, dt \right] = - K(t,\tau,t)\, d\, \nu(t).$$

Then we have the following theorem.

[THEOREM 3.24] Suppose that the conditions of Theorem 3.22 are satisfied. Then we have

$$K(t,\tau,t) = B(\tau|t)\, H^*(t)\, \mathcal{V}^{-1}(t), \quad \tau < t \tag{3.260}$$

where $B(\tau|t)$ is a solution of the following equation with the initial condition

$$B(\tau|\tau) = P(\tau|\tau) = \text{Cov}\ [\ \tilde{U}(\tau|\tau),\ \tilde{U}(\tau|\tau)\ ];$$

$$\frac{d\, B(\tau|t)}{dt} = B(\tau|t)\ [\ A^*(t) - \tilde{R}(t)\, P(t|t)\ ]. \tag{3.261}$$

Here, $P(t|t)$ is given by (3.238) or (3.251).

[PROOF] Let us set

$$y(\sigma) \triangleq \int_{t_0}^{\sigma} H(s)\, U(s)\, ds = \Delta Z(\sigma) - \int_{t_0}^{\sigma} d\, V(s).$$

Then we have by the direct computation

$$\frac{d}{d\sigma}\ \text{Cov}\ [\ \tilde{U}(\tau|t),\ y(\sigma)\ ] = \text{Cov}\ [\ \tilde{U}(\tau|t),\ H(\sigma)\, U(\sigma)\ ]$$

$$= \text{Cov}\ [\ \tilde{U}(\tau|t),\ U(\sigma)\ ]\ H^*(\sigma)$$

and by Theorem 3.21

$$\text{Cov}\ [\ \tilde{U}(\tau|t),\ y(\sigma)\ ] = \text{Cov}\ [\ U(\sigma) - \hat{U}(\tau|t),\ \Delta Z(\sigma) - \int_{t_0}^{\sigma} d\, V(s)\ ]$$

$$= \text{Cov}\ [\ \hat{U}(\tau|t), \int_{t_0}^{\sigma} d\, V(s)\ ] = \int_{t_0}^{\sigma} K(t,\tau,s)\, \mathcal{V}(s)\, ds.$$

Hence, it follows that for $\sigma < t$

$$K(t,\tau,\sigma)\, \mathcal{V}(\sigma) = V(\tau|\sigma)\, H^*(\sigma)$$

where

$$V(\tau|\sigma) = \text{Cov}\,[\,\tilde{U}(\tau|t),\ U(\sigma)\,].$$

Since any regulated function is equivalent in an almost everywhere sense to a function continuous on the left, we can take limits as σ approaches t from below in the above relation and thus deduce that

$$K(t,\tau,t) = V(\tau|t)\ H^*(t)\,\mathcal{V}^{-1}(t).$$

Let us now derive the time evolution of $V(\tau\,|t)$. Setting $\mu(t,s)$ as

$$\mu(t,s) = \int_s^t K(t,\tau,\alpha)\ H(\alpha)\ \mathcal{U}\,(\alpha,s)\ d\alpha$$

and using Theorem 3.22, we have

$$\frac{\partial\mu(t,s)}{\partial t} = K(t,\tau,t)\ H(t)\ (\,\mathcal{U}(t,s) - \psi(t,s)) \tag{3.262}$$

where $\psi(t,s)$ is given by (3.252).

We note that

$$\hat{U}(\tau|t) = \int_{t_0}^t K(t,\tau,\alpha)\ d\,Z(\alpha) = \int_{t_0}^{\tau} L(\tau,\alpha)\ d\,Z(\alpha) + \int_{\tau}^t K(t,\tau,\alpha)\ d\,Z(\alpha)$$

$$= \hat{U}(\tau|\tau) + \int_{\tau}^t K(t,\tau,\alpha)\ d\,Z(\alpha) \tag{3.263}$$

and

$$d\,Z(\alpha) = H(\alpha)\,\mathcal{U}(\alpha,\tau)\ U(\tau)\ d\alpha + d\,V(\alpha)$$

$$+ \left[\,\int_{\tau}^{\alpha} H(\alpha)\mathcal{U}(\alpha,s)\ C(s)\ d\,W(s)\,\right] d\alpha, \quad \text{for } \tau \leq s \leq \alpha \leq t.$$

Then we have

$$\int_{\tau}^t K(t,\tau,\alpha)\ d\,Z(\alpha) = \mu(t,\tau)\ U(\tau) + \int_{\tau}^t \mu(t,s)\ C(s)\ d\,W(s)$$

$$+ \int_{\tau}^t K(t,\tau,\alpha)\ d\,V(\alpha). \tag{3.264}$$

Hence, it follows that

$$\hat{U}(\tau|t) = \hat{U}(\tau|\tau) + \mu(t,\tau)\, U(\tau)$$

$$+ \int_\tau^t \mu(t,\alpha)\, C(\alpha)\, d\, W(\alpha) + \int_\tau^t K(t,\tau,\alpha)\, d\, V(\alpha).$$

On the other hand, it follows that

$$U(t) = \mathcal{U}(t,\tau)\, U(\tau) + \int_\tau^t \mathcal{U}(t,\alpha)\, C(\alpha)\, d\, W(\alpha).$$

Hence, from Lemma 3.5 we have

$$\text{Cov}\,[\, \hat{U}(\tau|t), U(t)\,] = (\,\text{Cov}\,[\, \hat{U}(\tau|\tau), U(\tau)] + \mu(t,\tau)\,\text{Cov}\,[\, U(\tau), U(\tau)\,]$$

$$+ \int_\tau^t \mu(t,s)\, \tilde{Q}(s)\, \mathcal{U}^*(\tau,s)\, ds\,)\, \mathcal{U}^*(t,\tau). \tag{3.265}$$

Continuing the same vein, we have

$$\text{Cov}\,[\, U(\tau), U(t)\,] = \text{Cov}\,[\, U(\tau), U(\tau)\,]\, \mathcal{U}^*(t,\tau). \tag{3.266}$$

It follows from (3.265) and (3.266) that

$$V(\tau|t) = (\, P(\tau|\tau) - \mu(t,\tau)\, P_\tau$$

$$- \int_\tau^t \mu(t,s)\, \tilde{Q}(s)\, \mathcal{U}^*(\tau,s)\, ds\,)\, \mathcal{U}^*(t,\tau) \tag{3.267}$$

where

$$P_\tau = \text{Cov}\,[\, U(\tau), U(\tau)\,].$$

Hence, it follows from (3.267) that

$$\frac{d\, V(\tau|t)}{dt} = V(\tau|t)\, A^*(t) - (\, \frac{\partial \mu(t,\tau)}{\partial t}\, P_\tau$$

$$+ \int_\tau^t \frac{\partial \mu(t,s)}{\partial t}\, \tilde{Q}(s)\, \mathcal{U}^*(\tau,s)\, ds\,)\, \mathcal{U}^*(t,\tau). \tag{3.268}$$

Substituting (3.262) into (3.268) and taking into consideration of (3.251), we have

$$\frac{d\,V(\tau|t)}{dt} = V(\tau|t)\,A^*(t) - K(t,\tau,t)\,H(t)\,[\,(\mathcal{U}(t,\tau) - \psi(t,\tau))\,P_\tau$$

$$+ \int_\tau^t (\mathcal{U}(t,s) - \psi(t,s))\,\tilde{Q}(s)\,\mathcal{U}^*(\tau,s)\,ds\,]\,\mathcal{U}^*(t,\tau)$$

$$= V(\tau|t)\,A^*(t) - K(t,\tau,t)\,H(t)\,P(t|t).$$

Furthermore, from (3.267) we have

$$V(\tau|\tau) = P(\tau|\tau).$$

Since the uniqueness of the solution for (3.261) is clear, using $K(t,\tau,t)\,H(t) = V(\tau|t)\;\tilde{R}(t)$ yields

$$B(\tau|t) = V(\tau|t) \quad \text{for any} \quad t > \tau .$$

Thus, the proof of the theorem is completed. Q.E.D.

Bearing (3.261) in mind, we have the following corollary.

[COROLLARY 3.8] Under the same hypotheses as Theorem 3.22, $B^*(\tau|t)$ is given by

$$B^*(\tau|t) = (\,\mathcal{U}(t,\tau) - \psi(t,\tau))\,P(\tau|\tau). \tag{3.269}$$

[PROOF] From (3.252) we have

$$\frac{\partial\psi(t,\tau)}{\partial t} = L(t,t)\,H(t)\,\mathcal{U}(t,\tau) + \int_\tau^t \frac{\partial L(t,\alpha)}{\partial t}\,H(\alpha)\,\mathcal{U}(\alpha,\tau)\,d\alpha.$$

Using (3.228) yields

$$\frac{\partial\psi(t,\tau)}{\partial t} = A(t)\,\psi(t,\tau) + L(t,t)\,H(t)\,(\,\mathcal{U}(t,\tau) - \psi(t,\tau)).$$

Hence, we have

$$\left(\frac{\partial \mathcal{U}(t,\tau)}{\partial t} - \frac{\partial \psi(t,\tau)}{t} \right) P(\tau|\tau) = A(t)(\mathcal{U}(t,\tau) - \psi(t,\tau))\, P(\tau|\tau)$$

$$- L(t,t)\, H(t)\, (\mathcal{U}(t,\tau) - \psi(t,\tau))\, P(\tau|\tau).$$

Let us define $N(\tau|t)$ by

$$N(\tau|t) = (\mathcal{U}(t,\tau) - \psi(t,\tau))\, P(\tau|\tau).$$

Then we have

$$\frac{d\, N(\tau|t)}{dt} = (A(t) - L(t,t)\, H(t))\, N(\tau|t).$$

Using (3.251) yields

$$\frac{d\, N^*(\tau|t)}{dt} = N^*(\tau|t)\, (A^*(t) - \tilde{R}(t)\, P(t|t)).$$

Furthermore, from the definition of $N(\tau|t)$ we have

$$N^*(\tau|\tau) = P(\tau|\tau).$$

Then it follows from (3.261) that $N(\tau|t) = B^*(\tau|t)$.

Thus, the proof of the corollary is completed. Q.E.D.

In order to derive the equation for the optimal smoothing error covariance operator, we shall first prove the following lemma.

[LEMMA 3.14] Suppose that $\hat{U}(\tau|t)$ and $\tilde{U}(\tau|t)$ are defined by (3.253) and (3.255), respectively. Then we have

$$\text{(a) } \mathrm{Cov}\,[\, \tilde{U}(\tau|t),\, \hat{U}(\tau|t)\,] = -\,\mu(t,\tau)\, \mathrm{Cov}\,[\, U(\tau),\, \hat{U}(\tau|\tau)\,] \tag{3.270}$$

and

$$\text{(b) } \mathrm{Cov}\,[\, \tilde{U}(\tau|t),\, U(\tau)\,] = P(\tau|\tau) - \mu(t,\tau)\, \mathrm{Cov}\,[\, U(\tau),\, U(\tau)\,]. \tag{3.271}$$

[PROOF] (a) It follows from (3.263) that

$$\tilde{U}(\tau|t) = U(\tau) - \hat{U}(\tau|t) = \tilde{U}(\tau|\tau) - \int_\tau^t K(t,\tau,\alpha)\, d\, Z(\alpha)$$

and

$$\mathrm{Cov}\,[\, \tilde{U}(\tau|t),\ \hat{U}(\tau|t)\,] = \mathrm{Cov}\,[\, \tilde{U}(\tau|t),\ \hat{U}(\tau|\tau)\,]$$
$$+ \mathrm{Cov}\,[\, \tilde{U}(\tau|t),\ \int_\tau^t K(t,\tau,\alpha)\, d\, Z(\alpha)\,].$$

Using (3.264) yields

$$\mathrm{Cov}\,[\, \tilde{U}(\tau|t),\ \hat{U}(\tau|t)\,] = -\, \mu(t,\tau)\, \mathrm{Cov}\,[\, U(\tau),\ \hat{U}(\tau|\tau)\,] \tag{3.272}$$

and

$$\mathrm{Cov}\,[\, \tilde{U}(\tau|t),\ \int_\tau^t K(t,\tau,\alpha)\, d\, Z(\alpha)\,] = P(\tau|\tau)\, \mu^*(t,\tau)$$
$$-\ \mu(t,\tau)\, \mathrm{Cov}\,[\, U(\tau),\ U(\tau)\,]\, \mu^*(t,\tau) - \int_\tau^t \mu(t,\alpha)\, \tilde{Q}(\alpha)\, \mu^*(t,\alpha)\, d\alpha$$
$$-\ \int_\tau^t K(t,\tau,\alpha)\, \mathcal{V}(\alpha)\, K^*(t,\tau,\alpha)\, d\alpha.$$

Substituting (3.260) into the above equation, we have

$$\mathrm{Cov}\,[\, \tilde{U}(\tau|t),\ \int_\tau^t K(t,\tau,\alpha)\, d\, Z(\alpha)\,] = 0. \tag{3.273}$$

Hence, from (3.272) and (3.273) the proof of (a) is completed.

As for (b) we have from (3.263) and (3.264)

$$\mathrm{Cov}\,[\, \tilde{U}(\tau|t),\ U(\tau)\,] = \mathrm{Cov}\,[\, \tilde{U}(\tau|\tau),\ U(\tau)\,]$$
$$-\ \mathrm{Cov}\,[\, \int_\tau^t K(t,\tau,\alpha)\, d\, Z(\alpha),\ U(\tau)\,]$$
$$= P(\tau|\tau) - \mu(t,\tau)\, \mathrm{Cov}\,[\, U(\tau),\ U(\tau)\,].$$

Thus, the proof of the lemma is completed. Q.E.D.

Note that (3.272) means that the usual orthogonality between $\tilde{U}(\tau|t)$ and $\hat{U}(\tau|t)$ does not hold although (3.273) shows that $\tilde{U}(\tau|t)$ is orthogonal to $\int_\tau^t K(t,\tau,\alpha)\, d Z(\alpha)$. From this lemma, we have the following theorem concerning with the smoothing error covariance operator $P(\tau|t) = \text{Cov}\,[\,\tilde{U}(\tau|t), \tilde{U}(\tau|t)\,]$.

[THEOREM 3.25] The optimal smoothing error covariance operator $P(\tau|t)$ is given by

$$P(\tau|t) = P(\tau|\tau) - \mu(t,\tau)\, P(\tau|\tau). \tag{3.274}$$

Furthermore, as the differential form of (3.274) we have

$$\frac{d\, P(\tau|t)}{dt} = -\, B(\tau|t)\, \tilde{R}(t)\, B^*(\tau|t) \tag{3.275}$$

with the initial condition $P(\tau|\tau)$.

[PROOF] From the definition of $P(\tau|t)$, we have

$$P(\tau|t) = \text{Cov}\,[\,\tilde{U}(\tau|t), U(\tau)\,] - \text{Cov}\,[\,\tilde{U}(\tau|t), \hat{U}(\tau|t)\,]$$

and using Lemma 3.14 yields

$$P(\tau|t) = P(\tau|\tau) - \mu(t,\tau)\, \text{Cov}\,[\,U(\tau), \tilde{U}(\tau|\tau)\,]$$

$$= P(\tau|\tau) - \mu(t,\tau)\, P(\tau|\tau).$$

Hence, (3.274) is established.

Differentiating (3.274) with respect to time t, we have

$$\frac{d\, P(\tau|t)}{dt} = -\frac{\partial \mu(t,\tau)}{\partial t}\, P(\tau|\tau)$$

and it follows from the definition $\mu(t,\tau)$ that

$$\frac{d\, P(\tau|t)}{dt} = -\, K(t,\tau,t)\, H(t)\, (\,\mathcal{U}(t,\tau) - \psi(t,\tau))\, P(\tau|\tau).$$

Using Corollary 3.8 and (3.260) yields

$$\frac{d\,P(\tau|t)}{dt} = -\,B(\tau|t)\,\tilde{R}(t)\,B^*(\tau|t).$$

Since the initial condition of $P(\tau|t)$ is $P(\tau|\tau)$, (3.275) is obtained. Thus, the proof of the theorem is completed. Q.E.D.

If the underlying spaces are finite dimensional, then $A(\cdot)$, $C(\cdot)$, and $H(\cdot)$ become matrices, and the results derived here can be reduced to those of the lumped parameter systems obtained by using the Kalman's limiting procedure [24].

Let us define the evolution operator of $A(t) - P(t|t)\,R(t)$ by $\mathcal{U}_A(t,\tau)$;

$$\frac{\partial\,\mathcal{U}_A(t,\tau)}{\partial t} = (\,A(t) - P(t|t)\,\tilde{R}(t)\,)\,\mathcal{U}_A(t,\tau) \tag{3.276}$$

$$\mathcal{U}_A(\tau,\tau) = \mathcal{I}.$$

Then the following lemma holds.

[LEMMA 3.15] The solution $B(\tau|t)$ of (3.261) is given by the following relation:

$$B(\tau|t) = P(\tau|\tau)\,\mathcal{U}_A^*(t,\tau). \tag{3.277}$$

[PROOF] By direct differentiation of (3.277) with respect to t, it is easily seen that $B(\tau|t)$ given by (3.277) satisfies (3.261). Since the solution of (3.261) is unique, $B(\tau|t)$ of (3.277) is a unique solution of (3.261). Thus, the proof of the lemma is completed. Q.E.D.

Then the following lemma holds.

[LEMMA 3.16] The solution $P(\tau|t)$ of (3.275) is given by the following relation:

$$P(\tau|t) = P(\tau|\tau) - P(\tau|\tau)\int_\tau^t \mathcal{U}_A^*(\alpha,\tau)\,\tilde{R}(\alpha)\,\mathcal{U}_A(\alpha,\tau)\,d\alpha\;P(\tau|\tau). \tag{3.278}$$

[PROOF] Integrating each side of (3.275) with respect to t, we have

$$P(\tau|t) = P(\tau|\tau) - \int_\tau^t B(\tau|\alpha)\,\tilde{R}(\alpha)\,B^*(\tau|\alpha)\,d\alpha.$$

Substituting (3.277) into the above equation yields (3.278).

Thus, the proof of the lemma is completed. Q.E.D.

Then the following theorem holds.

[THEOREM 3.26] The optimal smoothing estimator satisfies the following relations:

$$\hat{U}(\tau|t) = \hat{U}(\tau|\tau) + P(\tau|\tau)\,\lambda(\tau,t) \tag{3.279}$$

$$\lambda(\tau,t) = \int_\tau^t \mathcal{U}_A^*(\alpha,\tau)\,H^*(\alpha)\,\mathcal{V}^{-1}(\alpha)\,d\nu(\alpha) \tag{3.280}$$

$$B(\tau|t) = P(\tau|\tau)\,\mathcal{U}_A^*(t,\tau) \tag{3.281}$$

$$P(\tau|t) = P(\tau|\tau) - P(\tau|\tau)\int_\tau^t \mathcal{U}_A^*(\alpha,\tau)\,\tilde{R}(\alpha)\,\mathcal{U}_A(\alpha,\tau)\,d\alpha\,P(\tau|\tau). \tag{3.282}$$

[PROOF] From (3.259), (3.260), and Lemma 3.15, we have (3.279).

Thus, the proof of the theorem is completed. Q.E.D.

Based on these expressions, the various types of smoothing estimators can be derived.

Fixed-point smoothing

Substituting $\tau = t_1$ into (3.279)-(3.282) yields the following theorem.

[THEOREM 3.27] The fixed-point smoothing estimator $\hat{U}(t_1|t)$ satisfies the following equations:

$$d\,\hat{U}(t_1|t) = B(t_1|t)\,H^*(t)\,\mathcal{V}^{-1}(t)\,d\nu(t) \tag{3.283}$$

$$\frac{d\,B(t_1|t)}{dt} = B(t_1|t)\,(A(t) - P(t|t)\,\tilde{R}(t))^* \tag{3.284}$$

$$B(t_1|t_1) = P(t_1|t_1)$$

$$\frac{d\,P(t_1|t)}{dt} = -\,B(t_1|t)\,\tilde{R}(t)\,B(t_1|t). \tag{3.285}$$

Fixed-interval smoothing

Substituting $\tau = t$ and $t = T$ fixed, into (3.279)-(3.282) yields the following theorem.

[THEOREM 3.28] The fixed-interval smoothing estimator $\hat{U}(t|T)$ satisfies the following equations:

$$d\,\hat{U}(t|T) = A(t)\,\hat{U}(t|T)\,dt + \tilde{Q}(t)\,P^{-1}(t|t)\,(\,\hat{U}(t|T) - \hat{U}(t|t))\,dt \tag{3.286}$$

$$\frac{d\,P(t|T)}{dt} = (\,A(t) + \tilde{Q}(t)\,P^{-1}(t|t))\,P(t|T)$$
$$+\;P(t|T)\,(\,A(t) + \tilde{Q}(t)\,P^{-1}(t|t))^{*} - \tilde{Q}(t). \tag{3.287}$$

Fixed-lag smoothing

Substituting $\tau = t$ and $t = t + \nabla$, $\nabla > 0$ into (3.279)-(3.282) yields the following theorem.

[THEOREM 3.29] The fixed-lag smoothing estimate $\hat{U}(t|t+\nabla)$ satisfies the following equations:

$$d\,\hat{U}(t|t+\nabla) = A(t)\,\hat{U}(t|t+\nabla)\,dt + G(t+\nabla)\,P(t+\nabla|t+\nabla)\,H^{*}(t+\nabla)\,\mho^{-1}(t+\nabla)$$
$$(\,d\,Z(t+\nabla) - H(t+\nabla)\,\hat{U}(t+\nabla|t+\nabla)dt\,) + \tilde{Q}(t)\,P^{-1}(t|t)\,(\,\hat{U}(t|t+\nabla) - \hat{U}(t|t))\,dt$$
$$\tag{3.288}$$

$$\frac{d\,G(t+\nabla)}{dt} = \tilde{Q}(t)\,P^{-1}(t|t)\,G(t+\nabla) - G(t+\nabla)\,\tilde{Q}(t+\nabla)\,P^{-1}(t+\nabla|t+\nabla)$$
$$+\,A(t)\,G(t+\nabla) - G(t+\nabla)\,A(t+\nabla) \tag{3.289}$$

$$G(t_0+\nabla) = B(t_0|t_0+\nabla)$$

$$\frac{d\,P(t|t+\nabla)}{dt} = (\ A(t) + \tilde{Q}(t)\ P^{-1}(t|t)\ )\ P(t|t+\nabla)$$

$$+ P(t|t+\nabla)\ (\ A(t) + \tilde{Q}(t)\ P^{-1}(t|t)\ )^*$$

$$- B(t|t+\nabla)\ \tilde{R}(t)\ B^*(t|t+\nabla)\ - \tilde{Q}(t) \qquad (3.290)$$

with the initial condition $P(t_0|t_0+\nabla)$.

An application to a distributed parameter system

We now briefly give an application of the results in this section to a smoothing problem for a distributed parameter system of parabolic type with discrete observations on the spatial domain D. Let A(t) be an elliptic differential operator of order 2 in a bounded open domain D;

$$A(t) \triangleq \Sigma_{i,j=1}^{r}\ \partial/\partial x_i\ (\ a_{ij}(t,x)\ \partial/\partial x_j).$$

Assume that $a_{ij}(t,x)$ and the boundary of D denoted by S are sufficiently smooth. The domain $\mathcal{D}(A)$ of A(t) consists of all the smooth functions satisfying the Dirichlet boundary conditions or, in fact, any set of regular boundary conditions. Then A(t) can be extended into a closed operator in $L^p(D)$ for any $1 < p < \infty$ [14] and it satisfies the conditions (i)-(iii) in Section 3.2.1.

Hence, we can apply Theorems 3.27- 3.29 to the following distributed parameter system;

$$\frac{\partial U(t,x)}{\partial t} = \Sigma_{i,j=1}^{r}\ \frac{\partial}{\partial x_i}\ (\ a_{ij}(t,x)\ \frac{\partial U(t,x)}{\partial x_j}\ ) + C(t,x)\ \dot{W}(t,x) \qquad (3.290)$$

$$\Gamma_\xi U(t,\xi) = 0, \quad \forall \xi \in S$$

$$U(t_0,x) = U_0(x).$$

$$\dot{Z}(t) = U_m(t) + \dot{V}(t) \tag{3.291}$$

where

$$V(t) = (\, v_1(t), \cdots, v_m(t) \,)', \quad Z(t) = (\, z_1(t), \cdots, z_m(t) \,)$$

and

$$U_m(t) = (\, \int_{D_1} U(t,x)\, dx, \quad \cdots, \quad \int_{D_m} U(t,x)\, dx \,)'.$$

For simplicity of the expression, we assume that $R(t) = r\,I$, $r > 0$ where I denotes the $m \times m$ identity matrix. Then the fixed-point smoothing estimator $\hat{U}(t_1|t)$ is given by the following relation.

$$\frac{\partial \hat{U}(t_1,x|t)}{\partial t} = \frac{1}{r} \Sigma_{k=1}^{m} \int_{D_k} B(t_1,x,y|t)\, dy\, [\, \dot{z}_k(t) - \int_{D_k} \hat{U}(t,x|t) dx \,]$$

$$\Gamma_\xi \hat{U}(t_1,\xi|t) = 0, \ \forall \xi \in S$$

where

$$\frac{\partial B(t_1,x,y|t)}{\partial t} = \Sigma_{i,j=1}^{r} \frac{\partial}{\partial x_i} (\, a_{ij}(t,x) \frac{\partial B(t_1,x,y\ t)}{\partial x_j} \,)$$

$$- \frac{1}{r} \Sigma_{k=1}^{m} \int_{D_k} B(t_1,x,y|t)\, dy \int_{D_k} P(t,x,y|t)\, dx$$

$$\Gamma_\xi B(t_1,x,\xi|t) = 0, \quad \forall \xi \in S$$

$$B(t_1,x,y|t_1) = P(t_1,x,y|t_1).$$

Furthermore, the smoothing error covariance function $P(t_1,x,y|t)$ is given by

$$\frac{d\, P(t_1,x,y|t)}{dt} = -\frac{1}{r} \Sigma_{k=1}^{m} \int_{D_k} B(t_1,x,y|t)\, dy \int_{D_k} B(t_1,x,y|t)\, dx$$

$$\Gamma_\xi P(t_1,x,\xi|t) = 0, \ \forall \xi \in S.$$

3.2.3. Optimal prediction problems.

Let us suppose that the state U(t) and the observation Z(t) are given by (3.194) and (3.196), respectively. Then the prediction problem we consider is to find the best estimate of the state $U(\tau)$ based on the observed data Z(s), $t_0 \leqq s \leqq t$, $\tau > t$, which has the form

$$\hat{U}(\tau|t) = \int_{t_0}^{t} M(t,\tau,s)\, d\, Z(s) \tag{3.292}$$

where $M(t,\tau,\cdot) \in L^2([t_0,t_f] ; \mathcal{L}(\mathcal{K}, \mathcal{H}))$ for almost all t and τ, and which minimizes the following prediction estimation error variance function J;

$$J = E[\langle h, \tilde{U}(\tau|t) \rangle^2], \quad \forall h \in \mathcal{H} \tag{3.293}$$

$$\tilde{U}(\tau|t) = U(\tau) - \hat{U}(\tau|t). \tag{3.294}$$

Then the following Wiener-Hopf theorem holds.

[THEOREM 3.30] A necessary and sufficient condition for the estimate (3.292) to be optimal is that the Wiener-Hopf equation

$$\int_{t_0}^{t} M(t,\tau,\sigma)\, E[Z(\sigma)\, Z'(\alpha)]\, d\sigma = E[U(\tau)\, Z'(\alpha)] \tag{3.295}$$

holds for $t_0 \leqq \alpha < t$. (3.295) is equivalent to

$$E[\tilde{U}(\tau|t)\, Z'(\alpha)] = 0, \quad t_0 \leqq \alpha < t. \tag{3.296}$$

Furthermore, the optimal kernel $M(t,\tau,\sigma)$ is unique.

Since the proof of this theorem is directly obtained from Theorem 3.16, the proof of this theorem is omitted here.

Then the following theorem holds.

[THEOREM 3.31] The optimal prediction estimate $\hat{U}(\tau|t)$ is given by the following relation:

$$\frac{\partial \hat{U}(\tau|t)}{\partial \tau} = A(\tau)\ \hat{U}(\tau|t) \tag{3.297}$$

where the initial condition of (3.297) is $\hat{U}(t|t)$.

[PROOF]   Differentiating (3.295) with respect to τ yields

$$\int_{t_0}^{t} \partial M(t,\tau,\sigma)/\partial\tau\ E\ [\ Z(\sigma)\ Z'(\alpha)\ ]\ d\sigma\ = E\ [\ \partial U(\tau)/\partial\tau\ Z'(\alpha)\ ]$$

$$= A(\tau)\ E\ [\ U(\tau)\ Z'(\alpha)\ ].$$

Using the Wiener-Hopf equation (3.295) yields

$$\int_{t_0}^{t} (\ \partial M(t,\tau,\sigma)/\partial\tau\ + A(\tau)\ M(t,\tau,\sigma))\ E\ [\ Z(\sigma)\ Z'(\alpha)\ ]\ d\sigma\ = 0.$$

From the uniqueness of the kernel function $M(t,\tau,\sigma)$, we have

$$\frac{\partial M(t,\tau,\sigma)}{\partial \tau} = A(\tau)\ M(t,\tau,\sigma).$$

Then differentiating (3.292) with respect to τ and substituting the above relation, we have

$$\frac{\partial \hat{U}(\tau|t)}{\partial \tau} = \int_{t_0}^{t} A(\tau)\ M(t,\tau,\sigma)\ Z(\sigma)\ d\sigma\ = A(\tau)\ \hat{U}(\tau|t).$$

Thus, the proof of the theorem is completed.   Q.E.D.

Then the following theorem holds.

[THEOREM 3.32]   The optimal prediction error covariance operator $P(\tau|t)$ is given by the following relation:

$$\frac{d\,P(\tau|t)}{d\tau} = A(\tau)\ P(\tau|t) + P(\tau|t)\ A^*(\tau) + \tilde{Q}(\tau) \tag{3.298}$$

where the initial condition of (3.298) is $P(t|t)$.

[PROOF]   From (3.294) and (3.297), we have

$$d\,\tilde{U}(\tau|t) = A(\tau)\,\tilde{U}(\tau|t)\,d\tau + C(\tau)\,d\,W(\tau).$$

Using the evolution operator $\mathcal{U}(\tau,t)$ of $A(\tau)$ yields

$$\tilde{U}(\tau|t) = \mathcal{U}(\tau,t)\,\tilde{U}(t|t) + \int_t^\tau \mathcal{U}(\tau,\alpha)\,C(\alpha)\,d\,W(\alpha).$$

From Lemma 2.2 we have

$$P(\tau|t) = E\,[\,\tilde{U}(\tau|t)\circ\tilde{U}(\tau|t)\,] = \mathcal{U}(\tau,t)\,P(t|t)\,\mathcal{U}^*(\tau,t)$$

$$+ \int_t^\tau \mathcal{U}(\tau,\alpha)\,\tilde{Q}(\alpha)\,\mathcal{U}^*(\tau,\alpha)\,d\alpha.$$

Differentiating each side with respect to τ, we have

$$\frac{d\,P(\tau|t)}{d\tau} = A(\tau)\,P(\tau|t) + P(\tau|t)\,A^*(\tau) + \tilde{Q}(\tau).$$

Thus, the proof of the theorem is completed. Q.E.D.

3.2.4. Innovation processes.

We consider the innovation process $\nu(t)$ in detail in this section. This process $\nu(t)$ appears in the optimal estimators, that is, the filtering and smoothing estimators as shown in Theorems 3.20, 3.26 or Lemma 3.8 and plays a role of the inputs of the estimators.

[DEFINITION 3.1] The innovation process $\nu(t)$ is defined by the following relation [20, 27]:

$$d\,\nu(t) = d\,Z(t) - H(t)\,\hat{U}(t|t)\,dt = H(t)\,\tilde{U}(t|t)\,dt + d\,V(t). \tag{3.299}$$

Then the following theorem holds.

[THEOREM 3.33] The innovation process $\nu(t)$ possesses the following properties:

(i) $\nu(t)$ is continuous for almost all sample path.

(ii) Let $\mathcal{J}_t$ denote the minimal σ-field generated by the observation data $Z(s)$, $t_0 \leqq s \leqq t$. Then it follows that

$$E[\,\nu(t)|\,\mathcal{J}_s\,] = \nu(s) \quad \text{for } {}^{\forall}t \geqq s, \tag{3.300}$$

that is, $\nu(t)$ possesses the Martingale property.

(iii) $E[\,(\,\nu(t) - \nu(s))\circ(\,\nu(t) - \nu(s)\,)|\,\mathcal{J}_s\,]$

$$= E[\,(\,V(t) - V(s))\circ(\,V(t) - V(s))\,] = \int_s^t \mathcal{V}(\alpha)\,d\alpha. \tag{3.301}$$

(iv) $d\nu(t)$ is equivalent to $d\,Z(t)$. (3.302)

[PROOF] We have for $t_0 \leqq s \leqq t \leqq t_f$

$$\nu(t) = \nu(s) + \int_s^t H(\alpha)\,\tilde{U}(\alpha|\alpha)\,d\alpha + V(t) - V(s). \tag{3.303}$$

On the other hand, $\tilde{U}(t|t)$ is a solution of (3.236) and hence, is continuous with probability one as shown Theorem 2.2 or Theorem 2.7 and the Wiener process $V(t)$

is also continuous with probability one as shown in Theorem 2.1. Hence, the proof of (i) is completed.

Taking the conditional expectation of (3.303) conditioned with $\mathcal{T}_s$ and using the relation v) in Lemma 2.11;

$$E[\tilde{U}(\alpha|\alpha)|\mathcal{T}_s] = E[(E[\tilde{U}(\alpha|\alpha)|\mathcal{T}_\alpha])|\mathcal{T}_s] = 0, \quad \text{for } \alpha \geqq s,$$

we have

$$E[\nu(t)|\mathcal{T}_s] = \nu(s), \quad \text{for } {}^\forall t \geqq s.$$

Thus, the proof of (ii) is completed.

Setting $H(t)\tilde{U}(t|t) = Y(t)$ yields from (3.303)

$$\nu(t) - \nu(s) = \int_s^t Y(\alpha)\,d\alpha + V(t) - V(s).$$

Then we have

$$\begin{aligned} \operatorname{Cov}[(\nu(t)-\nu(s))\circ(\nu(t)-\nu(s))|\mathcal{T}_s] &= E[(V(t)-V(s))\circ (V(t)-V(s))|\mathcal{T}_s] + \int_s^t E[(V(t)-V(s))\circ Y(\alpha)|\mathcal{T}_s]\,d\alpha \\ &+ \int_s^t E[(Y(\alpha)\circ(V(t)-V(s)))|\mathcal{T}_s]\,d\alpha \\ &+ E[\int_s^t\int_s^t Y(\alpha)\circ Y(\beta)\,d\alpha d\beta\,|\mathcal{T}_s]. \end{aligned} \tag{3.304}$$

The second term of the right hand side of (3.304) becomes

$$\int_s^t E[(V(t)-V(\alpha))\circ Y(\alpha)|\mathcal{T}_s]\,d + \int_s^t E[(V(\alpha)-V(s))\circ Y(\alpha)|\mathcal{T}_s]\,d\alpha$$

$$= \int_s^t E[(V(\alpha)-V(s))\circ Y(\alpha)|\mathcal{T}_s]\,d\alpha.$$

The third term is also the same form as the second term. Since the fourth term can be rewritten as

$$\int_s^t \int_s^t Y(\alpha) \circ Y(\beta)\, d\alpha d\beta = \int_s^t Y(\alpha) \circ \int_s^\alpha Y(\beta)\, d\alpha d\beta$$

$$+ \int_s^t \int_s^\alpha Y(\beta)\, d\beta \circ Y(\alpha)\, d\alpha ,$$

the total sum of the second, third, and fourth terms becomes

$$\int_s^t E[\,(\, V(\alpha) - V(s) + \int_s^\alpha Y(\beta)\, d\beta\,) \circ Y(\alpha) \mid \mathcal{J}_s\,]\, d\alpha$$

$$+ \int_s^t E[\, Y(\alpha) \circ (\,(\, V(\alpha) - V(s)) + \int_s^\alpha Y(\beta)\, d\beta\,) \mid \mathcal{J}_s\,]\, d\beta. \qquad (3.305)$$

The first term of (3.305) becomes

$$\int_s^t E[\,(\,(\, V(\alpha) - V(s)\,) + \int_s^\alpha Y(\beta)\, d\beta\,) \circ Y(\alpha) \mid \mathcal{J}_s\,]\, d\alpha$$

$$= \int_s^t E[\,(\, \nu(\alpha) - \nu(s)\,) \circ Y(\alpha) \mid \mathcal{J}_s\,]\, d\alpha$$

$$= \int_s^t E[\, E[\,(\, \nu(\alpha) - \nu(s)\,) \circ Y(\alpha) \mid \mathcal{J}_\alpha\,] \mid \mathcal{J}_s\,]\, d\alpha = 0.$$

Similarly, the second term of (3.305) becomes zero. Since Wiener process $V(t)$ possesses the independent increment property as shown in Theorem 2.1, it follows that

$$E[\,(\, V(t) - V(s)\,) \circ (\, V(t) - V(s)\,) \mid \mathcal{J}_s\,]$$

$$= E[\,(\, V(t) - V(s)\,) \circ (\, V(t) - V(s)\,)\,] = \int_s^t \mathcal{V}(\alpha)\, d\alpha.$$

Thus, the proof of (iii) is completed.

To show that $\nu(t)$ is equivalent to $Z(s)$, $t_0 \leqq s \leqq t$, we must show that they can be obtained from the other by linear operations. Since $\hat{U}(t|t)$ can be given by the linear transformation of the observed data $Z(s)$, $t_0 \leqq s \leqq t$, we may write $H(t)\, \hat{U}(t|t)$ as

$$H(t)\ \hat{U}(t|t)\ dt = \int_{t_0}^{t} \bar{L}(t,s)\ d\ Z(s)\ dt = F(\ d\ Z(t))\ dt.$$

Hence, we have

$$d\ \nu(t) = d\ Z(t) - F(\ d\ Z(t)\ )\ dt = (\ \mathcal{J} - F\ )\ d\ Z(t) \qquad (3.306)$$

Since under the assumption that the kernel $\bar{L}(t,s)$ is square integrable, the operator $(\mathcal{J} - F)^{-1}$ exists and is given by the Neuman geometric series

$$(\mathcal{J} - F)^{-1} = \Sigma_{k=0}^{\infty} F^k.$$

Hence, from (3.306) the equivalence relation between $\nu(t)$ and $Z(t)$ is obtained. Thus, the proof of the theorem is completed. Q.E.D.

We note that the equivalence of $\nu(t)$ and $Z(t)$ may be proved based on the Kalman-Bucy filter. As $d\nu(t) = d\ Z(t) - H(t)\ \hat{U}(t|t)\ dt$ and $\hat{U}(t|t)$ is obtained from the observed data $Z(s)$, $t_0 \leqq s \leqq t$, $\nu(t)$ is determined completely from the observed data $Z(s)$, $t_0 \leqq s \leqq t$. Conversely, the Kalman-Bucy filter obtained by Theorem 3. 2 shows that $\hat{U}(t|t)$ is determined by the innovation process $\nu(t)$ and then $Z(t)$ can be obtained as $d\ Z(t) = d\ \nu(t) + H(t)\ \hat{U}(t|t)\ dt$. Thus, $\nu(t)$ and $Z(t)$ can each be obtained from the other by causal operation. These results are an extension of [27] to the distributed parameter system.

3.3. Optimal estimators by the parameter optimization technique.

3.3.1. Optimal filtering problems.

Let us consider the linear stochastic system in the Hilbert spaces described by

$$U(t) = \int_{t_0}^{t} A(\alpha)\, U(\alpha)\, d\alpha \;+\; \int_{t_0}^{t} C(\alpha)\, d\, W(\alpha) \;+ U_0 \qquad (3.307)$$

$$U_0 \in \mathcal{H} \triangleq L^2(\Omega, \mu; H).$$

Note that the unique solution of (3.307) exists and satisfies the following relation as shown in Theorem 2.5:

$$U(t) \in C(t_0, t_f ; \mathcal{V}') \cap L^\infty(t_0, t_f ; \mathcal{H}) \cap L^2(t_0, t_f ; \mathcal{V}) \qquad (3.308)$$

where

$$\mathcal{V} \triangleq L^2(\Omega, \mu; V) \subset \mathcal{H} \subset \mathcal{V}' \triangleq L^2(\Omega, \mu; V').$$

Usually, (3.307) is denoted by the following linear stochastic differential equation in Hilbert space $\mathcal{H}$;

$$d\, U(t) = A(t)\, U(t)\, dt + C(t)\, d\, W(t) \qquad (3.309)$$

$$U(t_0) = U_0. \qquad (3.310)$$

Assume that U_0 is independent of $W(t)$ and is Gaussian random variable in H which has the mean value and the covariance operator, respectively, given by

$$E[\, U_0\,] = U_1 \neq 0 \qquad (3.311)$$

$$\mathrm{Cov}[\, U_0, U_0\,] = E[\, (U_0 - U_1) \circ (U_0 - U_1)\,] = P_0 \qquad (3.312)$$

where P_0 is a nonnegative, self-adjoint, and nuclear operator.

The observation Z(t) of the state U(t) is given by

$$d\,Z(t) = H(t)\,U(t)\,dt + d\,V(t) \tag{3.313}$$

where V(t) is a Wiener process with a value in a Hilbert space and is independent of both W(t) and U_0. The Wiener processes W(t) and V(t) possess the following mean values and covariance operators;

$$E[\,W(t)\,] = 0, \quad E[\,V(t)\,] = 0$$

$$\mathrm{Cov}[\,W(t), W(s)\,] = E[\,W(t) \circ W(s)\,] = \int_{t_0}^{\min(t,s)} \mathcal{W}(\alpha)\,d\alpha$$

$$\mathrm{Cov}[\,V(t), V(s)\,] = E[\,V(t) \circ V(s)\,] = \int_{t_0}^{\min(t,s)} \mathcal{V}(\alpha)\,d\alpha$$

where $\mathcal{W}(\alpha)$ and $\mathcal{V}(\alpha)$ are positive, self-adjoint, and nuclear operators. Assume further that $\mathcal{V}(\alpha)$ is invertible. Then $\mathcal{V}(\alpha)$ is an invertible and nuclear operator and so, the dimension of V(t) becomes finite [9, 14] and is assumed to be $\mathbf{R}^m$. If we restrict our attention to the pointwise observation, H(t) may contain the term of Col [$\delta(x - x^1), \cdots, \delta(x - x^m)$] for $x, x^1, \cdots, x^m \in D$ where $\delta(\cdot)$ denotes Dirac's delta function defined on $D \subset \mathbf{R}^r$. Denoting the Sobolev space of order $n \in \mathbf{R}$ defined on D by $H^n(D)$ [5, 9, 14], it was proved in [9,14] that

$$\delta(x) \in (\,H^{[r/2]+1}(D)\,)'$$

where r and [r/2] denote the dimension of D and the integer part of r/2, respectively. Hence, if

$$V \subset H^{[r/2]+1}(D), \tag{3.314}$$

then the pointwise observation of $U(t) \in \mathcal{V}$ for almost all t is possible in the sense of Lions [13] and (3.313) has meaning as a time function.

Now the filtering problem is posed as follows: Given the measurement data $Z(s)$, $t_0 \leqq s \leq t$, find an estimate $\hat{U}(t|t)$ of the present state $U(t)$. Here, we assume that the filtering estimate $\hat{U}(t|t)$ is given by the following time evolution scheme;

$$d\, \hat{U}(t|t) = K(t,t)\, \hat{U}(t|t)\, dt + L(t,t)\, d\, Z(t) \tag{3.315}$$

where

$$K(t,t) \in L^2(\, t_0,t_f\, ;\ \mathcal{L}(V,V')) \quad \text{and} \quad L(t,t) \in L^\infty(\, t_0,t_f\, ; \mathcal{L}(\, \mathbf{R}^m, H\,)).$$

Furthermore, we assume that

$$< -\, K(t,t)\, z,\, z > + \lambda\, \|z\|_H^2 \geqq \alpha\, \|z\|_V^2 \quad \text{for } \forall t \in (t_0,t_f], \forall z \in V, \lambda \geqq 0, \text{ and } \alpha > 0. \tag{3.316}$$

Assume that the estimation error criterion is based on the unbiased and minimum variance estimations given by

$$E\, [\, \tilde{U}(t|t)\,] = 0 \tag{3.317}$$

and

$$\mathrm{Cov}\, [\tilde{U}^o(t|t), \tilde{U}^o(t|t)\,] \leqq \mathrm{Cov}\, [\, \tilde{U}(t|t),\, \tilde{U}(t|t)\,] \tag{3.318}$$

where $\tilde{U}^o(t|t)$ denotes the optimal estimation error function and

$$\tilde{U}(t|t) = U(t) - \hat{U}(t|t). \tag{3.319}$$

The notation $\Theta^o \leqq \Theta$ of (3.318) means that

$$(\, \phi,\, \Theta^o\, \phi\,) \leqq (\, \phi,\, \Theta\, \phi) \quad \text{for } \forall \phi \in H. \tag{3.320}$$

The intuitive meaning of the form of (3.315) is that the optimal estimate $\hat{U}(t|t)$ is adjusted by using the additionally obtained observed data $d\, Z(t)$. Alternately, the solution of (3.315) is represented by using the evolution operator $\mathcal{U}_k(t,t_0)$ of $K(t,t)$ as follows:

$$\hat{U}(t|t) = \mathcal{U}_K(t,t_0)\, U_1 + \int_{t_0}^{t} \mathcal{U}_K(t,\alpha)\, L(\alpha,\alpha)\, d\, Z(\alpha). \tag{3.321}$$

Thus, (3.321) means that $\hat{U}(t|t)$ is given by the linear transformation of $Z(s)$, $t_0 \leq s \leq t$. Since it is well-known that if $U(t)$ and $Z(t)$ are Gaussian, then the optimal minimum variance estimator is given by the linear transformation of $Z(s)$, $t_0 \leq s \leq t$, the assumption of the form of (3.315) holds without loss of generality.

Derivation of the optimal filter

In order to derive the optimal filter, it is necessary to obtain the time evolution of $\tilde{U}(t|t)$. It follows from (3.309), (3.313), and (3.315) that

$$d\, \tilde{U}(t|t) = A(t)\, U(t)\, dt + C(t)\, d\, W(t) - K(t,t)\, \hat{U}(t|t)\, dt - L(t,t)\, d\, Z(t)$$

$$= -\, (\, K(t,t) + L(t,t)\, H(t) - A(t))\, U(t)\, dt$$

$$+ K(t,t)\, \hat{U}(t|t)\, dt - L(t,t)\, d\, V(t) + C(t)\, d\, W(t).$$

Since it follows from (3.309) and (3.311) that

$$\frac{d\, E[\, U(t)\,]}{dt} = A(t)\, E\, [\, U(t)\,], \quad E\, [\, U(t_0)\,] = U_1 \neq 0,$$

$E\, [\, U(t)\,] \neq 0$ and from (3.317) we have the following relation in the weak sense;

$$K(t,t) = -\, L(t,t)\, H(t) + A(t) \tag{3.322}$$

where the weak sense means that

$$<\, (\, K(t,t) + L(t,t)\, H(t) + A(t)\,)\, \phi\, ,\ \phi\, > = 0 \qquad \text{for } \forall \phi \in V.$$

Then we have

$$d\, \hat{U}(t|t) = A(t)\, \hat{U}(t|t)\, dt + L(t,t)\, d\, \nu(t) \tag{3.323}$$

$$d\nu(t) \triangleq d\,Z(t) - H(t)\,\hat{U}(t|t)\,dt \tag{3.324}$$

$$d\,\tilde{U}(t|t) = A(t)\,\tilde{U}(t|t)\,dt - L(t,t)\,H(t)\,\tilde{U}(t|t)\,dt - L(t,t)\,d\,V(t)$$
$$+ C(t)\,d\,W(t). \tag{3.324}$$

On the other hand, it follows from (2.4) that

$$(\phi, \mathrm{Cov}[\,\tilde{U}(t|t), \tilde{U}(t|t)\,]\,\phi) = E[\,(\phi, \tilde{U}(t|t))\,(\tilde{U}(t|t), \phi)\,]$$
$$= (\phi, P(t|t)\,\phi) \qquad \text{for } \forall\phi \in H \tag{3.325}$$

where

$$P(t|t) \triangleq E[\,\tilde{U}(t|t) \circ \tilde{U}(t|t)\,]. \tag{3.326}$$

Accordingly, it is sufficient to determine L(t,t) such that (3.325) is minimized. Using Ito's lemma in Hilbert spaces, Theorem 2.3, and the following relation given by (2.6),

$$h_1 \circ (N\,h_2) = (h_1 \circ h_2)\,N^*$$

for $\forall h_1 \in H$, $\forall h_2 \in V$, and $\forall N \in \mathcal{L}(V, V')$, it follows that

$$d\,(\tilde{U}(t|t) \circ \tilde{U}(t|t)) = (d\,\tilde{U}(t|t)) \circ \tilde{U}(t|t) + \tilde{U}(t|t) \circ (d\,\tilde{U}(t|t))$$
$$+ L(t,t)\,\mathcal{V}(t)\,L^*(t,t)\,dt + \tilde{Q}(t)\,dt. \tag{3.327}$$

Using (3.324) and the following relation given by (2.5)

$$(h_1 \circ h_2)^* = h_2 \circ h_1 \quad \text{for } \forall h_1, h_2 \in H,$$

and taking the expectation of each side of (3.327), we have

$$\frac{d\,P(t|t)}{dt} = K(t,t)\,P(t|t) + P(t|t)\,K^*(t,t) + L(t,t)\mathcal{V}(t)\,L^*(t,t) + \tilde{Q}(t).$$

Substituting (3.322) into the above equation yields

$$\frac{d\,P(t|t)}{dt} = A(t)\,P(t|t) + P(t|t)\,A^*(t) + \tilde{Q}(t) - P(t|t)\,\tilde{R}(t)\,P(t|t) + \Sigma_\Delta(t) \tag{3.328}$$

where

$$\Sigma_\Delta(t) \triangleq T_\Delta(t)\,\mathcal{V}^{-1}(t)\,T_\Delta^*(t)$$

$$T_\Delta(t) \triangleq L(t,t)\,\mathcal{V}(t) - P(t|t)\,H^*(t). \tag{3.329}$$

Since $\mathcal{V}(t)$ is positive, $L(t,t)$ minimizes the scalar product (3.325) if and only if $T_\Delta(t)$ is null operator. This is shown as follows:
Let $M(t)$ be the solution of the following operator equation of Riccati type

$$\frac{d\,M(t)}{dt} = A(t)\,M(t) + M(t)\,A^*(t) + \tilde{Q}(t) - M(t)\,\tilde{R}(t)\,M(t) \tag{3.330}$$

$$M(t_0) = P(t_0|t_0) = P_0\,.$$

Let us define $D(t)$ to be the difference between $P(t|t)$ and $M(t)$

$$D(t) = P(t|t) - M(t) \tag{3.331}$$

Then we have from (3.328) and (3.330)

$$\frac{d\,D(t)}{dt} = \tilde{A}(t)\,D(t) + D(t)\,\tilde{A}^*(t) + \Sigma_\Delta(t) \tag{3.332}$$

where

$$\tilde{A}(t) \triangleq A(t) - 1/2\,(\,P(t|t) + M(t))\,\tilde{R}(t).$$

Let $\mathcal{U}_{\tilde{A}}(\,t,\,s\,)$ be the evolution operator of $\tilde{A}(t)$. Then the solution of (3.332) can be represented as follows:

$$D(t) = \int_{t_0}^{t} \mathcal{U}_{\tilde{A}}(t,\alpha)\ \Sigma_\Delta(\alpha)\ \mathcal{U}^*_{\tilde{A}}(t,\alpha)\ d\alpha. \tag{3.333}$$

Since $\Sigma_\Delta(t) \geqq 0$, it follows from (3.333) that

$$D(t) \geqq 0$$

where equality holds if and only if $T_\Delta(t) = 0$.

Thus, we have from (3.329)

$$L(t,t) = P(t|t)\ H^*(t)\ \mathcal{V}^{-1}(t). \tag{3.334}$$

Then the minimum variance filtering error covariance operator $P(t|t)$ is given by

$$\frac{d\ P(t|t)}{dt} = A(t)\ P(t|t) + P(t|t)\ A^*(t) + \tilde{Q}(t) - P(t|t)\ \tilde{R}(t)\ P(t|t) \tag{3.335}$$

$$P(t_0|t_0) = P_0\ . \tag{3.336}$$

Therefore, we have the following theorem.

[THEOREM 3.34] The optimal filtering estimate $\hat{U}(t|t)$ is given by the relation

$$d\ \hat{U}(t|t) = A(t)\ \hat{U}(t|t)\ dt + P(t|t)\ H^*(t)\ \mathcal{V}^{-1}(t)\ d\ \nu(t) \tag{3.337}$$

$$\hat{U}(t_0|t_0) = U_1 \tag{3.338}$$

$$\frac{d\ P(t|t)}{dt} = A(t)\ P(t|t) + P(t|t)\ A^*(t) + \tilde{Q}(t) - P(t|t)\ \tilde{R}(t)\ P(t|t) \tag{3.339}$$

$$P(t_0|t_0) = P_0. \tag{3.340}$$

Note that these results are the same results as Theorem 3.18.

3.3.2. Optimal smoothing problems.

Let us consider the same systems of the state and observation equations as the filtering problem. Now the smoothing problems are posed as follows: Given the measurement data $Z(s)$, $t_0 \leqq s \leqq t$, find an estimate $\hat{U}(\tau|t)$ of the state $U(\tau)$ at only particular time τ for $\tau < t$. Here, we assume that the estimation error criterion is based on the unbiased and minimum variance estimations given by

$$E [\tilde{U}(\tau|t)] = 0 \tag{3.341}$$

and

$$\mathrm{Cov} [\tilde{U}^o(\tau|t), \tilde{U}^o(\tau|t)] \leqq \mathrm{Cov} [\tilde{U}(\tau|t), \tilde{U}(\tau|t)] \tag{3.342}$$

where $\tilde{U}^o(\tau|t)$ denotes the optimal smoothing estimation error function and

$$\tilde{U}(\tau|t) = U(\tau) - \hat{U}(\tau|t). \tag{3.343}$$

Furthermore, we assume that the smoothing estimate $\hat{U}(\tau|t)$ is given by the following time evolution scheme:

$$d \hat{U}(\tau|t) = K(\tau,t) \hat{U}(t|t) dt + L(\tau,t) d Z(t) \tag{3.344}$$

where

$$K(\tau,\cdot) \in L^2(t_0,t_f ; \mathcal{L}(V, V')) \text{ and } L(\tau,\cdot) \in L^\infty(t_0,t_f ; \mathcal{L}(\mathbf{R}^m, H)).$$

Furthermore, assume that

$$< - K(\tau,t) z, z > + \lambda \|z\|_H^2 \geqq \alpha \|z\|_V^2$$

for $\tau \in (t_0, t_f]$, $z \in V$, $\lambda \geqq 0$, and $\alpha > 0$.

Integrating (3.343) from $\alpha = \tau$ to $\alpha = t$ yields

$$\hat{U}(\tau|t) = \hat{U}(\tau|\tau) + \int_\tau^t K(\tau,\alpha) \hat{U}(\alpha|\alpha) d\alpha + \int_\tau^t L(\tau,\alpha) d Z(\alpha).$$

Therefore, we can see that the optimal filtering estimate $\hat{U}(\tau|\tau)$ constitutes the initial value for the smoothing estimate $\hat{U}(\tau|t)$ and that $\hat{U}(\tau|\tau)$ is corrected by the linear transformation of the additionally available observed data $Z(s)$, $\tau \leq s \leq t$. But $\hat{U}(\tau|\tau)$ is a linear transformation of the observed data $Z(s)$, $t_0 \leq s \leq \tau$, and so, the smoothed estimate $\hat{U}(\tau|t)$ given by (3.344) is also the linear transformation of the observed data $Z(s)$, $t_0 \leq s \leq t$.

In order to derive the optimal smoothing estimator, it is necessary to obtain the time evolution of $\tilde{U}(\tau|t)$. It follows from (3.309), (3.313), (3.343), and (3.344) that

$$d\,\tilde{U}(\tau|t) = -\,(\,K(\tau,t) + L(\tau,t)\,H(t)\,)\,U(t)\,dt + K(\tau,t)\,\tilde{U}(t|t)\,dt$$

$$-\,L(\tau,t)\,d\,V(t). \tag{3.345}$$

Since $\hat{U}(\tau|t)$ and $\hat{U}(t|t)$ are unbiased estimates, we have in the weak sense

$$K(\tau,t) = -\,L(\tau,t)\,H(t). \tag{3.346}$$

Then we have

$$d\,\hat{U}(\tau|t) = L(\tau,t)\,(\,d\,Z(t) - H(t)\,\hat{U}(t|t)\,dt\,) = L(\tau,t)\,d\,\nu(t) \tag{3.347}$$

and

$$d\,\tilde{U}(\tau|t) = K(\tau,t)\,\tilde{U}(t|t)\,dt - L(\tau,t)\,d\,V(t). \tag{3.348}$$

On the other hand, it follows from (2.4) that

$$(\,\phi,\ \mathrm{Cov}\,[\,\tilde{U}(\tau|t),\ \tilde{U}(\tau|t)\,]\,\phi\,) = (\,\phi,\ P(\tau|t)\phi\,) \quad \text{for } \forall\phi \in H \tag{3.349}$$

where

$$P(\tau|t) = E\,[\,\tilde{U}(\tau|t)\circ\tilde{U}(\tau|t)\,]. \tag{3.350}$$

Hence, we must determine $L(\tau,t)$ such that (3.349) is minimized.

Using Ito's lemma in Hilbert spaces, Theorem 2.3, and (2.6), we have

$$d\,(\tilde{U}(\tau|t) \circ \tilde{U}(\tau|t)) = (d\,\tilde{U}(\tau|t)) \circ \tilde{U}(\tau|t) + \tilde{U}(\tau|t) \circ (d\,\tilde{U}(\tau|t))$$

$$+ L(\tau,t)\,\mathcal{V}(t)\,L^*(\tau,t).$$

Substituting (3.348) and taking the expectation of each side, we have

$$\frac{d\,P(\tau|t)}{dt} = K(\tau,t)\,B^*(\tau|t) + B(\tau|t)\,K^*(\tau,t) + L(\tau,t)\,\mathcal{V}(t)\,L^*(\tau,t) \quad (3.351)$$

where

$$B(\tau|t) = E\,[\,\tilde{U}(\tau|t) \circ \tilde{U}(t|t)\,]. \quad (3.352)$$

Substituting (3.346) into (3.351) yields

$$\frac{d\,P(\tau|t)}{dt} = -\,B(\tau|t)\,\tilde{R}(t)\,B^*(\tau|t) + \Sigma_s(t)$$

where

$$\Sigma_s(t) = T_s(t)\,\mathcal{V}^{-1}(t)\,T_s^*(t)$$

$$T_s(t) = L(\tau,t)\,\mathcal{V}(t) - B(\tau|t)\,H^*(t). \quad (3.353)$$

Then it is clear that $L(\tau,t)$ minimizes the scalar product (3.349) if and only if $T_s(t) = 0$. Hence, it follows from (3.353) that

$$L(\tau,t) = B(\tau|t)\,H^*(t)\,\mathcal{V}^{-1}(t). \quad (3.354)$$

Therefore, the minimum variance estimation error covariance operator satisfies

$$\frac{d\,P(\tau|t)}{dt} = -\,B(\tau|t)\,\tilde{R}(t)\,B^*(\tau|t). \quad (3.355)$$

Thus, we have the following relations:

$$P(\tau|t) = P(\tau|\tau) - \int_\tau^t B(\tau|\alpha)\,\tilde{R}(\alpha)\,B^*(\tau|\alpha)\,d\alpha \quad (3.356)$$

and

$$\hat{U}(\tau|t) = \hat{U}(\tau|\tau) + \int_{\tau}^{t} B(\alpha|t)\, H^{*}(\alpha)\, \mathcal{V}^{-1}(\alpha)\, d\, \nu(\alpha). \tag{3.357}$$

Let us now derive the time evolution of $B(\tau|t)$. Using Ito's lemma in Hilbert spaces, Theorem 2.3, yields

$$d\,(\,\tilde{U}(\tau|\alpha) \circ \tilde{U}(\alpha|\alpha)) = (\,d\,\tilde{U}(\tau|\alpha)) \circ \tilde{U}(\alpha|\alpha) + \tilde{U}(\tau|\alpha) \circ (\,d\,\tilde{U}(\alpha|\alpha))$$

$$+ L(\tau,\alpha)\, \mathcal{V}(\alpha)\, L^{*}(\alpha,\alpha)\, d\alpha.$$

Substituting (3.324) and (3.348) and taking the expectation of each side of the above equation, we have

$$\frac{d\, B(\tau|\alpha)}{d\alpha} = K(\tau,\alpha)\, P(\alpha|\alpha) + B(\tau|\alpha)(\,A(\alpha) - L(\alpha,\alpha)\, H(\alpha))^{*} + L(\tau,\alpha)\, \mathcal{V}(\alpha)\, L^{*}(\alpha,\alpha).$$

But from (3.346) we have

$$\begin{aligned} K(\tau,\alpha)\, P(\alpha|\alpha) &= -\, L(\tau,\alpha)\, H(\alpha)\, P(\alpha|\alpha) \\ &= -\, L(\tau,\alpha)\, \mathcal{V}(\alpha)\, (\, P(\alpha|\alpha)\, H^{*}(\alpha)\, \mathcal{V}^{-1}(\alpha)\,)^{*} \\ &= -\, L(\tau,\alpha)\, \mathcal{V}(\alpha)\, L^{*}(\alpha,\alpha). \end{aligned}$$

Hence, we have

$$\frac{d\, B(\tau|\alpha)}{d\alpha} = B(\tau|\alpha)\,(\,A(\alpha) - L(\alpha,\alpha)\, H(\alpha))^{*} \tag{3.358}$$

$$B(\tau|\tau) = P(\tau|\tau). \tag{3.359}$$

Letting the evolution operator of $A(\alpha) - L(\alpha,\alpha)\, H(\alpha)$ be $\mathcal{U}_A(\alpha,\tau)$ yields

$$\frac{d\, \mathcal{U}_A(\alpha,\tau)}{d\alpha} = (\,A(\alpha) - L(\alpha,\alpha)\, H(\alpha))\, \mathcal{U}_A(\alpha,\tau), \quad \mathcal{U}_A(\alpha,\alpha) = \mathcal{I}. \tag{3.360}$$

Then the following theorem holds.

[THEOREM 3.35] The optimal smoothing estimate $\hat{U}(\tau|t)$ satisfies the following relations:

$$B(\tau|t) = P(\tau|\tau)\,\mathcal{U}_A^*(t,\tau) \tag{3.361}$$

$$P(\tau|t) = P(\tau|\tau) - P(\tau|\tau)\int_\tau^t \mathcal{U}_A^*(\alpha,\tau)\,\tilde{R}(\alpha)\,\mathcal{U}_A(\alpha,\tau)\,d\alpha\,P(\tau|\tau) \tag{3.362}$$

$$\hat{U}(\tau|t) = \hat{U}(\tau|\tau) + P(\tau|\tau)\,\lambda(\tau,t) \tag{3.363}$$

$$\lambda(\tau,t) \triangleq \int_\tau^t \mathcal{U}_A^*(\alpha,\tau)\,H^*(\alpha)\mathcal{V}^{-1}(\alpha)\,d\,\nu(\alpha). \tag{3.364}$$

Based on these expressions, the various types of smoothing estimators can be derived.

Fixed-point smoothing

Substituting $\tau = t_1$ into (3.361)-(3.364) yields the following theorem.

[THEOREM 3.36] The fixed-point smoothing estimator $\hat{U}(t_1|t)$ satisfies the following equations:

$$d\,\hat{U}(t_1|t) = B(t_1|t)\,H^*(t)\mathcal{V}^{-1}(t)\,d\,\nu(t) \tag{3.365}$$

$$\frac{d\,B(t_1|t)}{dt} = B(t_1|t)\,(\,A(t) - P(t|t)\,\tilde{R}(t))^* \tag{3.366}$$

$$B(t_1|t_1) = P(t_1|t_1)$$

$$\frac{d\,P(t_1|t)}{dt} = -\,B(t_1|t)\,\tilde{R}(t)\,B^*(t_1|t). \tag{3.367}$$

Fixed-interval smoothing

Substituting $\tau = t$ and $t = T$ fixed, into (3.365)-(3.367) yields the following theorem.

[THEOREM 3.37] The fixed-interval smoothing estimator $\hat{U}(t|T)$ satisfies the following equations:

$$d\,\hat{U}(t|T) = A(t)\,\hat{U}(t|T)\,dt + \tilde{Q}(t)\,(\,\hat{U}(t|T) - \hat{U}(t|t))\,dt \tag{3.368}$$

$$\frac{d\,P(t|T)}{dt} = (\,A(t) + \tilde{Q}(t)\,P^{-1}(t|t)\,)\,P(t|T) + P(t|T)\,(\,A(t) + \tilde{Q}(t)\,P^{-1}(t|t)\,)^{*} - \tilde{Q}(t). \tag{3.369}$$

Fixed-lag smoothing

Substituting $\tau = t$ and $t = t + \nabla$, $\nabla > 0$ into (3.361)-(3.364) yields the following theorem.

[THEOREM 3.38] The fixed-lag smoothing estimate $\hat{U}(t|t+\nabla)$ satisfies the following equations:

$$d\,\hat{U}(t|t+\nabla) = A(t)\,\hat{U}(t|t+\nabla)\,dt + G(t+\nabla)\,P(t+\nabla|t+\nabla)\,H^{*}(t+\nabla)\,\mathcal{V}^{-1}(t+\nabla)\,(\,d\,Z(t+\nabla) - H(t+\nabla)\,\hat{U}(t+\nabla|t+\nabla)\,dt\,) + \tilde{Q}(t)\,P^{-1}(t|t)\,(\,\hat{U}(t|t+\nabla) - \hat{U}(t|t))\,dt \tag{3.370}$$

$$\frac{d\,G(t+\nabla)}{dt} = \tilde{Q}(t)\,P^{-1}(t|t)\,G(t+\nabla) - G(t+\nabla)\,\tilde{Q}(t+\nabla)\,P^{-1}(t+\nabla|t+\nabla) + A(t)\,G(t+\nabla) - G(t+\nabla)\,A(t+\nabla) \tag{3.371}$$

$$G(t_0+\nabla) = B(t_0|t_0+\nabla)$$

$$\frac{d\,P(t|t+\nabla)}{dt} = (\,A(t) + \tilde{Q}(t)\,P^{-1}(t|t))\,P(t|t+\nabla) + P(t|t+\nabla)\,(\,A(t) + \tilde{Q}(t)\,P^{-1}(t|t)\,)^{*} - B(t|t+\nabla)\,\tilde{R}(t)\,B^{*}(t|t+\nabla) - \tilde{Q}(t) \tag{3.372}$$

with the initial condition $P(t_0|t_0+\nabla)$.

3.3.3. Optimal prediction problems.

Let us consider the same systems of the state and observation equations as the filtering problem. Now the prediction problem is posed as follows: Given the measurement data $Z(s)$, $t_0 \leqq s \leqq t$, find an estimate $\hat{U}(\tau|t)$ of the future state $U(\tau)$ at only particular time τ for $\tau > t$. Here, we assume that the estimation error criterion is based on the unbiased estimation given by

$$E [\tilde{U}(\tau|t)] = 0 \tag{3.373}$$

where

$$\tilde{U}(\tau|t) = U(\tau) - \hat{U}(\tau|t). \tag{3.374}$$

Furthermore, the time evolution of the prediction value $\hat{U}(\tau|t)$ is assumed to be

$$d\hat{U}(\tau|t) = K(\tau,t)\, \hat{U}(t|t)\, d\tau \tag{3.375}$$

where

$$K(\tau,\cdot) \in L^2(t_0,t_f ; \mathcal{L}(V, V')).$$

Furthermore, assume that

$$< - K(\tau,t)\, z, z > + \lambda \|z\|_H^2 \geqq \alpha \|z\|_V^2 \quad \text{for } \tau > t, \ \forall z \in V, \ \lambda \geqq 0, \text{ and } \alpha > 0.$$

The form of $\hat{U}(\tau|t)$ given by (3.375) shows that the prediction value is obtained by transforming the observed data $Z(s)$, $t_0 \leqq s \leqq t$. It follows from (3.309), (3.374), and (3.375) that

$$d\, \tilde{U}(\tau|t) = (A(\tau) \mathcal{U}(\tau,t) - K(\tau,t))\, U(t)\, d\tau + K(\tau,t)\, \tilde{U}(t|t)\, d\tau$$

$$+ C(\tau)\, d\, W(\tau) + A(\tau) \int_t^\tau \mathcal{U}(\tau,\alpha)\, C(\alpha)\, d\, W(\alpha)\, d\tau.$$

Hence, we have from (3.373)

$$K(\tau,t) = A(\tau)\,\mathcal{U}(\tau,t). \tag{3.376}$$

Then it follows from (3.375) that

$$d\,\hat{U}(\tau|t) = A(\tau)\,\mathcal{U}(\tau,t)\,\hat{U}(t|t)\,d\tau \tag{3.377}$$

$$d\,\tilde{U}(\tau|t) = K(\tau,t)\,\tilde{U}(t|t)\,d\tau + C(\tau)\,d\,W(\tau)$$

$$+ A(\tau)\int_t^\tau \mathcal{U}(\tau,\alpha)\,C(\alpha)\,d\,W(\alpha)\,d\tau. \tag{3.378}$$

Hence, from (3.377) we have

$$d\,\hat{U}(\tau|t) = d\,\mathcal{U}(\tau,t)\,\hat{U}(t|t).$$

Integrating each side with respect to τ yields

$$\hat{U}(\alpha|t) = \mathcal{U}(\alpha,t)\,\hat{U}(t|t) \quad \text{for} \quad \alpha > t.$$

Thus, from (3.377) we have

$$d\,\hat{U}(\tau|t) = A(\tau)\,\hat{U}(\tau|t) \qquad \text{fot} \quad \tau > t. \tag{3.379}$$

It follows from (3.378) and Ito's lemma in Hilbert spaces, Theorem 2.3, that

$$d\,(\tilde{U}(\tau|t) \circ \tilde{U}(\tau|t)) = K(\tau,t)\,\tilde{U}(t|t) \circ \tilde{U}(\tau|t)\,d\tau$$

$$+ \tilde{U}(\tau|t) \circ \tilde{U}(t|t)\,K^*(\tau,t)\,d\tau + \tilde{Q}(\tau)\,d\tau\,. \tag{3.380}$$

Taking the expectation of each side of (3.380) yields

$$\frac{d\,P(\tau|t)}{d\tau} = A(\tau)\,P(\tau|t) + P(\tau|t)\,A^*(\tau) + \tilde{Q}(\tau), \quad P(\tau|t) = E[\tilde{U}(\tau|t) \circ \tilde{U}(\tau|t)]. \tag{3.381}$$

Thus, we have the following theorem.

[THOREM 3.39] The optimal prediction estimate $\hat{U}(\tau|t)$ satisfies the following relations:

$$d\,\hat{U}(\tau|t)/d\tau = A(\tau)\,\hat{U}(\tau|t) \tag{3.382}$$

and

$$\frac{d\,P(\tau|t)}{d\tau} = A(\tau)\,P(\tau|t) + P(\tau|t)\,A^{*}(\tau) + \tilde{Q}(\tau). \tag{3.383}$$

where the initial conditions of (3.382) and (3.383) are $\hat{U}(t|t)$ and $P(t|t)$, respectively.

Thus, we have derived the optimal estimators, that is, the filtering, the smoothing, and the prediction estimators in Hilbert spaces. The fundamental approach to solve the estimation problems is the Wiener-Hopf theory which was originated by Kalman [21, 22]. Although Kalman failed to derive the optimal smoothing estimator based on the Wiener-Hopf theory, the results in this chapter show that the optimal smoothing estimators can be derived by using the Wiener-Hopf theory.

The other method to solve the estimation problem is the approach to use the innovation theory [20, 27, 28]. Although the theory is elegant and powerful, the method necessitates also the Wiener-Hopf theory and the results obtained by using the Wiener-Hopf theory show that the innovation process can be derived by the orthogonal projection theory as a consequence of the Wiener-Hopf theory as shown in Theorems 3.20, 3.26. Therefore, the method stated here is classical, but the method is basic and is easily extended to the other estimation problems, for example, the estimation problems for a discrete-time distributed parameter system or a time-lag system. Furthermore, the method by the parameter optimization technique is proposed by us [7,8,23, 29, 30,31] and gives us the physical meaning of the optimal estimators.

3.3.4. Kernel representations of the operator equations.

Let us now apply the results for the optimal estimators in Hilbert spaces to the estimation problems for a distributed parameter system. Assume that

$V = H^1(D)$ and $H = L^2(D)$ and let M be $[t_0, t_f] \times D$ and assume that

$$< - A(t)\, z_1,\, z_2 > \triangleq \Sigma_{i,j=1}^{r} \int_D a_{ij}(t,x) \frac{\partial z_1(x)}{\partial x_i} \frac{\partial z_2(x)}{\partial x_j} dx \tag{3.384}$$

for $^\forall z_1, z_2 \in V$ and $a_{ij}(t,x) \in L(M)$ such that

$$\Sigma_{i,j=1}^{r} a_{ij}(t,x)\, y_i\, y_j \geqq \beta\, (y_1^2 + \cdots + y_r^2) \quad \text{for } \beta > 0 \text{ and } y_i \in \mathbf{R}.$$

In this case, it is easily verified from (3.38) that (2.54) is satisfied since $V = H^1(D)$. Then (3.309) is equivalent to the following equation:

$$d\, (U(t),\, z) = < A(t)\, U(t),\, z > dt + (C(t)\, d\, W(t),\, z) \quad \text{for } ^\forall z \in V.$$

Let $\mathcal{D}(D)$ be a space of infinitely differentiable functions with compact support in D. Since $^\forall \phi \in \mathcal{D}(D) \subset V$, it follows that

$$\int_D d\, U(t,x)\, \phi(x)\, dx = \int_D (A_x\, U(t,x))\, \phi(x)\, dx + \int_D C(t,x)\, d\, W(t,x)\, \phi(x)\, dx \tag{3.385}$$

where

$$A_x(\cdot) = \Sigma_{i,j=1}^{r} \frac{\partial}{\partial x_i} \left(a_{ij}(t,x) \frac{\partial(\cdot)}{\partial x_j} \right).$$

Therefore, it holds that

$$d\, U(t,x) = A_x\, U(t,x)\, dt + C(t,x)\, d\, W(t,x) \quad \text{for a.e. } (t,x) \in M \tag{3.386}$$

$$U(t_0,x) = U_0(x) \tag{3.387}$$

where a.e. denotes almost everywhere or almost surely.

Using Green's formula shown in Appendix, we have for $\forall z \in V$

$$< - A(t)\, U(t,x),\, z > \;=\; \int_S \frac{\partial U(t,\xi)}{\partial \mathbf{n}}\, z(\xi)\, d\xi \;+\; \int_D (\, A_x\, U(t,x))\, z(x)\, dx$$

where $\mathbf{n}$ denotes the normal vector to the boundary S and

$$\partial(\cdot)/\partial \mathbf{n} = \Sigma_{i,j=1}^{r}\; a_{ij}(t,\xi)\, \cos(\, \mathbf{n},\, x_i)\; \partial(\cdot)/\partial x_j .$$

Using (3.386) and the above equation, we have

$$\partial U(t,\xi)/\, \partial \mathbf{n} = 0 \quad \text{for } \forall \xi \in S. \tag{3.388}$$

Hence, the general formulation of (3.309) includes the distributed parameter system described by (3.386)-(3.388). Letting $H(t)(\cdot) = h(t) \int_D \mathrm{Col}\, [\, \delta(x-x^1),\, \cdots,\, \delta(x-x^m)\,]\, (\cdot)\, dx$ yields

$$d\, Z(t) = h(t)\, U_m(t)\, dt + d\, V(t) \tag{3.389}$$

$$U_m(t) = \mathrm{Col}\, [\, U(t,x^1),\, \cdots,\, U(t,x^m)\,]$$

where $h(t)$ is an $m \times m$ matrix.

In order for the pointwise observation to be possible, it is necessary from (3.314) that the dimension r of the spatial domain is equal to one. Note that if $V = H^2(D)$ which is possible if $a_{ij}(t,x)$ and $C(t,x)$ are sufficiently smooth on M [5, 13], then r can take the integers such that $1 \leqq r \leqq 3$. Because from (3.314) it is necessary for the pointwise observation to be possible that

$$[\, r/2\,] + 1 \leqq 2, \text{ that is, } \quad r = 1,2,3.$$

In order to find the optimal estimator described by the stochastic partial differential equations, Schwartz's kernel theorem will be reformulated to obtain a more suitable form for the estimation problems in the Hilbert spaces. Hence, the following lemma will be proved.

[LEMMA 3.17] The operator $h_1(t) \circ h_2(t)$ possesses the kernel representation given by

$$(h_1(t) \circ h_2(t)) \; h_3(t) = \int_D H(t,x,y) \, h_3(t,y) \, dy \tag{3.390}$$

$$H(t,x,y) = h(t,x) \, h(t,y)$$

for $\forall h_1(t), h_2(t), h_3(t) \in H$ and a fixed $t \in (t_0, t_f]$.

[PROOF] From the definition (2.4) of the operator " $\circ$ ", we have

$$\begin{aligned} (h_1(t) \circ h_2(t)) \; h_3(t) &= h_1(t)(h_2(t), h_3(t)) \\ &= h_1(t,x) \int_D h_2(t,y) \, h_3(t,y) \, dy \\ &= \int_D H(t,x,y) \, h_3(t,y) \, dy. \end{aligned}$$

Thus, the proof of the lemma is completed. Q.E.D.

[LEMMA 3.318] The operator $P(\theta|t) \, A^*(t)$ possesses the following kernel representation given by

$$P(\theta|t) \, A^*(t) \, \phi(t) = \int_D (A_y \, P(\theta,x,y|t)) \, \phi(t,y) \, dy \tag{3.391}$$

$$P(\theta,x,y|t) = E \, [\, \tilde{U}(\theta,x|t) \, \tilde{U}(\theta,y|t) \,] \tag{3.392}$$

for $\forall \phi(t) \in \mathfrak{D}(D)$ and a fixed $t, \theta \in (t_0, t_f]$ where

$$\tilde{U}(\theta|t) = U(\theta) - \hat{U}(\theta|t), \quad \theta = \tau \text{ or } t.$$

[PROOF] From the definitions (3.326), (3.350) or (3.381) of $P(\theta|t)$ and the property (2.6), it follows that

$$(P(\theta|t) \, A^*(t)) \, \phi(t) = E \, [\, \tilde{U}(\theta|t) < A(t) \, \tilde{U}(\tau|t), \, \phi(t) >]$$

$$= \int_D E [\tilde{U}(\theta,x|t)(A_y \tilde{U}(\theta,y|t))] \phi(t,y) dy$$

$$= \int_D (A_y P(\theta,x,y|t)) \phi(t,y) dy.$$

Thus, the proof of the lemma is completed. Q.E.D.

[LEMMA 3.19] For any $h(t) \in H$ and any $e_n(t) \in \mathbf{R}^n$, the operator $h(t) \circ e_n(t)$ possesses the following kernel representation:

$$(h(t) \circ e_n(t)) e_k(t) = F_n(t,x) e_k(t) \tag{3.393}$$

$$F_n(t,x) = h(t,x) e_n'(t)$$

for any $e_k(t) \in \mathbf{R}^n$ and any fixed $t \in (t_0, t_f]$.

This lemma will be obtained by the parallel way to the proof of Lemma 3.18 and hence, the proof is omitted here.

Then applying these lemmas to Theorem 3.34 yields the following theorem.

[THEOREM 3.40] The optimal filtering estimate $\hat{U}(t,x|t)$ is given by the relations

$$d \hat{U}(t,x|t) = A_x \hat{U}(t,x|t) dt + P_m(t,x) h(t) \mho^{-1}(t) d \nu(t) \tag{3.394}$$

$$\hat{U}(t_0,x|t_0) = U_1 = E [U(t_0,x)]$$

$$\frac{\partial P(t,x,y|t)}{\partial t} = A_x P(t,x,y|t) + A_y P(t,x,y|t) + \tilde{Q}(t,x,y)$$

$$- P_m(t,x t) \tilde{R}(t) P_m'(t,y t), \tilde{R}(t) = h(t) \mho^{-1}(t) h'(t) \tag{3.395}$$

$$P(t_0,x,y|t_0) = P_0(x,y) = E [U(t_0,x) U(t_0,y)]$$

where the boundary conditions of (3.394) and (3.395) are

$$\partial(\cdot)/ \partial \mathbf{n} = 0, \quad (\cdot) = \hat{U}(t,\xi|t) \text{ or } P(t,x,\xi|t), \ \forall \xi \in S.$$

As for the smoothing problems, especially the fixed-point smoothing problem, we have the following theorem from Theorem 3.36:

[THEOREM 3.41] The fixed-point smoothing estimate $\hat{U}(\tau,x|t)$ satisfies the following relations:

$$d\,\hat{U}(t_1,x|t) = B_m(t_1,x|t)\; h(t)\, \mathcal{V}^{-1}(t)\; d\,\nu(t) \tag{3.396}$$

$$\frac{\partial B(t_1,x,y\;t)}{\partial t} = A_y\; B(t_1,x,y|t) \;-\; B_m(t_1,x|t)\; \tilde{R}(t)\; P_m'(t,y) \tag{3.397}$$

$$B(t_1,x,y|t_1) = P(t_1,x,y|t_1)$$

$$\frac{\partial P(t_1,x,y\;t)}{\partial t} = -\; B_m(t_1,x|t)\; \tilde{R}(t)\, B_m'(t_1,y|t) \tag{3.398}$$

where the initial conditions of (3.396) and (3.398) are $\hat{U}(t_1,x|t_1)$ and $P(t_1,x,y|t_1)$, respectively and the boundary conditions are the same forms as the filtering problems. The other types of the smoothing estimates can be derived by the same way as Theorem 3.41.

For the prediction problem we have the following theorem.

[THEOREM 3.42] The optimal prediction estimate $\hat{U}(\tau,x|t)$ satisfies the following relations:

$$d\,\hat{U}(\tau,x|t) = A_x\; \hat{U}(\tau,x|t)\; d\tau, \quad \tau > t \tag{3.399}$$

$$\frac{\partial P(\tau,x,y|t)}{\partial \tau} = A_x\; P(\tau,x,y|t) + A_y\; P(\tau,x,y|t) + \tilde{Q}(\tau,x,y) \tag{3.400}$$

where the initial conditions of (3.399) and (3.400) are $\hat{U}(t,x|t)$ and $P(t,x,y|t)$, respectively and the boundary conditions are the same forms as the filtering problems.

APPENDIX: Green's formula.

Let us consider Green's formula which plays a central role to solve the boundary value problems. Let A(t) be defined as the following differential operator;

$$A(t) = \Sigma_{i,j=1}^{r} A_{ij}(t,x) \frac{\partial^2}{\partial x_i \partial x_j} + \Sigma_{i=1}^{r} B_i(t,x) \frac{\partial}{\partial x_i} + C(t,x)$$

where A_{ij}, B_i, and C are $n \times n$ symmetric matrices and $A_{ij} = A_{ji}$. Further, assume that $A^*(t)$ is the adjoint operator of A(t), that is,

$$A^*(t)(\cdot) = \Sigma_{i,j=1}^{r} \partial^2(A_{ij}(t,x)(\cdot))/\partial x_i \partial x_j$$

$$- \Sigma_{i,j=1}^{r} \partial(B_i(t,x)(\cdot))/\partial x_i + C(t,x)(\cdot).$$

Denoting the inner product of n-dimensional Euclidean space $\mathbf{R}^n$ by $(\cdot,\cdot)$, we have the following theorem.

[THEOREM 3.43] The following relation holds.

$$\int_D [(A(t) U(t,x), V(t,x)) - (U(t,x), A^*(t) V(t,x))] dx$$

$$= \int_S [(\beta_A(t,\xi) U(t,\xi), V(t,\xi)) - (U(t,\xi), \beta_A^*(t,\xi) V(t,\xi))] d\xi \quad (3.401)$$

where

$$\beta_A(\cdot) = \Sigma_{j=1}^{r} A_j(t,\xi) \frac{\partial(\cdot)}{\partial x_j}, \quad A_j(t,\xi) = \Sigma_{i=1}^{r} A_{ij}(t,\xi) \cos(\mathbf{n}, x_i)$$

$$\beta_A^*(\cdot) = \beta_A(\cdot) - L(t,\xi)(\cdot)$$

$$L(t,\xi) = \Sigma_{j=1}^{r} (B_i(t,\xi) - \Sigma_{j=1}^{r} \frac{\partial A_{ij}(t,)}{\partial x_j}) \cos(\mathbf{n}, x_i).$$

[PROOF] From the definitions of $A(t)$ and $A^*(t)$, we have

$$(V, A(t) U) - (U, A^*(t) V) = \Sigma_{i,j=1}^{r} [(V, A_{ij}\, \partial^2 U/\partial x_i \partial x_j)$$

$$- (\partial^2(A_{ij} V)/\partial x_i \partial x_j , U)] + \Sigma_{i=1}^{r} [(V, B_i\, \partial U/\partial x_i)$$

$$+ (\partial(B_i V)/\partial x_i , U)] + (V, C U) - (U, C V).$$

Using the symmetricity of the matrices yields

$$(V, A(t) U) - (U, A^*(t) v) = \Sigma_{i=1}^{r} \frac{\partial}{\partial x_i} [\Sigma_{j=1}^{r} ((\partial U/\partial x_j , A_{ij} V)$$

$$- (U, \partial(A_{ij} V)/\partial x_j)) + (U, B_i V)].$$

Setting H_i to be the following relation

$$H_i = \Sigma_{j=1}^{r} ((A_{ij}\, \partial U/\partial x_j , V) - (U, A_{ij}\, \partial V/\partial x_j))$$

$$+ (U, B_i V) - \Sigma_{j=1}^{r} (U, \partial A_{ij}/\partial x_j V),$$

we have

$$\int_D [(A(t) U, V) - (U, A^*(t) V)] dx = \int_D \Sigma_{i=1}^{r} \frac{\partial H_i}{\partial x_i} dx.$$

Using Green's formula yields

$$\int_D \Sigma_{i=1}^{r} \frac{\partial H_i(t,x)}{\partial x_i} dx = \int_S \Sigma_{i=1}^{r} H_i(t,\xi) \cos (\mathbf{n}, x_i) d\xi.$$

Thus, the proof of the theorem is completed. Q.E.D.

3.4. Concluding remarks.

We have derived the optimal estimators, that is, the filtering, smoothing, and prediction estimators for a linear distributed parameter system. The filtering results in Section 3.1.1 were obtained by Sakawa [32] and those of Sections 3.1.2-3.1.3 were derived by Omatu et al.,[33, 34]. The method by using the Ito integral in Hilbert spaces in Section 3.2 was proposed by Falb [2] and the results for the filtering problem in Section 3.2.1 was derived in [2]. The smoothing and prediction results in Sections 3.2.2-3.2.3 were obtained by Omatu et al., [35, 36]. The method by using the parameter optimization technique was proposed by Omatu et al., [7,8] and thus, the results of Section 3.3 were obtained in [7,8].

The results obtained in this chapter can be extended to the estimation and control problems for a linear discrete-time distributed parameter system by using the discretization method [37]. Furthermore, it is also possible to discuss the estimation problems from the information theoretical viewpoints [29, 30, 38]. The other derivations for the optimal estimators for a linear distributed parameter system are given by [66-68].

Chapter 4. EXISTENCE THEOREMS FOR THE OPTIMAL ESTIMATIONS.

4.1. Existence theorem for Riccati equation.

Let D be a bounded open domain of an r-dimensional Euclidean space, and let S, the boundary of D, consist of a finite number of (r - 1)-dimensional hypersurfaces of class C^3. The spatial coordinate vector will be denoted by $x = (a_1, \cdots, x_r) \varepsilon D$. We define Γ_ξ, $\xi \varepsilon S$ by

$$\Gamma_\xi [\cdot] = \alpha(\xi) [\cdot] + (1 - \alpha(\xi)) \partial[\cdot]/ \partial \mathbf{n}$$

where $\mathbf{n}$ is a function of class C^2 on S satisfying

$$0 \leqq \alpha(\xi) \leqq 1.$$

Let an operator A_x be given by

$$A_x u = (\Delta - q(x)) u \quad \text{if} \quad u \varepsilon \mathcal{D}(A_x) \tag{4.1}$$

where Δ is the Laplacian, $q(x) \geqq 0$ is Hölder-continuous on the compact domain $\bar{D} = D \cup S$, and $\mathcal{D}(A_x)$, the domain of the operator A_x is given by

$$\mathcal{D}(A_x) = (u ; \quad \Delta u \varepsilon L^2(D), \quad \Gamma_\xi u(\xi) = 0, \xi \varepsilon S).$$

In this section, we consider the existence theorem for the following partial differential equation of Riccati type:

$$\frac{\partial P(t,x,y)}{\partial t} = A_x P(t,x,y) + A_y P(t,x,y) + Q(t,x,y) - F_m(t,x,y,P) \tag{4.2}$$

$$F_m(t,x,y,P) = P_m(t,x) R(t) P_m'(t,y) \tag{4.3}$$

$$P_m(t,x) = [P(t,x,x^1), \cdots, P(t,x,x^m)] \tag{4.4}$$

$$P(t_0,x,y) = P_0(x,y) \tag{4.5}$$

$$\Gamma_\xi \, P(t,\xi,y) = 0, \forall \xi \in S, \forall y \in \bar{D} \tag{4.6}$$

where $R(t)$ is an $m \times m$ synnetric positive-definite matrix and " ' " denotes the transpose of the matrix.

Let us assume that $R(t)$ is continuous and bounded and

$$Q(t,x,y) = Q(t,y,x) \in L^1(\, t_0, \infty \,;\, L^\infty\,(\, D \times D\,)\,) \tag{4.7}$$

$$P_0(x,y) = P_0(y,x) \in L^2(\, D \times D\,). \tag{4.8}$$

Note that the Riccati equation given by (4.2)-(4.6) describes the optimal filtering error covariance function based on the observed data obtained from the measurement points $x^1, \cdots, x^m \in \bar{D}$ as shown in Theorem 3.3.

In order to prove the existence theorem for the Riccati equation, we introduce the following partial differential equation:

$$\frac{\partial M(t,x,y)}{\partial t} = A_x \, M(t,x,y) + A_y \, M(t,x,y) + Q(t,x,y) \tag{4.9}$$

$$M(t_0,x,y) = P_0(x,y) \tag{4.10}$$

$$\Gamma_\xi \, M(t,\xi,y) = 0, \forall \xi \in S, \forall y \in \bar{D}. \tag{4.11}$$

It is easily seen that the partial differential equation given by (4.9)-(4.11) describes the second order moment of the linear distributed parameter system of (3.81)-(3.84).

Then Ito [18, 19] proved that there exists a unique fundamental solution $\mathcal{U}(t,x,y)$ of (4.1) such that

$$\frac{\partial \mathcal{U}(t,x,y)}{\partial t} = A_x \, \mathcal{U}(t,x,y) \tag{4.12}$$

$$\mathcal{U}(0, x,y) = \delta(x - y) \tag{4.13}$$

$$\Gamma_\xi \mathcal{U}(t,\xi,y) = 0, \forall \xi \in S, \quad \forall y \in \bar{D}. \tag{4.14}$$

Furthermore, $\mathcal{U}(t,x,y)$ possesses the following properties [18,39]:

$$\mathcal{U}(t,x,y) = \mathcal{U}(t,y,x) \geqq 0 \tag{4.15}$$

$$0 \leqq \int_D \mathcal{U}(t,x,y)\, dx \leqq 1. \tag{4.16}$$

Let us now consider the existence theorem concerning a bounded unique solution for (4.2)-(4.4). Before proving this theorem, we shall prove the following lemma which plays the essential role to prove the theorem.

[LEMMA 4.1] If (2.5) is satisfied, then there exists a unique bounded solution $M(t,x,y)$ of (4.9)-(4.11) and $M(t,x,y)$ is given by the following relation:

$$M(t,x,y) = \Psi(t,x,y) + \int_{t_0}^{t} \int_{D^2} \mathcal{U}(t-\tau,x,z)\, Q(\tau,z,a)\, \mathcal{U}(t-\tau,a,y)\, dz\,da\,d\tau. \tag{4.17}$$

where $D^2 = D \times D$ and

$$\Psi(t,x,y) = \int_{D^2} \mathcal{U}(t-t_0,x,z)\, P_0(z,a)\, \mathcal{U}(t-t_0,a,y)\, dz\, da \tag{4.18}$$

[PROOF] By direct differentiation, it is clear from (4.12)-(4.14) that (4.17) satisfies (4.9)-(4.11). Hence, there exists a solution of (4.12)-(4.14). In order to show that the solution of (4.12)-(4.14) is always represented by the integral form (3.1), we assume that $M(t,x,y)$ satisfies (4.12)-(4.14) and let I_τ be defined by

$$I_\tau = \int_{D^2} \mathcal{U}(t-\tau,a,x)\, M(\tau,a,b)\, \mathcal{U}(t-\tau,y,b)\, da\, db.$$

Differentiating each side of I_τ with respect to τ yields

Substituting (4.9) and (4.12) into the above equation yields

$$\frac{d\,I_\tau}{d\tau} = \int_{D^2} [\,(-A_a\,\mathcal{U})\,M\,\mathcal{U} + \mathcal{U}(A_a M + A_b M + Q)\mathcal{U} + \mathcal{U}M\,(-A_b\,\mathcal{U})\,]\,dadb.$$

Using the boundary conditions (4.11) and (4.14), it follows from Green's formula as shown in Appendix that

$$\int_{D^2} [\,(A_a\mathcal{U})\,M\,\mathcal{U} - \mathcal{U}(A_a M)\,\mathcal{U}\,]\,dadb = 0.$$

Thus, we have

$$\frac{d\,I_\tau}{d\tau} = \int_{D^2} \mathcal{U}(t-\tau,a,x)\,Q(\tau,a,b)\,\mathcal{U}(t-\tau,y,b)\,da\,db.$$

Using the symmetricity (4.15) of $\mathcal{U}(t,x,y)$ and integrating each side of the above equation with respect to τ, we have

$$I_t - I_{t_0} = \int_{t_0}^{t}\int_{D^2} \mathcal{U}(t-\tau,a,x)\,Q(\tau,a,b)\,\mathcal{U}(t-\tau,b,y)\,da\,db\,d\tau.$$

On the other hand, it follows from (4.13) and the definition (4.18) of $\Psi(t,x,y)$ that

$$I_t = M(t,x,y) \quad \text{and} \quad I_{t_0} = \Psi(t,x,y).$$

Hence, it is shown that the solution of (4.9)-(4.11) is represented by the integral form (4.17). Thus, it is proved that the partial differential equation given by (4.9)-(4.11) is equivalent to the integral form (4.17).

In order to prove the uniqueness of the solution of (4.9)-(4.11), we assume that there exist two solutions $M_1(t,x,y)$ and $M_2(t,x,y)$ of (4.9)-(4.11). Letting $D(t,x,y)$ be the difference between $M_1(t,x,y)$ and $M_2(t,x,y)$, that is,

$$D(t,x,y) = M_1(t,x,y) - M_2(t,x,y),$$

it follows from (4.9)-(4.11) that

$$\frac{\partial D(t,x,y)}{\partial t} = A_x\, D(t,x,y) + A_y\, D(t,x,y)$$

$$D(t_0,x,y) = 0$$

$$\Gamma_\xi\, D(t,\xi,y) = 0, \quad \forall \xi \in S, \quad \forall y \in \bar{D}.$$

Applying the relation of (4.17) to the above equation yields

$$D(t,x,y) = 0, \text{ that is, } \quad M_1(t,x,y) = M_2(t,x,y).$$

Thus, it is proved that the solution of (4.9)-(4.11) is unique.

In order to prove the boundedness of $M(t,x,y)$, we note that we have from (4.15) and (4.17)

$$|M(t,x,y)| \leqq k_0 \int_{D^2} \mathcal{U}(t,x,a)\, \mathcal{U}(t,b,y)\, da\, db$$

$$+ \int_{t_0}^{t} k_1(\tau) \int_{D^2} \mathcal{U}(t-\tau,x,a)\, \mathcal{U}(t-\tau,b,y)\, da\, db\, d\tau$$

where

$$k_0 = \sup_{x,y \in D} |P_0(x,y)|$$

$$k_1(\tau) = \sup_{x,y \in D} |Q(\tau,x,y)|.$$

Then it follows from (4.7) and (4.16) that

$$|M(t,x,y)| \leqq k_0 + \int_{t_0}^{t} k_1(\tau)\, d\tau < \infty. \tag{4.19}$$

Thus, the proof of lemma is completed. Q.E.D.

Then we shall prove the following lemma.

[LEMMA 4.2] Let the sequence $P^n(t,x,y)$ be

$$\frac{\partial P^n(t,x,y)}{\partial t} = A_x P^n(t,x,y) + A_y P^n(t,x,y) + Q(t,x,y) - F_m(t,x,y,P^{n-1}), \quad n=1,2,\cdots \tag{4.20}$$

where

$$P^0(t,x,y) = \Psi(t,x,y) \tag{4.21}$$

$$P^n(t_0,x,y) = P_0(x,y) \tag{4.22}$$

$$\Gamma_\xi P^n(t,\xi,y) = 0, \quad \forall\xi \in S, \quad \forall y \in \bar{D}. \tag{4.23}$$

If $|P^{n-1}(t,x,y)| \leq K$ for a positive constant K, then for all $t \geq t_0$

$$|P^n(t,x,y)| \leq K. \tag{4.24}$$

[PROOF] Let T_1 be some finite time and let d_1 and d_2 be

$$d_1 = \sup_{\substack{t\in[t_0,T_1] \\ x,y\in D}} |Q(t,x,y)| \quad \text{and} \quad d_2 = \sup_{t\in[t_0,T_1]} \|R(t)\|$$

where for the (i,j)-th element $r_{ij}(t)$ of $R(t)$

$$\|R(t)\| = \Sigma_{i,j=1}^m |r_{ij}(t)|.$$

By using Lemma 4.1 the unique bounded solution $P^n(t,x,y)$ of (4.20)-(4.23) is represented as follows:

$$P^n(t,x,y) = \Psi(t,x,y) + \int_{t_0}^t \int_{D^2} \mathcal{U}(t-\tau,x,a)\,[\,Q(\tau,a,b) - F_m(\tau,a,b,P^{n-1})\,]\,\mathcal{U}(t-\tau,b,y)\,da\,db\,d\tau. \tag{4.25}$$

If $|P_0(x,y)| \leq K/2$, then from (4.16) and (4.25) we have

$$|P^n(t,x,y)| \leqq K/2 + T_1 (d_1 + K^2 d_2).$$

Thus, by taking $T_1 = K/ 2(d_1 + K^2 d_2)$ we have

$$| P^n(t,x,y) | \leqq K, \quad \forall t \in [t_0, T_1].$$

Repeating the same procedure by taking T_1 as the initial time and so on, we have

$$| P^n(t,x,y) | \leqq K, \quad \forall t \in [t_0, \infty).$$

Hence, the proof of the lemma is completed. Q.E.D.

Then we have the following existence theorem.

[THEOREM 4.1] Under the same condition as Lemma 4.1, there exists a unique bounded solution $P(t,x,y)$ of (4.2)-(4.6) and it satisfies

$$P(t,x,y) = \Psi(t,x,y) + \int_{t_0}^{t} \int_{D^2} \mathcal{U} (t-\tau,x,a) [Q(\tau,a,b) - F_m(\tau,a,b,P)] \mathcal{U} (t-\tau,b,y) \, da \, db \, d\tau. \tag{4.26}$$

[PROOF] In order to prove the existence theorem by using the successive approximation technique, let the sequence $P^n(t,x,y)$ be given by (4.20)-(4.23), that is, (4.25). From the boundedness of $P^n(t,x,y)$ it follows that

$$| F_m(t,x,y,P^n) - F_m(t,x,y,P^{n-1}) | \leqq k/2 \, (\sup_i | P^n(t,x,x^i) - P^{n-1}(t,x,x^i) | + \sup_i | P^n(t,x^i, y) - P^{n-1}(t,x^i, y) |) \tag{4.27}$$

where $k = 2 K d_2$.

Let $r_n(t)$ be defined by

$$r_n(t) = \sup_{\substack{\zeta \leqq t \\ x,y \in D}} | P^n(\zeta,x,y) - P^{n-1}(\zeta,x,y) | . \tag{4.28}$$

Since it is clear that

$$\sup_{i,\ y \in D} | P^n(t,x,^i_, y) - P^{n-1}(t,x,^i_,y)| \leq \sup_{x,y \in D} | P^n(t,x,y) - P^{n-1}(t,x,y) | ,$$

it follows from (4.25) that

$$r_{n+1}(t) \leq k \int_{t_0}^{t} r_n(\tau)\, d\tau, \quad n = 1, 2, \cdots. \tag{4.29}$$

Letting M be

$$M = \sup_{\substack{x,y \in D \\ \tau \in [t_0,t]}} | Q(\tau,x,y) - F_m(\tau,x,y,\Psi) | ,$$

it follows from (4.29) that

$$r_n(t) \leq k^{n-1}\, t^n\, M / n!, \quad n = 1, 2, \cdots.$$

Hence, $r_n(t)$ converges uniformly to zero if n goes to infinity, that is,

$$\lim_{n \to \infty} P^n(t,x,y) = P(t,x,y) \tag{4.30}$$

where (4.30) holds uniformly.

Since it was proved that $P^n(t,x,y)$ converges uniformly to $P(t,x,y)$ and from Lemma 4.2 $P^n(t,x,y)$ is bounded, (4.26) follows from (4.25) and the Lebesgue bounded convergence theorem [7, 14, 15]. Since it is clear that (4.26) satisfies the partial differential equation described by (4.2)-(4.6), it is proved that there exists a bounded solution of (4.2)-(4.6). By the similar way to Lemma 4.1, it is easily seen that the solution of (4.2)-(4.6) always satisfies the integral form (4.26). Hence, it is proved that (4.2)-(4.6) are equivalent to (4.26).

In order to prove the uniqueness of the solution of (4.2)-(4.6), let us assume that there exist two solutions $P_1(t,x,y)$ and $P_2(t,x,y)$ of (4.2)-(4.6).

Letting the difference between $P_1(t,x,y)$ and $P_2(t,x,y)$ be $D(t,x,y)$, it follows from (4.26) that

$$D(t,x,y) = \int_{t_0}^{t} \int_{D^2} \mathcal{U}(t-\tau,x,a) \, [\, F_m(\tau,a,b,P_2) - F_m(\tau,a,b,P_1) \,] \, \mathcal{U}(t-\tau,b,y) \, da \, db \, d\tau.$$

Using the inequality (4.27) yields

$$D(t,x,y) \leqq k \int_{t_0}^{t} \int_{D^2} \mathcal{U}(t-\tau,x,a) \, [\sup_{a,b \, \varepsilon \, D} | D(t,x,y) | \,] \, \mathcal{U}(t-\tau,b,y) \, da \, db \, d\tau. \qquad (4.29)$$

Letting $p_M(t)$ be

$$p_M(t) = \sup_{\substack{\zeta \leqq t \\ x,y \, \varepsilon \, D}} | D(\zeta,x,y) |,$$

it follows from (4.16) and (4.29) that

$$p_M(t) \leqq k \int_{t_0}^{t} p_M(\tau) \, d\tau.$$

Since it is clear from the definition of $p_M(t)$ that $p_M(t)$ is a non-negative and increasing function of t, it follows that

$$0 \leqq p_M(t) \leqq k \, t \, p_M(t).$$

Hence, it follows that

$$p_M(t) = 0, \quad \forall t \, \varepsilon \, [\, t_0, 1/k \,].$$

Repeating the same procedure by taking 1/k as the initial time and so on, it follows that

$$p_M(t) = 0, \quad \forall t \, \varepsilon \, [\, t_0, \infty \,).$$

Thus, it is proved that the solution of (4.2)-(4.6) is unique. The boundedness of $P(t,x,y)$ is clear from Lemma 4.2.

Thus, the proof of the theorem is completed. Q.E.D.

Accordingly, we proved that there exists a unique bounded solution of (4.2)-(4.6) not in the sense of the distribution such as [5, 13, 14] but in the sense of the usual function. Furthermore, Theorem 4.1 shows that there exists the strict solution of (4.2)-(4.6) although Datko [40] and Curtain et al. [41] proved the existence theorem of the mild or inner product solution.

4.2. Existence theorems for the optimal filtering and prediction estimates.

Using Theorem 4.1, we can easily seen in Theorem 3.40 that

$$L(t,x,t) = P_m(t,x)\, h'(t) \mathcal{V}^{-1}(t) \;\varepsilon\; L^{\infty}(t_0,t_f;\; \mathcal{L}(\mathbf{R}^m, H))$$

and

$$K(t,x,t) = A_x - P_m(t,x)\, h'(t) \mathcal{V}^{-1}(t) \;\varepsilon\; L^2(t_0,t_f;\; \mathcal{L}(V, V')).$$

Thus, from Theorem 2.5 we have the following theorem.

[THEOREM 4.2] There exists the unique solution $\hat{U}(t,x|t)$ of the filtering estimator equation (3.394) such that

$$\hat{U}(t,x|t) \;\varepsilon\; C(t_0,t_f;\mathcal{V}') \cap L^{\infty}(t_0,t_f;\mathcal{H}) \cap L^2(t_0,t_f;\mathcal{V}). \tag{4.30}$$

Theorem 4.2 means that the unique solution of (3.394) exists in the sense of the distribution. It is in general, difficult to physically interpret the solution in the sense of the distribution which may limit the usefulness of Theorem 4.2. However, it is well known that for the deterministic system the conditions under which the distribution is identified with the ordinary function are given by

Nikodym's theorem [14]. Hence, if Nikodym's theorem can be extended to the stochastic case, Theorem 4.2 will become more useful.

As for the optimal prediction problem, the following theorem holds from Theorem 2.4 and (3.399).

[THEOREM 4.3] There exists the unique solution $\hat{U}(\tau,x|t)$ for $\tau > t$ of the prediction estimator equation (3.399) such that

$$\hat{U}(\tau,x|t) \in C(t_0,t_f;\mathcal{V}') \cap L^{\infty}(t_0,t_f;\mathcal{H}) \cap L^2(t_0,t_f;\mathcal{V}). \qquad (4.31)$$

It is clear that the result of (4.31) may be improved if we can improve Theorem 4.2 since $\hat{U}(t,x|t)$ is the initial condition of $\hat{U}(\tau,x|t)$ for $\tau > t$.

4.3. Existence theorem for the smoothing gain function.

Let us now prove the existence theorem for the optimal smoothing gain function $B(\tau,x,y|t)$ given by (3.358), that is,

$$\frac{\partial B(\tau,x,y|t)}{\partial t} = A_y\, B(\tau,x,y|t) - B_m(\tau,x|t)\,\tilde{R}(t)\,P_m'(t,y) \qquad (4.32)$$

$$\frac{\partial B(\tau,x,\xi|t)}{\partial \mathbf{n}} = 0, \forall \xi \in S, \forall x \in \bar{D} \qquad (4.33)$$

$$B(\tau,x,y|\tau) = P(\tau,x,y|\tau). \qquad (4.34)$$

Then the following theorem can be proved.

[THEOREM 4.4] There exists the unique solution of (4.32)-(4.34) and the following relation holds:

$$B(\tau,x,y|t) = \Xi(t,x,y) - \int_\tau^t \int_D B_m(\tau,x|\sigma)\,\tilde{R}(\sigma)\,P_m'(\sigma,a|\sigma)\,\mathcal{U}(t-\sigma,y,a)\,da\,d\sigma \qquad (4.35)$$

where

$$\Xi(t,x,y) = \int_D P(\tau,x,a|\tau)\ \mathcal{U}(t-\tau,y,a)\ da.$$

[PROOF] Using the successive approximation technique, we have

$$\frac{\partial B^{n+1}(\tau,x,y|t)}{\partial t} = A_y\ B^{n+1}(\tau,x,y|t) - B_m^n(\tau,x|t)\ \tilde{R}(t)\ P_m'(t,y) \tag{4.36}$$

where $n = 0, 1, \cdots$ and

$$B^0(\tau,x,y|t) = \Xi(t,x,y),\quad \frac{\partial}{\partial \mathbf{n}} B^n(\tau,\xi,y|t) = 0,\ \forall \xi \in S,\quad \forall y \in \bar{D}$$

$$B^n(\tau,x,y|\tau) = P(\tau,x,y|\tau),\ n = 1, 2, \cdots.$$

Using the fundamental solution $\mathcal{U}(t,x,y)$, The solution of (4.36) can be written as follows:

$$B^{n+1}(\tau,x,y|t) = \Xi(t,x,y) - \int_\tau^t \int_D B_m^n(\tau,x|\sigma)\ \tilde{R}(\sigma)\ P_m'(\sigma,a|\sigma)\ \mathcal{U}(t-\sigma,y,a)\ da\ d\sigma. \tag{4.37}$$

Letting the function $r_{n+1}(t)$ be

$$r_{n+1}(t) = \sup_{\substack{\sigma \leq t \\ x,y \in D}} |\ B^{n+1}(\tau,x,y|\sigma) - B^n(\tau,x,y|\sigma)|\ ,$$

it follows from (4.16), (4.37), and the boundedness of $P(t,x,y|t)$ that

$$r_{n+1}(t) \leqq K \int_\tau^t r_n(\sigma)\ d\sigma$$

where

$$k = \sup_{\substack{\sigma \in [t_0,t_f] \\ x,y \in D}} |\ \mathbf{e}'\ \tilde{R}(\sigma)\ \mathbf{e}\ \ P(\sigma,x,y|\sigma)\ |,\quad \mathbf{e} = \mathrm{Col}\ [\ 1,\cdots,1\ ].$$

Hence, it follows that

$$r_n(t) \leqq K^{n-1} (t - \tau)^n M/ n!, \quad M = \sup_{\substack{\sigma \in [t_0, t_f] \\ x,y \in D}} | \mathbf{e}' \tilde{R}(\sigma) \mathbf{e} \, \Xi(\sigma,x,y)| ,$$

$n = 1, 2, \cdots.$

Then $r_n(t)$ converges uniformly to zero as n goes to infinity, that is,

$$\lim_{n \to \infty} B^n(\tau,x,y|t) = B(\tau,x,y|t). \tag{4.38}$$

Since (4.38) holds uniformly, it is possible to interchange the limit operation and the integration. Hence, it is concluded that $B(\tau,x,y|t)$ satisfies (4.35). Since $B(\tau,x,y|t)$ given by (4.35) satisfies the partial differential equations (4.32)-(4.34), it is proved that there exists a solution of (4.32)-(4.34). In order to show that $B(\tau,x,y|t)$ satisfying (4.32)-(4.34) is represented by (4.35), we assume that $B(\tau,x,a|\sigma)$ satisfies (4.32)-(4.34). Let us define I_σ by

$$I_\sigma = \int_D \mathcal{U}(t-\sigma,y,a) \, B(\tau,x,a|\sigma) \, da.$$

Differentiating I_σ with respect to σ yields

$$\frac{\partial I_\sigma}{\partial \sigma} = \int_D \left(\frac{\partial \mathcal{U}}{\partial \sigma} B + \mathcal{U} \frac{\partial B}{\partial \sigma} \right) da.$$

On the other hand, from (4.32) we have

$$\frac{\partial I_\sigma}{\partial \sigma} = \int_D \left[- (A_a \mathcal{U}) B + \mathcal{U} (A_a B - B_m(\tau,x|\sigma) \tilde{R}(\sigma) P_m(\sigma,a|\sigma)) \right] da.$$

Using the boundary condition (4.33) and Green's formula yields

$$\partial I_\sigma / \partial \sigma = - \int_D \mathcal{U}(t-\tau,y,a) \, B_m(\tau,x|\sigma) \, \tilde{R}(\sigma) \, P_m(\sigma,a|\sigma) \, da.$$

Integrating each side of the above equation yields

$$I_t = I_\tau - \int_\tau^t \int_D \mathcal{U}(t-\sigma,y,a)\, B_m(\tau,x|\sigma)\, \tilde{R}(\sigma)\, P_m(\sigma,a|\sigma)\, da d\sigma.$$

But

$$I_t = B(\tau,x,y|t) \quad \text{and} \quad I_\tau = \Xi(t,x,y).$$

Hence, it is proved that $B(\tau,x,y|t)$ satisfying (4.32)-(4.34) is represented by (4.35). Therefore, we can conclude that (4.32)-(4.34) are equivalent to (4.35). We must prove the uniqueness property of (4.32)-(4.34). If we assume that $B_1(\tau,x,y|t)$ and $B_2(\tau,x,y|t)$ are two solutions of (4.32)-(4.34) and $D(\tau,x,y|t)$ denotes the difference function between them, we have

$$D(\tau,x,y|t) = - \int_\tau^t \int_D \mathcal{U}(t-\sigma,y,a)\; D_m(\tau,x|\sigma)\, \tilde{R}(\sigma)\, P_m(\sigma,a|\sigma)\, da\, d\sigma \quad (4.39)$$

where

$$D_m(\tau,x|\sigma) = B_{1m}(\tau,x|\sigma) - B_{2m}(\tau,x|\sigma).$$

If we let $r(t)$ be

$$r(t) = \sup_{\substack{\sigma \leq t \\ x,y \in D}} | D(\tau,x,y|\sigma)| ,$$

then we have from (4.16) and (4.39)

$$0 \leqq r(t) \leqq K \int_\tau^t r(\sigma)\, d\sigma \leqq K\, r(t)\, (t - \tau).$$

Hence, we have for $\forall t \in (\tau , \tau + 1/K)$

$$r(t) = 0.$$

Repeating the same procedure by taking $\tau + 1/k$ as the initial time and so on, we have

$r(t) = 0 \quad \text{for} \quad {}^{\forall} t \in (\tau, t_f]$.

Therefore, it is proved that the solution of (4.32)-(4.34) is unique.
Thus, the proof of the theorem is completed. Q.E.D.

Since $K(\tau,x,t) = - B_m(\tau,x|t) h'(t) \mathcal{V}^{-1}(t) H(t) \in L^2(\tau, t_f; \mathcal{L}(V,v'))$ and $L(\tau,x,t) = - B_m(\tau,x|t) h'(t) \mathcal{V}^{-1}(t) \in L^{\infty}(\tau, t_f; \mathcal{L}(\mathbf{R}^m, H))$, the following theorem follows:

[THEOREM 4.5] There exists the unique solution $\hat{U}(\tau,x|t)$ of the optimal smoothing estimator equation (3.396) such that

$$\hat{U}(\tau,x|t) \in C(\tau,t_f; \mathcal{V}') \cap L^{\infty}(\tau,t_f; \mathcal{H}) \cap L^2(\tau,t_f; \mathcal{V}).$$

Thus, we have proved that there exists the unique solution of the optimal smoothing problem in the sense of the distribution.

4.4. Concluding remarks.

In this chapter, we prove the existence and uniqueness theorem concerning a solution of the partial differential equation of Riccati type. The existence and uniqueness theorem was proved by many authors from the several viewpoints [5, 13, 40, 41, 42]. The procedure for the proof of the existence theorem is based on the successive approximation technique and this method shows that the existence and uniqueness theorem can be proved for the case of the point-wise observation.

Chapter 5. Optimal sensor location problems.

5.1. Problem formulation.

Let D be a bounded open domain of an r-dimensional Euclidean space, and let S, the boundary of D , consist of a finite number of (r - 1)-dimensional hypersurface of Class C^3. Let the state U(t,x) be described by a linear partial differential equation of parabolic type

$$\frac{\partial U(t,x)}{\partial t} = A_x U(t,x) + C(t,x) \dot{W}(t,x) \tag{5.1}$$

$$U(t_0,x) = U_0(x) \tag{5.2}$$

$$\Gamma_\xi U(t,\xi) = 0, \ ^\forall\xi \in S, \ ^\forall y \in \bar{D} \tag{5.3}$$

where A_x is given by (4.1) and $\dot{W}(t,x)$ is a white Gaussian process.

Then it is well known that there exist the eigenvalues λ_i and the corresponding normalized eigenfunctions $\phi_i(x)$ of the operator A_x exist and satisfy the following conditions [18,39];

$$A_x \ \phi_i(x) = \lambda_i \phi_i(x), \quad i = 1, 2, \cdots \tag{5.4}$$

$$C \geqq \lambda_1 \geqq \cdots \geqq \lambda_i \geqq \cdots, \quad \lim_{i \to \infty} \lambda_i = -\infty \tag{5.5}$$

where $C = -\min_{x \in D} [q(x)]$ and that the family of eigenfunctions { $\phi_i(x)$, $i = 1, 2, \cdots$ } is complete and orthonormal in $L^2(D)$.

Now the function spaces $\mathfrak{F}(t_0,t)$ and $\mathfrak{F}_1(t_0,t)$ which will play an important role in the subsequent derivations of the optimality conditions are defined as follows:

$$\mathfrak{F}(t_0,t) = \{ f \ ; \ f(\tau,x,y) = \Sigma_{i,j=1}^{\infty} \ g_{ij}(\tau) \ \phi_i(x) \ \phi_j(y), \ g_{ij}(\tau) = g_{ji}(\tau) \in C^1(t_0,t) \text{ and } [g_{ij}]_N \geqq 0 \text{ for } ^\forall\tau \in [t_0, t] \} \tag{5.6}$$

and

$$\mathcal{F}_1(t_0,t) = \{ f; \quad f \in \mathcal{F}(t_0,t) \text{ and } g_{ij}(\tau) = h_i(\tau)\, \delta_{ij} \} \tag{5.7}$$

where δ_{ij} denotes the Kronecker delta and $[g_{ij}]_N$ is the $N \times N$ matrix with g_{ij} as the (i,j)-th element.

Note that the form on the spatial domain of the function in $\mathcal{F}(t_0,t)$ is completely determined by the eigenfunctions $\phi_i(x)$ of the partial differential operator A_x.

Assume that $U_0(x)$ is a Gaussian random function whose mean and covariance functions are given by

$$E[U_0(x)] = 0, \quad E[U_0(x)\, U_0(y)] = P_0(x,y). \tag{5.8}$$

Let the observed data be taken at fixed m points, $a^1, a^2, \cdots, a^m \in \overline{D}$ and let an m-dimensional column vector $U_a(t)$ be defined by

$$U_a(t) = \text{Col} [U(t,a^1), \cdots , U(t,a^m)]. \tag{5.9}$$

Assume that the observation equation is given by

$$Z_a(t) = H(t)\, U_a(t) + \dot{V}(t) \tag{5.10}$$

$$\dot{V}(t) = \text{Col} [\dot{V}(t,a^1), \cdots, \dot{V}(t,a^m)] \tag{5.11}$$

where $H(t)$ is a known $m \times m$ matrix and $\dot{V}(t,x)$ is a white Gaussian process.

The White Gauusian processes $\dot{W}(t,x)$ in (5.1) and $\dot{V}(t,x)$ in (5.11) are assumed to be stochastically independent of each other and also independent of the stochastic initial condition $U_0(x)$. Their mean and covariance functions are given by

$$E[\dot{W}(t,x)] = E[\dot{V}(t,x)] = 0, \quad E[\dot{W}(t,x)\, \dot{W}(s,y)] = q(t,x,y)\, \delta(t-s)$$

$$E[\dot{V}(t,x)\, \dot{V}(s,y)] = r(t,x,y)\, \delta(t-s).$$

It is easily seen from the definition of the covariance functions and the symmetric property of $\delta(\tau)$ with respect to τ that

$$q(t,x,y) = q(t,y,x) \quad \text{and} \quad r(t,x,y) = r(t,y,x).$$

Then the covariance matrix of $V_a(t)$ is given by

$$E[\dot{V}_a(t)\,\dot{V}_a'(s)] = R_a(t)\,\delta(t-s)$$

$$R_a(t) = [\, r(t,a^i, a^j)\,]_m \,. \tag{5.12}$$

Assume that $q(t,x,y)$ is bounded for almost all $x,y \in D$ and that $R_a(t)$ is positive-definite and $r(t,x,y)$ is continuous with respect to all x,y, and t. Note that the assumption for $q(t,x,y)$ is required to prove the existence and uniqueness theorem concerning a solution of (5.1)-(5.3) as shown in Theorem 2.5. Therefore, in order to prove the existence and uniqueness theorem, $W(t,x)$ must be a colored noise with respect to the spatial coordinate x since $q(t,x,y)$ excludes the Dirac delta function. This means intuitively that the system noise $W(t,x)$ is a smooth function on the spatial domain when there exists a unique state $U(t,x)$ of the system (5.1)-(5.3). Furthermore, it is shown later that the continuity assumption on $r(t,x,y)$ with respect to each variable x,y, and t is required to prove the existence theorem concerning a solution of the optimal sensor location problem.

Let the optimal estimate $\hat{U}_a(t,x|t)$ of the state $U(t,x)$ be determined from the viewpoint of the minimum variance estimation error criterion based on the observed data $Z_a(s)$, $t_0 \leq s \leq t$. Then the optimal filtering error covariance function $P_a(t,x,y)$ satisfies the following partial differential equation of Riccati type as shown in Theorem 3.3:

$$\partial P_a(t,x,y)/\partial t = A_x P_a(t,x,y) + A_y P_a(t,x,y) + Q(t,x,y) - F_a(t,x,y,P_a) \tag{5.13}$$

$$P_a(t_0,x,y) = P_0(x,y) \tag{5.14}$$

$$\Gamma_\xi \; P_a(t,\xi,y) = 0, \; \forall \xi \in S, \; \forall y \in \bar{D} \tag{5.15}$$

where

$$P_a(t,x,y) = E\,[\,\tilde{U}_a(t,x|t)\;\tilde{U}_a(t,y|t)\,]$$

$$\tilde{U}_a(t,x|t) = U(t,x) - \hat{U}_a(t,x|t)$$

$$Q(t,x,y) = C(t,x)\;q(t,x,y)\;C(t,y)$$

$$F_a(t,x,y,P_a) = P_a(t,x)\;\tilde{R}_a(t)\;P_a'(t,y) \tag{5.16}$$

$$\tilde{R}_a(t) = H'(t)\;R_a^{-1}(t)\;H(t) \tag{5.17}$$

$$P_a(t,x) = (\,P_a(t,x,a^1),\cdots,\,P_a(t,x,a^m)). \tag{5.18}$$

Let the fundamental solution of A_x be $\mathcal{U}(t,x,y)$. Then (4.12)-(4.16) hold and further, the following relation follows [18, 39]:

$$\mathcal{U}(t,x,y) = \Sigma_{i=1}^{\infty}\; \exp\,(\,\lambda_i\; t\,)\;\; \phi_i(x)\;\phi_i(y), \quad (\,t > 0\,) \tag{5.19}$$

where $\{\;\phi_i(x),\;\lambda_i\;\}$ are given by (5.4) and (5.5).

In order to define the optimal sensor location problem a performance index must be specified which is to be minimized by choice of a^i, $i = 1, 2, \cdots, m$. Since the location criterion is that of obtaining the best possible estimate of the state $U(t,x)$, it is adopted here to minimize the trace of the estimation error variance function $P_a(t,x,x)$ in the optimal filter. Hence, for any fixed time t_f the performance index $J_a(t_f)$ is defined by the following relation:

$$J_a(t_f) = \int_D \; P_a(t,x,x)\;dx \; = \; \text{trace}\;[\;P_a(t_f,x,x)\;]. \tag{5.20}$$

where trace $[\cdot]$ denotes the trace of the function given by

$$\text{trace}\,[\cdot] = \Sigma_{i=1}^{\infty} [\cdot]_{ii}$$

where $[\cdot]_{ii}$ is the (i,i)-th Fourier expansion coefficient.
In order to avoid the possibility that several measurement points might be clustered in a point of the spatial domain, it is assumed that $a^i \neq a^j \in \overline{D}$ for $i \neq j$.

Furthermore, assume that $b^1, b^2, \cdots, b^m \in \overline{D}$ are measurement points which differ from $a^1, a^2, \cdots, a^m$. Let $\tilde{R}_b(t)$ and $P_b(t,x)$ be defined by exchanging a^i for b^i in (5.17) and (5.18), respectively and let $F_b(t,x,y,P_b)$ be defined as follows:

$$F_b(t,x,y,P_a) = P_a(t,x)\,\tilde{R}_b(t)\,P_a'(t,y) \tag{5.21}$$

Let $P_b(t,x,y)$ denote the solution of (5.13)-(5.15) obtained by substituting $F_b(t,x,y,P_b)$ in place of $F_a(t,x,y,P_a)$. Then we note that there exists some constant k such that

$$| F_a(t,x,y,P_a) - F_a(t,x,y,P_b) | \leqq k/2 \,(\, \sup_i | P_a(t,x,a^i) - P_b(t,x,a^i)|$$

$$+ \sup_i |P_a(t,a^i, y) - P_b(t,a^i, y)| \,) \tag{5.22}$$

which is a direct consequence of (4.27).
From Theorem 4.1 and (5.19) we have the following lemma.
[LEMMA 5.1] The unique solution of (5.13)-(5.15) belongs to $\mathfrak{F}(t_0,t)$, that is,

$$P_a(t,x,y) \in \mathfrak{F}(t_0,t). \tag{5.23}$$

5.2. Comparison theorem.

Let us prove the comparison theorem which plays the essential role in the derivation of the optimality conditions for the sensor location problem.

[THEOREM 5.1] If the nonlinear terms $F_a(t,x,y,P_a)$ and $F_b(t,x,y,P_b)$ satisfy the following inequality

$$F_b(t,x,y,P) \geqq F_a(t,x,y,P) \tag{5.24}$$

for $\forall t \in [t_0,t_f]$, $\forall P \in \mathfrak{F}(t_0,t)$ and any measurement points ($a^1, a^2, \cdots, a^m$), then it follows that

$$P_b(t,x,y) \leqq P_a(t,x,y) \qquad \text{for} \quad \forall t \in [t_0,t_f]. \tag{5.25}$$

[PROOF] Let $D(t,x,y)$ be the difference between $P_a(t,x,y)$ and $P_b(t,x,y)$, that is,

$$D(t,x,y) = P_a(t,x,y) - P_b(t,x,y). \tag{5.26}$$

Letting $\bar{D}(t,x,y)$ be

$$\bar{D}(t,x,y) = D(t,x,y) \exp(\, k\, t\,) \tag{5.27}$$

where k is the constant in (5.22), it follows from (5.13)-(5.15) that

$$\frac{\partial \bar{D}(t,x,y)}{\partial t} = A_x \bar{D}(t,x,y) + A_y \bar{D}(t,x,y) + k \bar{D}(t,x,y)$$

$$+ \exp(\, k\, t\,)\, (\, F_b(t,x,y,P_b) - F_a(t,x,y,P_a)\,). \tag{5.28}$$

$$\bar{D}(t_0,x,y) = 0 \tag{5.29}$$

$$\Gamma_\xi \bar{D}(t,\xi,y) = 0, \ \forall \xi \in S, \ \forall y \in \bar{D}. \tag{5.30}$$

Then applying Theorem 4.1 to (5.28)-(5.30) yields

$$\overline{D}(t,x,y) = \int_{t_0}^{t} \int_{D^2} \mathcal{U}(t-\tau,x,a) \, [\, k \; \overline{D}(\tau,a,b)$$

$$+ \exp(\, k\tau \,)(\, F_b(\tau,a,b,P_b) - F_a(\tau,a,b,P_a))\,] \, \mathcal{U}(t-\tau,b,y) \; da \, db \, d\tau. \tag{5.31}$$

Taking into consideration from Lemma 5.1 that P_a and P_b belong to $\mathcal{F}(t_0,t)$, it follows from (5.22) and (5.24) that

$$\exp(\, k\tau \,)\,(\, F_b(\tau,a,b,P_b) - F_a(\tau,a,b,P_a))$$

$$\geqq \exp(\, k\tau \,)\,(\, F_a(\tau,a,b,P_b) - F_a(\tau,a,b,P_a)\,)$$

$$\geqq \exp(\, k\tau \,)\,(\, - k/2 \sup_i |P_b(\tau,a,a^i) - P_a(\tau,a,a^i)|$$

$$- k/2 \sup_i |P_b(\tau,a^i,b) - P_a(\tau,a^i,b)|\,). \tag{5.32}$$

Using (5.26) and (5.27), it follows from (5.32) that

$$\exp(\, k\tau \,)\,(\, F_b(\tau,a,b,P_b) - F_a(\tau,a,b,P_a)\,)$$

$$\geqq \; - k/2\,(\, \sup_i \; |\overline{D}(\tau,a,a^i)| \; + \; \sup_i |\overline{D}(\tau,a^i,b)| \;). \tag{5.33}$$

Let the functions $n_\Delta(t)$ and $n(t)$ be

$$- n_\Delta(t) = \inf_{\substack{\tau \leq t \\ a,b,i}} \;(\; \overline{D}(\tau,a,b) - |\, \overline{D}(\tau,a,a^i)| \;) \tag{5.34}$$

and

$$- n(t) = \inf_{\substack{\tau \leqq t \\ a,b}} \;(\; \overline{D}(\tau,a,b) - |\overline{D}(\tau,a,b)|\,). \tag{5.35}$$

Since it is clear that $\overline{D}(t,x,y)$ is symmetric with respect to x and y, it follows from (5.32)-(5.35) that

$$\bar{D}(t,x,y) \geqq - k \int_{t_0}^{t} \int_{D^2} \mathcal{U}(t-\tau,x,a)\; n_\Delta(\tau)\; \mathcal{U}(t-\tau,b,y)\; da\, db\, d\tau .$$

Using (4.16), (5.34), and (5.35) yields

$$\bar{D}(t,x,y) \geqq - k \int_{t_0}^{t} n_\Delta(\tau)\; d\tau \geqq - k \int_{t_0}^{t} n(\tau)\; d\tau . \tag{5.36}$$

Thus, it follows from (5.36) that

$$\bar{D}(t,x,y) - |\bar{D}(t,x,y)| \geqq - 2k \int_{t_0}^{t} n(\tau)\; d\tau . \tag{5.37}$$

Thus, we have from (5.35) and (5.37)

$$- n(t) \geqq - 2k \int_{t_0}^{t} n(\tau)\; d\tau \geqq - 2\, k\, t\, n(t).$$

Hence, it follows that

$$n(t) = 0 \quad \text{for } \forall t \in [\, t_0,\, 1/2k\,].$$

Repeating the same procedure by taking 1/2k as the initial time and so on, it follows that

$$n(t) = 0 \quad \text{for } \forall t \in [\, t_0,\, t_f\,], \text{ i.e., } \bar{D}(t,x,y) \geqq 0 \quad \text{for } \forall t \in [\, t_0,\, t_f\,].$$

Hence, (5.25) follows from (5.26), (5.27), and the above relation.
Thus, the proof of the theorem is completed. Q.E.D.

Taking $h_i(\tau) = \exp(\lambda_i \tau)$ in (5.7), it follows from (5.19) that $\mathcal{U}(t-\tau,x,a)$ and $\mathcal{U}(t-\tau,b,x)$ belong to $\mathcal{U}_1(t_0,t)$. Setting x = y in (5.31) and using the same procedure as the proof of Theorem 5.1, the following theorem holds.

[THEOREM 5.2] If the following relation holds in the weak sense

$$F_b(t,x,y,P) \geqq F_a(t,x,y,P) \tag{5.38}$$

for $^\forall t \in [t_0,t_f]$, $^\forall P \in \mathcal{F}(t_0,t)$ and any measurement points ($a^1, a^2, \cdots, a^m$), then it follows that

$$P_b(t,x,x) \to P_a(t,x,x) \qquad\qquad (5.39)$$

for $^\forall t \in [t_0,t_f]$ and $^\forall x \in \overline{D}$, where the weak sense in (5.38) means that for any $P_1 \in \mathcal{F}_1(t_0,t)$

$$\int_{D^3} P_1(t,x,a)\ F_b(t,a,b,P)\ P_1(t,b,x)\ da\ db\ dx$$

$$\geq \int_{D^3} P_1(t,x,a)\ F_a(t,a,b,P)\ P_1(t,b,x)\ da\ db\ dx. \qquad (5.40)$$

Thus, using the existence and uniqueness theorem concerning a solution of the partial differential equation of Riccati type, Theorem 4.1, the comparison theorem for the partial differential equations was proved.

Let us now prove the following theorem which will be required to prove the existence theorem for the optimal sensor location problem.

[THEOREM 5.3]   Under the preceding condition on $r(t,x,y)$ the solution $P_a(t,x,y)$ of (5.13)-(5.15) is continuous with respect to the measurement points $(a^1, a^2, \cdots, a^m)$, that is, if ($a^1, a^2, \cdots, a^m$) go to ($b^1, b^2, \cdots, b^m$), then

$$P_a(t,x,y) \to P_b(t,x,y) \quad \text{for} \quad ^\forall t \in [t_0, t_f].$$

[PROOF]   It follows from (5.13)-(5.15) and (5.26) that

$$\frac{\partial D(t,x,y)}{\partial t} = A_x D(t,x,y) + A_y D(t,x,y) + F_b(t,x,y,P_b) - F_a(t,x,y,P_a)$$

$$D(t_0,x,y) = 0$$

$$\Gamma_\xi D(t,\xi,y) = 0, \quad ^\forall \xi \in S, \quad ^\forall y \in \overline{D}.$$

Hence, it follows from Theorem 4.1 that

$$D(t,x,y) = \int_{t_0}^{t} \int_{D^2} \mathcal{U}(t-\tau,x,a) \; [\; F_b(\tau,a,b,P_b) - F_a(\tau,a,b,P_a) \;] \, \mathcal{U}(t-\tau,b,y) \; da\, db\, d\tau. \qquad (5.41)$$

On the other hand, it follows from (5.16) that

$$F_b(\tau,a,b,P_b) - F_a(\tau,a,b,P_a) = - P_d(\tau,a)\, \tilde{R}_b(\tau)\, P_b'(\tau,b) + P_a(\tau,a)(\, \tilde{R}_b(\tau) - \tilde{R}_a(\tau))\, P_b'(\tau,b) - P_a(\tau,a)\, \tilde{R}_a(\tau)\, P_d'(\tau,b) \qquad (5.42)$$

where

$$P_d\,(\tau,a) = (\; P_a(\tau,a,a^1) - P_b(\tau,a,b^1),\; \cdots,\; P_a(\tau,a,a^m) - P_b(\tau,a,b^m))$$

$$= P_a(\tau,a) - P_b(\tau,a).$$

Since the solution $P_a(t,x,y)$ of (5.13)-(5.15) is bounded, there exists a constant m_1 such that

$$|\; P_a(\tau,x,y)\;|\;,\;\; |\; P_b(\tau,x,y)| < m_1.$$

Letting $q(t)$ be defined by

$$q(t) = \sup_{x,y\,\varepsilon\, D} \;|\; D(t,x,y)|\;, \qquad (5.43)$$

it follows from (5.41) and (5.42) that

$$|D(t,x,y)| \leqq \int_{t_0}^{t} \int_{D^2} \mathcal{U}(t-\tau,x,a)(\; q(\tau)\; \Delta_b(\tau)\; m_1 \;+ m_1^2 \;|\; \Delta_b(\tau) - \Delta_a(\tau)| + m_1\; \Delta_a(\tau)\; q(\tau))\; \mathcal{U}\,(t-\tau,b,y)\; da\, db\, d\tau \qquad (5.44)$$

where

$$\Delta_c(\tau) = \mathbf{e}\ \tilde{R}_c(\tau)\ \mathbf{e}', \quad \mathbf{e} = (1, \cdots, 1), \quad c = a \text{ or } b.$$

Since $\tilde{R}_c(\tau)$ is continuous with respect to τ from the assumption on $r(\tau,x,y)$, there exists a constant m_2 such that

$$0 \leqq \Delta_c(\tau) \leqq m_2 \qquad \text{for } \forall\, \tau \in [\, t_0, t_f \,].$$

Using the property (4.16) yields

$$q(t) \leqq m_3 \int_{t_0}^{t} q(\tau)\, d\tau + m_1^2 \int_{t_0}^{t} |\, \Delta_b(\tau) - \Delta_a(\tau) |\, d\tau \qquad (5.45)$$

$$m_3 = 2\, m_1\, m_2.$$

Applying Gronwall-Bellman's inequality which will be proved in the next lemma, from (5.45) we have

$$q(t) \leqq m_1^2 \int_{t_0}^{t} |\, \Delta_b(\tau) - \Delta_a(\tau) |\, d\tau \ \exp(\, m_3 t\,). \qquad (5.46)$$

Using the assumption that $r(\tau,x,y)$ is continuous with respect to x and y yields the continuity of $\Delta_a(\tau)$ with respect to the measurement points $(\, a^1, \cdots, a^m\,)$. Therefore, it is easily seen from (5.46) that if $(\, a^1, \cdots, a^m\,)$ go to $(\, b^1, \cdots, b^m)$, then for $\forall\, t \in [t_0, t_f\,]$

$$q(t) \to 0, \text{ i.e., } D(t,x,y) \to 0.$$

Thus, the proof of the theorem is completed. Q.E.D.

[LEMMA 5.2] Gronwall-Bellman's lemma

Let $a(t) \in L^1(\, t_0, t_f\,)$, $a(t) \geqq 0$, and $b(t)$ be absolutely continuous on $[t_0, t_f]$. If $c(t) \in L^{\infty}(\, t_0, t_f\,)$ satisfies

$$c(t) \leqq b(t) + \int_{t_0}^{t} a(s)\, c(s)\, ds, \qquad (5.47)$$

then

$$c(t) \leqq b(t_0) \exp \left(\int_{t_0}^{t} a(s)\, ds \right) + \int_{t_0}^{t} \dot{b}(s) \exp \left(\int_{s}^{t} a(\tau)\, d\tau \right) ds. \tag{5.48}$$

[PROOF] Let H(t) be

$$H(t) = \int_{t_0}^{t} a(s)\, c(s)\, ds$$

then

$$\dot{H}(t) = a(t)\, c(t) \leqq a(t)\, b(t) + a(t)\, H(t) \quad \text{almost everywhere.}$$

Hence,

$$\frac{d}{dt} \left(H(t) \exp \left(- \int_{t_0}^{t} a(s)\, ds \right) \right) \leqq a(t) \exp \left(- \int_{t_0}^{t} a(s)\, ds \right) b(t).$$

Thus, we have

$$H(t) \exp \left(- \int_{t_0}^{t} a(s)\, ds \right) \leqq \int_{t_0}^{t} - \frac{d}{ds} \left[\exp \left(- \int_{t_0}^{s} a(\tau)\, d\tau \right) \right] b(s)\, ds,$$

and so

$$H(t) \leqq - b(t) + b(t_0) \exp \left(\int_{t_0}^{t} a(s)\, ds \right)$$
$$+ \exp \left(\int_{t_0}^{t} a(s)\, ds \right) \int_{t_0}^{t} \dot{b}(s)$$
$$\exp \left(- \int_{t_0}^{s} a(\tau)\, d\tau \right) ds.$$

Using (5.47) , it follows from the above equation that

$$c(t) \leqq b(t) + H(t) \leqq b(t_0) \exp \left(\int_{t_0}^{t} a(s)\, ds \right)$$
$$+ \int_{t_0}^{t} \dot{b}(s) \exp \left(\int_{s}^{t} a(\tau)\, d\tau \right) ds.$$

Thus, the proof of the theorem is completed. Q.E.D.

5.3. Existence theorem and optimality conditions.

In this section, it is proved that there exists a solution of the optimal sensor location problem and the necessary and sufficient conditions for optimality are derived by using the theorems proved in the previous section.

[THEOREM 5.4] Under the same condition as Theorem 5.2, there exists an optimal solution of the sensor location problem.

[PROOF] Since from Theorem 5.3 $J_a(t_f)$ defined by (5.20) is continuous with respect to the measurement points $(a^1, a^2, \cdots, a^m)$ which range in the compact set $\overline{D}^m$, the optimal measurement points such that $J_a(t_f)$ is minimized always exist [9, 14].

Thus, the proof of the theorem is completed. Q.E.D.

Now consider the necessary and sufficient conditions for optimality of the sensor location problem. The sufficient condition for optimality is directly obtained from Theorem 5.2.

[THEOREM 5.5] If the measurement points $(b^1, b^2, \cdots, b^m)$ satisfy the following condition;

$$\int_D F_b(t,x,x,\overline{P})\, dx \geqq \int_D F_a(t,x,x,\overline{P})\, dx \tag{5.49}$$

for $\forall t \in [t_0,t_f]$, $\forall \overline{P} \in (t_0, t)$, and any measurement points $(a^1, a^2, \cdots, a^m)$, then $(b^1, b^2, \cdots, b^m)$ are the optimal measurement points.

[PROOF] Letting $\overline{P}(t,x,y)$ be defined by

$$\overline{P}(t,x,y) = \int_D P_1(t,x,a)\, P(t,a,y)\, da, \tag{5.50}$$

then (5.40) is reformulated from (5.16) as follows:

$$\int_D \overline{P}_b(t,x)\, \tilde{R}_b(t)\, \overline{P}_b'(t,x)\, dx = \int_D F_b(t,x,x,\overline{P})\, dx$$

$$\geqq \int_D F_a(t,x,x,\overline{P})\,dx = \int_D \overline{P}_a(t,x)\,\tilde{R}(t)\,\overline{P}_a'(t,x)\,dx$$

where

$$\overline{P}_c(t,x) = (\ \overline{P}(t,x,c^1),\ \cdots,\ \overline{P}(t,x,c^m)\ ),\quad c = a \text{ or } b.$$

On the other hand, it is easily seen from (5.6), (5.7), and (5.50) that

$$\overline{P}(t,x,y) \in \mathcal{F}(t_0,t)$$

and that $\overline{P}(t,x,y)$ can span $\mathcal{F}(t_0,t)$ by ranging the functions P_1 and P in $\mathcal{F}(t_0,t)$ and $\mathcal{F}_1(t_0,t)$, respectively.
Thus, the proof of the theorem is established. Q.E.D.
Note that the criterion (5.49) of this theorem means intuitively that the optimal measurement points maximize the nonlinear term in the right hand side of (5.13).

Consider the necessary condition for optimality based on the existence and uniqueness theorem in the previous section.

[THEOREM 5.6] It is necessary for the measurement points ($b^1, \cdots, b^m$) to be optimal that

$$\int_{t_0}^{t_f} \int_{D^2} \mathcal{U}_A(t_f-\tau,x,a)\,P_b(\tau,a)\,[\,\tilde{R}_b(\tau) - \tilde{R}_a(\tau)\,]\,P_b'(\tau,b)\,\mathcal{U}_A(t_f-\tau,b,x)\,da\,db\,d\tau \geqq 0 \tag{5.51}$$

where $\mathcal{U}_A(t,x,y)$ is the fundamental solution for the differential operator $\overline{A}_x$ given by

$$\overline{A}_x u = A_x u - P_b(t,x)\,\tilde{R}_a(t)\,u_m(y) \tag{5.52}$$

$u_m(y) = (\ u(a^1, y),\ \cdots,\ u(a^m, y)\ )$ for $u(x,y) \in L^2(\ D \times D\ )$, that is,

$$\frac{\partial \mathcal{U}_A(t,x,y)}{\partial t} = \overline{A}_x\,\mathcal{U}_A(t,x,y) \tag{5.53}$$

$$\mathcal{U}_A(0,x,y) = \delta(\, x - y \,) \tag{5.54}$$

$$\Gamma_\xi\, \mathcal{U}_A(t,\xi,y) = 0, \quad \forall \xi \in S, \quad \forall y \in \bar{D}. \tag{5.55}$$

[PROOF] As $D(t,x,y)$ is defined by (5.26), it follows from (5.13)-(5.15) that

$$\frac{\partial D(t,x,y)}{\partial t} = \bar{A}_x\, D(t,x,y) + \bar{A}_y\, D(t,x,y) - D_a(t,x)\, \tilde{R}_a(t)\, D_a'(t,y)$$

$$+ P_b(t,x)\, (\, \tilde{R}_b(t) - \tilde{R}_a(t))\, P_b'(t,y) \tag{5.56}$$

$$D_a(t,x) = (\, D(t,x,a^1), \cdots, D(t,x,a^m))$$

$$D(t_0,x,y) = 0 \tag{5.57}$$

$$\Gamma_\xi\, D(t,\xi,y) = 0, \quad \forall \xi \in S, \quad \forall y \in \bar{D}. \tag{5.58}$$

Using the assumption that $\tilde{R}_a(t)$ is positive-definite, it follows that

$$\int_{t_0}^{t} \int_{D^2} \mathcal{U}_A(t-\tau,x,a)\, P_b(\tau,a)(\, \tilde{R}_b(\tau) - \tilde{R}_a(\tau))\, P_b'(\tau,b)\, \mathcal{U}_A(t-\tau,b,x)$$

$$da\, db\, d\tau \geqq D(t,x,x). \tag{5.59}$$

Since it is necessary for the measurement points $(\, b^1, \cdots, b^m\,)$ to be optimal that $D(t,x,x) \geqq 0$, (5.51) follows from (5.59).

Note that if $\mathcal{U}_A(t,x,y)$ possesses the time reverse property, then setting $\hat{\mathcal{U}}_A(t,x,y) = \mathcal{U}_A(t_f-t,x,y)$ yields

$$-\frac{\partial\, \hat{\mathcal{U}}_A(t,x,y)}{\partial t} = \bar{A}_x\, \hat{\mathcal{U}}_A(t,x,y) \tag{5.60}$$

$$\hat{\mathcal{U}}_A(t_f,x,y) = \delta(\, x - y\,) \tag{5.61}$$

$$\Gamma_\xi \hat{\mathcal{U}}_A(t,\xi,y) = 0, \forall \xi \in S, \forall y \in \bar{D}. \tag{5.62}$$

Thus, Theorem 5.6 reduces to Bensoussan's result [43] which was obtained by using the concept of functional analysis. Note that from Theorems 5.5-5.6 the sufficient condition (5.49), of course, satisfies the necessary condition (5.51). Furthermore, the necessary condition (5.51) corresponds to that of Chen & Seinfeld [44] by using the maximum principle for the distributed parameter system. Thus, it can be seen that the procedure adopted here derives the result of Chen & Seinfeld's work [44] from the viewpoint of the existence and uniqueness properties of the Riccati equation. It is clear from Theorem 5.6 that the present method necessitates only to find the adjoint state $\mathcal{U}_A(t,x,y)$ defined by (5.5.53)-(5.55) for the partial differential operator A_x while the method by Chen & Seinfeld [44] must determine the adjoint state for two partial differential operators A_x and A_y .

Since it is difficult to solve the optimal sensor location problem by directly using the optimality conditions obtained here, an approximation technique based on the preceding theorems is proposed. Assume that the distributed parameter system (5.1)-(5.3) can be approximated as the N-dimensional system by using the Fourier expansion method. Then it was proved in (3.80) that the optimal filtering error covariance matrix is given by

$$\frac{d\, P_a(t)}{dt} = \Lambda\, P_a(t) + P_a(t)\,\Lambda - P_a(t)\, \Phi_a' \,\tilde{R}_a(t)\, \Phi_a\, P_a(t) + Q(t) \tag{5.63}$$

$$P_a(t) = [\, p^a_{ij}(t) \,]_N \,, \quad Q(t) = [\, q_{ij}(t) \,]_N, \; \Lambda = \mathrm{Diag}\, [\, \lambda_1, \cdots, \lambda_N \,]$$

where

$$P_a(t,x,y) = \Sigma_{i,j=1}^{\infty} \; p^a_{ij}(t)\, \phi_i(x)\, \phi_j(y)$$

$$Q(t,x,y) = \Sigma_{i,j=1}^{\infty} \; q_{ij}(t) \; \phi_i(x) \; \phi_j(y)$$

$$\Phi_a = \begin{pmatrix} \phi_1(a^1) & \phi_2(a^1) & \cdots & \phi_N(a^1) \\ \phi_1(a^2) & \phi_2(a^2) & \cdots & \phi_N(a^2) \\ \vdots & & & \vdots \\ \phi_1(a^m) & \phi_2(a^m) & \cdots & \phi_N(a^m) \end{pmatrix}.$$

In this case, the performance index $J_a(t_f)$ defined by (5.20) is approximated by

$$J_a^N(t_f) = \Sigma_{i=1}^{N} \; p_{ij}^a(t_f) = \mathrm{tr}\,[\, P_a(t_f) \,] \tag{5.64}$$

where tr $[\cdot]$ denotes the trace of the matrix.

Let $(a_1^1, \cdots, a_N^m)$ and $(b_N^1, \cdots, b_N^m)$ be the measurement points for the N-approximated system which correspond to $(a^1, \cdots, a^m)$ and $(b^1, \cdots, b^m)$, respectively. Thus, assume that $(b_N^1, \cdots, b_N^m)$ are the optimal measurement points for $J_a^N(t_f)$ of (5.64). Then the following theorem holds from Theorem 5.5.

[THEOREM 5.7] If the following inequality holds for $\forall t \in [t_0, t_f]$ and any measurement points $(a_N^1, \cdots, a_N^m)$

$$\Phi'_{b_N} \tilde{R}_{b_N}(t) \; \Phi_{b_N} \geqq \Phi'_{a_N} \; \tilde{R}_{a_N}(t) \; \Phi_{a_N} \, , \tag{5.65}$$

then the measurement points $(b_N^1, \cdots, b_N^m)$ are optimal.

[PROOF] From the definition (5.6), it follows that for any $P \in \mathcal{F}(t_0,t)$

$$P(t,x,y) = \Sigma_{i,j=1}^{\infty} \; p_{ij}(t) \; \phi_i(x) \; \phi_j(y). \tag{5.66}$$

Let $P_a(t,x) = (P(t,x,a^1), \cdots, P(t,x,a^m))$ and let F_a^N and $P_a^N(t,x)$ be the corresponding functions to F_a and $P_a(t,x)$ for the N-dimensional system by the Fourier expansion method, respectively. Then it follows from (5.16) and

and (5.66) that

$$F_a^N\ (t,x,x,P) = P_a^N(t,x)\ \tilde{R}_{a_N}(t)\ P_a^{N\,'}(t,x) \tag{5.67}$$

$$P_a^N(t,x) = \Sigma_{i,j=1}^{N}\ p_{ij}(t)\ \phi_i(x)\ (\ \phi_j(a_N^1),\ \cdots,\ \phi_j(a_N^m)\ ). \tag{5.68}$$

Substituting (5.68) into (5.67) yields

$$F_a^N = (\ \phi_1(x),\ \cdots,\ \phi_N(x))\ P(t)\ \Phi_{a_N}'\ \tilde{R}_{a_N}(t)\ \Phi_{a_N}\ P(t)\ (\ \phi_1(x),\ \cdots,\ \phi_N(x)\ )' \tag{5.69}$$

where

$$P(t) = [\ p_{ij}(t)\ ]_N. \tag{5.70}$$

Note that P(t) does not depend on the measurement points ($a_N^1, \cdots, a_N^m$) since $p_{ij}(t)$, i,j=1, ⋯, N can be determined as the arbitrary function satisfying (5.6). Denoting $\Theta(x,t)$ by

$$\Theta(x,t) = (\ \phi_1(x),\ \cdots,\ \phi_N(x))\ P(t), \tag{5.71}$$

it follows from (5.69) that if (5.65) is satisfied, then for $\forall x \in D$ and $\forall t \in [t_0,t_f]$

$$F_b^N - F_a^N = \Theta(x,t)\ [\ \Phi_{b_N}'\ \tilde{R}_{b_N}(t)\ \Phi_{b_N} - \Phi_{a_N}'\ \tilde{R}_{a_N}(t)\ \Phi_{a_N}\ ]\ \Theta'(x,t) \geqq 0. \tag{5.72}$$

Therefore, if ($b_N^1, \cdots, b_N^m$) satisfy (5.65), it follows from Theorem 5.5 that the measurement points ($b_N^1,\ \cdots,\ b_N^m$) are optimal.

Thus, the proof of the theorem is completed. Q.E.D.

Taking into consideration that P(t) is an arbitrary symmetric positive-semidefinite matrix, the following theorem holds from Theorem 5.5.

[THEOREM 5.8] If the following inequality holds

$$\mathrm{tr}\,[\,P(t)\ \Phi_{b_N}'\ \tilde{R}_{b_N}(t)\ \Phi_{b_N}\ P(t)\,] \geqq \mathrm{tr}\,[\,P(t)\ \Phi_{a_N}'\ \tilde{R}_{a_N}(t)\ \Phi_{a_N}\ P(t)\,] \tag{5.73}$$

for $\forall t \in [t_0, t_f]$, any symmetric positive-semidefinite matrix $P(t)$, and all measurement points ($a_N^1, \cdots, a_N^m$), then the measurement points ($b_N^1, \cdots, b_N^m$) are optimal.

[PROOF] Integrating each side of (5.69) with respect to x and using the orthogonality condition of $\phi_i(x)$, it follows that

$$\int_D F_a^N(t,x,x,P)\, dx = \mathrm{tr}\,[\, P(t)\, \Phi'_{a_N}\, \tilde{R}_{a_N}(t)\, \Phi_{a_N}\, P(t)\,]. \tag{5.74}$$

Applying Theorem5.5 and using (5.74), the measurement points ($b_N^1, \cdots, b_N^m$) are optimal. Thus, the proof of the theorem is completed. Q.E.D.

Note that this theorem corresponds to that of [45] for the discrete-time distributed parameter system. From Theorem 5.6 the following theorem holds.

[THEOREM 5.9] It is necessary for the measurement points ($b_N^1, \cdots, b_N^m$) to be optimal that

$$\int_{t_0}^{t_f} U_\Lambda(t_f,\tau)\, P_{b_N}(\tau)\, [\, \Phi'_{b_N}\, \tilde{R}_{b_N}(\tau)\, \Phi_{b_N} - \Phi'_{a_N}\, \tilde{R}_{a_N}(t)\, \Phi_{a_N}\,]\, P_{b_N}(\tau)\, U'_\Lambda(t_f,\tau)\, d\tau \geqq 0 \tag{5.75}$$

$$P_b(t) = [\, p_{ij}^b(t)\,]_N, \quad P_b(t,x,y) = \Sigma_{i,j=1}^{\infty}\, p_{ij}^b(t)\, \phi_i(x)\, \phi_j(y)$$

where $U_\Lambda(t,\tau)$ is the transition matrix of $\Lambda - P_{b_N}(t)\, \Phi'_{a_N}\, \tilde{R}_{a_N}(t)\, \Phi_{a_N}$.

Note that the necessary condition of Theorem 5.9 corresponds to that of Athans' work [46] which was derived by using the matrix maximum principle. It can be seen that the new matrix term Φ_{b_N} is contained in the criterion of Theorem 5.9 compared with that of Athans' work [46]. This difference results from the fact that Athans [46] considers only the optimal switching time determination problem for the sensor location. However, the necessary condition of Theorem 5.9 shows that by solving the two-point boundary value problem by suitable methods, both the optimal timing and the optimal measurement points can be determined at the same time.

5.4. Numerical examples.

In this section, numerical examples are illustrated to determine the optimal sensor location by using the sufficient condition of Theorem 5.7. For the purpose of the facilitating the comparison of the approach presented here with the method of Chen & Seinfeld's work [44], the same system models are adopted. Hence, we consider a one-dimensional heat conduction system described by

$$\frac{\partial U(t,x)}{\partial t} = 0.5 \ \frac{\partial^2 U(t,x)}{\partial x^2} + \dot{W}(t,x), \quad x \in D = (0, 1). \tag{5.76}$$

The initial and boundary conditions of (5.76) are given by

$$U(t_0,x) = U_0(x) \tag{5.77}$$

and

$$\partial U(t,0)/\partial x = \partial U(t,1)/\partial x = 0. \tag{5.78}$$

The observation process is represented by

$$Z_a(t) = H(t)\ U_a(t) + \dot{V}(t) \tag{5.79}$$

where m-dimensional vector $U_a(t)$ and $\dot{V}(t)$ are given by

$$U_a(t) = [\ U(t,a^1),\ U(t,a^m)\ ]' \text{ and } \dot{V}(t) = [\ V(t,a^1),\ V(t,a^m)\ ],\ m = 1 \text{ or } 2.$$

Assume that $Q(t,x,y) = 2.66$, $P_0(x,y) = 6$, and $H(t) = I_m$ where I_m denotes the identity $m \times m$ matrix. The following two cases are considered:

Case 1. $r(t,a^i,a^j) = \exp\ (\ 2\ |a^i - 0.5|\ )\ \delta_{ij},\quad i,j = 1, m.$

Case 2. $r(t,a^i,a^j) = \exp\ (\ -\ 2\ |a^i - 0.5|\ )\ \delta_{ij},\quad i,j = 1, m.$

The eigenfunctions $\phi_i(x)$ and eigenvalues λ_i for (5.76)-(5.78) are given by

$$\phi_i(x) = k_i \cos (i - 1) \pi x \quad \text{and} \quad \lambda_i = 0.5 (i - 1)^2 \pi^2, \quad i = 1, 2, \cdots$$

where $k_1 = 1$ and $k_2 = \sqrt{2}$ for $i \geqq 2$.

In these examples, the (i,j)-th Fourier expansion coefficients $q_{ij}(t)$ and $p_{ij}(t_0)$ of $Q(t,x,y)$ and $P_0(x,y)$ are given by

$$q_{ij}(t) = \begin{cases} 2.66, & i = j = 1 \\ 0, & \text{otherwise} \end{cases} \qquad p_{ij}(t_0) = \begin{cases} 6.0, & i = j = 1 \\ 0, & \text{otherwise.} \end{cases}$$

Hence, the performance index $J_a(t_f)$ can be approximately given by $p^a_{11}(t_f)$.

Consider first the one-point observation case, that is, m = 1, under the assumption that a^1 is restricted to a set of [0.0, 0.1, ⋯, 0.9, 1.0]. Then it follows from Theorem 5.7 that if $r^*_t = r^{-1}(t,a^1,a^1)$ is maximized with respect to a^1, then the measurement point a^1 which maximizes r^*_t for $\forall t \in [t_0, t_f]$ is optimal for the one-point observation case. Hence, the optimal measurement point b^1 is given by

$$b^1 = 0.5 \text{ for Case 1} \quad \text{and} \quad b^1 = 0.0 \text{ or } 1.0 \text{ for Case 2.}$$

Consider next the two-point observation case, that is, m = 2, under the assumption that a^1 and a^2 are restricted to the interior points [0.1, 0.2, ⋯, 0.9] of the spatial domain (0, 1). Then it follows from Theorem 5.7 that the measurement points which maximize $r^*_t = r^{-1}(t,a^1,a^1) + r^{-1}(t,a^2,a^2)$ for $\forall t \in [t_0, t_f]$ are optimal. Hence, the optimal measurement points b^1 and b^2 are given by

$$(b^1, b^2) = (0.5, 0.4 \text{ or } 0.6) \text{ for Case 1}$$

and

$$(b^1, b^2) = (0.9, 0.1) \text{ or } (0.1, 0.9) \text{ for Case 2.}$$

The trajectories of trace [$P_a(t,x,x)$] in the case of the one-point observation and $a^1 \in$ [0.0, 0.1,$\cdots$, 1.0] are depicted in Figs. 5-1 and 5-2 where P(r) denotes trace [$P_a(t,x,x)$] for $a^1 = r$. Tables V-1 and V-2 show the values of trace [$P_a(t,x,x)$] in the case of the two-point observation and a^1, a^2 $\in$ [0.1, 0.2, $\cdots$, 0.9] when the one measurement point a^1 is a fixed at 0.5 for Case 1 and at 0.1 for Case 2. It is clear that the numerical results give the same measurement points as the optimal values obtained by Theorem 5.7. Note that these results are identical with those of Chen & Seinfeld's work [47] which were obtained by using the maximum principle for the distributed parameter system. The main advantage of the method proposed here lies in the computational simplicity and the mathematical exactness which are mainly due to the elimination of the computation of the two-point boundary value problem for the distributed parameter system. Furthermore, the present method has an advantage that the optimal measurement points can be determined without solving the partial differential equation of Riccati type if the eigenvalue problem can be solved. Since it was shown [47, 48] that the optimal measurement points for the other type boundary conditions can be determined by the present method, Theorems 5.7-5.8 seem to give a powerful technique for solving the optimal sensor location problem.

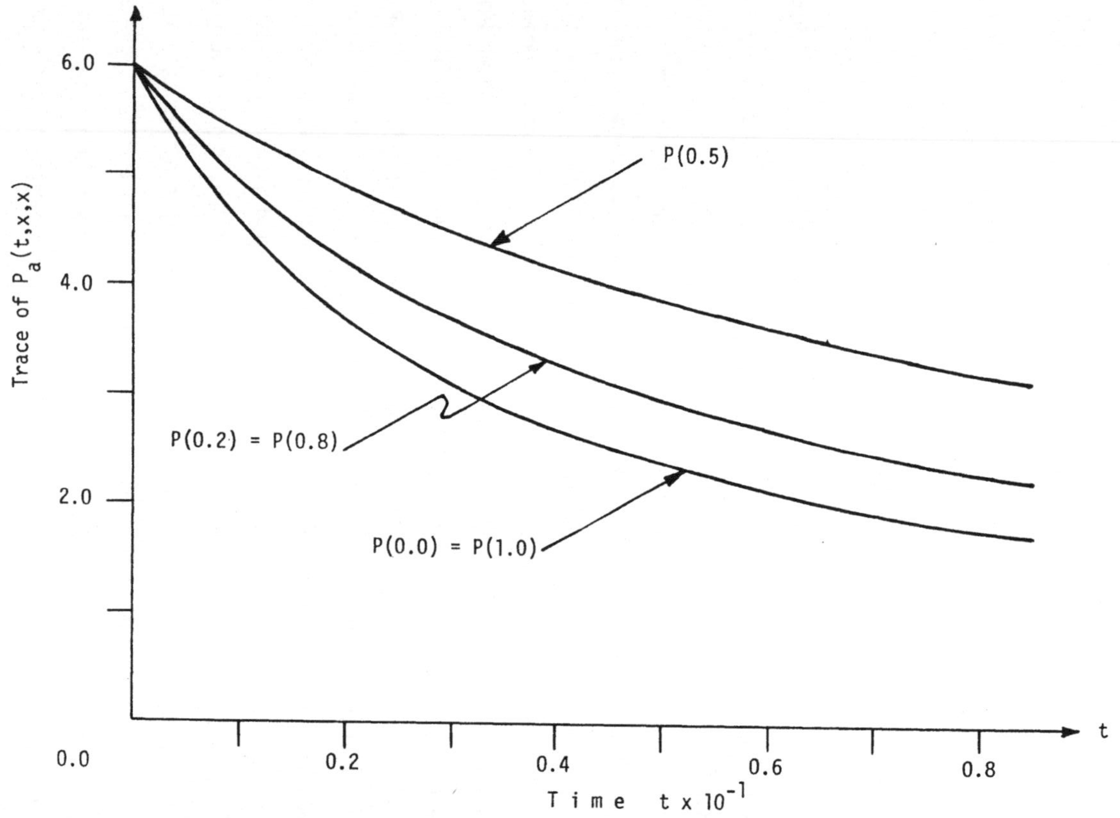

Fig. 5-1. Trace of the estimation error variance function $P_a(t,x,x)$ with one-point observation for Case 1.

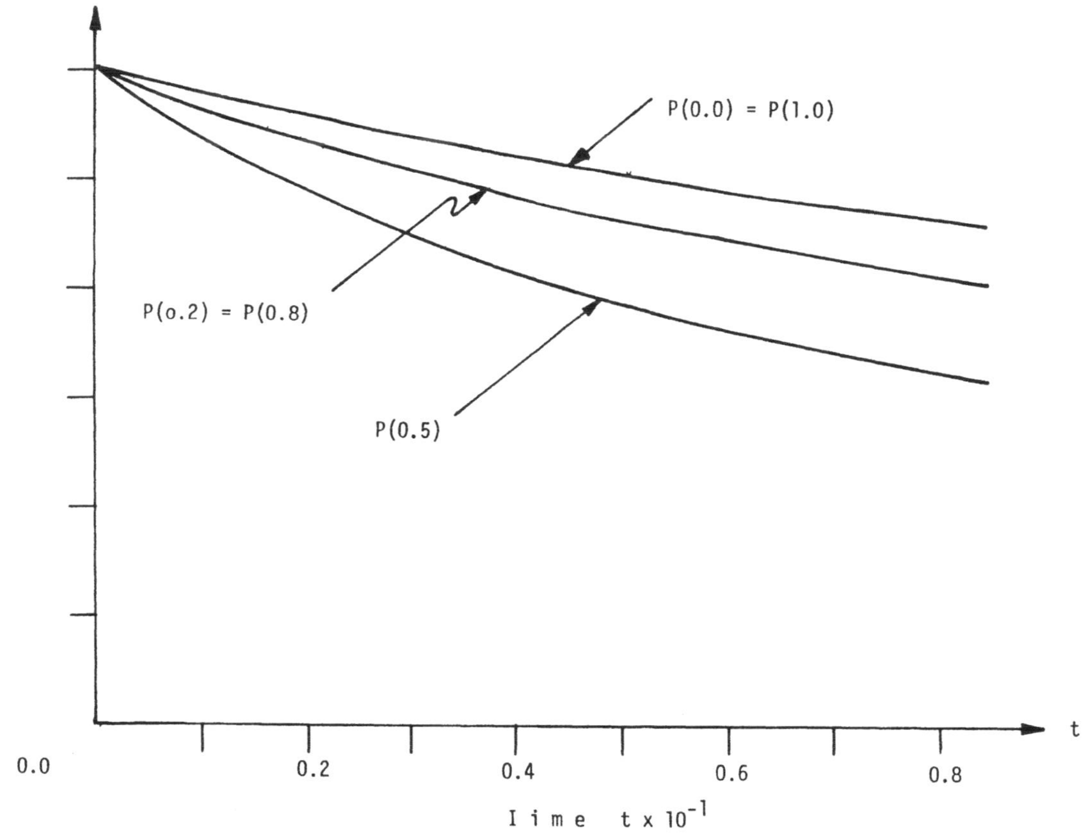

Fig. 5-2. Trace of the estimation error variance function $P_a(t,x,x)$ with one-point observation for Case 2.

TABLE V-1. trace [$P_a(t,x,x)$] with the two-point observation and $a^1 = 0.5$ for Case 1.

a^2	Trace of $P_a(t,x,x)$ for $a^1 = 0.5$				
	t = 0.005	t = 0.025	t = 0.045	t = 0.065	t = 0.085
0.1	5.557	4.230	3.440	2.913	2.538
0.2	5.502	4.144	3.341	2.812	2.441
0.3	5.466	4.044	3.226	2.698	2.332
0.4	5.422	3.928	3.097	2.571	2.211
0.6	5.422	3.928	3.097	2.571	2.211
0.7	5.466	4.044	3.226	2.698	2.332
0.8	5.502	4.144	3.341	2.812	2.441
0.9	5.557	4.230	3.440	2.913	2.538

TABLE V-2. trace [$P_a(t,x,x)$] with the two-point observation and $a^1 = 0.1$ for Case 2.

a^2	Trace of $P_a(t,x,x)$ for $a^1 = 0.1$				
	t = 0.005	t = 0.025	t = 0.045	t = 0.065	t = 0.085
0.2	4.838	2.746	1.939	1.517	1.261
0.3	4.917	2.874	2.052	1.614	1.345
0.4	4.983	2.988	2.155	1.703	1.423
0.5	5.038	3.088	2.248	1.784	1.494
0.6	4.983	2.988	2.155	1.703	1.423
0.7	4.917	2.874	2.052	1.614	1.345
0.8	4.838	2.746	1.939	1.517	1.261
0.9	4.746	2.605	1.818	1.414	1.173

5.5. Concluding remarks.

We have proved the existence theorem concerning a solution for the optimal sensor location problem and then derived the optimality conditions. This problem was discussed by various authors from the different viewpoints [43-52] and its survey has been given in detail in [52]. The method described here shows that the procedure to prove the existence theorem for the optimal sensor location problem is more direct and simpler than that of [43] by using Lions' compactness result [13] and the variational inequality.

An advantage of the present approach to derive the optimality conditions is that the necessary and sufficient conditions for optimality of the sensor location problem can be derived by the same procedure as the proof of the existence theorem and that the derivation can be done in a more strictly mathematical sense than those of [44, 45].

Chapter 6. STOCHASTIC OPTIMAL CONTROL PROBLEMS.

6.1. Problem formulation.

In this chapter, we consider the stochastic optimal control problems in Hilbert spaces. Let us give the definitions of $L_n^2(D)$ and $H_n^m(D)$ needed in this chapter by

$$L_n^2(D) = \{ \phi(t,x) | \int_D \| \phi(t,x) \|_n^2 \, dx < \infty \} \tag{6.1}$$

$$H_n^m(D) = \{ \phi(t,x) | \frac{\partial^{|\alpha|} \phi(t,x)}{\partial x_1^{k_1} \cdots \partial x_r^{k_r}} \in L_n^2(D), \ | \alpha | \leq m \} \tag{6.2}$$

where $\| \cdot \|_n$ denotes the n-dimensional Euclidean norm, $|\alpha| = k_1 + \cdots + k_r$ for $\alpha = (k_1, \cdots, k_r)$, and m,n, and k_i are nonnegative integers. Similarly, $L_n^2(S)$ and $H_n^m(S)$ are defined by exchanging S for D in (6.1) and (6.2), respectively. We define the norms of $L_n^2(D)$ and $H_n^m(D)$ by

$$\| \phi(t,x) \|_{L_n^2(D)}^2 = (\phi(t,x), \phi(t,x))_{L_n^2(D)}$$

$$= \int_D \phi'(t,x) \phi(t,x) \, dx \tag{6.3}$$

$$\| \phi(t,x) \|_{H_n^m(D)}^2 = (\phi(t,x), \phi(t,x))_{H_n^m(D)}$$

$$= \sum_{|\alpha| \leq m} \left(\frac{\partial^{|\alpha|} \phi(t,x)}{\partial x_1^{k_1} \cdots \partial x_r^{k_r}} , \frac{\partial^{|\alpha|} \phi(t,x)}{\partial x_1^{k_1} \cdots \partial x_r^{k_r}} \right)_{L_n^2(D)}. \tag{6.4}$$

Thus, $L_n^2(D)$ and $H_n^m(D)$ are Hilbert spaces endowed with inner products defined by (6.3) and (6.4), respectively. Let us assume that the state U(t) is assumed to be an element in $\mathcal{U}_1 = H_n^2(D)$;

$$U(t) \in \mathcal{U}_1 = H_n^2(D), \text{ for any } t \in [t_0, t_f]. \tag{6.5}$$

Similarly, we denote the system noise by W(t) and assume it to be an element in $\mathcal{U}_2 = L_p^2(D)$:

$$W(t) \in \mathcal{U}_2 = L_p^2(D), \quad \text{for any } t \in [\, t_0, t_f \,]. \tag{6.6}$$

The control laws $f_d(t)$ and $f_b(t)$ are assumed to be elements of $\mathcal{U}_3 = L_k^2(D)$ and $\mathcal{U}_4 = L_k^2(S)$:

$$f_d(t) \in \mathcal{U}_3 = L_k^2(D) \quad \text{and} \quad f_b(t) \in \mathcal{U}_4 = L_k^2(S), \quad \text{for any } t \in [\, t_0, t_f \,] \tag{6.7}$$

where $f_d(t)$ and $f_b(t)$ denote the distributed control input on the spatial domain D and the boundary control input on the boundary S, respectively. Furthermore, the state $U_b(t)$ on the boundary S is assumed to be an element of $\mathcal{U}_5 = L_n^2(S)$. Then the state of the system is assumed to be given by

$$d\,U(t) = F(t, U(t), f_d(t)\,)\,dt + G(t, U(t), f_d(t))\,d\,W(t) \tag{6.8}$$

where W(t) is a $\mathcal{U}_2$-valued Wiener process, F(·) maps $[t_0,t_f] \times \mathcal{U}_1 \times \mathcal{U}_3$ into $\mathcal{U}_6 = L_n^2(D)$, and G(·) defined on $[t_0,t_f] \times \mathcal{U}_1 \times \mathcal{U}_3$ is an element of $\mathcal{L}(\mathcal{U}_2, \mathcal{U}_6)$. Furthermore, the stochasitc differential equation in Hilbert spaces of (6.8) is assumed to be Ito type as shown in chapter 2.

The initial and boundary conditions are assumed to be described by

$$U(t_0) = U_0 \in \mathcal{U}_1 \tag{6.9}$$

and

$$B(t, U_b(t), f_b(t)) = 0, \tag{6.10}$$

respectively, where B(·) is the mapping defined on $[t_0,t_f] \times \mathcal{U}_5 \times \mathcal{U}_4$.

The covariance function of W(t) is given by

$$E [W(t) \circ W(s)] = Q \min (t - t_0, s - t_0) \tag{6.11}$$

where Q is a compact, positive, bounded, and trace class operator mapping $\mathcal{U}_2$ into $\mathcal{U}_2$.

The cost functional $J(\cdot)$ is assumed to be the following form:

$$J(U(t_0), t_0) = E_{U,t_0} [K(t_f, U(t_f)) + \int_{t_0}^{t_f} L(\tau, U(\tau), f_d(\tau), f_b(\tau))\, d\tau] \tag{6.12}$$

where $E_{U,t_0} [\cdot]$ denotes the conditional expectation of $[\cdot]$ with respect to the σ-fields generated by $[U(\tau), t_0 \leqq \tau \leqq t]$ and $K(\cdot)$ and $L(\cdot)$ are well-defined real-valued integrable function with respect to time t.

Then the optimal control problem is now posed as follows: Given a stochastic system described by (6.8)-(6.10), find such a control $f_d^o(t)$ and $f_b^o(t)$ that minimizes the functional $J(U(t_0), t_0)$ given by (6.12).

6.2. Hamilton-Jacobi equations.

We define $V(U(t), t)$ as the minimum of $J(\cdot)$ with respect to $f_d(t) \in \mathcal{U}_3$ and $f_b(t) \in \mathcal{U}_4$:

$$V(U(t),t) = \min_{\substack{f_d(\tau),\, f_b(\tau) \\ t \leqq \tau \leqq t_f}} [J(U(t),t)]. \tag{6.13}$$

Let us assume that $V(U(t),t)$ is continuously differentiable on $[t_0,t_f]$ and continuously two-times Fréchet differentiable on $\mathcal{U}_1$. Dividing the integral in (6.12) into two parts and applying the principle of optimality by Bellman [13, 53] to (6.12), we have

$$\min_{\substack{f_d(\tau),\ f_b(\tau)\\ t \leqq \tau \leqq t+a}} [\ E_{U,t}[\ \int_t^{t+a} L(\tau, U(\tau), f_d(\tau), f_b(\tau))\, d\tau + V(U(t+a),t+a)\ ] - V(U(t),t)\ ] = 0. \tag{6.14}$$

Describing the first term in the conditional expectation in (6.14) by I_1 and using the mean value theorem [9, 54], we have

$$I_1 = E_{U,t}[\ L(t+a\theta,\ U(t+a\theta),\ f_d(t+a\theta),\ f_b(t+a\theta))\ ]\ a, \quad (0 < \theta < 1). \tag{6.15}$$

Moreover, we define I_2 by

$$I_2 = E_{U,t}[\ V(U(t+a),\ t+a)\ ], \tag{6.16}$$

and using the Taylor expansion theorem [9, 54], we have

$$I_2 = V(U(t),t) + a\ (\ \partial V(U(t),t)/\partial t) + V_c(U(t),t)\ E_{U,t}[\ \Delta U(t)\ ] + 1/2\ E_{U,t}[\ V_{cc}(U(t),t)[\ \Delta U(t),\ \Delta U(t)\ ]\ ] + O\ (\ \|\Delta U(t)\|^3_{\mathcal{U}_6}) \tag{6.17}$$

$$\Delta U(t) = U(t+a) - U(t) \tag{6.18}$$

where $V_c(\cdot)$ denotes the first-order Fréchet derivative on $\mathcal{U}_1$ which is a linear mapping from $\mathcal{U}_1$ into the real-valued **R**, and $V_{cc}(\cdot)$ the second-order Fréchet derivative on $\mathcal{U}_1$ which is a bilinear mapping from $\mathcal{U}_1 \times \mathcal{U}_1$ into **R**, and $O(\cdot)$ shows the same order infinitesimal. From (6.8) we have

$$E_{U,t}[\ \Delta U(t)\ ] = \int_t^{t+a} F(\tau,U(\tau),\ f_d(\tau))\, d\tau \tag{6.19}$$

$$E_{U,t}[\Phi[\Delta U(t), \Delta U(t)]] = \tilde{tr}(\Phi)(G\sqrt{Q})\,a \tag{6.20}$$

$$\tilde{tr}(\Phi)(G\sqrt{Q}) = \Sigma_{i=1}^{\infty} [G(t,U(t),f_d(t))\sqrt{\lambda_i}\, e_i, G(t,U(t),f_d(t))\sqrt{\lambda_i}\, e_i] \tag{6.21}$$

where Φ is a bilinear mapping from $\mathcal{V}_6 \times \mathcal{V}_6$ into $\mathbf{R}$ and $\{e_i, \lambda_i, i = 1, 2, \cdots\}$ is an orthonormal set of eigenfunctions and eigenvalues of the operator Q:

$$Q\, e_i = \lambda_i\, e_i, \quad i = 1, 2, \cdots. \tag{6.22}$$

Hence, substituting (6.19) and (6.20) into (6.17),

$$I_2 = V(U(t),t) + a\,(\partial V(U(t),t)/\partial t) + V_c(U(t),t) \int_t^{t+a} F(\tau,U(\tau),f_d(\tau))\, d\tau$$

$$+ 1/2\ \tilde{tr}(V_{cc}(U(t),t))(G\sqrt{Q})\,a + O(\|\Delta U(t)\|^3_{\mathcal{V}_6}). \tag{6.23}$$

On the other hand, (6.8), (6.11), and (6.18) yield

$$O(\|\Delta U(t)\|^3_{\mathcal{V}_6}) = O(a^{3/2}). \tag{6.24}$$

Accordingly, utilizing (6.24) we have from (6.14)-(6.16) and (6.23)

$$-\frac{\partial V(U(t),t)}{\partial t} = \min_{f_d(t+a\theta),\, f_b(t+a\theta)} [\ E_{U,t}[L(t+a\theta, U(t+a\theta), f_d(t+a\theta),$$

$$f_b(t+a\theta))] + V_c(U(t),t)\, a^{-1} \int_t^{t+a} F(\tau,U(\tau),f_d(\tau))\, d\tau$$

$$+ 1/2\ \tilde{tr}(V_{cc}(U(t),t))(G\sqrt{Q}) + O(a^{1/2})\ ]. \tag{6.25}$$

Using the Bochner theorem [9, 10], we have

$$\lim_{a \to 0} a^{-1} \int_t^{t+a} F(\tau,U(\tau), f_d(\tau))\, d\tau = F(t,U(t),f_d(t)). \tag{6.26}$$

When $a \to 0$ in (6.25), we have the following Hamilton-Jacobi equation in the

Hilbert space,

$$-\frac{\partial V(U(t),t)}{\partial t} = \min_{f_d(t),\ f_b(t)} [\ H(t,U(t),\ f_d(t),\ f_b(t),\ V_c,\ V_{cc})\ ] \quad (6.27)$$

where H(·) is called the Hamiltonian of the system which is a real-valued functional defined by

$$H(\cdot) = L(t,U(t),\ f_d(t),\ f_b(t)) + V_c(U(t),t)\ F(t,U(t),f_d(t))$$
$$+\ 1/2\ \tilde{tr}\ (\ V_{cc}(U(t),t)(\ G\sqrt{Q}\ )). \quad (6.28)$$

The first- and second-order Fréchet derivatives of the functional on $\mathcal{U}_1$ are called gradient denoted by $\nabla_c(\cdot)$ and Hessian denoted by $\Theta_{cc}(\cdot)$, respectively. Hence, H(·) defined by (6.28) yields

$$H(\cdot) = L(t,U(t),f_d(t),f_b(t)) + (\nabla_c\ V(U(t),t),\ F(t,U(t),f_d(t)))_{\mathcal{U}_6}$$
$$+\ 1/2\ tr\ [(\ G(t,U(t),f_d(t))\ Q\ G^*(t,U(t),f_d(t)))\Theta_{cc}V(U(t),y)\ ] \quad (6.29)$$

where tr[·] denotes the trace of the operator.

Therefore, using (6.29), we can also write (6.27) as follows:

$$-\frac{\partial V(U(t),t)}{\partial t} = \min_{f_d(t),\ f_b(t)} [\ H(t,U(t),f_d(t),f_b(t),\ \nabla_c V,\ \Theta_{cc}V\ )]. \quad (6.30)$$

If the underlying spaces are finite dimensional, then F(·) and G(·) become a vector and a matrix in the finite dimensional space, respectively, and (6.30) can be reduced to the results in lumped parameter systems [24, 55, 56]. Furthermore, comparing (6.30) with the known Hamilton-Jacobi equation in the Hilbert space for the deterministic case [13, 57, 58], it is easy to see that (6.30) contains the new term $\Theta_{cc}V(U(t),t)$ resulted from the stochastic property of Wiener process W(t).

6.3. Optimal boundary control problems.

Let us now consider the optimal boundary control problem based on a quadratic cost functional for a linear distributed parameter system subject to the additive noise disturbance. Thus, we treat the state equation given by

$$\frac{\partial U(t,x)}{\partial t} = A(\partial/\partial x)\ U(t,x) + C(t,x)\ \dot{W}(t,x) \tag{6.31}$$

$$U(t_0,x) = U_0(x) \tag{6.32}$$

$$\alpha(\xi)\ U(t,\xi) + \Sigma_{i,j=1}^{r}\ A_{ij}(t,\xi)\ \partial U(t,\xi)/\partial \mathbf{n} = B_b(t,\xi)\ f_b(t,\xi),\ \forall\xi \in S \tag{6.33}$$

where

$$A(\partial/\partial x) = \Sigma_{i,j=1}^{r}\ A_{ij}(t,x)\ \partial^2/\partial x_i \partial x_j + \Sigma_{i=1}^{r} A_i(t,x)\ \partial/\partial x_i + A_0(t,x) \tag{6.34}$$

and $A_{..}(t,x)$, and $A_.(t,x)$ are $n \times n$ symmetric matrix functions defined on $[t_0,t_f] \times D$. Assume that $A_{ij} = A_{ji}$ and let $W(t,x)$ be the wiener process whose intensity $Q(x,y)$ of the covariance matrix function defined by (6.11). Let $K(\cdot)$ and $L(\cdot)$ of (6.12) be given by

$$K(t_f,\ U(t_f,x)) = 1/2 \int_D\ (\ U(t_f,x),\ K_1(x,y)\ U(t_f,x))_{L_n^2(D)}\ dy \tag{6.35}$$

$$L(t,U(t,x),f_b(t,\xi)) = 1/2 \int_D\ (\ U(t,x),\ L_1(x,y)\ U(t,y)\ )_{L_n^2(D)}\ dy$$

$$+\ 1/2 \int_S\ (\ f_b(t,\xi),\ L_2(\xi,\eta)\ f_b(t,\eta))_{L_k^2(S)}\ d\xi \tag{6.36}$$

where $K_1(x,y)$ and $L_1(x,y)$ are $n \times n$ positive-definite matrix functions and $L_2(\xi,\eta)$ is a $k \times k$ similar matrix function.

Then we can rewrite (6.31)-(6.36) as follows:

$$d\,U(t) = A(t)\,U(t)\,dt + C(t)\,d\,W(t) \tag{6.37}$$

$$U(t_0) = U_0 \tag{6.38}$$

$$\alpha\,U(t) + \Sigma_{i,j=1}^{r}\,A_{ij}(t)\,\partial U(t)/\partial \mathbf{n} = B_b(t)\,f_b(t) \tag{6.39}$$

$$K(t_f, U(t_f)) = 1/2\,(\,U(t_f),\,K_1\,U(t_f))_{L_n^2(D)} \tag{6.40}$$

$$L(t,U(t),f_b(t)) = 1/2\,(\,U(t),\,L_1\,U(t))_{L_n^2(D)}$$

$$+\,1/2\,(\,f_b(t),\,L_2\,f_b(t))_{L_k^2(S)}. \tag{6.41}$$

Hence, Hamiltonian $H(\cdot)$ of the system is given from (6.29) by

$$H(\cdot) = 1/2\,(\,U(t),\,L_1\,U(t))_{L_n^2(D)} + 1/2\,(\,f_b(t),\,L_2\,f_b(t))_{L_k^2(S)}$$

$$+\,(\,\nabla_c\,V(U(t),t),\,A(t)\,U(t)\,)_{L_n^2(D)}$$

$$+\,1/2\,\mathrm{tr}\,[\,\tilde{Q}(t)\,\Theta_{cc}\,V(U(t),t)\,] \tag{6.42}$$

where

$$\tilde{Q}(t) = C(t)\,Q(t)\,C^*(t).$$

Let $V(U(t),t)$ be the following form:

$$V(U(t),t) = 1/2\,(\,U(t),\,P_2(t)\,U(t))_{L_n^2(D)} + 1/2\,P_0(t) \tag{6.43}$$

where $P_2(t) \in \mathcal{L}(\,\mathcal{U}_1,\,\mathcal{U}_1)$ is a self-adjoint positive-definite trace class operator with its kernel $P_2(t,x,y)$ and $P_0(t)$ is a real-valued function of t. Then ∇_c and Θ_{cc} of $V(U(t),t)$ are given by

$$\nabla_c\,V(U(t),t) = P_2(t)\,U(t) \tag{6.44}$$

$$\Theta_{cc}\,V(U(t),t) = P_2(t). \tag{6.45}$$

Hence, we have

$$H(\cdot) = 1/2\ (\ U(t),\ L_1\ U(t))_{L_n^2(D)} + 1/2\ (\ f_b(t),\ L_2\ f_b(t))_{L_k^2(S)}$$

$$+\ (\ P_2(t)\ U(t),\ A(t)\ U(t)\ )_{L_n^2(D)} + 1/2\ \mathrm{tr}\ [\ \tilde{Q}(t)\ P_2(t)\ ]. \qquad (6.46)$$

Using Green's formula as shown in Appendix in Chapter 3, we have

$$(\ P_2(t)\ U(t),\ A(t)\ U(t)\ )_{L_n^2(D)} = (\ A^*(t)\ P_2(t)\ U(t),\ U(t)\ )_{L_n^2(D)}$$

$$-\ (\ (\partial/\partial\nu + \partial/\partial\nu_a\ )\ P_2(t)\ U(t),\ U(t))_{L_n^2(S)}$$

$$+\ (\ P_2(t)\ U(t),\ \partial U(t)/\partial\nu\ )_{L_n^2(S)} \qquad (6.47)$$

where

$$\partial(\cdot)/\partial\nu = \Sigma_{i,j=1}^{r}\ A_{ij}(t)\ \partial(\cdot)/\ \partial\mathbf{n}$$

$$\partial(\cdot)/\ \partial\nu_a = \Sigma_{i,j=1}^{r}\ \partial(\ A_{ij}(t)(\cdot))/\partial\mathbf{n} - \Sigma_{i=1}^{r}\ A_i(t)\ \cos\ (\ \mathbf{n},\ x_i)(\cdot)$$

$$A^*(t)(\cdot) = A^*(\partial/\partial x)(\cdot) = \Sigma_{i,j=1}^{r}\ \partial^2(\ A_{ij}(t,x)(\cdot))/\partial x_i\partial x_j$$

$$-\ \Sigma_{i=1}^{r}\ \partial(\ A_i(t,x)(\cdot))/\partial x_i + A_0(t,x)(\cdot).$$

Let us now seek the optimal control $f_b^o(t)$. In order to do so, we assume that $\mathcal{U}_4$ is convex. Then we have

$$H_c(\ f_b^o(t))\ (\ f_b(t) - f_b^o(t)\ ) \geqq 0 \qquad (6.48)$$

where $f_b(t)$ is any element of $\mathcal{U}_4$ and $H_c(\cdot)$ is the Fréchet derivative of $H(\cdot)$ with respect to $f_b(t)$. Since we have taken $\mathcal{U}_4$ as $L_k^2(S)$, that is, no constraint control, $f_b(t) = f_b^o(t) \pm \phi(t)$ are also elements of $\mathcal{U}_4$ for any $\phi(t)$

$\varepsilon\ \mathcal{U}_4$. Hence, from (6.48) we have

$$H_c(\ f_b^o(t))\ \phi(t) = 0. \tag{6.49}$$

Therefore, it follows that the optimal control $f_b^o(t)$ which minimizes $H(\cdot)$ is characterized by (6.49). Accordingly, from (6.46) and (6.47), we can easily find $f_b^o(t)$ given by

$$f_b^o(t) = -\ L_2^{-1}\ B_b^*(t)\ P_2(t)\ U(t). \tag{6.50}$$

Using (6.30), (6.43), and (6.50), the unknown functions $P_2(t)$ and $P_0(t)$ can be characterized by

$$-\frac{d\ P_2(t)}{dt} = A^*(t)\ P_2(t) + (\ A^*(t)\ P_2(t))^* + L_1$$

$$-\ P_b(t)\ B_b(t)\ L_2^{-1}\ B_b^*(t)\ P_2(t) \tag{6.51}$$

$$-\frac{d\ P_0(t)}{dt} = tr\ [\ \tilde{Q}(t)\ P_2(t)\ ] \tag{6.52}$$

where $(\ A^*(t)\ P_2(t))^*$ and $P_b(t)$ are the adjoint of $(\ A^*(t)\ P_2(t))$ and the element of $\mathcal{L}(\ L_n^2(S),\ L_n^2(D))$, respectively, and satisfy the following relations:

$$(\ U(t),\ A^*(t)\ P_2(t))_{L_n^2(D)} = (\ (\ A^*(t)\ P_2(t))^*\ U(t),\ U(t))_{L_n^2(D)}$$

$$(\ P_2(t)\ U(t),\ U(t)\ )_{L_n^2(S)} = (\ U(t),\ P_b(t)\ U(t)\ )_{L_n^2(D)}.$$

Final conditions of them are given from (6.40), (6.41), and (6.43) by

$$P_2(t_f) = K_1 \tag{6.53}$$

$$P_0(t_f) = 0. \tag{6.54}$$

The boundary condition for $P_2(t)$ is given from (6.39) and (6.47) by

$$(\partial/\partial\nu + \partial/\partial\nu_a)\, P_2(t) + \alpha\, P_2(t) = 0. \tag{6.55}$$

Thus, we have seen that the optimal control $f_b^o(t)$ can be characterized by a system of (6.51)-(6.55).

Let us now transform the system of ordinary differential equations in Hilbert spaces into the partial differential equations. Denoting the space of infinitely differentiable functions with compact support in D by $\mathcal{D}(D)$, with the aid of the kernel theorem due to Schwartz [5, 10], $P_2(t)$ and its inverse $P_2^{-1}(t)$ can be represented by

$$P_2(t)\phi = \int_D P_2(t,x,y)\,\phi(y)\,dy \tag{6.56}$$

and

$$P_2^{-1}(t)\phi = \int_D \overline{P}_2(t,x,y)\,\phi(y)\,dy \tag{6.57}$$

where $\phi(x) \in \mathcal{D}(D)$.

Then applying these formula to (6.51), (6.53), and (6.55), it follows that $P_2(t,x,y)$ satisfies the partial integro-differential equations;

$$-\frac{\partial P_2(t,x,y)}{\partial t} = A^*(\partial/\partial x)\, P_2(t,x,y) + (A^*(\partial/\partial y)\, P_2(t,x,y))' + L_1(x,y)$$

$$- \int_D \int_D P_2(t,x,\xi)\, B_b(t,\xi)\, \overline{L}_2(\xi,\eta)\, B_b'(t,\eta)\, P_2(t,\eta,y)\, d\xi d\eta \tag{6.58}$$

$$P_2(t_f,x,y) = K_1(x,y) \tag{6.59}$$

$$(\partial/\partial\nu + \partial/\partial\nu_a)\, P_2(t,\xi,x) + \alpha(\xi)\, P_2(t,\xi,x) = 0, \quad \forall\xi \in S, \ \forall x \in \overline{D}. \tag{6.60}$$

Similarly we have from (6.52) and (6.54)

$$- \frac{d\, P_0(t)}{dt} = \int_D \int_D \tilde{Q}(t,x,y)\, P_2(t,y,x)\, dx\, dy \tag{6.61}$$

$$P_0(t_f) = 0. \tag{6.62}$$

It is easy to see that the optimal control $f_b^o(t,\xi)$ can be determined from (6.50) by

$$f_b^o(t,\xi) = - \int_S \int_D \overline{L}_2(\xi,\eta)\, B_b'(t,\eta)\, P_2(t,\eta,x)\, U(t,x)\, dx\, d\eta \tag{6.63}$$

and the minimum cost functional $V(U(t),t)$ can be given from (6.43) by

$$V(U(t,x), t) = 1/2 \int_D \int_D U'(t,x)\, P_2(t,x,y)\, U(t,y)\, dx\, dy + 1/2\, P_0(t). \tag{6.64}$$

Thus, it has been shown that a family of (6.58)-(6.64) determines the optimal control of the system subject to additive noise disturbance, and these results become the boundary control versions of the results of Tzafestas & Nightingale's [59-61] and Kushner's [42, 68].

On the other hand, it is difficult to realize the optimal control law given by (6.63) by using the physical device since it contains the infinite numbers of the control devices. Thus, we treat the distributed parameter system whose inputs are located at the finite numbers of discrete points on the boundary S, that is, $\xi^i \in S$, $i = 1, \cdots, m$. Then the control $f_b(t,\xi)$ can be given by the following form:

$$f_b(t,\xi) = - \Sigma_{i=1}^m F_i(t)\, \delta(\xi - \xi^i). \tag{6.64}$$

Following the same procedures as the preceding paragraph, we can determine the optimal control $f_b^o(t,\xi)$ as follows:

$$f_b^o(t,\xi) = - \Sigma_{i=1}^m F_i^o(t)\, \delta(\xi - \xi^i) \tag{6.65}$$

$$F_i^o(t) = \Sigma_{j=1}^m \bar{L}_{ij} B_j'(t) \int_D P_j(t,x) U(t,x) dx \tag{6.66}$$

where

$$L_{ij} = L_2(\xi^i, \xi^j)$$

$$B_j(t) = B_b(t, \xi^j)$$

$$P_j(t,x) = P_2(t, \xi^j, x)$$

and

$$L_2(\xi) = [L_{ij}]_m , \quad \bar{L}_2(\xi) = L_2^{-1}(\xi) = [\bar{L}_{ij}]_m.$$

Here, $P_2(t,x,y)$ is formulated by

$$- \frac{\partial P_2(t,x,y)}{\partial t} = A^*(\partial/\partial x) P_2(t,x,y) + (A^*(\partial/\partial y) P_2(t,x,y))' + L_1(x,y)$$

$$- \Sigma_{i,j=1}^m P_i'(t,x) B_i(t) \bar{L}_{ij} B_j'(t) P_j(t,y). \tag{6.67}$$

It is easy to see that the other relations required for the determination of the optimal controller remain unchanged.

Next, in order to facilitate numerical computations of the integro-differential equation (6.67), we further assume that the differential operator $A^*(\partial/\partial x)$ has a set of complete orthonormal eigenfunctions and eigenvalues $\{ \phi_i(x), \lambda_i, i = 1, 2, \ldots \}$. Let us now set $P_2(t,x,y)$ by the following form:

$$P_2(t,x,y) = \Sigma_{i,j=1}^\infty p_{ij}(t) \phi_i(x) \phi_j'(y). \tag{6.68}$$

Substituting (6.68) into (6.67) and with the aid of the orthonormality of the eigenfunctions we have

$$- \frac{d p_{ij}(t)}{dt} = (\lambda_i + \lambda_j) p_{ij}(t) + a_{ij} - \Sigma_{k,n=1}^\infty p_{ik}(t) b_{kn}(t) p_{nj}(t) \tag{6.69}$$

where

$$a_{ij} = \int_D \int_D \phi_i'(x)\ L_1(x,y)\ \phi_j(y)\ dx\ dy$$

$$b_{ij}(t) = \Sigma_{k,n=1}^{m}\ \phi_i'(\xi^k)\ B_k(t)\ \overline{L}_{kn}\ B_n'(t)\ \phi_j(\xi^n).$$

It follows that the final condition of (6.69) is given from (6.59) by

$$p_{ij}(t_f) = \int_D \int_D \phi_i'(x)\ K_1(x,y)\ \phi_j(y)\ dx\ dy. \qquad (6.70)$$

Thus, the optimal control can be determined by solving the simultaneous ordinary differential equations (6.69) with final conditions (6.70). Of course, it is possible to describe (6.69) by the matrix form as before. Then we have the following results:

$$-\frac{d\,P(t)}{dt} = \Lambda\, P(t) + P(t)\,\Lambda + A - P(t)\, B(t)\, P(t) \qquad (6.71)$$

$$P(t_f) = P_{t_f}$$

where

$$P(t) = [\ p_{ij}(t)\ ]_N, \qquad \Lambda = \text{Diag}\ [\ \lambda_1, \lambda_2, \cdots, \lambda_N\ ],$$

$$A = [\ a_{ij}\ ]_N,$$

$$B(t) = [\ b_{ij}(t)\ ]_N,$$

and

$$P_{t_f} = [\ p_{ij}(t_f)\ ]_N.$$

These results correspond to those of the Meditch's work [24].

6.4. Optimal distributed control problems.

Let us consider the optimal distributed control problems based on a quadratic cost functional for a linear distributed parameter system subject to the additive noise disturbance. Thus, we treat the state equation given by

$$\frac{\partial U(t,x)}{\partial t} = A(\partial/\partial x)\ U(t,x) + B_d(t,x)\ f_d(t,x) + C(t,x)\ \dot{W}(t,x) \tag{6.72}$$

$$U(t_0,x) = U_0(x) \tag{6.73}$$

$$\alpha(\xi)\ U(t,\xi) + \Sigma_{i,j=1}^{r}\ A_{ij}(t,\xi)\ \partial U(t,\xi)/\partial \mathbf{n} = 0 \tag{6.74}$$

where $A(\partial/\partial x)$ is given by (6.33) and we assume that the assumptions in Section 6.3 hold. $K(\cdot)$ and $L(\cdot)$ of (6.12) are assumed to be the following form:

$$K(t_f,\ U(t_f,x)) = 1/2 \int_D (\ U(t_f,x),\ K_1(x,y)\ U(t_f,x))_{L_n^2(D)}\ dy \tag{6.75}$$

$$L(t,U(t,x),f_d(t,x)) = 1/2 \int_D (\ U(t,x),\ L_1(x,y)\ U(t,y))_{L_n^2(D)}\ dy$$

$$+ 1/2 \int_D (\ f_d(t,x),\ L_2(x,y)\ f_d(t,y))_{L_k^2(D)}\ dx \tag{6.76}$$

where K_1, L_1, and L_2 are assumed to satisfy the same assumption as those of Section 6.3.

Using the same procedures as those in Section 6.3, we have the following optimal distributed control law:

$$f_d^o(t) = -\ L_2^{-1}\ B_d^*(t)\ P_2(t)\ U(t) \tag{6.77}$$

Where $P_2(t)$ satisfies the following Riccati equation

$$-\frac{d\ P_2(t)}{dt} = A^*(t)\ P_2(t) + (\ A^*(t)\ P_2(t))^* + L_1 - P_2(t)\ B_d(t)\ L_2^{-1}\ B_d^*(t)\ P_2(t) \tag{6.78}$$

$$- \frac{d\, P_0(t)}{dt} = \mathrm{tr}\,[\, \tilde{Q}(t)\, P_2(t)\,]. \tag{6.79}$$

Terminal conditions of (6.78) and (6.79) are given by

$$P_2(t_f) = K_1 \tag{6.80}$$

$$P_0(t_f) = 0. \tag{6.90}$$

The boundary condition of (6.78) is give by

$$(\partial/\partial\nu + \partial/\partial\nu_a)\, P_2(t) + \alpha\, P_2(t) = 0. \tag{6.91}$$

Using the kernel representation of $P_2(t)$, we have the following relations:

$$- \frac{\partial P_2(t,x,y)}{\partial t} = A^*(\partial/\partial x)\, P_2(t,x,y) + (\, A^*(\partial/\partial y)\, P_2(t,x,y))^* + L_1(x,y)$$

$$- \int_D \int_D \; P_2(t,x,a)\, B_d(t,a)\, \bar{L}_2(a,b)\, B_d'(t,b)\, P_2(t,b,y)\, da\, db \tag{6.92}$$

$$P_2(t_f,x,y) = K_1(x,y) \tag{6.93}$$

$$(\, \partial/\partial\nu + \partial/\partial\nu_a)\, P_2(t,\xi,x) + \alpha(\xi)\, P_2(t,\xi,x) = 0, \forall \xi \in S, \forall x \in \bar{D}. \tag{6.94}$$

Furthermore, the optimal control $f_d^o(t,x)$ can be represented as follows:

$$f_d^o(t,x) = - \int_D \int_D \; \bar{L}_2(x,a)\, B_d'(t,a)\, P_2(t,a,b)\, U(t,b)\, da\, db. \tag{6.95}$$

Thus, by solving (6.92)-(6.95) we can determine the optimal controller for a linear distributed parameter system with distributed controls on the spatial domain D.

6.5. Optimal control with noisy observations.

Let the state equation and the observation equation be described by the following relations:

$$d\,U(t) = A(t)\,U(t)\,dt + B_d(t)\,f_d(t)\,dt + C(t)\,d\,W(t) \tag{6.96}$$

and

$$d\,Z(t) = H(t)\,U(t)\,dt + d\,V(t). \tag{6.97}$$

Now we denote by $U_f(t,s;c)$ the solution of (6.96) for $t \geqq s$ with the initial state $U(s) = c$ and the control input $f_d(t)$. The cost functional $J(\cdot)$ is given by

$$J(\hat{U}(s), s) = E_{U,s}\,[\,K(t_f, U(t_f,s;c)) + \int_s^{t_f} L(\tau, U_f(\tau,s;c), f_d(\tau))\,d\tau\,] \tag{6.98}$$

where

$$K(t_f, U(t_f)) = 1/2\,(\,U_f(t_f,s;c),\,K_1\,U_f(t_f,s;c))_{L_n^2(D)} \tag{6.99}$$

$$L(\tau, U_f, f_d) = 1/2\,(\,U_f(\tau,s;c),\,L_1\,U_f(\tau,s;c))_{L_n^2(D)}$$

$$+\,1/2\,(\,f_d(\tau),\,L_2\,f_d(\tau))_{L_k^2(D)} \tag{6.100}$$

and

$$\hat{U}(s) = E\,[\,U(s)|\,\Omega_s\,] = \hat{U}(s|s). \tag{6.101}$$

Here we have denoted by Ω_s the σ-field generated by the observed data, $Z(\tau)$, $t_0 \leqq \tau \leqq s$. Similarly, we shall denote by $\hat{U}_f(t,s;c)$ the optimal estimate of $U_f(t,s;c)$ based on the observed data, $Z(\tau)$, $t_0 \leqq \tau \leqq t$;

$$\hat{U}_f(t,s;c) = E\,[\,U_f(t,s;c)|\,\Omega_t\,]. \tag{6.102}$$

Since $\hat{U}_f(t,s;c)$ is the unbiased and minimum variance estimate of $U_f(t,s;c)$ [24,62], it satisfies the following Kalman-Bucy filter as shown in Chapter 3:

$$d\,\hat{U}_f(t,s;c) = A(t)\,\hat{U}_f(t,s;c)\,dt + B_d(t)\,f_d(t)\,dt$$
$$+ P(t|t)\,H^*(t)\,\mathcal{V}^{-1}(t)\,d\nu(t) \qquad (6.103)$$

where

$$d\,\nu(t) = d\,Z(t) - H(t)\,\hat{U}_f(t,s;c)\,dt. \qquad (6.104)$$

Denoting by $\tilde{U}_f(t,s;c)$ the optimal filtering error function

$$\tilde{U}_f(t,s;c) = U_f(t,s;c) - \hat{U}_f(t,s;c), \qquad (6.105)$$

we have proved in Chapter 3

$$E\,[\,\tilde{U}_f(t,s;c)\,\hat{U}_f'(t,s;c)\,] = 0. \qquad (6.106)$$

Thus, we have

$$K(t_f,\,U_f(t_f)) = 1/2\,(\,\tilde{U}_f(t_f,s;c),\,K_1\,\tilde{U}_f(t_f,s;c))_{L_n^2(D)}$$
$$+ 1/2\,(\,\hat{U}_f(t_f,s;c),\,K_1\,\hat{U}_f(t_f,s;c))_{L_n^2(D)} \qquad (6.107)$$

and

$$L(\tau,U_f,f_d) = 1/2\,(\,\tilde{U}_f(\tau,s;c),\,L_1\,\tilde{U}_f(\tau,s;c))_{L_n^2(D)}$$
$$+ 1/2\,(\,\hat{U}_f(\tau,s;c),\,L_1\,\hat{U}_f(\tau,s;c))_{L_n^2(D)}$$
$$+ 1/2\,(\,f_d(\tau),\,L_2\,f_d(\tau))_{L_k^2(D)}. \qquad (6.108)$$

Since $\tilde{U}_f(t,s;c)$ is independent of Ω_s for $s \leqq t$, we have

$$E\,[\,(\,\tilde{U}_f(\tau,s;c),\,L_1\,\tilde{U}_f(\tau,s;c))_{L_n^2(D)}|\;\Omega_s\,]$$

$$= E [(\tilde{U}_f(\tau,s;c), L_1 \tilde{U}_f(\tau,s;c))_{L_n^2(D)}] = E [(\tilde{U}_f(\tau,t_0;U_0), L_1 \tilde{U}_f(\tau,t_0;U_0))_{L_n^2(D)}]$$

$$= \mathrm{tr} [L_1 P(\tau,t_0; P_0)]$$

where $P(\tau,t_0;P_0)$ denotes the solution of the Riccati equation (3.238) with the initial condition P_0.

Thus, $J(\cdot)$ of (6.98) can be rewritten as follows:

$$J(U(s), s) = 1/2\, E [(\hat{U}_f(t_f,s;c), K_1 \hat{U}_f(t_f,s;c))_{L_n^2(D)} | \Omega_s]$$

$$+ 1/2\, E [\int_s^{t_f} \{ (\hat{U}_f(\tau,s;c), L_1 \hat{U}_f(\tau,s;c))_{L_n^2(D)}$$

$$+ (f_d(\tau), L_2 f_d(\tau))_{L_k^2(D)} \} d\tau \ | \ \Omega_s]$$

$$+ 1/2\, \mathrm{tr} [K_1 P(t_f,t_0;P_0)]$$

$$+ 1/2 \int_s^{t_f} \mathrm{tr} [L_1 P(\tau,t_0;P_0)] d\tau. \tag{6.109}$$

Then the following separation theorem holds.

[THEOREM 6.1] The optimal control law such that the cost functional $J(\cdot)$ given by (6.98) is minimized is given by the following relations:

$$f_d^o(t) = - L_2^{-1} B_d'(t) P_2(t) \hat{U}(t|t) \tag{6.110}$$

$$d \hat{U}(t|t) = A(t) \hat{U}(t|t) dt + B_d(t) f_d^o(t) dt + P(t|t) H^*(t) \mathcal{V}^{-1}(t) d \nu(t)$$

$$\hat{U}(t_0|t_0) = \hat{U}_0 = 0 \tag{6.111}$$

$$\frac{d P(t|t)}{dt} = A(t) P(t|t) + P(t|t) A^*(t) + \tilde{Q}(t) - P(t|t) \tilde{R}(t) P(t|t)$$

$$P(t_0|t_0) = P_0 \tag{6.112}$$

$$- \frac{d P_2(t)}{dt} = A^*(t) P_2(t) + P_2(t) A(t) + L_1 - P_2(t) B_d(t) L_2^{-1} B_d^*(t) P_2(t)$$

$$P(t_f) = K_1. \tag{6.113}$$

[PROOF]   The cost functional given by (6.98) can be reformulated as follows:

$$J(U(s), s) = 1/2 \text{ tr } [K_1 P(t_f, t_0; P_0)]$$

$$+ 1/2 \int_s^{t_f} \text{tr } [L_1 P(\tau, t_0; P_0)] d\tau + J_1(f_d)$$

$$J_1(f_d) = 1/2 E [(U_f(t_f, s; c), K_1 U_f(t_f, s; c))_{L_n^2(D)} | \Omega_s]$$

$$+ 1/2 E [\int_s^{t_f} (U_f(\tau, s; c), L_1 U_f(\tau, s; c))_{L_n^2(D)}$$

$$+ (f_d(\tau), L_2 f_d(\tau))_{L_k^2(D)} d\tau | \Omega_s].$$

On the other hand, $P(t, t_0; P_0)$ does not depend on the control policy $f_d(t)$. Hence, we can determine the optimal control $f_d^0(t)$ which minimizes $J(\cdot)$ by only minimizing $J_1(f_d)$.   But we have shown in the preceding sections that the optimal control $f_d^0(t)$ which minimizes the cost functional $J_1(f_d)$ can be given by

$$f_d^0(t) = - L_2^{-1} B_d'(t) P_2(t) \hat{U}(t|t)$$

where $P_2(t)$ is the solution of (6.112).

Thus, the proof of the theorem is completed.   Q.E.D.

This theorem means that the optimal controller for the noisy observation system can be determined by the two-stage processes, that is, the first process is to determine the optimal estimate $\hat{U}(t|t)$ by using (6.111) and (6.112), and the second process is to determine the optimal controller $f_d^0(t)$ by using (6.110) and (6.113).   Therefore, this theorem is called the separation theorem. Furthermore, the relations between (6.112) and (6.113) are said to be dual and hence, it is called that the estimation and control problems are dual problems.

6.6. Concluding remarks.

We have derived the optimal controller for a linear stochastic distributed parameter system by using functional analysis. The results in this chapter were derived by Omatu et al. [6] and Omatu [17]. The numerical solutions of the optimal control problems for a linear distributed parameter system were given in [17] and [63].

More recently, Ichikawa [64] derived the similar results by using the abstract evolution theory and Curtain & Ichikawa [65] proved the separation theorem in Hilbert spaces based on the evolution theory. These results of [64] and [65] correspond to those of this chapter. Furthermore, it seems to be possible to derive the optimal controller at the discrete points on the spatial domain D based on the noisy measurements at the discrete points on the spatial domain D.

REFERENCES

[1] Doob,J.L., Stochastic Processes, Wiley, New York, 1963.

[2] Falb,P.L., *Infinite-dimensional filtering: The Kalman-Bucy filter in Hilbert space,* Information and Control, Vol.11, No.1, pp.102-137, 1967.

[3] Curtain,R.F., *Infinite-dimensional estimation theory for linear systems*, Rep. No.40, Control Theory Centre, Univ. of Warwick, England, 1975.

[4] Curtain,R.F., *A survey of infinite dimensional filtering*, SIAM Review, Vol.17, No.3, pp.395-411, 1975.

[5] Bensoussan,A., Filtrage Optimal des Systèmes Linéaires, Dunod, Paris, 1971.

[6] Omatu,S.,Shibata,H., and Hata,S., *Optimal boundary control for a linear stochastic distributed parameter system using functional analysis*, Information and Control, Vol.24, No.3, pp.264-278, 1974.

[7] Omatu,S., Soeda,T., and Tomita,Y., *Linear fixed-point smoothing by using functional analysis*, IEEE Trans. on Automatic Control, Vol.AC-22, No.1, pp.9-18, 1977.

[8] Omatu,S. and Soeda,T., *Estimation problems for a linear stochastic differential equation in Hilbert space*, Proc. of Intern. Symp. on Stochastic Differential Equation, K. Ito ed., Kyoto, 1976.

[9] Yosida,K., Functional Analysis, Springer-Verl., New York, 1968.

[10] Dunford,N. and Schwartz,J.T., Linear Operators, Part I: General Theory, Intersci., New York, 1958.

[11] Scalora,F.S., *Abstract martingale convergence theorems*, Pacific J. Math., Vol.11, pp.347-374, 1961.

[12] Gikhman,I.I. and Skorokhod,A.V., Introduction to the Theory of Random Processes, W.B.Saunders Co., London, 1965.

[13] Lions,J.L., Optimal Control of Systems Governed by Partial Differential Equations, Springer-Verl., New York, 1971.

[14] Mizohata,S., The Theory of Partial Differential Equations, Cambridge Univ. Press., London, 1973.

[15] Kato,T., Perturbation Theory for Linear Operators, Springer-Verl., New York, 1966.

[16] Curtain,R.F. and Falb,P.L., *Ito's Lemma in infinite dimensions*, J.Math.Anal.,its Appl., Vol.31, pp.434-448, 1970.

[17] Omatu,S., Studies of Optimal Synthesis of the Stochastic Control Systems, Ph.D. thesis, Dept. of Electronics Eng., Univ. of Osaka Pref., 1974.

[18] Ito,S., *Fundamental solutions of parabolic differential equations and boundary value problems*, Japan J. Math., Vol.27, pp.55-102, 1957.

[19] Omatu,S., Koide,S., and Soeda,T., *Optimal sensor location problem for a linear distributed parameter system, to appear in* IEEE Trans. on Automatic Control, Vol.AC-23, No.4, 1978.

[20] Kailath,T. and Frost,P., *An innovation approach to least-squares estimation: Part II. Linear smoothing in additive white noise*, IEEE Trans. on Automatic Control, Vol.AC-13, NO.6, pp.655-660, 1968.

[21] Kalman,R.E., *A new approach to linear filtering and prediction problems*, Trans. ASME, Series D, J. Basic Eng., Vol.82, pp.35-45, 1960.

[22] Kalman,R.E. and Bucy,R.S., *New results in linear filtering and prediction theory*, Trans. ASME, Series D, J. Basic Eng., Vol.83, pp.95-108, 1961.

[23] Tomita,Y., Omatu,S., and Soeda,T., *An application of the information theory to the fixed-point smoothing problems*, Int. J. Control, Vol.23, No.4, pp.525-534, 1976.

[24] Meditch,J.S., Stochastic Optimal Linear Estimation and Control, McGraw-Hill Comp., New York, 1969.

[25] Kalman,R.E., Falb,P.L., and Arbib,M.A., Topics in Mathematical System Theory, McGraw-Hill Comp., New York, 1967.

[26] Falb,P.L. and Kleinman,D.L., *Remarks on the infinite dimensional Riccati equation*, IEEE Trans. on Automatic Control, Vol.AC-11, pp.534-536, 1966.

[27] Kailath,T., *An innovation approach to least-squares estimation. Part I: Linear filtering in additive white noise*, IEEE Trans. on Automatic Control, Vol.AC-13, No.6, pp.646-655, 1968.

[28] Kailath,T., *An innovation approach to detection and estimation theory*, Proc. IEEE, Vol.58, pp.680-695, 1970.

[29] Tomita,Y., Omatu,S., and Soeda,T., *An application of the information theory to the estimation problems*, Information and Control, Vol.32, No.2, pp.101-111, 1976.

[30] Tomita,Y., Omatu,S., and Soeda, T., *An application of the information theory to the filtering problems*, Information Sciences, Vol.11, No.1, pp.13-27, 1976.

[31] Omatu,S., Kikuchi,A., and Soeda,T., *State estimations and mutual information for a continuous-time linear system*, Trans. Inst. of Electronics and Commun. Eng. of Japan, Vol.60-D, No.7, pp.539-546, 1977.

[32] Sakawa,Y., *Optimal filtering in linear distributed-parameter systems*, Int. J. Control, Vol.16, No.1, pp.115-127, 1972.

[33] Omatu,S., Tomita,Y., and Soeda,T., *Fixed-point smoothing problems for a linear distributed parameter system*, Trans. Instrument and Control Eng. of Japan, Vol.11, No.6, pp.682-687, 1975.

[34] Omatu,S., Nagamine,H., and Soeda,T., *Fixed-interval smoothing problems for a linear distributed parameter system*, ibid, Vol.13, No.6, pp.539-546, 1977.

[35] Omatu,S., Tomita,Y., and Soeda,T., *Fixed-point smoothing in Hilbert spaces*, Information and Control, Vol.34, No.4, pp.324-338, 1977.

[36] Omatu,S., Tomita,Y., and Soeda,T., *Smoothing problems of distributed parameter systems with fixed-point observations*, Trans. Inst. of Electrical Eng. of Japan, Vol.97-c, No.5, pp.77-84, 1977.

[37] Omatu,S., Tomita,Y., and Soeda,T., *Optimal filtering for discrete-time nonlinear systems*, IEEE Trans. on Automatic Control, Vol.AC-21, No.1, pp. 116-118, 1976.

[38] Omatu,S., Tomita,Y., and Soeda,T., *An alternative expression of the mutual information for Gaussian processes*, IEEE Trans. on Information Theory, Vol. IT-22, No.5, pp.593-595, 1976.

[39] Ito,S., Partial Differential Equations (in Japanese), Baifukan, Tokyo, 1966.

[40] Datko,R., *A linear control problem in abstract Hilbert space*, J. Differential Equations, Vol.9, pp.346-359, 1971.

[41] Curtain,R.F. and Pritchard,A.J., *The infinite-dimensional Riccati equation*, J. Math. Anal. its Appl., Vol.47, pp.43-57, 1974.

[42] Kushner,H.J., *On the optimal control of a system governed by a linear parabolic equation with white noise inputs*, SIAM J. Control, Vol.6, pp. 596-614, 1968.

[43] Bensoussan,A., *Optimization of sensors' location in a linear filtering problem*, Proc. Int. Symp. on Stab. of Stoch. Dyn. Sys., pp.62-84, 1972.

[44] Chen,W.H. and Seinfeld,J.H., *Optimal location of process measurements*, Int. J. Control, Vol.21, No.6, pp.1003-1014, 1975.

[45] Aidarous,S.E. and Gevers,M.R., *Optimal sensors' allocation strategies for a class of stochastic distributed systems*, Int. J. Control, Vol.22, No.2, pp. 197-213, 1975.

[46] Athans,M., *On the determination of optimal costly measurement strategies for linear stochastic systems*, Prep. of IFAC V Conf., 1972.

[47] Omatu,S., Koide,S., and Soeda,T., *Optimal sensor location in a linear distributed parameter system*, Proc. of IFAC Symp. on Environmental Systems Planning, Design and Control, Kyoto, pp.233-240, 1977.

[48] Omatu,S., Koide,S., and Soeda,T., *Optimal measurement locations*, Proc. of 6th SICE Symp. on Control Theory, Hachioji, Tokyo, 1977.

[49] Omatu,S.,Koide,S., and Soeda,T., *Optimization of the sensor location for linear distributed parameter systems*, Trans. Inst. of Electrical Eng. of Japan, Vol.98-c, No.1, pp.9-16, 1978.

[50] Yu,T.K. and Seinfeld,J.H., *Observability and optimal measurement location in linear distributed parameter system*, Int. J. Control, Vol.18, No.4, pp.785-799, 1973.

[51] Cannon,J.R. and Klein,R.E., *Optimal selection of a measurement location in a conductor for approximate determination of temperature distribution*, Proc. JACC, pp.750-756, 1970.

[52] Cavarini,P. and Pillo,G.D., *Optimal location of a measurement point in a diffusion process*, Prep. of IFAC VI Conf., 1975.

[53] Bellman,R.E., Adaptive Control Processes; A Guided Tour, Princeton Univ. Press., New Jersey, 1961.

[54] Dieudonné,J., Foundations of Modern Analysis, Acad. Press., New York, 1960.

[55] Kushner,H.J., Stochastic Stability and Control, Acad. Press, New York, 1967.

[56] Bryson,A.E. and Ho,Y.C., Applied Optimal Control, John Wiley & Sons, New York, 1975.

[57] Erzberger,H. and Kim,M., *Optimal boundary control of distributed parameter systems*, Information and Control, Vol.9, pp.265-278, 1966.

[58] Greenberg,S.G., *On quadratic optimization in distributed parameter systems*, IEEE Trans. on Automatic Control, Vol.AC-16, No.2, pp.153-159, 1971.

[59] Tzafestas,S.G. and Nightingale,J.M., *Optimal control of a class of linear stochastic distributed-parameter systems*, Proc. IEE, Vol.115, No.8, pp.1213-1220, 1968.

[60] Tzafestas,S.G., *Optimal distributed parameter control using classical variational theory*, Int. J. Control, Vol.12, No.4, pp.593-608, 1970.

[61] Tzafestas,S.G., *Distributed parameter control in function space*, J. Franklin

Institute, Vol.295, No.4, pp.317-342, 1973.

[62] Bucy,R.S. and Joseph,P.D., Filtering for Stochastic Processes with Application to Guidance, Interscience Pub., New York, 1968.

[63] Omatu,S., Kawakami,H., Shibata,H., and Hata,S., *Numerical analysis of the point-wise control*, Bull. of Univ. of Osaka Pref., Vol.22, No.1, pp.49-56, 1973.

[64] Ichikawa,A., *Dynamic programming approach to stochastic evolution equations*, Rep. No.60, Control Theory Centre, Univ. of Warvick, 1977.

[65] Curtain,R.F. and Ichikawa,A., *The separation principle for stochastic evolution equations*, SIAM J. Control & Opt., Vol.15, No.3, pp.367-383, 1977.

[66] Tzafestas,S.G. and Nightingale,J.M., *Optimal filtering, smoothing, and prediction in linear distributed-parameter systems*, Proc. IEE, Vol.115, No.8, pp.1207-1212, 1968.

[67] Tzafestas,S.G. and Nightingale,J.M., *Concerning optimal filtering theory of distributed-parameter systems*, Proc. IEE, Vol.115, No.11, pp.1737-1742, 1968.

[68] Kushner,H.J., *Filtering for linear distributed parameter systems*, SIAM J. Control, Vol.8, No.3, pp.346-359, 1970.

Lecture Notes in Economics and Mathematical Systems

For information about Vols. 1–104 please contact your bookseller or Springer-Verlag

Vol. 105: Optimal Control Theory and its Applications. Part I. Proceedings 1973. Edited by B. J. Kirby. VI, 425 pages. 1974.

Vol. 106: Optimal Control Theory and its Applications. Part II. Proceedings 1973. Edited by B. J. Kirby. VI, 403 pages. 1974.

Vol. 107: Control Theory, Numerical Methods and Computer Systems Modeling. International Symposium, Rocquencourt, June 17–21, 1974. Edited by A. Bensoussan and J. L. Lions. VIII, 757 pages. 1975.

Vol. 108: F. Bauer et al., Supercritical Wing Sections II. A Handbook. V, 296 pages. 1975.

Vol. 109: R. von Randow, Introduction to the Theory of Matroids. IX, 102 pages. 1975.

Vol. 110: C. Striebel, Optimal Control of Discrete Time Stochastic Systems. III. 208 pages. 1975.

Vol. 111: Variable Structure Systems with Application to Economics and Biology. Proceedings 1974. Edited by A. Ruberti and R. R. Mohler. VI, 321 pages. 1975.

Vol. 112: J. Wilhlem, Objectives and Multi-Objective Decision Making Under Uncertainty. IV, 111 pages. 1975.

Vol. 113: G. A. Aschinger, Stabilitätsaussagen über Klassen von Matrizen mit verschwindenden Zeilensummen. V, 102 Seiten. 1975.

Vol. 114: G. Uebe, Produktionstheorie. XVII, 301 Seiten. 1976.

Vol. 115: Anderson et al., Foundations of System Theory: Finitary and Infinitary Conditions. VII, 93 pages. 1976

Vol. 116: K. Miyazawa, Input-Output Analysis and the Structure of Income Distribution. IX, 135 pages. 1976.

Vol. 117: Optimization and Operations Research. Proceedings 1975. Edited by W. Oettli and K. Ritter. IV, 316 pages. 1976.

Vol. 118: Traffic Equilibrium Methods, Proceedings 1974. Edited by M. A. Florian. XXIII, 432 pages. 1976.

Vol. 119: Inflation in Small Countries. Proceedings 1974. Edited by H. Frisch. VI, 356 pages. 1976.

Vol. 120: G. Hasenkamp, Specification and Estimation of Multiple-Output Production Functions. VII, 151 pages. 1976.

Vol. 121: J. W. Cohen, On Regenerative Processes in Queueing Theory. IX, 93 pages. 1976.

Vol. 122: M. S. Bazaraa, and C. M. Shetty, Foundations of Optimization VI. 193 pages. 1976

Vol. 123: Multiple Criteria Decision Making. Kyoto 1975. Edited by M. Zeleny. XXVII, 345 pages. 1976.

Vol. 124: M. J. Todd. The Computation of Fixed Points and Applications. VII, 129 pages. 1976.

Vol. 125: Karl C. Mosler. Optimale Transportnetze. Zur Bestimmung ihres kostengünstigsten Standorts bei gegebener Nachfrage. VI, 142 Seiten. 1976.

Vol. 126: Energy, Regional Science and Public Policy. Energy and Environment I. Proceedings 1975. Edited by M. Chatterji and P. Van Rompuy. VIII, 316 pages. 1976.

Vol. 127: Environment, Regional Science and Interregional Modeling. Energy and Environment II. Proceedings 1975. Edited by M. Chatterji and P. Van Rompuy. IX, 211 pages. 1976.

Vol. 128: Integer Programming and Related Areas. A Classified Bibliography. Edited by C. Kastning. XII, 495 pages. 1976.

Vol. 129: H.-J. Lüthi, Komplementaritäts- und Fixpunktalgorithmen in der mathematischen Programmierung. Spieltheorie und Ökonomie. VII, 145 Seiten. 1976.

Vol. 130: Multiple Criteria Decision Making, Jouy-en-Josas, France. Proceedings 1975. Edited by H. Thiriez and S. Zionts. VI, 409 pages. 1976.

Vol. 131: Mathematical Systems Theory. Proccedings 1975. Edited by G. Marchesini and S. K. Mitter. X, 408 pages. 1976.

Vol. 132: U. H. Funke, Mathematical Models in Marketing. A Collection of Abstracts. XX, 514 pages. 1976.

Vol. 133: Warsaw Fall Seminars in Mathematical Economics 1975. Edited by M. W. Loś, J. Loś, and A. Wieczorek. V. 159 pages. 1976.

Vol. 134: Computing Methods in Applied Sciences and Engineering. Proceedings 1975. VIII, 390 pages. 1976.

Vol. 135: H. Haga, A Disequilibrium – Equilibrium Model with Money and Bonds. A Keynesian – Walrasian Synthesis. VI, 119 pages. 1976.

Vol. 136: E. Kofler und G. Menges, Entscheidungen bei unvollständiger Information. XII, 357 Seiten. 1976.

Vol. 137: R. Wets, Grundlagen Konvexer Optimierung. VI, 146 Seiten. 1976.

Vol. 138: K. Okuguchi, Expectations and Stability in Oligopoly Models. VI, 103 pages. 1976.

Vol. 139: Production Theory and Its Applications. Proceedings. Edited by H. Albach and G. Bergendahl. VIII, 193 pages. 1977.

Vol. 140: W. Eichhorn and J. Voeller, Theory of the Price Index. Fisher's Test Approach and Generalizations. VII, 95 pages. 1976.

Vol. 141: Mathematical Economics and Game Theory. Essays in Honor of Oskar Morgenstern. Edited by R. Henn and O. Moeschlin. XIV, 703 pages. 1977.

Vol. 142: J. S. Lane, On Optimal Population Paths. V, 123 pages. 1977.

Vol. 143: B. Näslund, An Analysis of Economic Size Distributions. XV, 100 pages. 1977.

Vol. 144: Convex Analysis and Its Applications. Proceedings 1976. Edited by A. Auslender. VI, 219 pages. 1977.

Vol. 145: J. Rosenmüller, Extreme Games and Their Solutions. IV, 126 pages. 1977

Vol. 146: In Search of Economic Indicators. Edited by W. H. Strigel. XVI, 198 pages. 1977.

Vol. 147: Resource Allocation and Division of Space. Proceedings. Edited by T. Fujii and R. Sato. VIII, 184 pages. 1977.

Vol. 148: C. E. Mandl, Simulationstechnik und Simulationsmodelle in den Sozial- und Wirtschaftswissenschaften. IX, 173 Seiten. 1977.

Vol. 149: Stationäre und schrumpfende Bevölkerungen: Demographisches Null- und Negativwachstum in Österreich. Herausgegeben von G. Feichtinger. VI, 262 Seiten. 1977.

Vol. 150: Bauer et al., Supercritical Wing Sections III. VI, 179 pages. 1977.

Vol. 151: C. A. Schneeweiß, Inventory-Production Theory. VI, 116 pages. 1977.

Vol. 152: Kirsch et al., Notwendige Optimalitätsbedingungen und ihre Anwendung. VI, 157 Seiten. 1978.

Vol. 153: Kombinatorische Entscheidungsprobleme: Methoden und Anwendungen. Herausgegeben von T. M. Liebling und M. Rössler. VIII, 206 Seiten. 1978.

Vol. 154: Problems and Instruments of Business Cycle Analysis. Proceedings 1977. Edited by W. H. Strigel. VI, 442 pages. 1978.

Vol. 155: Multiple Criteria Problem Solving. Proceedings 1977. Edited by S. Zionts. VIII, 567 pages. 1978.

Vol. 156: B. Näslund and B. Sellstedt, Neo-Ricardian Theory. With Applications to Some Current Economic Problems. VI, 165 pages. 1978.

Vol. 157: Optimization and Operations Research. Proceedings 1977. Edited by R. Henn, B. Korte, and W. Oettli. VI, 270 pages. 1978.

Vol. 158: L. J. Cherene, Set Valued Dynamical Systems and Economic Flow. VIII, 83 pages. 1978.

Vol. 159: Some Aspects of the Foundations of General Equilibrium Theory: The Posthumous Papers of Peter J. Kalman. Edited by J. Green. VI, 167 pages. 1978.

Vol. 160: Integer Programming and Related Areas. A Classified Bibliography. Edited by D. Hausmann. XIV, 314 pages. 1978.

This series aims to report new developments in the fields of control and information sciences – quickly, informally and at a high level. The type of material considered for publication includes:

1. Preliminary drafts of monographs and advanced textbooks
2. Lectures on a new field, or presenting a new angle on a classical field
3. Research reports
4. Reports of meetings, provided they are
   a) of exceptional interest and
   b) devoted to a specific topic.

The timeliness of a manuscript is more important than its form, which may be unfinished or tentative. If possible, a subject index should be included. Publication of Lecture Notes is intended as a service to the international scientific and engineering community, in that a commercial publisher, Springer-Verlag, can offer a wider distribution to documents which would otherwise have a restricted readership. Once published and copyrighted, they can be documented in the scientific literature.

Manuscripts

Manuscripts should comprise not less than 100 pages. They are reproduced by a photographic process and therefore must be typed with extreme care. Symbols not on the typewriter should be inserted by hand in indelible black ink. Corrections to the typescripts should be made by pasting the amended text over the old one, or by obliterating errors with white correcting fluid. Authors receive 75 complimentary copies and are free to use the material in other publications. The typescript is reduced slightly in size in the process of reproduction. Best results will not be obtained unless the text on any one page is kept within the overall limit of 18 x 26,5 cm (7 x 10½ inches). The publishers will be pleased to supply on request special typing sheets with the typing area outlined.

Manuscripts, preferably in English, should be sent to Prof. Dr. A. V. Balakrishnan, Department of System Science, University of California, 4531 Boelter Hall, Los Angeles, Ca. 90024, Professor Dr.-Ing. M. Thoma, Institut für Regelungstechnik, Technische Universität, Appelstrasse 11, D-3000 Hannover, or directly to Springer-Verlag Berlin Heidelberg GmbH

Springer-Verlag Berlin Heidelberg GmbH

ISBN 978-3-540-09142-4   ISBN 978-3-540-35401-7 (eBook)
DOI 10.1007/978-3-540-35401-7